JAZZ

and Its

DISCONTENTS

ALSO BY FRANCIS DAVIS

Afterglow: A Last Conversation with Pauline Kael

Like Young: Jazz, Pop, Youth, and Middle Age

Bebop and Nothingness: Jazz and Pop at the End of the Century

Outcats: Jazz Composers, Instrumentalists and Singers

In the Moment: Jazz in the 1980s

JAZZ
and Its
DISCONTENTS

A FRANCIS DAVIS READER

FRANCIS DAVIS

DA CAPO PRESS
A Member of Perseus Books Group

Set in 11 point Adobe Garamond by the Perseus Books Group

Cataloging-in-Publication data for this book is available from the
Library of Congress.

First Da Capo Press edition 2004
ISBN 0-306-81055-7

Published by Da Capo Press
A Member of the Perseus Books Group
http://www.dacapopress.com

Da Capo Press books are available at special discounts for bulk
purchases in the U.S. by corporations, institutions, and other
organizations. For more information, please contact the Special
Markets Department at the Perseus Books Group, 11 Cambridge
Center, Cambridge, MA 02142, or call (800) 255-1514 or
(617) 252-5298, or e-mail special.markets@perseusbooks.com.

1 2 3 4 5 6 7 8 9—08 07 06 05 04

For
DOROTHY DAVIS
AND
TERRY GROSS,
always

Contents

===

Only Myself to Blame

"Promise them a concept album and give them your greatest hits." This was my advice to a fellow jazz critic about fifteen years younger than me who said he'd like to interest a publisher in bringing out a book by him, preferably without having to write one entirely from scratch. He foolishly assumed that because I had published four collections of my newspaper and magazine articles on jazz I knew the ropes, and I was so flattered I found myself playing along. "You need to give them something they think they can use as a sales hook," I said, as if I knew what the hell I was talking about.

Well, it had worked for me. In 1984, I promised the august Sheldon Meyer, of Oxford University Press, a book on musicians born after World War II. I began work on *In the Moment* intending to give Sheldon the book we'd agreed on—one with a rather obvious sales hook, given the attention then being lavished on Wynton Marsalis and other players in their twenties or thirties whose emergence supposedly proved that jazz wasn't yet ready for the morgue. (Unlike Marsalis, the younger musicians who most intrigued me were loosely affiliated with the jazz avant-garde.) But the manuscript I delivered a year later was something else altogether. Along with profiles of about a dozen upstarts, it included pieces on Sonny Rollins, Ornette Coleman, Miles Davis, Warne Marsh, Abbey Lincoln, and a host of others born before my arbitrary starting point of 1946. Vanity, disguised as something much nobler, had taken over somewhere along the way. I wanted my book on jazz to include my favorite living musicians regardless of age, and the subtitle "Jazz in the 1980s" more than justified their inclusion, since all of them were still making vital contributions to jazz. But more than anything else, I wanted *In the Moment* to be a collection of what I considered to be my best writing on jazz to that point. Sheldon published what I sent him without protest, and I was suddenly not just a writer but an author—a bump in status that doesn't necessarily bring a boost in income, I should have remembered to caution my younger colleague.

This current book *is* my greatest hits. It features my own choice of the best material from my first three collections, and my name is part of the subtitle, which effectively makes *me* one of the hooks. Yet I find myself wishing I could

pull a fast one on John Radziewicz, my current editor, similar to the fast one
I pulled on Sheldon nearly twenty years ago. Instead of a greatest hits album,
I wish this could be a tombstone-size Mosaic box set of my complete work,
including a generous sampling of my uncollected pieces. Or at the very least,
an omnibus of *In the Moment* (1986), *Outcats* (1990), and *Bebop and Nothingness* (1996) like those recent editions of Mickey Spillane that each offered
three complete vintage Mike Hammer novels. How about all of my pieces on
singers in one volume, the giants of swing and bop in another, and so on? Or
Francis Davis Remixed, three volumes of raw interview transcripts in place of
the chapters that drew selectively from them?

"Musicians presuppose that all critics are frustrated musicians," I quipped
in my introduction to *In the Moment*. "That's incorrect: the good ones are frustrated novelists." Over the years, my friend Howard Mandel has quoted this
every time we've been on a panel together or shared the stage at an awards ceremony—he'll get me into Bartlett's yet, Howard will. But what I should have
written was that music journalism at its highest level is a valid literary genre,
not a vicarious alternative to mastering an instrument. Howard is no frustrated novelist—he's writing a mystery I can't wait to read—and neither am I.
I dropped the false modesty in my introduction to *Bebop and Nothingness*,
pointing out that I tried "to crowd even those pieces that begin as record
reviews with what Dwight Macdonald, in his essay on Hemingway, described
as 'the subject matter of the novel: character, social setting, politics, money
matters, human relations, all the prose of life.'" I think of the kind of writing
I do as fiction by other means—fiction with the added burden of factual accu-
racy. I favor narrative and mood over thesis, even in my more straightforward
critical essays, where narrative takes the form of one thought following
another and the only "character" is myself.

But it isn't pride in my work that makes me wish everything I've ever published could remain in print and be readily accessible. Quite the opposite: a
good deal of what I've written embarrasses me. It's just that I hate choosing
among my pieces. I'm too close to them to be sure I'm choosing intelligently.
Inasmuch as those of us who become critics tend to define ourselves by our
taste, criticism is also autobiography by other means—an ongoing account of
what recordings and books and movies delighted us or troubled us or pissed
us off enough to make us write about them, in an effort to figure out exactly
how they fit into our lives. In choosing the best material from my first three
collections for this "reader," I'm probably dooming the rest of it to obscurity—
more or less ensuring that those three books will remain out of print and dis-
owning many of my earlier passions in the bargain. For the most part, I've
chosen those pieces I feel best represent me as a writer. But I've also given
precedence to those major figures it's every critic's responsibility to weigh in

on, and this has forced me to bypass any number of less celebrated musicians whose work has given me endless pleasure and whom I've written about at some length. Feeling as though I was turning my back on them, along with part of my life, I turned to Robert Lowell for commisseration. "I am not an authoritative critic of my own poems, except in the most pressing and urgent way," Lowell wrote in 1977:

> I have spent hundreds and hundreds of hours shaping, extending and changing hopeless or defective work. I lie on a bed staring, crossing out, writing in, crossing out what was written in, again and again, through days and weeks. . . .
>
> I know roughly what I think are my better poems, and more roughly and imperfectly why I think they are; and roughly too, which are my worst and where they fail. I have an idea how my best fall short. To have to state all this systematically, and perhaps with controversial argument, would be a prison sentence to me. It would be an exposure. . . .

Enough brooding. Maybe all an author needs to do in a book introduction is to rip your ticket, smile, and say "enjoy the show." But the contents of this book require some explanation. *In the Moment, Outcats,* and *Bebop and Nothingness* were books "on" jazz, but jazz wasn't all they were about. Among other things, *In the Moment* was about money and race, *Outcats* about alienation (mine and that common to jazz musicians and their devotees), and *Bebop and Nothingness* about age (a theme I continued in *Like Young*). There is nothing here from *The History of the Blues, Like Young,* or *Afterglow*; these books are still in print, and I'd like to keep it that way. The order here is chronological in the sense that pieces from *In the Moment* come before those from *Outcats,* which in turn precede those from *Bebop and Nothingness.* But the pieces from each of those books aren't necessarily in their original order. I wanted this book to begin with my piece on Sonny Rollins, because this piece was a turning point for me as a writer. It was originally commissioned by *Esquire,* and when they decided against running it and paid me an insulting kill fee, I decided it was time to get an agent and start thinking about a book. It was the first piece I ever sent to Bill Whitworth, of *The Atlantic Monthly,* and although he didn't use it, this marked the beginning of a close friendship as well as my longest professional affiliation. "An Improviser Prepares" taught me to trust my intuition. Before killing the piece, my editors at *Esquire* kept telling me I needed to lure readers in by showing Rollins in performance near the beginning. I resisted giving them what they wanted because—even though I wasn't able to articulate it then—I knew the piece had to *end* with Rollins finally cutting loose.

xii   **Only Myself to Blame**

(Like many of the pieces here, the one on Rollins is a hybrid—half profile, half critical meditation. In common with newspaper movie critics, jazz journalists routinely pull double duty, interviewing and providing a sounding board for the same performers whose concerts and recordings they review. But who says an artist profile has to be uninterrupted puffery? My instinct has always been to have two voices alternating, mine and my subject's.)

Though I borrowed the word from the obscure beatnik pianist Paul Knopf, "outcat" has become my contribution to the jazz lexicon. (I can also take credit for "hipster doofus," a phrase I used to describe Kramer in my piece on *Seinfeld* for *The Atlantic Monthly*; the show's writers subsequently used the phrase in a couple of episodes.)

What else do I need to explain here? The long chapter from *In the Moment* on Anthony Davis and the genesis of his opera about Malcom X will have to stand for the many younger musicians who offered something new in the early 1980s but were subsequently rejected by the jazz establishment. My reviews of books by Whitney Balliett and Amiri Baraka have not been collected before, nor has the piece on Jim Hall, which I inexplicably left out of *In the Moment*. I hope it's eternal, like Hall himself. Sun Ra, Miles Davis, and Wynton Marsalis are inexhaustable subjects; I've grouped together pieces on them of different vintages. There might be too much here about singers, but so be it; this is the one branch of music in which I can claim to have some background. Jazz isn't the only music I listen to, and the penultimate section has nothing to do with jazz per se. Nor is it the only subject I write about, and since a "reader" might be understood to be a kind of sampler of a writer's work, I wanted to include in the very final section pieces on film, television, and comedy that would have no place in a collection dedicated to music. Though not originally conceived as such, the final three pieces—on Bob Hope, *The Best Years of Our Lives*, and action movies—form a sort of war trilogy. They are presented here *Memento*-style, in reverse sequence, for reasons that became clear to me only after I decided to do it that way. The last piece was written not long after the September 11 terrorist attacks, before our military invasion of Iraq dissipated the unfamiliar sense of unity and purpose we felt as Americans. (It was common then for people to say that if they refrained from traveling or celebrating the Christmas holidays with as much enthusiasm as usual "the terrorists will have already won." But wouldn't their ultimate victory be George W. Bush's reelection this November?) I also knew I wanted this book to end as "Only in the Movies" does, with my mother's death. I happened to spend a lot of time in New York in the months just after the attacks, when people talked of smelling burning flesh in the air. Their grief was so palpable I hesitated to tell them the horrible truth that no matter how close to home it strikes, death remains an abstraction until you find yourself in the same room with it.

I've put off commenting on the current state of jazz because it's too damn depressing. Twenty-five years ago, when I started writing about jazz, it was in decent shape artistically; the problem was its lack of exposure. But Gary Giddins was writing about David Murray and Birili Legrene for *Vanity Fair*, Ornette Coleman or Sun Ra might be the musical guest on *Saturday Night Live*, and it was at least possible to sell a magazine such as *Esquire* on the *idea* of a piece on Sonny Rollins. None of this would be very likely today. I hear people complain that the audience for jazz is getting older, but isn't the audience for anything interesting and a little out of the way, including art and repertory film? You can blame the mass media as much as you want, but it's difficult not to conclude that much of the blame lies with the entrenched tastes of the jazz faithful. This simply isn't a very exciting time for the music, and if something potentially earthshaking does happen to come along, the odds are good that the guardians of tradition at Lincoln Center and the Thelonious Monk Institute and the various funding agencies are going to ignore it—and go out of their way to ensure that everybody else does too.

In his introduction to *Ecstacy at the Onion*, a collection of his pieces published in 1971, Whitney Balliett informed his readers that this would probably be his last book on jazz. "I have been writing about the music since 1947, a more than ample time to say what has to be said on any subject," he explained. "And jazz itself, in its present dwindling, defenseless state, can no longer bear much critical weight—if, indeed, it ever could." Balliett—whose writing has had an enormous influence on mine, even though he might be surprised (or even appalled) to hear it—wanted to move on to other subjects, and so do I. But he never really gave up his regular beat, and just five years later, in his introduction to *New York Notes*, he felt justified in announcing that "the music seems to be in good health." I hope I can begin my next collection on a similar note of optimism, though this remains to be seen.

A few final things. To thank everyone who helped these pieces along in some way would fill an entire chapter, but I owe special debts of gratitude to the Pew Fellowship in the Arts; my agent Mark Kelley; Corby Kummer and everyone else at *The Atlantic Monthly*; Andrea Schulz; John Radziewicz and his staff at Da Capo Press; my father-in-law, Irving Gross; and (most of all) my late mother, Dorothy Davis, and my wife, Terry Gross. Journalism is very much like jazz, a spur-of-the-moment thing that only sometimes endures. I don't know if everything here has stood the test of time, but I'm hoping the pieces that haven't at least evince a certain period flavor. As much perverse enjoyment as I take in "staring, crossing out, writing in, crossing out what was written in, again and again, through days and weeks," I haven't indulged in any of it here, because to groom pieces written (and first published) as long as twenty years ago would be pathetic, not to say pathological.

Oh, and about the title—John Radziewicz looked me in the eye and said, "You know, you're often very funny. You should think of a funny title for the *Reader.*" Great, I thought: punchlines on demand. I thought of *Only Myself to Blame* too late for the catalog, but *Jazz and Its Discontents*, if not so hard-boiled and not exactly hilarious, at least captures the tone of some of the pieces in this collection.

Philadelphia,
December 2003

from
IN THE MOMENT

An Improviser Prepares

A fter a summer tour of Japan with the guitarist Pat Metheny and a string of West Coast concerts in early autumn, the tenor saxophonist Sonny Rollins accepted no more work the rest of 1983. Something of a homebody anyway, he needed time to brace himself for a January record date, and time to reflect on a close call.

In April, Rollins had played New York's Town Hall, with the cocky young trumpeter Wynton Marsalis on the bill as his special guest. Rollins says that he was so preoccupied with rehearsals the afternoon of the concert that he had forgotten to eat: he had recently made several personnel changes in his band, and he wanted to give the new recruits ample opportunity to familiarize themselves with one another, their leader, and added starter Marsalis. Rollins may have been edgy for another reason that he is understandably reluctant to express: many male jazz fans invest as much ego in rooting for their favorite soloists as other men invest in prizefighters, and a segment of the audience that night wanted a clear-cut victor to emerge from what was being talked about as a fight to the finish between Rollins and Marsalis, the reigning heavyweight champion and the newest pretender to his throne.

Lucille Rollins, who has been married to Sonny Rollins for over 20 years and managed him for the last 11, says she knew something was wrong when, from her post backstage, she heard the rhythm section slam to a halt following a curious pause in her husband's solo on Charlie Parker's "Big Foot," the third number of the evening. Sonny Rollins had landed on his back, his head about three inches from Tommy Campbell's bass drum. "I whispered, *'Get up, man,'* thinking he was spoofing, before realizing that he was out cold," Campbell remembers. "I looked over at Wynton, who was shaking uncontrollably. We were all so petrified it was easier to go on playing for a few seconds than it was to stop."

Upon regaining consciousness in his dressing room, Rollins's first thought was fear his horn might be stolen, what with so many strangers milling around. An ambulance rushed him to the cardiovascular wing of Bellvue Hospital; *Bellvue,* a name that shrieks bedlam within the jazz community, the hospital to which Rollins's friend Charles Mingus had gone to seek psychiatric counseling

3

and been locked away for weeks until a lawyer intervened. Asked to remain overnight for tests, a shaken and superstitious Rollins refused and checked himself out. His private physician subsequently ruled out heart attack or stroke—everyone's unspoken fear. But Rollins was found to be suffering from hypertension aggravated by nervous exhaustion.

When I caught up with Rollins before his concert in Boston six months later, his memory of the evening in question was hazy. He speculated that his heel must have caught on a wire, causing him to topple over backwards and bump his head—but Lucille Rollins reminded him that no one, her least of all, was buying that fanciful scenario. Still radiating youthful power and vitality in his mid fifties, Rollins perhaps finds it difficult to admit to physical infirmity (his wife reveals that, like many victims of hypertension surprise attacks, he has to be reminded to take his daily medication now that his blood pressure has returned to normal). Even so, he was only too happy to follow doctor's orders to lighten up on travel, since that meant spending more time at home in Germantown, New York, a few miles north of Woodstock, where he and Lucille (his second wife), who have no children, enjoy a quiet, bucolic existence.

One could work up a lather about how the scarcity of jazz nightclubs everywhere but New York City has made the presentation of jazz a catch -as-catch-can proposition, citing as evidence Sonny Rollins's itinerary in the waning months of 1983 (he played a Greenwich Village rock showcase, two Southern universities, and a pink-and-white wedding cake of a room in the Copley Plaza, one of Back Bay Boston's most patrician hotels). But Rollins is no typical jazz musician, be the yardstick creative temperament or earning capacity. His inactivity was strictly a matter of choice, the few dates he accepted one-nighters designed not to keep him away from home too long.

"There are certain things to be said in favor of the old days, when you played a club for an entire week before moving on," Rollins told me as he fit a mouthpiece over his horn before going on stage in Boston. "After a few nights, you knew the audiences you could expect, you knew where to find whatever you needed around town, and you built up a special kind of rapport with your musicians from being away from home together so long. But as you get older, you miss sleeping in your own bed every night, and you miss the mundane activities that constitute your daily routine. And frankly, I just don't *want* to spend a week of the time I've got left in Cleveland or Detroit or wherever."

The road has traditionally symbolized freedom for professional musicians, an opportunity to carouse in the company of one's fellows; and bad habits born of the road have claimed scores of casualties from rock 'n' roll as well as jazz. Though he makes his living from it, nightlife is not Rollins's style, and one doubts it ever was: the road is an experience to be endured, not relished, so far as he is concerned. He spent most of his 36 hours in Boston in his hotel room, looking forward to the flight out. Not even the lure of hearing Sammy Price and Dave McKenna, the Copley's resident pianists, both of whom Rollins admires, was sufficient enticement for him to stay up late.

What he seems to resent most about performances on the road is not being able to practice his instrument (an odd thought, when one considers that performance is supposed to be the end result of practice—and that few musicians his age who perform as often as he does bother to practice at all). "At home, I usually get up around 4:00 A.M. to feed our two dogs and three cats—Lucille has them so spoiled they won't let us sleep later than that—the visiting cats, the visiting chickens, the visiting whatever else comes around, because a lot of the area around us is farmland, and you see a lot of animals. Then I go back to sleep for an hour or so and spend the rest of the day practicing. You can't practice in hotel rooms, though, for fear of annoying someone who might be trying to sleep in the next room. All you can do is watch soap operas and try to relax, and I can take only so much of that." His voice was losing some of its viscosity, becoming weightless in abstraction, and I thought it better to take leave of him, realizing that he was itching to get in a few minutes of practice now that he had the chance.

ROLLINS'S LIST OF ASSOCIATES OVER THE LAST 35 YEARS READS LIKE A modern jazz who's who: Charlie Parker, Thelonious Monk, Bud Powell, Dizzy Gillespie, Miles Davis, Max Roach, Clifford Brown. But simple cross-referencing of this sort fails to convey Rollins's true significance. Unlike Parker, Louis Armstrong, or Ornette Coleman, Rollins did not alter the rhythmic syntax of jazz. Unlike Davis, he has never been a reliable bellwether of new trends. Although a number of his compositions (the calypso "St. Thomas" and the blues derivatives "Oleo," "Doxie," and "Airegin") have become jam-session standbys, he has not set a standard other jazz writers have sought to emulate (unlike Monk, Duke Ellington, and Charles Mingus). He has never succeeded in forming a band in his own image, and although countless saxophonists have aped his stylistic mannerisms, his influence has never been as all-pervasive as John Coltrane's was in the mid-1960s. Yet when conjuring up an image of the quintessential jazzman—heroic, inspired, mystical, obsessed—as often as not, it is Rollins we picture, because no other jazz instrumentalist better epitomizes the lonely tightrope walk between spontaneity and organization implicit in taking an improvised solo. Everyone who listens to jazz can tell a story of a night when Rollins could do no wrong, when ideas poured out of him so effortlessly that a comparison to Leopold Bloom seemed in order, until one realized that it was James Joyce one was thinking of—that Rollins was blessed with an angbite of inwit far more ruthless and sophisticated and formal than the quaint phrase "stream of consciousness" could hope to convey. The irony is that the nights when Rollins is at wit's end can be just as thrilling for illuminating the perils endemic to improvisation. The great thing about Rollins—as the critic Gary Giddins once put it—is that even when he's off, he's on.

Rollins is the greatest living jazz improviser (no arguments please), and if we redefine virtuosity to include improvisational cunning as well as instrumental finesse (as we probably should when discussing jazz), he may be the greatest virtuoso that jazz has ever produced. But listening to him is rarely the unequivocal pleasure it ought to be, for not only is he the least predictable of jazz artists, he is in one way the most perverse: the ecstasy his playing arouses in others he seems stubbornly unwilling to partake of himself. He is a notorious perfectionist, and the pressure he creates for himself sometimes pulls him up short. Most jazz musicians, including some of the great ones, simply turn on the charm and let technique take over when inspiration fails to visit them, confident that few in their audiences will be able to tell the difference between manual dexterity and divine intercession. Not Rollins, bless him and curse him. He will bring a solo to a halt if the grand design he has been tracing eludes him even momentarily.

On such occasions, Rollins's default shifts the burden of giving the customers their money's worth to his sidemen, which can lead to comic scenes like one I witnessed in Philadelphia a decade ago. Rollins led an unrealistic round of applause each time his pianist climaxed a solo and began comping for the Rollins solo he thought would ensue. Looking over and noticing Rollins's saxophone dangling from its strap, the harried pianist had no choice but to nod graciously to the audience and launch another chorus, as if by popular demand.

"I don't remember that particular incident, but I have to plead guilty anyway," Rollins said when I asked him about it. "People have admonished me for pulling stunts like that, so I try not to anymore. Around the time you're talking about, I was playing two or three sets a night in clubs, and I always hoped that people would hang around for the next set, and that the next set would be better. Now I'm usually in town for one show only, and knowing that people have come out to hear *me* play, I play for them, even when I'm displeased with what I hear myself playing. But you know, there are times when things aren't clicking and I play *extended* solos out of sheer frustration, but nobody ever complains about *that*. Which makes me wonder, because it's like I'm forcing the music instead of letting it flow, and that's no good. But maybe that's what people like—they sense the tension I'm feeling and it excites them."

If Rollins's self-doubt makes him seem the stereotypical modern artist, his music betrays thankfully little of the anomie associated with modern art. He can be the jolliest of improvisers. His best solos are full of jeering subterranean moans, cheeky falsetto whistles, and pecking staccato phrases that recall the bar-walking rhythm 'n' blues saxophonists popular in black neighborhoods 30 years ago. Although he may be the most abstract thinker in jazz, he has never turned his back on blues and popular song forms, not even during his brief flirtation with free form in the early '60s; and one of the dizziest thrills jazz has to offer is following the lines of a familiar melody as they expand and contract in the funhouse mirror of a Rollins improvisation. In recent years, his populism has led him to such unlikely but felicitous vehicles as Stevie Wonders "Isn't She Lovely" and the jouncy Dolly Parton hit "Here You Come Again." From the outset of his career, he has delighted in pop confections of the sort many of his more priggish jazz colleagues would think beneath their dignity.

"Songs like 'Toot, Toot, Tootsie,' 'Wagon Wheels,' 'There's No Business Like Show Business,' . . . songs hardly anyone had recorded before. Or *since*, for that matter," he cracked the afternoon I visited him and Lucille in the Tribeca penthouse efficiency they lease as a combination business office and home away from home when he plays New York. "Those are the songs that first made me love music, and I guess I heard most of them in the movies on Saturday afternoons when I was a kid. I tend to enjoy humorous, lighthearted things," he said, gesturing to the coffee table and sofa, which were piled high with books on genre films of every description. A hardback copy of Diane Johnson's biography of Dashiell Hammett lay open, spine up, on the daybed. "Old movies, *Mad* magazine, Bob and Ray—pure escapism, I know. But I guess it's okay, since I work hard at my music and have no real hobbies."

Rollins, who looks wary even when smiling, has a reputation as an unapproachable loner, an image he has done little to cultivate but nothing to dispel. Still, he and Lucille seemed genuinely pleased to be entertaining company, as we sat gazing down at gridlocked traffic. "It's so difficult readjusting to the pace of the city, even though I was born here and lived here most of my life," Rollins said. He had spent his week in New York taking care of errands—buying reeds, having his horn repaired, running clothes to the tailor. He hadn't looked up any old musician friends, and he hadn't been out to hear any live music. Next door, a teenage heavy metal band ran down their Led Zeppelin and Van Halen, occasionally eclipsing our conversation. "My protégés," Rollins winced. "They keep at it all day long." He was born Theodore Walter Rollins in 1929 (no one has called him that in years), to a Harlem family he describes as "middle class, with a piano in the living room and everything." His childhood ambition was to become a professional illustrator, but by the time he was graduated from high school, he was already earning money as a musician, playing in "kid bands with the other young guys from the neighborhood" (some of whom have also achieved adult renown, including alto saxophonist Jackie McLean, pianist Kenny Drew, and drummer Art Taylor) "and sitting in with the older guys who were kind enough to let me, like Bud Powell and Thelonious Monk." His role model was tenor patriarch Coleman Hawkins, "a forceful player with a big ripe sound, but a thoughtful player, too, very sophisticated in his knowledge of alternate chords—that was a good combination. He was a very classy fellow, always impeccably dressed and very patient with everyone, and that was something else I tried to emulate." I asked Rollins if he ever worried that his country isolation deprives today's young musicians of similar access to *him*. "Oh, you're making me feel guilty now," he complained, rubbing his goatee and fooling with the shapeless woolen cap he always seems to be wearing, even indoors. "But you see, Coleman Hawkins and Lockjaw Davis and those guys didn't just make themselves available to me. I practically camped out on their doorsteps until they took pity on me and invited me in."

The critic and composer Gunther Schuller once praised Rollins for knowing that "well-timed silence can become part of a musical phrase"; as a corollary, one might add that Rollins's frequent sabbaticals have played as large a part as his improvised solos in defining his mystique. The first hiatus came in 1954, and no one much noticed. "There was a scourge of drugs around that time," Rollins told me, "and like everybody else, I was part of it." It was a dressing down from Charlie Parker, of all people, that persuaded Rollins to enroll in an experimental methadone program at the federal prison in Lexington, Kentucky. Rollins and Parker were together in a New Jersey recording studio as sidemen on a Miles Davis date, and Parker—who knew that Rollins revered him—asked him if he was clean. Rollins lied and said yes, but Parker learned the truth from a hushed conversation he overheard between Rollins and another musician on the date. Ironically, it had been Parker's example that had induced many musicians of Rollins's generation to shoot up in the first place. "But you have to realize Charlie Parker wasn't just a great musician. He was a very sick man who was dying from self-abuse and feeling guilty about the example he had set for others," Rollins explained. He decided that the best way to show his love for Parker was to do as he said, not as he did.

In 1959, dissatisfaction with the jazz business and his own playing prompted Rollins to interrupt his career just as it was taking off. (Speculation had it that the acutely self-conscious Rollins had become too inhibited to play after reading Schuller's close structural analysis of one of his solos in the *Jazz Review*. Rollins admits only that he resolved to stop reading his notices soon after coming across Schuller's "Sonny Rollins and the Art of Thematic Improvisation." He still carries clippings of his reviews for the purpose of identification: not so much to prove that he is Sonny Rollins as to prove that Sonny Rollins is *somebody*—a nice distinction that might occur only to a black musician idolized in jazz but scarcely recognized outside of it, and traveling with a white wife.) Although unintended as such, his second vanishing act amounted to a major publicity coup. In abandoning his audience, he had not abandoned his instrument, and not wishing to subject the neighbors in his Brooklyn apartment house to the torture of his marathon practice sessions, he would practice in the dead of night on the pedestrian level of the Williamsburg Bridge, as private a rehearsal hall as he could ever hope to find. But one night the jazz critic Ralph Berton wandered by, and the anonymity that Rollins had hoped for was gone forever. Soon, the TV networks were sending camera crews to the bridge and portraying Rollins as a lofty and mystical idealist, a man who had turned his back on worldly riches to pursue self-knowledge. When he returned to the jazz scene in 1961, he was able to parlay his status as a media curiosity into a lucrative recording contract with RCA Victor.

By the end of the '60s, he had again turned away from public performance, though he continued to practice every day. He attended to chronic dental problems caused by a hard embouchere and journeyed to India to study yoga "not so much for the betterment of my music as for greater peace of mind, but my playing has benefited as a side effect, I think, in terms of greater wind capacity and greater mental concentration," he told me; and I noticed that his legs were folded up beneath him on the sofa, in the classic lotus position, even as we talked.

When Rollins began recording and accepting engagements again in 1972, his wife became his manager strictly by default: there was no one else he trusted to do the job. "I know of countless instances in which a musician's wife has taken an active role in her husband's career, usually with disastrous results to both the career and the marriage," says Orrin Keepnews, Rollins's close friend and his record producer from 1972 until 1980. "Lucille is one of the shining exceptions."

Many of the jazz wives who represent their husbands do so because their husbands have seduced them into thinking it's part of their wifely obligation, "or because they think it'll be fun, working so closely with their husbands, but they wind up hating it," explained Lucille Rollins as Sonny stared straight ahead. "You've got to know what you're doing, or you'll do more harm than good. At first, I felt like such an amateur dealing with club-owners and record producers that I used the pseudonym Janice Jesta for a while—Jesta was one of our cats. But I became more self-confident once I realized how much I love this business."

In addition to retaining veto power over her husband's bookings (he signed with an agency in 1979), Lucille Rollins, who worked as an office adminis-trator before their marriage, handles the payroll and travel arrangements for his band. (Rollins prefers staying at whatever hotel is closest to the airport and taking a limousine to the concert—that way he can make a faster getaway and he doesn't have to wander around a strange city.) Since the incident at Town Hall, she has traveled with him to most of his jobs; backstage in Boston, she made it a point to remind him to eat before going on stage.

The couple were co-producers of Rollins's last three albums, and even before that, Lucille had become Sonny's proxy at playbacks and mixdowns, because he cannot bear to listen to his own recordings—a point that emerged from our conversation when Lucille told me that the best performance she had ever heard her husband give was at the June 1983 makeup for the aborted Town Hall concert with Marsalis. Even Rollins had to admit that he played "okay." Lucille rolled her eyes and gasped "*Okay?* It was *fantastic!*" Too bad it wasn't recorded, I said, and a look of resignation settled on Rollins's face: "If it had been recorded, it might not have been okay."

"SONNY WILL ADMIT THAT RECORDING HAS ALWAYS BEEN A TRAUMATIC experience for him, and as the years have passed and he feels that he has more of a reputation to uphold, it's become even more traumatic, to use his own word," says Orrin Keepnews. "To some extent, every musician I've ever worked with has felt that he never put anything of value on a record. But Sonny is the supreme example. If the essence of jazz is improvisation, then the whole concept of recording—freezing a particular moment and calling it definitive—violates that essence. And Sonny, who is the most intuitive musician I've ever met as well as the most intellectual, is the musician most acutely aware of that contradiction."

Rollins's phobia hasn't prevented him from recording a goodly number of albums commonly regarded as classics, including *Saxophone Colossus, Worktime, A Night at the Village Vanguard, The Freedom Suite,* and *Way Out West,* all dating from a fertile period in the mid- to late '50s, when he was also in the studio regularly as a sideman with Miles Davis, Thelonious Monk, and Clifford Brown and Max Roach. From the 1960s, there are such still disputed masterpieces as *Our Man in Jazz,* with sidemen enlisted from Ornette Coleman's group, and *Sonny Meets Hawk,* a Mexican standoff with father figure Coleman Hawkins.

Toward the mid-'70s, Rollins began to employ younger musicians whose first allegiance was to amplified jazz-rock fusion, and one listened to his new records with enthusiastic ambivalence and exasperated awe, much the way earlier jazz listeners must have greeted the mature work of Louis Armstrong, who also embraced the most dubious musical conventions of his day. (This comparison is relevant in another way: as Armstrong had, Rollins began overindulging his technique at the cost of continuity, climaxing too many of his solos with gratuitous high notes sustained beyond purpose.) "I've always been a very rhythmic player," Rollins pointed out when I asked him about this change in direction, "and I want the rhythms beneath me to be rhythms you can feel throughout your entire system, not just something you can tap your foot to. I know that some people think I should be using a '50s kind of rhythm section, with upright bass walking a straight four beats to the measure, the piano blocking out chords, and the drummer going 'ta-da, ta-da,' or whatever, very discreetly on his cymbals. But that's tired, and it just doesn't appeal to me anymore. I want energy and constant propulsion, and I find only young players can give that to me. And rock rhythms or funk rhythms or whatever you want to call them are what the young guys are interested in today, along with electric instruments. So it's all been a natural progression for me, if you look at it that way."

Even if one looks at it Rollins's way, his logic is riddled with holes. He talks as though there are no options beyond bop and fusion, which is simply not the case. His present drummer's beat is chunky and metronomic compared with the drummers he recorded with in the '50s and '60s (you won't catch Max Roach or Billy Higgins or Elvin Jones going "ta-da, ta-da"). The bass guitarists he has been using tend to favor disruptive, guitar-like filigree rather than earthy, locomotive bass lines. Contrary to what Rollins believes, there are younger musicians playing hard bop who could follow him better and give him a higher lift than the fusioneers he insists on hiring, but it's doubtful if he has heard them. Talking to him, one gets the impression that he no longer monitors developments in jazz the way he did when he was younger—or the way Coleman Hawkins did throughout his career. In this, Rollins is no guiltier than most of his contemporaries, and in all fairness, it's as much lack of opportunity as lack of curiosity that's to blame. There's no 52nd Street anymore—no golden strip where musicians cross paths and trade secrets—and no one predominant jazz style. In its maturity, jazz has become both a bewilderingly pluralistic form of expression and a commercially marginal enterprise, a combination that effectively rules against an apprentice system or a chain of command. It's not surprising that outside of their own cliques, most veteran musicians have no better idea than the casual listener of who the hot young players are.

If Rollins's secret motive is to woo rock audiences, he has overestimated his capacity for the ordinary—his records have not been "commercial" in the simplest, most accurate sense: they haven't sold in enormous quantities. Yet with *No Problem* (Milestone M-9014) and *Reel Life* (Milestone M-9018), both released in 1982, Rollins's advocacy of a modified back beat began to pay unexpected artistic dividends. He was swinging more ferociously than ever, and he had escaped the sham democracy of modern jazz, which entitles each band member to solo to his heart's content on every single number. Rollins was now the star; his sidemen were relegated to back-up positions; and that was the way it should have been all along. Long portions of the 1984 release *Sunny Days and Starry Nights* (Milestone M-9122) are given over to exuberant, jabbing exchanges between Rollins and the drummer Tommy Campbell, with the rest of the band laying low or laying out. It's such a pleasure to hear Rollins duking it out with a drummer this way again that one is willing to ignore the fact that Campbell doesn't pack very much punch. The record also demonstrates Rollins's increased mastery of pop recording techniques. Multi-tracking enables him to be his own duet partner on Noel Coward's "I'll See You Again," and to weave a luxurious improvisation around his own held notes on an original ballad dedicated to Wynton Marsalis. (The pianist Mark Sloskin's overdubbed celeste is an especially nice touch on "Wynton," recalling Thelonious Monk's use of the delicate instrument on his 1957 recording of "Pannonica" with Rollins.) Also boasting a wickedly inventive chromatic orbit on Jerome Kern's "I'm Old Fashioned," and three snorting "St. Thomas"-like calypsos, *Sunny Days and Starry Nights* is the first Rollins LP in ages that one can enjoy from start to finish without first scaling down one's expectations. But like all of his records, it captures only the echo of his genius. To catch him in full cry, one must hear him live. And even then, there are no guarantees.

ON AN OVERHANGING WALL OPPOSITE THE BAR AT THE BOTTOM LINE ARE framed color glossies of Elvis Costello, Van Morrison, Philip Glass, and Phoebe Snow. A large, dark, characterless room near Washington Square, the Bottom Line is not a jazz club, but it is Rollins's club of preference in New York, because he can attract as many people there in one night as he would over several nights in a smaller jazz venue like Sweet Basil or the Village Vanguard. When I heard him at the Bottom Line in November 1983, all the tables were full an hour before showtime, the crowd was three deep in front of the bar, and SRO tickets were all that were available for the late show. It was at the Bottom Line that Mick Jagger heard Rollins and asked him to add saxophone tracks to the Rolling Stones' *Tattoo You.* Jagger was nowhere to be seen the night I was there, and whatever musicians were in the crowd respected Rollins's desire for privacy. In his dressing room between sets, he greeted only relatives and two close friends, a journalist and a physician, both there socially rather than professionally.

Rollins began playing well before the audience was admitted, hunching his shoulders and pacing the short runway between his dressing room and the stage, part fullback and part expectant father, as he worried over a long aching phrase that eventually blossomed into the old chestnut "Where Are You?" His sidemen ordered cold sandwiches and fried chicken dishes from the club's dinner menu, and the sound and lighting crews ran around shouting instructions to one another . . . "He doesn't like much follow coverage, not much saturation. Just create an environment and let it happen . . ." "The sax on top with everything else below it, right? . . ." Rollins was oblivious to all of them.

Without breaking stride, he played "Where Are You?" at the sound check, too, chipping away at the melody until nothing was left but a luminous, abstract, imperishable paraphrase, a point of departure for the stupendous choruses that seemed ready to come brimming out of his horn as the band began chording for him and he began tugging at their beat. But when Rollins surged into double time, he left the others clutching at air, and everything broke down. It was painfully obvious that his sidemen were not conversant enough with "Where Are You?" (which Rollins recorded in 1961 and perhaps heard Gertrude Niessen sing in the 1937 film *Top of the Town* at a Saturday matinee when he was in grade school) to take liberties with it.

After their leader left the stage, the guitarist Bobby Broom jumped into Tommy Campbell's vacated drum chair; and together, he and bass guitarist Russell Blake hammered out a funk rift that brought a smile to both their faces. The whole bizarre scene portrayed with a vengeance the difference in age between Rollins and his charges, all of whom are in their mid- to late twenties. The camaraderie one listens for in a good band was missing from this unit, perhaps as a result of their not having spent much off time together on the road. ("I just *practiced* with Coleman Hawkins," Rollins had told me. "I never hung out with him or anything, because I was just a kid and he was a grown man. What could we possibly have had in common?") Frequently, Rollins and his sidemen even take separate flights, because he prefers arriving in town a day early so that he won't have to battle travel fatigue when it comes time to play—quite a departure from the days when a whole band would travel together on a bus. The trombonist Clifton Anderson—Rollins's nephew, sometimes practice partner, and newest member of his band—told me that there had not been a full group rehearsal in the four months he had been with Rollins. "Everyone in the band realizes that Sonny is a master, and the people turn out mainly to hear him, not us," Anderson said. "So as long as he's in a good mood and really feels like playing, we just try to keep up with him. But it can be hard. He can throw you, seguing from number to number the way he does and trying out tunes in different keys."

Once the show started, Rollins continued to pace, the shadow cast by the brim of his floppy red velvet hat forming a hood over his eyes. On some numbers, he played an aural game of hide-and-seek with the crowd, offering nothing that could be considered an improvised chorus. Yet his sweet and sour theme recapitulations were so delicious, his movements which cheered on the rhythm section so disarming, and his habit of cradling his horn in his arms and announcing song titles directly into the lipstick mike mounted in the bell at once so distancing and so benign (talk about star presence!) that the audience rewarded him with rapturous ovations for these pieces anyway, shouting their approval of solos they had only imagined hearing.

But on "Cabin in the Sky," "I'll Be Seeing You," and "I'm Old Fashioned," Rollins unloosed solos beyond anyone's power of imagining save his own. His band gave him all the energy and propulsion he could have wished for, creating grooves that had this jazz audience dancing in its seats and might have had a rock audience dancing in the aisles. But Rollins's barking crescendos carried such vehement rhythmic impact and shone with such harmonic iridescence as to render all accompaniment superfluous. And indeed, the most satisfying moments of the evening came when he dispensed with the band altogether for twisting out-of-tempo intros and lapidary cadenzas which he tossed off with an astonishing and somehow reassuring what–me–worry? nonchalance. He was in such high spirits that as he bit into the roguish "Alfie's Theme," he motioned Anderson to weave a counterpoint behind him, and what had served as a brief and perfunctory sign-off riff in Boston just a week before stretched out over 15 minutes with bubbling solos all around. The set fell short of perfection (there was nothing as magnificent as those few tentative measures of "Where Are You?"), but Sonny Rollins accomplished two things only he could have: he convinced you that the next set might be the best live jazz concert you'd ever hear; and more important, he convinced you that, coming from an improviser, that's a promise as thrilling for the making as for the keeping.

(APRIL 1984)

No Success Like Failure:
Ornette Coleman's
Permanent Revolution

W hen Ornette Coleman made his East Coast nightclub debut opposite the Art Farmer–Benny Golson Jazztet at the Five Spot Cafe in Greenwich Village on November 18, 1959, "all hell broke loose," in Coleman's apt phrase. "Everybody in New York was saying you've got to go down to the Five Spot and hear this crazy alto player from Texas. It was like I was E.T. or something, just dropped in from the moon, and everybody had to come take a look at me."

The 29-year-old alto saxophonist arrived in New York having already won the approval of some of the period's most influential jazz opinion-makers. "Ornette Coleman is doing the only really new thing in jazz since the innovations in the mid '40s of Dizzy Gillespie and Charlie Parker, and those of Thelonious Monk," John Lewis, the pianist and musical director of the Modern Jazz Quartet, told an interviewer after hearing Coleman in Los Angeles. (Lewis later helped Coleman secure a contract with Atlantic Records.) Coleman's other champions included the critics Nat Hentoff and Martin Williams and the composer Gunther Schuller, all of whom wrote for the magazine *Jazz Review*. "I believe that what Ornette Coleman is playing will affect the whole character of jazz music profoundly and pervasively," Williams editorialized a month before Coleman opened at the Five Spot.

Not all of Williams's colleagues shared his enthusiasm once they were given the opportunity to hear Coleman for themselves. In *Down Beat*, George Hoefer described the reactions of an audience at a special press preview at the Five Spot: "Some walked in and out before they could finish a drink, some sat mesmerized by the sound, others talked constantly to their neighbors at the table or argued with drink in hand at the bar." Many critics, finding Coleman's

music strident and incoherent, feared that his influence on jazz would be dele-
terious. Others doubted that he would exert any influence on jazz at all. Still
others, bewildered by Coleman's music and preferring to take a wait-and-see
position on its merits, accused his supporters at *Jazz Review* of touting him
for their own aggrandizement. Musicians—always skeptical of newcomers
and envious of the publicity that Coleman was receiving—denounced him
even more harshly than critics did. Some questioned his integrity as well as his
instrumental competence; the outspoken Miles Davis went so far as to question his sanity.

"Every night the club would be jammed, with some people hating what I
was doing and calling me a charlatan, and other people loving it and declaring me a genius," Coleman says. "I remember one well established musician—
a drummer, and I'm not going to name any names—becoming so upset he
kicked down the door to the men's room, then coming after me and landing
a punch on my jaw before the bartender could pull him off. Incredible isn't a
strong enough word for it."

"Many musicians were terrified that what Ornette was doing would render
their music obsolete. That was the absurd part of it," remembers Martin
Williams, now a Special Editor at Smithsonian Institution Press. It was
Williams who landed Coleman the Five Spot engagement by playing an acetate
of his music for Joe and Iggy Termini, the club's owners. "Some musicians had
studied for years to learn everything it was possible to know about chord
changes, and here comes a man whose approach was highly intuitive, reaping
all that publicity, and telling them, in essence, that harmony wasn't as all-
important as they assumed. He sounded like a primitive to them. Yet if you
gave him the benefit of the doubt, it was obvious that he knew his instrument
inside out. I remember hearing him at the Five Spot one night during a bliz-
zard, when he played a blues exactly as Charlie Parker might have—and I mean
exactly, the embouchere, the attack, all of it—and the few people who braved
the weather that night just sat there with their mouths open in astonishment,
because this was something he was supposed to be incapable of doing. Sonny
Rollins was there, listening intently at the end of the bar, and I looked around
at the end to see his reaction, but he had disappeared into the night."

Infighting over the merits of historical movements and geographical
schools was nothing new in the jazz world. But not since the short-lived vogue
for the decrepit New Orleans trumpeter Bunk Johnson (and perhaps not even
then) had one musician split opinion so dramatically. Coleman was either a
visionary or a fraud, and there was no middle ground between advocacy and
disapprobation. The controversy raged, spreading from the music journals to
daily newspapers and general-interest magazines, where it gradually turned
comic. Every VIP in Manhattan, from Leonard Bernstein to Dorothy Kil-

gallen, seemed to have been to the Five Spot and to have emerged with wisdom to offer on the subject of Ornette Coleman. In Thomas Pynchon's first novel *V.*, there is a character named McClintic Sphere, who plays an alto saxophone of hand-carved ivory (Coleman's was made of white plastic) at a club called the V Note:

> "He plays all the notes Bird missed," somebody whispered in front of Fu. Fu went through the motions of breaking a beer bottle on the edge of the table, jamming it into the speaker's back and twisting.

This was the closest modern jazz would ever come to Beatlemania or the premiere of *Le Sacre du Printemps.*

THE SILVER ANNIVERSARY OF COLEMAN'S FIVE SPOT OPENING PASSED virtually unnoticed toward the end of 1984. Coleman wasn't even aware that it was coming up, and if there had been an official commemoration, he would probably have been too busy to attend. As November 18 approached, he had just returned from a European tour with his band Prime Time. Following a 72-hour stopover in New York, he flew to Fort Worth, Texas (his birthplace), to mix two albums he hopes eventually to sell to an independent label—one a live performance by Prime Time, the other a eulogy for Buckminster Fuller with the Fort Worth Symphony. After running into endless financial roadblocks, the filmmaker Shirley Clarke had finally completed *Made in America,* the bio-documentary on Coleman which she started shooting in 1968; Coleman was making plans to attend the world premiere in West Berlin early the following year. When he found a spare moment, he worked on "The Oldest Language," a piece calling for the participation of 130 musicians from Europe, North America, and the Third World, all of whom would have to live together for six months and reconcile their cultural and linguistic differences before learning Coleman's score. Coleman is no fool; he knows that the cost of such a project is prohibitive. "I've got to find an angel," he muses in his soft Texas drawl. "I know it can be done. Philip Glass has written things like *Einstein on the Beach* which must have cost a million dollars to stage. That proves it's possible."

The disarray of Coleman's loft, which occupies the top floor of a public schoolhouse on New York's Lower East Side and doubles as living quarters and rehearsal space, mirrors Coleman's vagabond lifestyle and his perilous financial station. One wall is nothing but windows looking out on grim streets still awaiting the first signs of gentrification. The sparsely and indifferently furnished room is dominated by professional-quality sound equipment, including a mixing board and speakers the size of small manned spacecraft, and by Coleman's own paintings, many of them photorealist renderings of his album jackets. In

part, Coleman's interest in classical music, poetry, and the visual arts is the result
of the interest classical composers, poets, and visual artists displayed in his work
when he arrived in New York in 1959 (the Five Spot was a popular watering
hole for artists long before the Termini brothers adopted a jazz policy). The
open hostility of fellow jazz musicians wounded Coleman, but it was nothing
new: he had been a pariah in Los Angeles in the 1940s and on the Southern
chitlin circuit before that. At least in New York, he was able to make friends
outside of jazz. The attention from famous artists surprised and delighted him.
"You have to realize I wasn't trying to be an intellectual or anything like that. I
had very little formal schooling, and coming from Texas, I had never even spoken as an equal to a white person until I moved out to California when I was
21," he says. As a self-made man, he is quite a piece of work.

FOR THOSE OF US WHO BEGAN LISTENING TO JAZZ AFTER 1959, IT IS
difficult to imagine that Coleman's music was once the source of animus and
widespread debate. Given the low visibility of jazz today, a figure as heretical
as Coleman arriving on the scene might find himself in the position of shouting "Fire" in an empty theater. Looking back, it also strains belief that so many
of Coleman's peers initially failed to recognize the suppleness of his phrasing
and the keening vox-humana quality of his intonation. Jazz musicians have
always respected instrumentalists able to "talk" on their horns, and they have
always sworn by the blues (although as jazz has increased in sophistication, the
blues has come to signify a feeling or tonal coloring, in addition to specific
forms). Coleman's blues authenticity—the legacy of the Texas juke joints he
had played as a teenager—should have scored him points instantly, especially
in 1959 when hard boppers were writing sanctified ditties with titles like
"Work Song" and "Dat Dere," to celebrate their Southern roots (and, not
coincidentally, to cash in on a trend). But Coleman was too much the genuine article; his ragged, down-home sound cast him in the role of country
cousin to his slicker, more urbanized brethren—as embarrassing a reminder
of their second-class status as a Yiddish-speaking relative might have been to
a newly assimilated Jew. In 1959 the old country for most black musicians was
the American South, and few of them wanted any part of it.

   Still, what must have bothered musicians more than the unmistakable
Southern dialect of Coleman's music was its apparent formlessness, its flout-
ing of rules that most jazz modernists had invested time and effort in learning (as Martin Williams suggests). In the wake of bebop, jazz had become a
music of enormous harmonic complexity. By the late '50s it also seemed to be
in danger of becoming a playground for virtuosos, as the once liberating practice of running the chords became routine. If some players sounded at times
as though they lacked commitment and were merely going through the

motions, it was because the motion of making each chord change was what they had become most committed to.

In one sense, the alternative that Coleman proposed amounted to nothing more drastic than a necessary (and, in retrospect, inevitable) suppression of harmony in favor of melody and rhythm. But this amounted to heresy in 1959. It has often been said that Coleman dispensed with recurring chord patterns altogether, in both his playing and his writing. This is not entirely accurate, however. Rather, he treated a harmonic sequence as just one of many options for advancing a solo. Coleman might improvise from the chords or, as inspiration moved him, instead use as his point of departure "a mood, fragment of melody, an area of pitch, or rhythmic fragment," to quote Williams. Moreover, Coleman's decision to dispense with a chordal road map also permitted him rhythmic trespass across bar lines. The stealthy rubato of his phrases and his sudden accelerations of tempo implied liberation from strict meter, much as his penchant for hitting notes a quarter-tone sharp or flat and his refusal to harmonize his saxophone with Don Cherry's trumpet during group passages implied escape from the well-tempered scale.

Ultimately, rhythm may be the area in which Coleman has made his most significant contributions to jazz. Perhaps the trick of listening to his performances lies in an ability to hear rhythm as melody, and melody as rhythm, the way he seems to, and the way jazz pioneers did. Some of his phrases, like some of King Oliver's or Sidney Bechet's, sound as though they were scooped off a drumhead.

Coleman was hardly the only musician to challenge chordal hegemony in 1959. John Coltrane, Miles Davis, Sonny Rollins, Horace Silver, Thelonious Monk, and Max Roach, among others, were looking beyond Charlie Parker's harmonic discoveries to the melodic and contrapuntal implications of bop. Cecil Taylor and George Russell were experimenting with chromaticism and pantonality, and a Miles Davis sextet featuring Coltrane and Bill Evans had just recorded *Kind of Blue,* an album that introduced a new spaciousness to jazz by replacing chords with modes and scales. But it was Coleman who was making the clearest break with convention, and Coleman whose intuitive vision of the future bore the most natural relationship with jazz's pragmatic country origins. He was a godsend, as it turned out.

IN 1959 COLEMAN'S MUSIC TRULY REPRESENTED "SOMETHING ELSE" (TO quote the title of his first album). Whether it also forecast "the shape of jazz to come" (another early album title) is still problematical. Certainly, Coleman's impact on jazz was immediate, and it has proved long-lasting. Within a few years of Coleman's first New York engagement, established saxophonists like Coltrane, Rollins, and Jackie McLean were playing a modified free form, often in the company of former Coleman sidemen. The iconoclastic bassist Charles Mingus (initially one of the skeptics) was leading a piano-less quartet featuring the alto saxophonist Eric Dolphy and the trumpeter Ted Curson, whose open-ended dialogues seemed inspired by those of Coleman and Cherry.

Over the years, Coleman has continued to cast a long shadow as he has extended his reach to symphonies; string quartets, and experiments in funk. By now, he has attracted two generations of disciples. There are the original sidemen in his quartet and their eventual replacements: the trumpeters Cherry and Bobby Bradford; the tenor saxophonist Dewey Redman; the bassists Charlie Haden, Scott LaFaro, Jimmy Garrison, and David Izenzon; and the drummers Billy Higgins, Ed Blackwell, and Charles Moffett. They were followed in the late '70s by musicians who brought to Coleman's bands the high voltage of rock and funk, most notably the guitarist James Blood Ulmer, the electric bassist Jamaaladeen Tacuma, and the drummer Ronald Shannon Jackson. Some of Coleman's early associates in Texas and California, including the clarinetist John Carter and the flutist Prince Lawsha, have gone on to produce work that bears Coleman's influence, as have Albert Ayler, Anthony Braxton, and the others whom Coleman put up when they first arrived in New York, and lent money to so that they could produce their own concerts. Coleman planted the seed for the free jazz movement of the 1960s, which in turn gave rise to a school of European "instant" composers led by the guitarist Derek Bailey and the saxophonist Evan Parker. Since 1965, Coleman has performed on trumpet and violin in addition to alto and tenor saxophones, and several young violinists have taken him as their model: Billy Bang, for example, whose jaunty, anthem-like writing also bespeaks an affection for Coleman. A relatively new form in jazz is the tempo-less ballad, the offspring of onrushing Coleman dirges like "Sadness," "Lonely Woman," and "Beauty Is a Rare Thing" (they could be described as mournful ballad performances, except that no one is playing in strict ballad tempo, and no one is mourning). And for all practical purposes, the idea of collective group improvisation, which has reached an apex in the work of groups affiliated with the AACM, began with the partial liberation of bass and drums from chordal and timekeeping duties in the first Ornette Coleman Quartet.

IF ONE LISTENS FOR THEM, ONE CAN HEAR COLEMANESQUE ACCENTS IN THE most unlikely places: the maundering piano soliloquies of Keith Jarrett, the space age meditations of the guitarist Pat Metheny, and the Socratic dialogues of young hard boppers like Wynton and Branford Marsalis. It is impossible to imagine how jazz might have evolved without Coleman, and he has even affected the way we listen to jazz that predates him. Yet for all of that, his way has never replaced Charlie Parker's as the lingua franca of jazz, as many hoped and others feared it might.

One reason could be that Coleman's low visibility has denied the jazz avant-garde a figurehead. "He hasn't played enough, especially in America," says Neshui Ertegun, president of WEA International and Coleman's record producer from 1959 to 1961. "I'm not saying that he's wrong to demand the things he demands from record companies and concert promoters, but it's made him invisible for long periods of time. As a consequence, his impact hasn't been as enormous as it might have been."

Coleman's Five Spot engagement, originally scheduled to last two weeks, ran six months; in all, he played a year and a half at the club between 1959 and 1961. But his failure to negotiate the controversy he caused into hard cash left him bitter and suspicious. "I was a patsy," he says now. "I never made more than two hundred dollars a week at the Five Spot, and when I would play a job in another city, I would wind up working for nothing after I paid travel expenses and hotel bills, even though there would be people lined up around the block waiting to hear me. Booking agents would tell me I wasn't in the business long enough to ask for top dollar, that I was just a creation of the press, a novelty that would pass."

"All of us were naive, not just Ornette," says the bassist Charlie Haden. "All we cared about was music. Joe and Iggy Termini were sweet guys, nice guys, but they were paying us practically nothing. We couldn't even pay our rents. And they were making lots of money off us. That club was jammed every single night we were there."

"I started asking for good money when I realized how the system works," says Coleman. "You see Coca-Cola all over the world, right? You know what else you see? My records. Record companies tell me my albums don't sell, but if that was true, they wouldn't be all over the place. Somebody's making a living from them, and it isn't me. I haven't found one person in the record business willing to deal with me in an equitable way, as a person rather than a commodity."

Since the early '60s, Coleman has set a price for concerts and recordings that reflects what he perceives to be his artistic merit rather than his limited commercial appeal. Needless to say, he has had very few takers. Even with over 30 albums on the market (not counting bootlegs) some of the best music he has recorded (including a 1977 reunion of his original quartet, with Cherry, Haden, and Higgins) remains unissued. Despite receiving numerous grants, including Guggenheim Fellowships in 1967 and 1974, he has been insolvent for most of his career. In 1984, the Internal Revenue Service slapped him with a $5,000 fine for failing to file tax returns for 1977 and 1978. Because he suffered net losses from bad investments for those years, he assumed he did not have to declare his earnings as a performer. The IRS was not charmed by his naiveté. The neighborhood he lives in is drug-infested, and he has been

burglarized twice since moving there in 1982. The second incident was especially scary. Two neighborhood youths he hired to help him lug sound equipment up the five flights to his apartment broke in later that night when he was
out. When he walked in on them, they hit him on the head with a crowbar
and stabbed him in the back. Hospitalized with a collapsed lung, he was
unable to play his saxophone for six months, and he says that the scar tissue
still itches. Not that it would have made a difference to them, but it is unlikely
that his teenage assailants had any idea that their victim was a celebrity of sorts.

JUST A FEW YEARS AGO IT APPEARED THAT COLEMAN'S STAR WAS ON THE
rise again. In 1977 his former sidemen Cherry, Redman, Haden, and Blackwell formed the band Old and New Dreams. Coleman compositions, old and
new, accounted for roughly half their repertoire. If the myth that Coleman
had to be physically present in order for his music to be played properly persisted in some quarters, Old and New Dreams dispelled it once and for all.
They played his music with a joy and heart of purpose that bore witness to his
omniscience as a composer. The reaction to Old and New Dreams showed
that the music once both hailed and reviled as the wave of the future had taken
a firm enough hold in the past to inspire nostalgia.

The rapture with which jazz audiences greeted the band's reinterpretations
of vintage Coleman owed something to the fact that Coleman himself had
moved on to other frontiers—appearing with two electric guitarists, two bass
guitarists, and two drummers in a configuration he called Prime Time. This
band provided the working model for a cryptic (and, one suspects, largely
after-the-fact) theory of tonality that Coleman calls harmolodics, based on the
premise that instruments can play together in different keys without becoming tuneless or exchanging the heat of the blues for a frigid atonality. (As the
critic Robert Palmer pointed out in *The New York Rocker*, Coleman's music
had always been "harmolodic" in a sense.) In practice the harmolodic theory
functioned like a McGuffin in a Hitchcock film: if you could follow what it
was all about, good for you; if you couldn't, that wasn't going to hamper your
enjoyment one iota. What mattered more than any amount of theorizing was
that Coleman was leading jazz out of a stalemate, much as he had in 1959.
He had located indigenous jazz rhythms that played upon the reflexes of the
body the way the simultaneously bracing and relaxing polyrhythms of funk
and New Wave rock 'n' roll do.

"In jazz, it's when the drummer sounds like he's playing with everybody else
that people say the music is swinging," Coleman says. "In rock 'n' roll and
funk, it's when everybody else sounds like they're playing with the drummer."
With Prime Time, he combined the best of both worlds. "In my band, all the

instruments are independent and equal. Lots of drummers think that time is rhythm, but rhythm is independent of time. When I'm playing time, the drummers can play rhythm; when I'm playing rhythm, they can play time."

Unlike most of the jazz musicians who embraced dance rhythms in the '70s, Coleman wasn't slumming or taking the path of least resistance in search of a mass following. Nonetheless, a modest commercial breakthrough seemed imminent in 1981, when he signed with Island Records and named Stan and Sid Bernstein as his managers (the latter was the promoter who brought the Beatles to Shea Stadium in 1965). There is some disagreement among the principal parties about what happened next. "Nothing is simple for Ornette when it comes to money," says Stan Bernstein. "He made demands that are unrealistic in this business unless you're Michael Jackson." According to Coleman, "my managers sold *Of Human Feelings,** which was the first digital jazz album recorded in the U.S., for less money than it had cost me to make it, and I never saw a penny of the royalties." Coleman was paid $25,000 for the rights to *Of Human Feelings,* "not a terrific sum but not a modest sum, either, for a jazz artist," according to Ron Goldstein, who was at that time in charge of Antilles, Island's jazz custom label. 'The figure was based on what we realistically thought we could sell, not what it had cost Ornette to record the album." Goldstein says that Coleman was given a $25,000 "one fund" advance to record a follow up to *Of Human Feelings*—one fund meaning that whatever was left over from recording costs was Coleman's to pocket. This much is clear: Coleman went over budget, asked for more money, and was refused. What should have been his second record for Island Antilles has never been released, and there is now some question of who owns the rights to the masters. The label did not pick up its option on him. In 1983, he severed his ties with the Bernstein Agency and again went into partial eclipse.

Lately, the task of shedding Coleman's light has fallen to his acolytes Ulmer, Jackson, and Tacuma. They have not sold very many records either, despite a greater willingness to accommodate public tastes—and despite reams of publicity from the intellectual wing of the rock press. When Coleman next makes a move, harmolodics may be an idea whose time has come and gone, so far as the critics and record companies are concerned. In the photographer Carol Friedman's book *A Moment's Notice,* there is a haunting portrait of Coleman facing the camera with his hands up over his face. It is recognizably him, but for all he lets us see of himself, he might as well not be there. No doubt Coleman's grievances are real. But if he is a neglected artist, it is impossible to avoid the conclusion that he bears complicity for his neglect.

---

*Antilles AN-2001, recorded in 1979 and released in 1982.

SEVERAL MILES WEST OF COLEMAN'S LOFT, A NEW HIGH RISE CONDO-
minium is going up at 5 Cooper Square, where the Five Spot used to be. Sometimes Coleman's influence is as difficult to trace as the club where he made his
heroic stand. Still, in the final analysis, his failure to redefine jazz as decisively
as many predicted he would is more the result of the accelerated pace at which
jazz was evolving *before* he arrived in New York than of his relative lack of activity since then. During the 50 years before 1959, a series of upheavals had taken
jazz from its humble folk origins and made of it a codified art music. It was as
though jazz has imitated the evolution of European concert music in a frac-
tion of the time. Just as the term "classical music" has come to signify European concert music of the late eighteenth and early nineteenth century, the
words "modern jazz" have become synonymous with the style of jazz originally called bebop.

With Ornette Coleman, jazz established its permanent avant-garde, its
"new" that would always remain new—comparable to the ongoing attack on
tonality in classical music, on narrative in post-First World War fiction, and
on representation in twentieth-century art. If one measures a player's influence solely by the number of instrumentalists who adopt aspects of his style
(the standard yardstick in jazz), Coleman finishes a distant third among his
contemporaries to John Coltrane and Miles Davis. Yet his accomplishment
seems somehow greater than theirs, for they merely showed which elements
of free form the jazz mainstream could absorb—modality; approximate harmonies, saxophone glossolalia, the sixteenth note as a basic unit of measure-
ment, the use of auxiliary percussion and horns once considered
"exotic"—and which elements it finally could not—variable pitch, free meter,
collective improvisation. Coleman's early biography is replete with stories of
musicians packing up their instruments and leaving the bandstand when he
tried to sit in. If Coleman showed up now incognito at a jam session presided
over by younger followers of Parker, Davis, and Coltrane, chances are he
would still be given the cold shoulder. Bebop seems to be invincible, though
Coleman and those who have taken their cue from him continue to challenge
its hegemony. The bop revolution of the '40s was the last in a series of successful coup d'etats. Coleman's revolution will never wholly succeed or fail. It
is going to be a permanent revolution, its skirmishes marking the emergence
of jazz as a full-fledged modern art, with all of modernism's dualities and
contradictions.

And jazz is only part of it. Coleman's idiosyncratic symphonies and string
quartets and his espousal of funk have helped demolish the barriers between
what he calls "the three kinds of Western music—racial or ethnic, popular,
and classical. I've transcended racial distinctions and stylistic divisions," he
says, a tape of a recent performance of "The Skies of America" (the symphonic

work that introduced the concept of harmolodics) booming out as he talks, doing more to warm up his chilly loft than the space heater in the middle of the bare floor. "I haven't had much material success, but I'm not a failure, either. I created music that's better than was there before," he says with the satisfaction of an artist who knows that his music has endured a quarter of a century and the wisdom of a prophet who knows it shall probably endure the ages as well. What does not change for him is the will to change, this man who seems bent on proving Bob Dylan's axiom: There's no success like failure, and failure's no success at all.

(NOVEMBER 1984/SEPTEMBER 1985)

Leading Lady

W hen the singer Abbey Lincoln gives her autograph, she appends the name *Aminata Moseka*. During her pilgrimage to Africa in 1975, the president of Guinea christened her "Aminata" in recognition of her inner strength and determination, and Zaire's minister of education likened her to "Moseka," the god of love in female form. "I love Aminata Moseka. I've added her to myself. But I can't say that's my one and only name," says Lincoln, who has taken many names, experienced several rebirths, in her fifty-five years, and who invests as much thought and feeling in conversation as she does in her songs. "It's more like a title—something to live up to. That's why I recorded Stevie Wonder's 'Golden Lady.' It gave me the opportunity to sing to a female god. But I'm still Abbey Lincoln—I still like to wear makeup and glittering dresses and look attractive for an audience. And in many ways, I'm still Anna Marie."

Anna Marie Wooldridge was the name she was born with in Chicago in 1930, the tenth of twelve children. Before she started school, her family moved to rural Calvin Center, Michigan. "My parents were city folk, but the story goes that because my mother insisted that the country was the only place to raise children, my father saved up and built a house for us on the eleven and a half acres he bought. I still remember the sound of my father's voice as he sang lullabies to me and my baby sister. He was a fine singer who might have become a professional if he and my mother hadn't had so many children. But they had a wonderful, lifelong love affair, and we were the result. He did odd jobs around the community, taking care of people's gardens and such, and my first exposure to music was from the records that neighbors would give to him instead of throwing them away. The one I remember best went 'Take them up in the air, boys. Take them up in the air.' It was by [the black vaudevillian] Bert Williams, and I guess it was recorded just after air travel became commonplace. The point was that's how men could impress women—take 'em up in the air.

"I sang in school pageants and in the church choir, though I never much enjoyed that. I preferred to sing alone—to be the centerpiece, for lack of a better word. The living room piano was my private space, once I discovered that singing could win me attention and admiration."

At nineteen, she began her professional career as Gabby Wooldridge. "I was Gabby for two years, because the owners of the Moulin Rouge in Los Angeles wanted all their girls to have French-sounding names. They didn't realize that Anna Marie *was* French; it was Wooldridge that was the problem. They knew less about their European heritage than I knew about my African heritage, which was nothing." She discarded the surname soon after an aged white millionaire also named Wooldridge spotted a mention of her in a newspaper and wrote to inquire whether she was his long-lost heir. "That's when I realized that although Wooldridge was the name my father handed down, it wasn't really ours."

At that time, her manager was Bob Russell, best known for his lyrics to Duke Ellington's "Do Nothing 'Til You Hear from Me" and "Don't Get Around Much Anymore," and pop standards including "Time Was" and "Crazy, She Calls Me."

"Recognizing something potentially fierce and proud and independent in me, Bob renamed me Abbey Lincoln. He said, jokingly, 'Well, Abe Lincoln didn't really free the slaves, but maybe you will,'

When I signed with Liberty Records, as a promotional gimmick, they sent the disc jockeys a photo of me wearing one of Marilyn Monroe's skin-tight dresses superimposed over President Lincoln's face on a penny. It was ridiculous, and, of course, nobody got the joke. But the name worked magic on my life. As Abbey Lincoln, I acquired a reputation as a woman warrior."

> But for the painted lady,
> There is a point and stare,
> And eyes that ask a question:
> Is she going anywhere?
> (*Painted Lady*,
> Moseka Music, BMI)

The covers of Lincoln's first few albums (most are still available in facsimile editions) mirror her growing self-awareness. *Affair*, her debut, released in 1957 and subtitled *A Story of a Girl in Love*, shows her lounging centerfold-style, like a sepia Julie London, a come-hither look in her eyes, her breasts barely contained in her lowcut blouse. "That was the way they packaged women singers then, and I went along with it because I didn't know any better. I didn't yet think of myself as a serious artist—or as a serious person, either. All I wanted was to be thought of as beautiful and desirable."

Although the covers of the three albums she made for Riverside in the late '50s after becoming romantically involved with the drummer Max Roach (whom she married in 1962) made no secret of the fact that she was a shapely woman, the fortitude that was coming to light in her singing was also becoming manifest in the poses she struck for the camera. Gaining a sense of herself as a black woman, she took herself off the sexual auction block. "Through Max, I met a circle of black artists—not only musicians, but actors, novelists, poets and playwrights. It was the early days of the civil rights movement, and we were all asking the same questions. But they were questions that glamour girls weren't supposed to ask. As I toured the country, I noticed that black people everywhere were living in slums, in abject poverty. I wanted to know why."

Gone were the strings that had accompanied her on *Affair*. Her delivery never really changed, but she was recording with jazz pacesetters like Roach, Sonny Rollins, Wynton Kelly, and Kenny Dorham now, often performing topical material. Although she continued to do standards, she banished from her repertoire songs about unrequited love and "no-good men who didn't know how to treat women. I discovered that you *become* what you sing. You can't repeat lyrics night after night as though they were prayer without having them come true in your life."

By 1961, when she collaborated with Roach and the lyricist Oscar Brown, Jr., on *We Insist: The Freedom Now Suite* (the original cover showed a reenactment of a sit-in at a segregated Southern lunch counter), she'd been branded an outspoken, intractable militant. Record companies considered her too hot to handle. "I would run into my old show-business associates who would be surprised to see me looking pretty much the way I had always looked, and they would say 'Abbey, we heard you were living in Greenwich Village, wearing black wooly stockings, and sleeping with musicians.' The word was out on me, and I was in plenty of trouble. But at least it was trouble of my own choosing. As the woman of easy virtue I was encouraged to portray earlier, I was on the road to loneliness and despair."

Over the last two decades, Lincoln's records have been few, less the result of a lingering backlash than of the American record industry's antipathy toward jazz. The records that have originated from Europe and Japan since *We Insist* and its companion album *Straight Ahead* show Lincoln wearing her hair natural or in dreadlocks or cornrows. "My straightened hair was the last curse left on my body. I started wearing a natural long before it became fashionable, and people would tell me I was a pretty woman, why didn't I make myself more presentable? But I was determined to find my hair beautiful, to find myself and the people I was representing up there on stage beautiful just as we were—even if no one else did."

I think about the life I live,
A figure made of clay,
And think about the things I lost,

Things I gave away
And when I'm in a certain mood,
I search the halls and look.
One night I found these magic words
In a magic book:

Throw it away!
You can throw it away.
Give your love,
Live your life,
Each and every day,

And keep your hands hide open,
And let the sun shine through,
'Cause you can never lose a thing
If it belongs to you.
                    (*Throw It Away*, Moseka
                        Music, BMI)

In concert, with her regal bearing and forthright declamation, Lincoln conveys an actress's riveting stage presence, without indulging in salacious flirtation, histrionic bathos, or sociopolitical cant. The jazz critic Martin Williams once saluted Billie Holiday as an actress without an act—and that accolade also describes Lincoln, who did in fact enjoy a sporadic film career, singing one number in the 1956 rock exploitation flick *The Girl Can't Help It;* co-starring in the acclaimed, independently produced 1964 civil-rights-of-passage film *Nothing But A Man,* and playing Sidney Poitier's love interest in the 1968 romantic comedy *For Love of Ivy.*

"With *Ivy*, my life reached a peak," she says. "Then it slid right into the valley again." *Ivy*'s producers optioned the rights to Billie Holiday's autobiography *Lady Sings the Blues* for Lincoln, but finally they were resold to Motown's Berry Gordy, who cast his own star, Diana Ross, in the lead. "I always loved Billie," Lincoln says, "but I was scared of her, too. She came to hear me once in Honolulu and just sat at the bar staring at me without saying a word. Years later, she came to Birdland one night when Dizzy Gillespie was playing and Max and I were in the audience. 'I'm so lonely,' she told me. 'Louis is in California on business, and I'm sitting at home washing my hair and polishing my nails and going crazy.' And everybody in the club knew that Louis McKay, her husband, was a few blocks away living it up with a woman who called herself Broadway Betty. That's the worst lie they told in the movie version of her life. Why give her one husband, when in real life she had four or five? If she'd had a man as faithful to her as the Billy Dee Williams character in the movie, her life might not have been so tragic. The problem was that although she could have had any man she wanted, she was only attracted to men who mistreated her.

"In a way, it's best that I didn't play Billie, because I don't know how to do anything half way. I was in such a sorry state myself at the time that portraying Billie's sorrow might have killed me. Max and I were divorced in 1970, and I was like a wounded animal. It's difficult recovering from a broken marriage, especially when it throws your career up into the air. I needed sanctuary, so I signed myself into a psychiatric hospital in upstate New York for five weeks, which turned out to be one of the best things that's ever happened to me."

Moving to Los Angeles to care for her ailing mother in 1973, Lincoln laid low for eight years, rarely performing. "I went underground, though I never intended to. I did community work and taught drama at Northridge University, where I felt a little out of place because I hadn't attended college myself. The good part about being in California was spending my mother's last years by her side. Oscar Brown, Jr., had shown me how to use the *I Ching,* and I would take comfort in the hexagram that said you cannot lose something that belongs to you *even if you throw it away.* I had thrown away my career, my relationship with Max—and I thought I had thrown away my life."

> *I'm a world away, it seems,*
> *From the one who haunts my dreams,*
> *Like the distance that*
> *The earth is to the sun.*
>
> *And he holds me in his love,*
> *Like the light that shines above,*
> *And he's everywhere*
> *and everything to me*
>
> *He makes the day begin,*
> *Just like the rising sun,*
> *An elemental fellow*
> *Who gets the job done*
>
> *He's simple and he's super,*
> *Oh, and what I wouldn't do for*
> *Just a smile from the early rising sun.*
> (Moseka Music, BMI)

"I wrote a love song to a man not of this world, a man who doesn't even exist," Lincoln says of the title track of her 1984 album *Talking to the Sun* (Enja 4060), the implication being that no lover under the sun could be as steadfast. Although her lyrics generally strive for social uplift, she does not consider herself a message singer. "Gil Scott-Heron is a message singer, not me. My songs are autobiographical, about the world as I encounter it. For example, 'People on the Street' [also from *Talking to the Sun*] is about the plight of the homeless, but it's based on personal observation—and sometimes I think I should be doing more to help those people than just singing about them. When I moved back to New York in 1981, I was shocked to see women younger than I was huddled on the streets like zombies, and my friends laughing at them, as if there was anything to laugh about. In the '60s, people used to at least feign social conscience, even if they didn't have any. It proves that we've taken more steps backward than forward since then. We demanded a say, and it was given to us. But some of the very people the revolution was fought for have sold it out. Black people like to wear the white hats—we're very good at pointing our fingers at others and pretending that we can do no wrong. But we can."

As a songwriter, Lincoln's greatest gift is her knack for hearty melodies and quick, pointed, telling observations. *The people in the houses ain't got long,* "I cried when that line came to me, because I realized I could wind up out there someday too. Composing music is the difficult part for me. I've come to think of lyrics as poems, some of which I find melodies for and some of which I don't." She has written an unpublished volume of poetry called *In a Circle, Everything Is Up* and an un-produced play called *A Pig in a Poke* "about an odd jobs man who stumbles on to a large fortune and doesn't know what to do with it. The character is partly based on my father and partly on myself. In my case, the fortune is my career, the musical gift it's taken me this long to figure out how to use properly."

Lincoln reclaimed the career she had thrown away in 1979, when Inner City Records released *People in Me* (IC-6040), an album she had recorded with Miles Davis the sidemen in Japan six years earlier. Since 1983, her backup band has included the alto saxophonist Steve Coleman, the pianist James Weidman, bassist Billy Johnson, and the drummer Mark Johnson, all promising young musicians in their late twenties. "Even though I don't perform often enough to give them steady work, they're there for me whenever I call, and that thrills me. I worry about them, though—whether they can hold out against the commercial pressures that young musicians face today. Nobody pays them any attention, and I'm afraid that's going to make them bitter and discouraged. That's why I'm glad I arrived on the scene in the '50s, when things were better. In those days, a lot of decisions were made for you by your management, and you just played along. But now that I'm out here by my lonesome, I miss that in a way—someone to hold my hand and tell me everything will be all right."

She lives alone now, in an apartment building on Central Park West, ten floors below her ex-husband, still a trusted friend. She has no children. "I never intended to. What sort of mother would I have been, traveling all the time? My mother was always there for me, and I knew I couldn't do that. I've gone through so much madness that I'm glad I didn't drag anyone else through it.

"That's why I'm thankful I've got my music. In a sense, it's all I've ever had. After *For Love of Ivy,* people predicted a big film career for me, but I knew it wouldn't happen. It wasn't even something I dreamt about, because it wasn't practical, and you have to temper idealism with practicality in real life. There are no roles for a black woman unless you're willing to play the buffoon, like Nell Carter in *Gimme a Break!*—not to knock her, you understand, because she has to make a living. I was offered plenty of parts as the sassy maid, but I turned them all down. I decided that if I was going to be in the movies, it would have to be as a leading lady. "Because that's what I've been off-screen, for better or worse—the leading lady in my own life."

(MAY 1986)

Anthony Davis's New Music

Anthony Davis's music—as documented on the albums he has made as a leader, as well as those to which he has brought an organizing intelligence as a sideman—summarizes the last 20 years of innovation in jazz and offers an optimistic prognosis for the future. Davis is in the forefront of a new generation of musicians who can claim the hard-won advances of Ornette Coleman, Cecil Taylor, and the Art Ensemble of Chicago as their birthright, who can embrace the distant jazz past without jeopardizing their standing as modernists, and who can borrow structural devices and instrumental procedures from Europe without relinquishing their places in the Afro-American continuum.

"But I'm not really a jazz musician," Davis cautions those of us eager to hail him as the most important pianist and composer to emerge from the jazz avant-garde since Cecil Taylor. "I've never related my conception of music—or Cecil Taylor's music, either, for that matter—to the term *jazz*. To a lot of jazz audiences, the music I play is very alienating. They still come expecting to hear solos on 'I Got Rhythm' changes, and I'm not interested in that. All the labels they put on music are stupid, but so long as there are labels, if I could be associated with *new music* instead of jazz, it would give me more freedom to create, and I wouldn't be tied down to pre-existing forms, the way I am with *jazz*."

That Davis voices such dissatisfaction with jazz and its audiences says something about his own biases and ambitions, but it also raises pertinent questions about where jazz is headed in the 1980s and what sort of audience it can expect to take with it.

One fluffy summer afternoon, Davis and I chatted over lunch in a French cafe across the street from the Manhattan high-rise where he lives with his wife, the fantasy novelist Deborah Atherton, and their young son. As Davis spoke of his beginnings and his current prospects, several recognizable themes kept surfacing: his role as a composer in what has traditionally been considered an improvisatory music; the increasingly conservative mood of jazz audiences and many of his contemporaries; the need to locate a new, less parochial audience with whom he can communicate on his own terms; and the ambiguous position in which reawakened interest in the jazz tradition places the innovative black musician.

DAVIS'S BACKGROUND AND CONSEQUENTLY HIS FRAME OF REFERENCE ARE more cosmopolitan than those of most musicians associated with jazz. The son of a university professor, he was born in Paterson, New Jersey, in 1951, and lived in New York, "up on 138th and Madison," until he was five. Except for a year in Italy when his father was awarded a Fulbright Fellowship, Davis spent his adolescence in a succession of campus towns, including Princeton, New Jersey, and State College, Pennsylvania. "Was I an academic brat?" he winced. "A *campus* brat? I don't know. I guess so. The parents of most of the people I grew up with were also involved with academia, especially once we moved to Penn State. There are a lot of advantages to growing up in an academic environment, however insular it might be. They had a really good music department at Penn State, so I had the opportunity, while still in junior high, to study with professors from the music faculty.

"I was a music major at Yale—finally. I started out in English and Philosophy, but in my senior year I switched, so my B.A. is in Music. Most of my instruction at Yale was in classical music, though, and it didn't really have that much of a bearing on my development, although I was exposed to some things I wouldn't have known about otherwise, like Medieval music, which still interests me, and Indian music, which I studied both at Yale and at Wesleyan with Amrad Raghaven, a fantastic South Indian drummer."

Davis remained in New Haven for a few years following his graduation from Yale, postponing the inevitable move to New York until 1977: "I came here because the music's here, the musicians are here, because I wouldn't have been able to make a living as a musician in New Haven. It was an important move. But if I had come here earlier, I think I'd have a far more conservative outlook now, especially since I started off with the same influences every pianist my age started off with—McCoy Tyner, Herbie Hancock, Andrew Hill. There are many conformist pressures that you face in New York. They go beyond commercial pressures; it has to do with winning approval from other musicians. If you come to New York with a pretty strong sense of your own identity, as I did, it's a lot easier to deal with. Being in New Haven, within a protective academic environment, I was able to develop my own ideas."

Davis has been fortunate enough to find something resembling an academic sanctuary even in the wilds of Manhattan; living in separate units within the same dormitory-like high-rise complex as he and his wife are such musicians as the trombonist George Lewis, the pianists Muhal Richard Abrams and Amina Claudine Myers, and tenor saxophonists Frank Lowe and Ricky Ford, as well as a number of dancers, writers, and visual artists. It recalls the creative company Davis kept at Yale. Matriculating at the university around the same time as he—or living in town—were several other young musicians with whom he was to form enduring alliances: Lewis, the saxophonist Dwight Andrews, the guitarist Allan Jaffe, the vibraphonist Jay Hoggard, the drummer Gerry Hemingway, and the bassists Wes Brown, Mark Dresser, and Mark Helias. The drummer Ed Blackwell and alto saxophonist Marion Brown—older, better-established figures from the jazz avant-garde's first wave—had settled in nearby Connecticut hamlets to teach. But the most decisive influence on Davis during his stay in New Haven was the transplanted Chicago trumpeter, composer, and theorist Leo Smith.

"Leo's wife was the director of a private high school in Orange, Connecticut, so he was living just outside of New Haven. I became involved with him when I was a student and joined New Delta Ahkri, an ensemble with Leo and Wes Brown. Leo introduced me to a different concept of playing, which involved the idea of composition, rather than improvisation, being of central importance in the ongoing development of black music. I think that Leo is one of the most important and underrated composers to emerge since Ornette Coleman. I think that Leo, along with Anthony Braxton, laid the foundation for what's happening in music now. We're in a new period, and some people are confused by what they're hearing, because the music is developing chiefly in the area of composition, not in terms of what people have been taught to listen for—new directions in improvisation.

"Most of my music is composed—written out. I think that improvisation is just one available option within the larger framework of a given piece. As a composer, the dynamic of a piece is more important to me, in a sense, than the performances of the individuals playing the piece. It's almost closer to the classical tradition of interpretation, of *realizing* a given work of music, than it is to the jazz-oriented concept of showcasing a soloist or creating a vehicle for a group of different individuals."

When Davis says that most of his music is written, he means literally that—that it is notated. He is aware that notation is anathema for Cecil Taylor, as it was for the late Charles Mingus—two of the composers he most admires. "I think they were upset with the limitations of notation, with the preconceptions it brings to a performance. They were trying to bring immediacy back into the music—that sense of creating in the moment—and they were also trying to create a collective music. I think that was important in that cycle, but what's important now is to reassert some control, because, at this point in the music, there's been too much random noise. I'm not saying that about Mingus or Cecil Taylor. But what I am saying is that I want everything that's played to be related to what's been played before and what will happen later; when you think like that, you have to deal with compositional form and planning. I find it inadequate just to say 'play like this' or 'play like that,' because finally what you're saying, when you try to communicate your ideas that way, is 'play something I've heard you play before.'"

AT THE TIME I SPOKE WITH HIM, DAVIS WAS PREPARING TO RECORD A longer, orchestrated version of "Under the Double Moon (Wayang No. 4)" (a piece from his solo piano album *Lady of the Mirrors*)* with the octet he calls Episteme: George Lewis, trombone; Dwight Andrews, woodwinds; Shem Guibbory, violin; Jay Hoggard, vibraphone; Abdul Wadud, cello; Warren Smith and Pheeroan Aklaff, percussion. "I'm interested in scoring some of my ideas—not only my compositional ideas but my improvisational ideas too— for an ensemble of that size. The piece will involve improvisation—it would have to, because there are some wonderful improvisers in the ensemble—but there will be an organic link between what I've written and what the soloists play. What I'm trying to do, really, is to take what I've learned as an impro- viser, take that unified concept one has as a soloist, and communicate that to other improvisers."

Davis said he feels he has reached the stage as a composer where he can write music that doesn't call for his own participation as an instrumentalist— music for solo voice, for example, or for violin, cello, or chamber orchestra. "eventually, I would like to write orchestral works which would involve impro- visation, but *scored* improvisation, so those works could he played by impro- visers and non-improvisers alike. One of my dreams is to write a ballet, and I'd like to compose more film music." (He has scored three independent films, including Carolyn Emmons's *Man Around the House,* winner of a 1980 Oscar as best student film.) He also envisions writing a musical drama; one model for it would be Stephen Sondheim's *Sweeney Todd,* which Davis called "a rev- elation. It's great music and great theater."

Also on the agenda are more solo piano recitals, although his efforts in this direction will not be totally improvised, as in the manner of Keith Jarrett. "The danger with that practice is that the music can become a progression of clichés. I mean, you go from doing one style you know how to do well to another style you know how to do. I hear him playing within himself; everything's within his fingers. Composed music faces the same barriers; there's always the prob- lem of getting beyond your own limitations, beyond what to you has already become a cliché, but I like to approach that through premeditation. I think it's possible to go beyond yourself when playing in the moment, but compo-

---

*Davis has recorded "Under the Double Moon (Wavang No. 4)" three times: a duet with the vibraphonist Jay Hoggard on *Under the Double Moon* (Pausa 7120), the octet performance on *Episteme* (Gramavision GR-8108), and the solo version on *Lady of the Mirrors* (India Navigation IN-1047).

sition can set the stage for you. I've done some things with George Lewis that were hardly notated at all. But even when I'm improvising freely, I'm still thinking compositionally, in terms of the overall structure, so it amounts to the same thing. The important influences on my playing have all been compositional—Ellington, Monk, Mingus; there were early classical influences, too—Messiaen, Chopin, and Stravinsky,"

DAVIS'S *LADY OF THE MIRRORS* IS AN ALBUM OF UNAPOLOGETIC PIANO music. No inaudible orchestra lies in waiting in Davis's left hand, and no invisible horn soloists line up in his right. The keyboard which bears the curve and pressure of his fingers is neither the well-tempered scale nor the skin of a drum. In the contact between pianist and piano, no graven image is permitted. Describing the programmatic content of each of the pieces in his liner insert, Davis draws analogies to the music of Duke Ellington and the blues, to science fiction and Balinese "shadow" (or "puppet") theater, and the arts of dance, painting, and still photography. Yet even as these performances succeed in delineating their stated subjects and moods, their "content" seems wholly musical, with Davis testing his powers of concentration as an instrumentalist, an improviser, and a composer. "Under the Double Moon," for example, is a movement from a dance suite based on the Balinese Wayang, titled after one of Deborah Atherton's unpublished novels. In performance, however, "the piece really addresses itself to the technical problem of hand independence," as Davis admits in the notes; it is actually the right hand that can be said to "accompany" the left for long stretches, as Davis generates percussive suspense by jabbing repeatedly at a shell-like note at the piano's high end. The title piece gathers similar tension from bass and treble clef oppositions, and from clusters, broken rhythms, and leaping intervals that reflect Davis's fascination with modern dance. "Five Moods from an English Garden," though beginning with an evocation of trilling birds, is non-representational, as befits a piece inspired by the Russian non-objectivist painter Vasily Kandinsky. "Beyond Reason," with its swirling tremolos and ostinatos and slivers of icicle-blue dissonance, is Davis's vindication of European Romanticism, and "Man on a Turquoise Cloud" is a modernist structure erected upon another magnificent ruin—a bedrock blues tribute to Ellington that also nods in the general direction of Thelonious Monk.

Reviewers have compared Davis to Ellington, Monk, and Cecil Taylor, not so much because he sounds like any of them but because his best writing proposes, as each of theirs did in its time, a formal consolidation of recent improvisatory gains. And he has dared to use the legacy of those pianists as the raw material for bold original works.

"It's natural you should," Davis said when I told him I thought I detected the shadow of Ellington in his "Crepescule: A Suite for Monk," and traces of

Monk and Taylor in his homages to Ellington, "On an Azure Plane" and "Man on a Turquoise Cloud."* "Those figures are all historically linked. There's a whole Ellington piano tradition. It extends from Ellington to Monk to Cecil Taylor, not to mention Randy Weston and Abdullah Ibrahim [Dollar Brand] and several other important pianists who are also composers. It goes back beyond Ellington, too. Historically, pianists have been the best educated of musicians—that sounds condescending, and I don't mean it to be. But pianists have had to deal with arranging, harmonies, comping—the whole structure of the music. That's been true from Scott Joplin on, and I think it explains the importance pianists have had as composers. The piano has a long tradition that parallels the history of the music, from the development of ragtime to the later development of stride and onward, and I'm part of that tradition."

DAVIS'S CONTINUED APPLICATION OF HIS EARLY CLASSICAL TRAINING links him to the Ellington tradition in yet another, more ironic way. In 1939 Ellington was branded a social climber by those former admirers who thought they detected the taint of European influence on "Reminiscing in Tempo." Over the years, John Lewis and Cecil Taylor have also been censured for their assimilationist tendencies. Now Davis is becoming a target of those who fear that black music barters too much of its root energy when it conducts trade with Europe.

"Of course European music has influenced me," Davis said. "I think that Europe has influenced everything in the world at this point. But there's an African influence in my work, too, and the influences aren't mutually exclusive. After all, the early 20th-century European composers like Stravinsky and Debussy drew from ragtime, and jazz composers have borrowed in turn from them. By this point, there's an American musical tradition that includes both European and African strains, and that's all there is to it—I mean, we haven't been a colony now for some zoo years. It's ridiculous that any new development in black music is assumed to have some hidden connection to European consciousness. It advances a stereotypical image of what the Afro-American experience is all about. It's unfortunate that certain parties are subverting the Afro-American tradition—which is a strong and very positive force for change—as a means of maintaining the status quo, of limiting the connection that jazz has to other musics and to the world of ideas.

"There's suddenly a lot of pressure to do music from 'in the tradition.' But the truest homage to Charlie Parker, for example, isn't to play his tunes or play

---

*"Crepescule: A Suite for Monk" and "On an Azure Plane" are both included on *Past Lives* (Red VPA-134).

just like him, but to do what George Lewis has done, to play something *new* that wouldn't be possible *without* Charlie Parker's example.* The most vital contribution you can make to furthering the jazz tradition is to create your own music, create a new music."

If Davis's slant on tradition is less sanctimonious than that of many of his black music contemporaries—if he is inclined to view it as a dynamic and not as a totem—perhaps it is because the idea of a tradition isn't so recent an acquisition for him as it is for many of them. He is a descendant of the Hampton Davises, the family that founded Hampton Institute, one of the country's oldest black colleges. His father was Charles T. Davis, the author of an influential book on Richard Wright, co-editor of the anthology *On Being Black*, first black faculty member at Princeton University, and chairman of Afro-American Studies at Yale from the inception of the program in the early '70s until his death in March 1981. In the estimation of Dr. John F. Szwed, a former colleague of Dr. Davis's at Yale, Dr. Davis established "the strongest and only serious black studies program in the country, with the possible exception of the one at Stanford, which was copied from Yale's model, with Dr. Davis' guidance."

"My father contributed a lot," said Davis, with understandable pride, "and, of course, he was very important to me individually, not only in terms of eventually being very supportive of my career in music—which upset him at first and caused some arguments when we found ourselves on the same campus— but also in maintaining my interest in other fields, in teaching me that music is just part of the whole spectrum of the Afro-American experience. My family wasn't rich, but there was always a lot of pride in what our ancestors had accomplished, and a lot of pressure on the younger members of the family to achieve distinction, which I think is why so many of us became artists of one sort or another—my younger brother Christopher is an actor, director, and playwright; my cousin Thulani is a poet and editor; another cousin is an architect; and another is a photographer and filmmaker. With our background, we were spared the burden that artists usually face of having to scuffle to make a living early in their careers. A whole generation of Davises—including my father and my Uncle Arthur, who is chairman of the English Department at Howard—was involved with the academic world, and I suppose I let the family down on that score. But I'm sort of making amends for that now. I'm teaching Composition and History of Creative Music from 1900 two days a week at my alma mater, and I'm trying to decide whether to go on with my education and earn some degrees. The university setting offers all kinds of

---

*On *Homage to Charles Parker* (Black Saint BSR-0029), with Lewis, Davis, Richard Teitelbaum, and Dwight Andrews.

opportunities for a composer, and some of the excitement my students feel about music rubs off on me—I become very excited sharing what I know with them. The paycheck from teaching also allows me the independence to say no, to do only those projects I really want to do."

One of the offers to which Davis would say no is the opportunity to play commercial music. "I'm just not interested in that at all. I know there are aspects of my music that are more commercial than others—that sounds presumptuous, but it's something every musician knows about himself. I want the freedom to present the most experimental aspect of my work, as well as those that are more immediate. I don't want to feel as though I can't play music that I like. I think you have to give the audience your best. Play the best music you can. I'm interested in communicating with audiences on other levels too, through the use of words, text, dance, and visuals.

"Being a musician doesn't make me better than anyone else. I'm a human being, and I'm thinking about a lot of things that other people are also thinking about. You have your own perceptions as an artist because you're put on this planet to create mystery, but you're put here to unravel mysteries, too. So I think you have to trust that the audience will have the sophistication to understand you, and you can't afford to condescend to them. And your ultimate audience, when you think about it, is God—however you conceive it. You're not only playing for people here and now; you're playing for past generations, for the people who have died. When I'm playing or writing music now, I'm thinking about my father, about Duke Ellington, about the contributions they made, and I feel compelled to create to my fullest capacity. I'd be letting them down if I didn't. That's how I feel."

(JANUARY 1982)

II

Hemispheres (Gramavision GR-8303) is a dance suite in five movements, a collaboration between pianist/composer Anthony Davis and dancer/choreographer Molissa Fenley that was premiered in 1883 as, part of the Brooklyn Academy of Music's Next Wave Festival. Although Fenley's contributions were of necessity sacrificed in the recording studio, one intuits a dancer's involvement in the rippling physicality and agitated panache of the accompaniment Davis has scored for a 10-member ensemble of winds, percussion, and strings. With its undulations and repetitions, its interlocking meters and shifting, layered harmonies, the music on *Hemispheres* initially sounds like Davis's proprietary stroll through the territory he staked out for himself between the kingdoms of Duke Ellington and Philip Glass on his hypnotic 1981 release

Episteme. But what ultimately divorces *Hemispheres* from the tough-minded mysticism of its predecessor is its theatricality, its hearty acceptance of Fenley's invitation to dance.

In the sense that *Hemispheres* is jazz dance music, it is, with its learned allusions to the Broadway stage and the European concert hall, dance music of a radically different stripe from that currently being purveyed by disparate jazz funkateers like Herbie Hancock, Ronald Shannon Jackson, and Oliver Lake. Still, some comparison is in order inasmuch as both sides (whatever their different motives) attempt to restore balance between soloist and ensemble. Jazz has always borrowed indiscriminately, from sources both high and low, and the net result of its many borrowings has always been the setting of improvisational boundaries. Jackson's Decoding Society and Davis's group Episteme are both precision units in which improvisers are called upon to relinquish some of their autonomy in the name of group order.

It is surprising, therefore, that *Hemispheres* owes much of its vigor and élan to the jabbing trumpet solos of Leo Smith—and not only because Davis usually permits his performers very little interpretive leeway. Smith has long seemed one of those problematical figures destined to register greater impact as a theorist and mentor (indeed, Davis is one of his disciples) than as a player. But on the flamboyant "Little Richard's New Wave" and the ominously tranquil "A Walk Through the Shadow," Davis manages to elicit scintillating work from his trumpeter by denying him the longuers that have marred so many of his solo LPs. Distinguishing the improvised passages in Davis's music from those passages that have been sketched out beforehand can be as tricky as telling the dancer from the dance, so insistent is he that improvised solos maintain the narrative continuity of his compositions, but the few choruses here that *sound* improvised are of a uniformly high order. Trombonist George Lewis paces Smith with fluttering, starkly drawn solos on both of the aforementioned titles. "Ifa the Oracle—Esu the Trickster" climaxes with agitated, nimble turns by J. D. Parran and Dwight Andrews (on contrabass clarinet and soprano saxophone respectively) over a treadmill rhythm rolled out by the leader's piano, David Samuels's vibraphone, and Pheeroan Aklaff's lashing drums. (It is surely no coincidence that Aklaff has been the drummer on so many of the 1980s' most provocative albums. Without the steady gallop the sensitive and sorely underrated Aklaff brings to *Hemispheres,* it might have become ponderous and top heavy, particularly the finale, "Clonetics," a piece whose lurching forward motions recall the pianistics and foot work of Thelonious Monk, as well as Leonard Bernstein's score for *Candide.*) The opening "Esu at the Crossroads" is a combination overture and miniature piano concerto, with Davis weaving gracefully around the massed strings and horns.

Still, it's the balance of instruments and the intricate musculature of Davis's writing that makes *Hemispheres* so seductive. "A Walk Through the Shadows" is the most beguiling piece of all, with keening, finely sifted passages for the strings (the violinist Shem Guibbory, the cellist Eugene Friesen, and the arco bassist Rick Rozie). "A Walk" appeared on *Episteme* as a rather cloistered piano exercise; expanded to 13 minutes here and opened up for orchestra, it acquires some of the majesty of Ellington's devotionals (and its recurring drone and pedal establish once and for all that Davis's style of minimalism is hardly a heretical, classical-music affectation, that jazz has its own history of minimalism in works like Ellington's "It Don't Mean a Thing" and "La Plus Belle Africaine" and Monk's "Skippy" and "Friday the Thirteenth").

Davis can hardly be held accountable for *Hemispheres'* one nagging flaw. Listening to this ravishing and at times robust music, one begins to wonder how Molissa Fenley described its rhythms with her body. If ever a work cried out for video preservation, this is it, but video technology now seems to be the exclusive property of rock image makers and chi-chi conceptualists like Laurie Anderson and Nam June Paik. (If the recent PBS special *Good Morning, Mr. Orwell* confirmed George Russell's observation that the avant-garde is the last refuge of the untalented, it also announced that video is quickly becoming the last refuge of the avant-garde.) Even minus its visual correlative, however, *Hemispheres* is a musical triumph, because its expansive body language demonstrates that the most provocative composer to emerge from jazz in the last decade and a half is not going to settle for the anemically modern or the fashionably recondite.

(JANUARY 1984)

III

Anthony Davis was no more than a spectator at a rehearsal I attended for *X,* his three-act opera based on the life of Malcolm X. *X* was scheduled to premiere as a work-in-progress in Philadelphia a month later, one of five productions to be mounted by the American Music Theater Festival during its maiden season. But on this clutching hot day in SoHo, Philadelphia was still far enough in the future that Davis could be forgiven if he seemed preoccupied with more immediate concerns. He was to perform his piece "Still Waters" with the New York Philharmonic the following evening, and he owed commissioned pieces—due before the end of the summer—to the Houston Symphony and the pianist Ursula Oppens. For that matter, the second and third acts of *X* still needed work—work that begged to be completed in solitude, at the piano bench. But the first act was already out of Davis's hands, and he looked as though he was trying to get used to the idea of being an onlooker, the role he would have to assume on opening night.

Davis watched in silence as director Rhoda Levine blocked out the Terpsichore for a scene in which a character named Street (a fictional composite of the various Stagger Lee-types the young Malcolm X ran with in Boston and Harlem) entices Malcolm with a dissonant aria extolling the spoils of "the life." (Although the aria had no title, it did have a hook, and Levine and the cast referred to it as "My Side of Town.") Around and around the actors playing Malcolm and Street (Avery Brooks and Peter Lightfoot, respectively), the other cast members writhed in flailing dance steps that were half slowed down lindy hop, half speeded-up Twyla Tharpe. Levine is a former choreographer, and anyone stumbling in on her rehearsal unaware might have assumed she was preparing her company for an avant garde deconstruction of *Guys and Dolls*, not a night at the opera. She was making them sweat.

During a lull, Davis walked over to the rehearsal pianist whose tone clusters, pedal points, and trills—the bare bones of the score—were substituting for Davis's in-member group Episteme, which would be in the orchestra pit on opening night. "Relax those sixteenth notes up a little bit," he advised, his bushy Afro bobbing as he illustrated the hambone rhythm he desired with fluid gyrations of his shoulders and hips.

"Rhythm is very important in this score," he remarked after taking a seat again. "There's going to be a contrabass clarinet improvisation over that figure, and a guitar riffing underneath. I want to evoke the music that Malcolm danced to when he was a shoe shine boy at the Roseland Ballroom in Boston, and I want to cue the audience right away what the character of Street represents, so I've found myself writing viper music—music vaguely reminiscent of Fats Waller and Cab Calloway.

"This will be the first time my music has been performed without me as one of the performers," said Davis, who comes from a tradition in which bridging the gap between composition and execution usually depends on the laying on of hands. "[The pianist] Marilyn Crispell will take my place with Episteme, and Peter Aaronson, the show's musical director and a much more experienced conductor than I am, will conduct. I'm just going to sit in the front row and watch, which I know will be difficult, but I want to maintain an objective eye. I'm learning to delegate responsibility—that's part of what appeals to me about collaborative works.

"*X* is still in the process of being written, and probably will be for years to come. When the American Music Theater Festival gave me the go ahead to write an opera, they had no idea I was planning *Tristan and Isolde!* We hope to present *X* in as complete a fashion as possible in Philadelphia, with the understanding that it will go on developing after it closes. This is my first opera, after all—my first dramatic work of any kind—and I need to gain some sense of which of the music I'm writing translates into stage action and which doesn't. I'm learning as I go along."

X IS A FAMILY AFFAIR: IT IS ALSO THE FIRST OPERA FOR DAVIS'S BROTHER Christopher, who wrote the story, and for their cousin Thulani Davis, who wrote the libretto. "It was originally Christopher's idea," says Anthony Davis. "He has experience as a stage actor and director, and he wanted to base a musical on the life of Malcolm X, which isn't as impractical a notion as it might sound, now that Stephen Sondheim has shown that it's possible to do all sorts of things in the commercial theater. I liked the idea, because I had always wanted to apply my music to a larger dramatic form, the way Sondheim did in *Sweeney Todd,* and I had always wanted to write a work around a political theme. But after thinking it over, I suggested to Christopher that Malcolm's life might play better as opera, with singing, rather than spoken dialogue, furthering the narrative. I also thought that doing it as an opera would enable us to do it on a larger scale. And as Thulani pointed out, scale was necessary if we were going to give a sense of how many millions of people were galvanized by Malcolm's message—and not just those people who converted to Islam because of him, either."

Although *X* draws on incidents depicted in *The Autobiography of Malcolm X,* Christopher Davis hastens to point out that he and Thulani Davis also drew from countless other sources, so their opera is in no sense an adaptation of *The Autobiography* (the dramatic rights to which belong to Warner Brothers). Nevertheless, autobiography as a concept is one of *X*'s themes. "My father taught a course in black autobiography, which is the oldest black literary tradition, from slave narratives and Frederick Douglass on through *The Autobiography of Malcolm X, Soul on Ice,* and *Manchild in the Promised Land,*" says Christopher. "Transformation is always the key theme in those books, and the transformation always means gaining the power of the word—learning how to read and write and express yourself, so that you can define yourself on your own terms. The author always begins by telling who his parents were in the very first sentence. The writing is always powerful and direct, and there's always the use of repetition to reflect the way black people create their own version of history in the telling and retelling of certain stories."

"It's a literary tradition that stems from an oral tradition, and it was Malcolm's principal tool as a recruiter for the Nation of Islam," adds Thulani Davis. "Instead of handing of leaflets, or reading from the Quram, he would tell people his life story in order to convince them to join his mosque."

X BEGINS WITH THE OFF-STAGE DEATH OF MALCOLM'S FATHER, THE REVEREND Earl Little, in East Lansing, Michigan, in 1931. Reverend Little was cut in half by a trolley; the police said he stumbled under its wheels by accident, but his family suspected he had been beaten and left on the tracks to die by the Ku Klux Klan, in retribution for his pro-Marcus Garvey sermons—the authors of X take the latter point of view. It ends with Malcolm's assassination at the Audubon Ballroom in Harlem in 1965, after his falling out with Muslim leader (and surrogate father) Elijah Muhammad. (What tacit part, if any, Elijah played in Malcolm's murder is a subject the authors leave open to conjecture.)

In the aftermath of Malcolm's assassination, several black composers associated with the free jazz movement (but unaffiliated with the Nation of Islam) embraced him as their sage and dedicated works to him; whatever their level of political involvement or spiritual attainment, they recognized in Malcolm a rage equal to their own. Anthony Davis, a representative of a later wave of avant-gardists and a product of the black bourgeoisie, views the slain Muslim leader with more detachment. "I was only 14 when he was gunned down. Growing up in a family that was active in the church and civil rights movement, I gravitated more toward Martin Luther King and the doctrine of non-violent integration. Later, after I left home and read Malcolm's speeches and autobiography, I began to understand that, by raising the issues of separatism and economic self-determination, Malcolm addressed the discontinuity of the black urban experience in a way that Dr. King, from his Southern agrarian frame of reference, could not. Dr. King was a great inspirational figure, a moralist, but Malcolm represented the more pragmatic side of the struggle, and I think you can measure his impact on history by looking at his impact on the thinking of Jesse Jackson, who is supposedly Dr. King's disciple.

"What makes Malcolm so compelling a dramatic protagonist, beyond his politics, though, are the many transformations you see him making over the course of his life—from country boy to street hustler to spiritual leader, world statesman, and political martyr. He combined violence and contemplation, the intuitive and the intellectual, mother wit and the groping for a more philosophical foundation—which is why he continues to be a force twenty years after his death, because those are the twin poles of black experience in America. His story is one of the great stories of our century, and it's also a story that I think begs to be *sung*.

"Malcolm had a link to music, and that link was probably John Coltraine, who symbolized musically what Malcolm symbolized on a social level—the intersection of the spiritual and the political. I tried to acknowledge that in the opera—the concurrence of Coltrane and Malcolm in the 1960s. For example, when Malcolm's brother Reginald, who has already joined the Nation of Islam, visits Malcolm in prison in the beginning of the second act, he sings

'Elijah is the messenger/the messenger of Allah.' It's meant to have the sweep of John Coltrane's tenor saxophone. Coltrane's phrasing was a style of preaching, and so were Malcolm's speeches. That's something else they had in common—and I tried to capture that without drawing from Baptist church music, which is antithetical to Muslim devotional music."

"MALCOLM HAD A GREAT SENSE OF RHETORIC, A WAY OF USING HOMEY expressions and giving them a double-edged meaning: 'the chickens coming home to roost,' for example, which he said to reporters about the Kennedy assassination," says Thulani Davis. The author of two volumes of poetry, she has contributed texts to pieces by her cousin, Anthony Davis, and her husband, the saxophonist Joseph Jarman, of the Art Ensemble of Chicago. "For the libretto, I tried to echo Malcolm's phrasing without using too much of his actual phraseology. I wanted a distillation of his speech, not the actual speeches. I tried to keep the language simple and direct, without too much embellishment or metaphor. I know that some of Malcolm's followers are probably worried that we're going to declaw Malcolm in order to make him safe for opera. Those people are going to be surprised. They're going to be impressed with the amount of research we've done on the subtle differences between the Black Muslims and the orthodox Muslims in the way they worship and what they believe, with the care we've taken to ensure that the prayers are right, the pronunciations are correct."

When I was little / They called me 'nigger,' / Called me 'nigger' so much, / I thought it was my name, Malcolm (who was born Malcolm Little) sings to a potential convert on the corner of 125th Street and Seventh Avenue in the second act. "That was a joke he used to tell," Thulani Davis explains, "and it's a very telling joke. The importance of *naming* is one of the thematic links in the libretto. Malcolm experienced several rebirths, each involving the taking of a new name, a new way of defining who he was—Malcolm Little, Detroit Red, Malcolm X, and finally El Hajj Malik El-Shabazz, Islamic for 'one who is reborn.' When the Muslims hit on the idea of renaming themselves, they tapped into something very old and powerful and almost forgotten. Naming is an Africanism—in some African religions, the belief is that a woman becomes pregnant because the man whispers the name of their offspring in her ear while they're making love. So names are sacred. But when we were brought to America, our names were taken away from us. Slaves often had successions of names not of their own choosing—they would be given another name every time they were sold. This was something Elijah Muhammad talked about, and it struck a responsive chord in Malcolm and untold numbers of other black Americans—the idea that the names they were born with said nothing about who they were or what they might become.

WHICH COMES FIRST? THE WORDS OR THE MUSIC? "THE WORDS," Anthony Davis said, in response to the clichéd question I was almost too embarrassed to ask. "To do it the opposite way would restrict Thulani too much, though I might have a figure in mind that I'll play for her to see if she can do anything with it, and, of course, we both confer with Christopher about what he's trying to depict. But Thulani's blank verse lends itself very readily to music, and she has a foolproof ear for what music can and cannot be sung—and no reluctance to tell me which is which."

"Anthony's score is a remarkable accomplishment," says Thulani Davis. "The opera spans thirty years in Malcolm's life, which were also thirty years during which black music was evolving at a rapid pace. When Malcolm was wearing a zoot suit and running numbers, the big bands were still popular; by the time he was murdered, another kind of jazz was taking form with John Coltraine and Ornette Coleman, and whether or not Malcolm was aware of them is unimportant. The point is that their music reflected the black consciousness of that period, no less than Malcolm's philosophy did. Another composer might have taken the easy way out and simply recreated those different musical styles, but Anthony has filtered them through the prism of his own music to create an exciting and original work."

(JUNE 1984)

IV

Only the first act was staged when *X* debuted as a work-in-progress in Philadelphia in 1984. (In addition, there was an oratorio-like presentation of choral numbers from the second act.) In my review in the following morning's *Philadelphia Inquirer,* I wrote that as an idealistic attempt to couch a story from black America in the lofty diction of the opera house, *X* was heir to *Treemonisha,* the Scott Joplin opera which folded after a single performance in Harlem in 1911 and was not resurrected until 1974, when Joplin was awarded a posthumous Pulitzer Prize. I wished *X* and its composer a kinder fate, but if you read between the lines, you could tell that I doubted that a kinder fate was in store.

Happily, I was wrong. *X* received its first full-length production in Philadelphia fifteen months later, on its way to its grand premiere by the New York City Opera in 1986. (What's the difference between a first full-length production and a grand premiere? Cultural politics. Beverly Sills and City Opera have more clout than the Philadelphia-based American Music Theater Festival. Regardless of who wins custody, however, *X* is clearly AMTF's baby, and the opera's speedy reappearance is eloquent testimony to AMTF's willingness to nurture a major work from conception to maturity—the ultimate measure of a company's stature, long after the overnight reviews have yellowed and the box office receipts have been tallied.)

The full-length *X* offers more than operatic sound and fury. As directed by Rhoda Levine, it's kinetic drama; John Conklin's set design is more Spartan than it needs to be (what a friend of mine calls Regulation Experimental Theater, with chair slats serving as cell bars, etc.), but Levine's blocking and Curt Osterman's spectral lighting fill in a lot of the blank spaces. And Christopher Davis's story, in combination with Thulani Davis's taut, fierce, declamatory libretto, passes the fundamental test of drama, in the process of underlining Malcolm's bitter and ironic twist on Horatio Alger: even though Malcolm's life and death are matters of public record, one sits waiting to see what's going to happen next, what motives and psychological consequences the authors are going to attribute to events taken from yesterday's headlines.

The most obvious level on which *X* succeeds, however, is as an evening of intricate and propulsive music by one of America's most gifted and adamantly uncategorizable younger composers. Major new operas are rare enough, but works of this scale by black composers are all but non-existent, because so few black composers have been given the necessary carte blanche. The staggering cost of mounting three performances of *X* in Philadelphia, with a 35-piece orchestra and a 40-member cast (including figurants)—estimated at $250,000 by an unofficial source close to the AMTF—perhaps provides a clue to Anthony Davis's displeasure with the word "jazz." Unlike their classical and theatrical counterparts, who enjoy the benefit of well-established institutional support systems, jazz composers must apply for funding as individuals, which effectively rules out the possibility of a jazz composer raising a quarter of a million dollars for a single project. Ironically, though—as Davis points out—if there were not separate categories for jazz, black composers might not be funded at all. (Along the way to its full-length debut at the Walnut Street Theater in October 1985, *X* received grants from the Ford Foundation; the National Institute for Music Theater; the Kitchen Center for Video, Music, Dance, Performance and Film; the Opera Music Theater Program of the National Endowment for the Arts; and various other public and corporate funding programs.)

To put an unfortunate misconception to rest once and for all, *X* is no ersatz "jazz" opera, unlike another of 1984's AMTF offerings, Noah Ain's *Trio*, which was jazz only in the sense that its all black cast sang melismatic drivel, and opera only in the sense that it said it was. Although Davis's score for *X* involves some improvisation by the members of Episteme, functioning concerto-grosso style from inside the orchestra, none of the singing is in the vernacular, not even the few bars of atonal scat the character of Street unleashes in the opening act. Like Philip Glass and Steve Reich, Davis favors inner-moving harmonies and cyclical, busy-bee rhythms borrowed from Indonesia; and the calculated disparity in scale between a "minimalist" score and a larger-than-life mise-en-scène with a twentieth-century archetype at the center is bound to tempt some to compare *X* to *Satyagraha* and *Einstein* on the Beach. But Davis's voicings are sleeker and more cosmopolitan than Glass's, and a comparison to Duke Ellington or Charles Mingus might be more in order. Davis's score echoes Glass and Reich; Ellington, Mingus, and John Coltrane; the ballads from *West Side Story* and *Sweeney Todd*. It recycles some of Davis's own chamber and solo works, including "Clonetics," "A Walk through the Shadow," and "Middle Passage," and there are probably references to Wagner and Stravinsky that fly right over my head. But finally, the score is all Davis, and it's like nothing one has heard before, even from him. Here at last is that Third Stream, that confluence of the idiomatic and the formal, that John Lewis and Gunther Schuller prophesized in the 1960s but were never successful in achieving in their own works. Although *X* might not *be* jazz, it is of obvious potential importance *to* jazz, if only for the glorious passages accompanying Malcolm's conversion to Islam and his pilgrimage to Mecca, in which Davis redeems Coltrane-like glossalalia and billowing modal textures that one had come to think of as devalued through over-use.

It might not be common practice in reviewing opera to single out individual members of the orchestra for praise, but X is no ordinary opera, and Episteme is no ordinary pit orchestra. (Besides, send a jazz critic to the opera, and you see what happens.) The saxophonists Dwight Andrews and Marty Ehrlich turned in several molten, wailing improvisations; and trombonist Ray Anderson shook the walls with his tailgating during the sequences set in the Boston ghetto demimonde in the 1940s.

In its own way, of course, opera is as empirical an art form as jazz, which is to say that an opera—*any* opera—is only as good as the cast which sings it. In this respect, Davis has been lucky. *X* proves that there is no shortage of talented black opera singers and stage actors, even if roles created specially for them have been at a premium. (The credits under the performers' names in *Playbill* include *Evita, Jesus Christ Superstar, Sophisticated Ladies, The Cotton Club,* and even *Miami Vice,* in addition to *Porgy and Bess, Treemonisha, Faust, Cavalleria Rusticana,* and *The CIVIL warS.*) As Malcolm, Avery Brooks was magic, riveting the eye from the word go, even though he didn't get to sing a note until the final number of the first act. Brooks, who stole the show in a minor role when X was presented as a work-in-progress in 1984, was promoted to the lead for workshop performances in Harlem and Brooklyn in the summer of 1985, but left the cast when ABC tapped him to play Hawk, Robert Urich's fly, glowering alter-ego in the fall series *Spenser: For Hire,* based on the detective novels of Robert B. Parker. Following Brooks's defection, the Metropolitan Opera's Michael Smartt—a 1984 Tony nominee for the Houston Grand Opera's production of *Porgy and Bess*—signed on as Malcolm. But Smartt bowed out before opening night in Philadelphia, and Brooks stepped back in at the last minute. What a gruelling week it must have been for Brooks, who flew back and forth from Boston to Philadelphia daily, shooting his TV series in the mornings and performing a role that required him to be on stage three solid hours at night. If Brooks had found it necessary to look at a crib sheet, one would have been inclined to forgive him under the circumstances. But he didn't, at least not during the performance I attended. In Brooklyn over the summer, Brooks bore an uncanny physical resemblance to Malcolm; in Philadelphia, with his pate shaved clean for his TV role, he forfeited that advantage. Yet he conveyed so much inner turmoil and determination with his carriage, his hand gestures, and the set of his jaw that he still recalled the charisma of the real Malcolm X. It had little to do with the doo rag that Brooks affected during the prison scenes or the rimless glasses he donned later on to signal Malcolm's spiritual and intellectual awakening—these were merely props a more literal-minded performer might have used to launch an impersonation. What Brooks was doing was *acting,* and it was a treat to watch in a day and age when TV docu-dramas have persuaded actors that impersonation is good enough.

Brooks exudes such star power that one suspects he has to work overtime not to upstage other actors. In *Spenser: For Hire,* with the doughnut-hole they call Robert Urich as his only competition, Brooks chews up the scenery. *X* proved his ability to fit into an ensemble. As Street—the role Brooks originated in 1984—Thomas Young had a tough act to follow, but he succeeded in making the part his own. Young was also Elijah Muhammad, a daring bit of dual casting (sin and salvation as opposite sides of the same coin) intended to provide Brooks's Malcolm with a consistent antagonist, a recurring father figure, from act to act. It worked because Young is such a versatile singer and actor, and because his tenor blended so melifluously with Brooks's bass baritone, and there was such physical chemistry between them. Priscilla Baskerville, whose boundless soprano was put in frivolous uses in the film *The Cotton Club* and the original Broadway production of *Sophisticated Ladies,* brought a restrained pathos to her role as Malcolm's mother; and there was fine singing by Kevin Maynor and Deborah Ford as Malcolm's brother and sister, Reginald and Ella. In fact, the only principal cast member whose singing left anything to be desired was Avery Brooks, an all-arounder who lacks only an opera singer's verismo—a shortcoming that was unnoticeable at the Brooklyn Academy of Workshop performances over the summer but occasionally proved telling in Philadelphia's thousand-seat Walnut Street Theater. Difficult though it might have been to imagine a more convincing Malcolm, given Brooks's countless other attributes, it would have been interesting to hear a traditional opera singer like Michael Smartt in the role (and, as Christopher Davis pointed out before Smartt's withdrawal, this is precisely what is going to have to happen if X is to enter the standard repertoire).

Apart from Brooks's lack of operatic credibility, I spotted two other flaws, both of them minor. Because Christopher Davis's story telescopes 30 years of Malcolm's life (and 30 years of American panorama) into some 3,500 bars of music and three hours of real time, some of the transitions are bumpy—for example: on the basis of what they saw depicted on stage, those members of the audience who haven't thumbed *The Autobiography of Malcolm X* lately might have assumed that the Boston police jailed the pre-Black Nationalist Malcolm for miscegenation, not burglary. And Anthony Davis's overture, although an estimable piece of music given a buoyant reading by pianist Marilyn Crispell, is just too lengthy to fulfill its intended dramatic purpose. As the overture builds to a succession of crescendos, the cast assembles on stage in groups of two and three in anticipation of the action—a beginning borrowed from *Sweeney Todd*, most likely. The only problem is that we don't yet know who any of these people are, and their dress doesn't give their identities away, the way it might in a *Sweeney*-esque period piece. Still, this static mode of introduction at least serves notice that the actors will be doubling as witnesses to history (the entire cast is on stage a good deal of the evening, with spotlights isolating the featured singers in any given scene). It also contributes to a Brechtian distancing effect which, though already something of an avant-garde cliché, is a welcome development in black musical theater, which—following the box office grosses of *Ain't Misbehavin'*, *Dream Girls*, and even *The Gospel at Colonus*—seems in constant jeopardy of signifying nothing more than a nostalgic trip uptown with those folks who sure do love to sing and dance.

In the long run, though, it might be audiences who choose to keep a distance—white opera-goers because of the volatility of Christopher Davis's story, the resolute modernism of Anthony Davis's score, and the Muslim esoterica in Thulani Davis's libretto; blacks and jazz fans because of the air of privilege and foppish refinement surrounding opera. In my original review, I worried that X might not soon find its ideal audience. Frankly, I still worry. The opening nighters I saw it with (the usual fat cats, with a heavier black delegation than normal) grew restless as the evening went on, and I thought it churlish of them to withhold from Avery Brooks and the rest of the cast the standing ovations and endless curtain calls they so richly deserved. Despite the imprimatur of City Opera, some companies are going to see *X* as nothing more than an equal-opportunities write-off: Anthony Davis tells me that one prestigious West Coast company asked if he could stage his opera in inner city playgrounds next summer (his response was to ask if they would expect Philip Glass and Robert Wilson to mount a portable *Einstein on the Beach* outdoors), and Thulani Davis adds that many classical-music types have asked her why her cousin can't do the opera with just his band and a small choir. I'm not sure the world is ready for a full-fledged black opera, much less an opera about Malcolm X, but I hope that my skepticism proves unwarranted. I ended my first review by saying that *X* had the potential for greatness, and on that score I think the full-length version proved me right. This is a show at once so subtle and overpowering that you leave the theater whistling the chord changes. Like Sweeney Todd, it convinces you that, if what they say is true—that all art aspires to music—all music should aspire to opera.

(OCTOBER 1985)

from
OUTCATS

Surviving Ellington

There's no business like show business. An *opéra bouffe* that Duke Ellington conceived in leisure—beginning work on it as a vehicle for Lena Horne in the late 1950s, and returning to it periodically, between more urgent deadlines, until his death in 1974—was being executed in haste. Six weeks before *Queenie Pie* was scheduled to open in Philadelphia as part of the American Music Theater's third season in 1986, not a single part had been cast.

"The key to the whole situation is finding our Queenie Pie. Once we know who she is, we'll know who Lil Daddy, her lover, and Cafe O'Lay, her younger rival, should be," explained Mercer Ellington, a white-haired man in his late sixties, sitting at a table littered with bios and eight-by-ten glossies in a sub-basement of New York's Lincoln Center. The auditions were over, and now Mercer and the others—the musical director Maurice Peress, the choreographer and director Garth Fagan, the co-director Robert Kalfin, the librettist George C. Wolfe, the lyricist George David Weiss, and Marjorie Samoff and Eric Salzman of the American Music Theater Festival—had assembled to judge the "callbacks." Each member of this braintrust was looking for something different, and some compromise would have to be reached between the actors who couldn't sing, the singers who couldn't dance very well, the dancers who couldn't sing or act, and the "gypsies" who did a little bit of everything, although not very well.

Something that no one else had noticed (or, at least, mentioned) was bothering Mercer Ellington. All of the talent parading before the tribunal was black, and that would never do. "Every show my father was ever involved with was racially integrated, and this one will be, too, if I'm going to have anything to do with it," Mercer said quietly, but in a tone of voice designed to indicate that the point was nonnegotiable, looking directly at Kalfin, who had wondered aloud whether white characters belonged in a show set in 1920s Harlem and on an imaginary island in the West Indies. "Ellington wouldn't have wanted anything to do with a log-cabin revue—that's what he would have called this, the way it seems to be going—and I don't want anything to do with it either, if that's what you have in mind."

"Was *Sophisticated Ladies* integrated, Mercer?" asked Peress, peering at Ellington over his bifocals.

"Of course it was! You know that, Maurice," Mercer replied.

"Yes, and look how awful that turned out," Peress quipped. The tension dissolved in laughter, and Elissa Meyers, the show's casting agent, promised to scare up some white faces before nightfall.

"Just make sure they're qualified," Mercer warned her. "I've seen the reverse situation too often in the old days, when agents would send black singers and dancers who were all wrong for the parts, in order to ensure that no blacks would be hired."

Mercer Ellington was listed in the festival's program as *Queenie Pie's* production coordinator, a job that no one, least of all Ellington himself, could define. The Duke Ellington Orchestra would be the pit band, but Mercer Ellington would not be holding the baton, as he had since assuming leadership of the orchestra upon his father's death. Instead, Peress would be the conductor, which seemed only proper as it was he who worked closely with Duke Ellington on the orchestrations and the vocal score.

Still, everyone agreed that Mercer Ellington was indispensable to the production, even if his role was merely to advise and consent. "He's standing in for the great presence," Peress explained. "He's here to make sure that what happened with *Sophisticated Ladies* doesn't happen again. That show was an entertainment which didn't really give a full account of Duke Ellington's genius. The ideal situation would be to have Duke himself involved in every aspect of the production, but, of course, that isn't possible. So Mercer is here because he's kept the flame burning."

"THE FIRST TIME I HEARD ELLINGTON'S MUSIC ON THE RADIO, IT DIDN'T make that big an impression on me, to tell you the truth. What did impress me was that we even *owned* a radio. You have to remember that this was back in the days when radio was considered an electronic marvel, when our home and the streetlamps outside were still being lit by gas," Mercer Ellington remembered over coffee one morning in his apartment across the street from Lincoln Center. He was due to hear more *Queenie Pie* hopefuls later that day. Three likenesses of his father (a silkscreen, a watercolor by Mercer's daughter Gaye, and the K. Abe photograph that served as model for the Ellington postage stamp) hung on one of the living room walls. Otherwise, there was surprisingly little Ellington memorabilia (his manuscripts are in a sealed vault in the Irving Trust, along with the Medal of Freedom bestowed on him by President Nixon), and unless one happened to notice the small electric piano next to the ironing board in the hallway corner, there was no apparent evidence that the man of the house was himself a musician and composer.

For anyone enamored of Duke Ellington's music, an audience with his son is a thrill, because no one else living knows that music so intimately. Even so, no one would want to trade places with Mercer Ellington, because more than anyone else, he also knew the man behind the music, and theirs was an unusually adversarial father-son relationship. Still, Mercer seems to have survived relatively unscarred, with his sense of humor intact—his reminiscences are punctuated by laughter, sometimes rueful, but never really bitter. Dressed haphazardly, as he was that morning, in knit shirt, track pants, and sneakers, he conveyed none of his father's seignorial air. Although he has a smoker's cough, he didn't once reach for his cigarettes during the two hours or so I spent with him. He generally refers to his father as "Ellington"—a sign, perhaps, that the debonair bandleader kept his son at the same distance that he kept the rest of the world (as well as a tacit admission by Mercer that the name "Ellington" inevitably evokes Duke, not Mercer).

"He called me 'the brat,' and I addressed him as 'Fadu,' for Father Duke, until I was about twenty. After that, I called him Pop, although we mostly talked to each other without calling each other anything. Ironically, although I always knew he was popular, even revered, it only fazed me how truly important Ellington was in the music business during one of his low periods, around 1950, when big bands were folding right and left, including mine. I had a mortgage to pay off, and three children to send through school. Borrowing money from Pop was out, because he wasn't doing so well himself. I would ask other bandleaders to give me a job, they'd say 'Why should you collect a paycheck that someone else really needs? You're Duke Ellington's son.' Everybody assumed he was rich, and he might have been if not for the problem of back taxes and keeping his men on salary, come rain or shine, as the saying goes, forty-eight weeks a year. If he hadn't been so determined to keep his band, his song royalties would have made him a millionaire several times over."

Duke Ellington never went out of his way to make the road easier for his son. If anything, he put hurdles across the path. "Duke Ellington would make certain he remained on top regardless of whom he knocked down, including me," Mercer wrote in his 1978 memoir, *Duke Ellington in Person* (written with the jazz critic Stanley Dance), an uneasy mix of *Daddy Dearest* and *Father Knows Best*. If only one Ellington could have his name in lights, Duke wasn't going to let it be Mercer, who remembered in his book that when he formed his own band in the 1940s, Duke insisted that he join him on the Musicraft label, then saw to it that only the band's inferior material was released. According to Mercer, Duke feared that *two* Ellington bands would confuse the public and devalue the name.

Mercer Ellington was born in 1919 in Washington, D.C., the first child of Edward Kennedy and Edna Thompson Ellington, who were both under twenty-one. Mercer doubts that his parents would have married except to legitimize his birth. "There was too much pulling them apart. My mother's folks were from a higher station of black society than my father's. They were all schoolteachers and principals, and they considered all musicians, including Duke Ellington, low-life. Ironically, though, Ellington's parents thought my mother wasn't good enough for *him*. You know how parents are, and his were even more so."

Two years later, Duke and Edna had another son, who died in infancy. So Mercer grew up as an only child, but without the unlimited devotion usually lavished on only children. He was left behind with his paternal grandparents in Washington when his parents set out for New York to launch Duke's career. His parents sent for Mercer when he was nine, but separated soon after, and although they never divorced, they were never reconciled, either. "I came home from school one day, and there was a strange woman [the dancer Mildred Dixon, the first of Duke's many paramours] living with my father and taking care of me and Ruth [Duke's younger sister, only four years older than Mercer, to whom she was more a sibling than an aunt]. My mother, it turned out, had moved back into the building up the street, where we had lived before. They had separated without telling us. Nobody in my family liked to be the bearer of bad news."

Until he entered college, Mercer spent six months a year with each parent, an unusual custody arrangement for the period. "But it wasn't a legal arrangement, you see. It was just something I decided on my own," says Mercer, who remained close to his mother until her death in 1966. What kept drawing him back to his father was their mutual love of music, although, ironically, it was his mother—a good friend of Fats Waller's——who gave him his first piano lessons, showing him the chords to Duke's "Solitude." "When I was staying with her as a kid, I would have to shine shoes, or whatever, to bring some extra money into the house. She was a lonely woman who liked to entertain just to have company, and although my father supported her to some degree, her friends would drink up every penny that she had. In a way, it's good that Ellington wasn't more generous with her, or she might have drunk herself into an early grave, with those friends of hers around."

Mercer also enjoyed a warm relationship with Beatrice "Evie" Ellis, a former Cotton Club showgirl who became Duke Ellington's mistress in the late thirties, and whose death followed his by two years (she is buried beside him in New York's Woodlawn Cemetery). "Poor Evie," Mercer says. "She was typical of many attractive black women at the Cotton Club; very intelligent but not very well educated. The goal for these women was to snare a handsome black bandleader, because if they fooled around with the white patrons, the best they could hope to become would be mistresses. Evie latched on to Ellington, who refused to divorce my mother and had no intention of remarrying after she died. So Evie wound up as a mistress anyway. She felt very exploited, and worried that she wouldn't be taken care of if he died, because he didn't believe in wills. She acquired a reputation as a grump, which enabled Ellington to use her as a shield. If he invited someone over and then changed his mind, he'd send her to the door to chase them away. The next time he ran into them, he'd act like Mister Sunshine and ask them why they hadn't shown up, giving the impression that she kept people away from him because she wanted him all to herself.

"You try to give your own kids what you never had when you were growing up, and, in my case, that was a feeling of closeness to my father. That's why I've always tried to take my kids on the road with me, whenever possible. I remember when *Sophisticated Ladies* opened on Broadway in 1980, I was sipping champagne at the celebration party with Paul, my youngest, wrapped up in my arms. He was only a year old then—you see, I wanted a grandchild, and since none of my kids were making any progress in that direction, I decided to take matters into my own hands." (In addition to Paul and teenage stepson Ralph, Mercer has three grown children from his first marriage: daughters Mercedes, a dancer, and Gaye, a painter; and son Edward Kennedy Ellington III, until recently the guitarist in the Duke Ellington Orchestra. "So, altogether, I have five children, although some people think I have six when they see me with Lene," Mercer jokes, referring to his second wife, a Danish airline hostess who pronounces her name "Lena" and is a good twenty-five years Mercer's junior.) In *Duke Ellington in Person,* Mercer recalls that sight of himself in uniform during World War II triggered an uncharacteristic show of fatherly affection from Duke. He can now guess what went through his father's mind. "I never knew fear until my first child was born. The most horrifying thing I can imagine is to outlive my children."

. . . The photographers cocked their shutters and snapped the picture, Duke happily looking paternal, right index finger pointing in the air as he admonished Mercer.

"Now grow up," he told Mercer, "and be a great composer," Duke laughed.

"As you say, Father Duke," Mercer smiled back.

Barry Ulanov, *Duke Ellington* (1946)

Although Duke Ellington studied art in high school and was offered a scholarship to Pratt Institute, he was musically self-taught, with an autodidact's scorn for formal education. Yet he saw to it that Mercer studied music at Juilliard, Columbia, and New York University. "I think it was his way of

keeping up with advancements in music theory through me," Mercer speculates. "I remember one day he handed me two huge volumes and said, 'Read
these and tell me about them.' It was the Schillinger System, and it took me
three years to digest it. When I started to explain it to him, he cut me off. 'Oh,
yeah, I was doing that back in 1928.' And, truthfully, he had." Predictably,
Mercer's greater education deepened the rift between them. "I've valued the
intuitive approach, and I'm belatedly coming around to his way of thinking.
Because unless you count the hit version of 'Bill Bailey' I did for Della Reese,
which was just an arrangement of a song in the public domain, the only things
I've written that've had any lasting impact were all written for the Ellington
Orchestra *before* I went to music school," Mercer laughs, referring to "Things
Ain't What They Used to Be" and "Blue Serge," which are often mistaken for
his father's work. "I take it as a compliment when people assume that some-
thing of mine was written by him. That's given me tremendous confidence."

Mercer, a competent musician, was a disappointment to his father, a genius
who, in terms of professional encouragement treated Billy Strayhorn—a composer of uncommon ability, only four years older than Mercer—more like a
son. Still, Duke never banished Mercer from the fold, and Mercer showed little inclination to leave. In 1964, after being on the fringes of his father's organization for two decades, Mercer joined the Duke Ellington Orchestra as its
road manager and a member of its trumpet section. "As road manager, I was
a combination psychologist, mathematician, and private detective. In order to
get everyone on the bus or plane in the mornings, I had to keep track of who
everybody had shacked up with the night before. With Paul [Gonsalves], who
had a drinking problem, although it never interfered with his playing, I'd have
to look for him on the floor of his hotel room if he wasn't in his bed. Or, once
or twice, in the alley outside the hotel. Paul was a special challenge to my
father, which is why he loved him so much. The guys prided themselves on
being an unruly bunch, and since each man had been responsible for his own
hotel bills, the band had acquired an undesirable reputation for skipping out
the back windows without settling its accounts. I changed all that by taking
care of all the travel expenses myself and deducting the costs from each man's
salary every week. I felt my father had a dignified image that had to be maintained. What made the job really difficult was that I was riding herd on the
men who had helped to raise me: Cootie Williams, Johnny Hodges, Harry
Carney. When someone knows you as a kid, it doesn't matter how much you
age. You'll always be the brat to them. It's like spending your whole life in your
hometown. Did they resent me telling them it was time to go to work? You
bet they did. They wouldn't do what Ellington told them to do, so why should
they listen to me? That's why he had this opening vamp that he would play
that eventually wound up being copyrighted as 'Kinda Dukish.' The idea was

for the audience to think that the band was waiting for Ellington to make up his mind what tune he wanted to play first. But he was actually waiting for the stragglers to take their chairs."

Would Duke Ellington ever second-guess his son? "Not really, because he didn't want to be bothered with the sort of details I was handling for him, if that meant taking away time from composing. But once I almost got into trouble for giving Russell Procope a five-dollar-a-night raise without consulting him. Russell was the lowest-paid man in the band, even though he had been with us for years. I liked him very much, so I snuck the extra money into his check without saying anything. After about three weeks, Russell said to my father, 'I've been getting too much money. What am I supposed to do? Give it back?' To my surprise, Ellington said, 'Well, Russell was honest about it, let's leave it that way.' Afterwards, I said to Russell, 'You know, if this were any other band, you could have cost me my job. You weren't giving me a chance to save my own skin by giving me the opportunity to correct what could have been an error on my part. From now on, come to me if you have any problems with your paycheck.' Of course, Russell became my enemy after that."

Did Duke ever compliment Mercer on a job well done? "No, and as a matter of fact, if anyone else would start to praise me in his presence, he would immediately shush them or change the subject, afraid that I would ask him for a raise. But he showed his appreciation in other ways. He would call me on the phone in my hotel room, ostensibly to argue about one thing or another, but really just to talk. I think he beckoned me mostly to keep him company, though he was too stubborn to admit that. We knew each other too well by that point for him to expect that he was getting a yes-man. From time to time, he would ask me if I loved him, and I would tell him that I did."

Thankless as the job sounds, it at least enabled Mercer to spend his father's last decade by his side, an opportunity given few sons. "That was important because I had never had the chance to know him that well at home. He was always on the road. Mine had always been the gruesome job in the family—I had to bury the relatives while Ellington worked. And when he was diagnosed as having cancer, there was the gradual shock of realizing that I would be burying him. Even before Ellington died, there were times when we would be on a bill with singers, and it was understood that we were to back them up. And he would call on me to lead the band so that he could save his energy for his own set. He also insisted that the band fulfill its contractual obligations even when he was in the hospital. He had promised the president of IBM that the band would fly down to Bermuda for an IBM convention with or without him. So a few days after his funeral, I was on a plane for Bermuda. Churches all over the country were inviting the band to play his Concerts of Sacred Music, and I gradually found myself holding a baton instead of a trumpet."

Mercer Ellington has been a semipro football player, a disc jockey, and a traveling salesman as well as a musician. He gives the impression that he would be just as happy behind the scenes, except for one thing: "Ever since I walked out on stage to take a peek at the audience when I accompanied Ellington on a New England tour when I was around seven years old, I've wanted to be on stage from time to time. I used to tell my mother's folks that I was interested in a career in aeronautics, but that was just to appease them. I always wanted to be a musician. That's why I learned both trumpet and saxophone as a kid. I wanted to he ready for whatever vacancy opened up in Pop's band. I never dreamed of leading his band. I just wanted to be in it with him."

"HE PASSED AWAY ABOUT A WEEK BEFORE WE WENT TO BERMUDA FOR IBM, and I discovered when we got there that we were in danger of losing our way. Paul Gonsalves was dead. Harry Carney was ailing. Cootie [Williams] was planning to retire. There were new men coming into the band, and the men who knew his music by heart were on the way out. We had only about twelve arrangements written down on paper for the new men to learn, and maybe a dozen others we could fake. What I had to do was restore the library, by hiring arrangers to transcribe older pieces from records, including "Caravan" and "Perdido," both of which were licks that guys in the band had come up with that just grew and grew, like Topsy, but had never been written down. Through the process, I began to catch up with him. I'm still catching up with him. But it's too big a job to accomplish in my lifetime, which is why it's important that his original arrangements be written down."

Under Mercer's direction, the Ellington Orchestra has revived "Ko-Ko," "Birmingham Breakdown," "East St. Louis Tootle-oo," "Hot and Bothered," "Daybreak Express," "Ring Dem Bells," "Echoes of Harlem"—innovative works from the twenties, thirties, and forties that Duke himself neglected in later decades. These reinterpretations leave much to be desired. The ensemble blend is usually too brassy, and in the absence of Hodges, Carney, Gonsalves, Lawrence Brown, and Cootie Williams, the solos are nondescript. Moreover, record companies, when bringing the Duke Ellington Orchestra into the studio, have inevitably requested new versions of Duke Ellington's Greatest Hits: "Caravan," "Satin Doll," "Sophisticated Lady," and "Take the 'A' Train." This has been a source of frustration for Mercer. So was *Sophisticated Ladies,* although with this show he succeeded in giving his father the Broadway smash that eluded him during his lifetime.

"When I was in the army, we produced what we called 'blueprint' shows, which meant that you went from base to base with just the score for a show— no cast. So the songs were tailored for the average serviceman to sing. What we would do is decide which songs should be in the show, then lay the sheet music on a table and keep shuffling it around until the song titles suggested a story. I preached the idea to Pop of doing the same thing with his songs when I got out of the service. I said, 'Your track record of unsuccessful shows is what they're holding against you. You should make your success as a songwriter work for you by putting all of your best-known numbers in one show.' But it was no sale. He said that would be cheating. He wanted each of his shows to contain all new songs specifically written for it." *Sophisticated Ladies* was to have been a "blueprint" show. "Let the songs tell a story. I got the idea again from seeing my daughter Mercedes in *No, No, Nanette*. It was such a pleasure to sit there hearing songs that were already familiar. But that was the last time [the show's producers] listened to me."

Although Mercer was listed as music director and conducted the Duke Ellington Orchestra for most of *Sophisticated Ladies'* Broadway run and many of the subsequent revivals, He had no creative control. "What I objected to about the show was that there was a bit too much Broadway in it. The music wasn't the star of the show, the way it should have been. The dancing and the staging took precedence. The best singers in the cast, like Priscilla Baskerville, were given the least to do, and they often had to sing at tempos all wrong for them, and all wrong for my father's music, because of the dancers, who argued that the tempos should be suited to them, since they were the ones risking injury. My argument was, make the dance fit the music, instead of the other way around. That's what Alvin Ailey had always done with Ellington's music. We wound up compromising on the issue, but nobody was happy. Every night, there would be either a singer or dancer waiting to chew me out.

"What I liked about *Sophisticated Ladies,* though, was that it presented Ellington to a contemporary audience. It meant that an additional generation would be familiar with his work. But, you know, every time he had a big hit song, he felt that that permitted him the luxury to do something major which might not go over so big. I feel that one of my obligations is to expose every side of Ellington, and that's why *Queenie Pie* is so important."

QUEENIE PIE DIDN'T BECOME ONE OF DUKE ELLINGTON'S PRIORITIES until 1970, when New York's WNET-TV commissioned its completion. Two years later, Ellington recruited Maurice Peress—former maestro of the Kansas City Philharmonic and the Corpus Christi Symphony, and once Leonard Bernstein's understudy with the New York Philharmonic—to assist him in orchestrating the vocal parts.

"The television people did not renew their option after Duke's death," Peress explains, "presumably because they felt the piece wasn't valuable without his presence on camera as the narrator, which is really what they were paying for." Patti LaBelle and Robert Guillaume (TV's "Benson") sang a few numbers from the score on *Love You Madly,* a 1983 PBS special. But it looked as though *Queenie Pie* would never be performed in its entirety—until Peress brought Mercer Ellington together with Marjorie Samoff and Eric Salzman of the American Music Theater Festival.

Queenie Pie had "American Music Theater Festival" written all over it in large letters—as a lavish amusement by a serious composer who doubled as a pop songwriter (like Gershwin's *Strike Up the Band,* which the festival had revived in 1984), and as a jazz composer's attempt to hurdle the racial and class prejudices segregating jazz from the other performing arts (like Anthony Davis's opera X, which the festival had debuted that same year). "We fell in love with the idea," Samoff says. Still, *Queenie Pie* was hardly ready to be staged, although Ellington had left among his personal effects what appeared to be a finished score, a libretto, and a plot synopsis neatly typed by Betty McGettigan. ("Another of his girlfriends, with a literary gift," Mercer says. "He believed in putting them to work.") The show wasn't long enough at sixty minutes (the length of the proposed TV presentation). So Peress interpolated "Creole Love Call," as well as four new songs culled from Ellington's note-books and given lyrics and dramatic rationale by George David Weiss and George C. Wolfe, respectively..

The title character was loosely based on Madame C. J. Walker, a key figure in the Harlem Renaissance of the 1920s, a beauty-products entrepreneur believed to have been the first woman in the United States to earn a million dollars. But Ellington's scenario was pure fantasy. As the show opens, Quee-nie Pie has reigned as Harlem's leading cosmetician and most beautiful woman for longer than anyone can remember. Suddenly facing stiff competition from a conniving young arrival from New Orleans, she sails off in her yacht and washes ashore on an imaginary island where she learns of a magic elixir that will bestow the eternal youth she needs to retain her throne.

Those involved with the American Music Theater production saw *Queenie Pie* as a metaphor for Ellington's own soul-searching during his final years. Per-ess says, "My sense of it is that like a lot of famous people who have been every-where and done everything, Ellington still felt somehow unfulfilled." Samoff says, "He was looking at the success of the Beatles and coming to terms with his own mortality, although I don't want to make the opera sound too heavy, because so much of it is tongue-in-cheek. But it deals with a mature and suc-cessful person coming to terms with a younger generation, asking the ques-tion, What is timeless and what is ephemeral?" Mercer Ellington says, "What [Queenie Pie] is really searching for [is] love, although she's not even aware of this need."

But this sounds like post–Phil Donahue pop psychology. Ellington made his peace with the Beatles with a delicious arrangement of Lennon and

McCartney's "All My Lovin'" on *Ellington '66,* and a backbeat gave him nothing to fear—witness "Acht O'Clock Rock" from *The Afro-Eurasian Eclipse* and the irresistible "Blue Pepper" from *The Far East Suite,* both from the mid-sixties (to say nothing of "Happy Go Lucky Local," from 1946). And would Ellington have depicted a feminine alter ego, given what his son describes as "a basic contempt for women. He considered them a necessary evil. The only women he ever had anything good to say about were Ruth and his mother, both of whom he put on a pedestal." More likely, Ellington's conscious theme was vanity, which he thought of as a feminine trait—although it was really a family trait, according to Mercer, who grew up calling his paternal grandparents Aunt Daisy and Uncle Ed so they wouldn't feel old. "Ellington was the same way. You can imagine how he felt when I made him a grandfather. When reporters would assume that I was his brother, or that my children were his, he would never correct them."

Would Duke have been happy with the American Music Theater Festival's production of *Queenie Pie?* For that matter, was Mercer happy with the way it was shaping up? "I argue with Bob [Kalfin] and Garth [Fagan] that since there are very few people in the theater who can sing, dance, and act equally well, we should go with the singers. But I have to honor their decisions. I believe what Ellington would have done is to wait until all the parts were cast, then overhauled everything to suit the abilities of the performers, just like he did with his orchestra. Whenever something turns out differently than you first expected it to, you know you're being faithful to the spirit of Duke Ellington," says Mercer, who, by his own admission, has spent the last twelve years trying to think exactly like his father, after spending his first fifty-five years doggedly thinking just the opposite.

And so, on with the show.

IS *QUEENIE PIE* MAJOR ELLINGTON? ON THE BASIS OF A GALA PREVIEW I attended, the answer would have been an unequivocal no. The jerry-built sets inspired by Romare Bearden's background scrim of Harlem in the 1920s (itself something any hack magazine illustrator might have come up with) looked like they would topple, and so did the dancers, in the oversized period costumes they wore in the first act. The choreography was a dire mix of jazz, ballet, and *Solid Gold.* Worst of all, Ellington's melodies had been only sketchily orchestrated. The show was inert, and everyone knew it. When an AMTF staffer with a good memory and a theatrical flair passed me on her way back to her seat after intermission, she looked me in the eye and paraphrased a line from *Tea and Sympathy:* "When you write about this—and you will—be kind."

But following a return visit a week later, I was no longer so sure that *Queenie Pie* was hopeless. A lot of hard work had gone into the production, and it showed; although the book—as dated and patronizing in its assumptions about "primitive" cultures and what women really want as Ellington's earlier *A Drum Is a Woman* (another TV project)—was dead weight no amount of effort was going to salvage. But perhaps it was a mistake to take the story too seriously. Just as some of the trills that Ellington wrote for his title character affectionately mocked Verdi and Puccini, it's possible that the ludicrous scenario was a send-up of classic opera's farfetched and superfluous story lines. (Queenie's real-life model made her fortune selling pomade to black Americans who wanted straight hair, but Ellington—or Wolfe—reversed the pattern by having Queenie show island folk how to let their hair grow natural. She introduces them to the concept of soul. Talk about American know-how!)

In any case, the book hardly mattered. The story was merely scaffolding for the music, which was majestic, although one would never have guessed that early in the show's run. From sumptuous balladry of the kind that casual listeners most associate with Ellington ("Truly a Queen"), to the minor-key mysterioso he bequeathed to Thelonious Monk and other contemporary jazz composers ("My Father's Island"), to the modal, percussive exotica that dominated the later suites ("Stix"), every conceivable genre and subgenre of Ellingtonia was represented in the score. Knowing that Peress, a staunch Ellingtonphile, had left the production over "creative" disagreements, I feared the worst; but the Ellington Orchestra, under Roy Glover's direction, succeeded in bringing to the surface melodies that had been hopelessly submerged during the previews. In most cases this involved stripping away excess orchestration. But "My Father's Island," which had earlier pivoted on a minimalistic organ vamp, had been re-harmonized for brass and reeds, and now sounded royal. It was fitting that the members of the orchestra took their places alongside the singers and dancers during the curtain calls. They were among the stars of the show, and they deserved a hand.

"Truly a Queen" and the three other previously unpublished Ellington songs that Peress and Wolfe had interpolated in the score fit comfortably, even if Weiss's lyrics were frequently banal (not surprising, given that he wrote the words for "What a Wonderful World" and "Can't Help Falling in Love," dreck hits for Louis Armstrong and Elvis Presley, respectively). Throughout *Queenie Pie* there were references to earlier Ellington, including the opening fanfare from *Harlem*, impeccably played by the trumpeter Barry Lee Hall to bring down the final curtain. "Jam with Sam" became "Harlem Scat." "Rhumbop" was reprised from *A Drum Is a Woman*. Only the inclusion of the wordless "Creole Love Call" seemed a misjudgment, though not because of its earlier vintage. Patty Holley gave it a boffo delivery that stirred up pleasant memories of Adelaide Hall on the original 1927 recording. The only problem was that Holley was playing Queenie's rival, Café O'Lay, and Teresa Burrell as

Queenie had no comparable first-act showstopper to win the audience over to her side. After seeing the preview, I wrote Burrell off as a graduate of the Phyllis Hyman School of Soulfulness and Charm. But once she gained assurance, she turned out to be a diverting singer with a voice full of weird dissonances ideally suited to Ellington. Larry Marshall and Ken Prymus were amiable enough in the male leads, and the energetic Lillias White and the Billy Eckstine-like baritone and former Ellington band singer Milt Grayson almost stole the show in minor parts (she took the lead vocal on "Stix," the second act's big dance number, and he sang "Oh, Gee," a *Sophisticated Lady* offspring). The entire cast deserved applause for scrupulously avoiding the pop-eyed gesticulation of other black shows set in Harlem of yesteryear, including the original production of *Sophisticated Ladies.*

After its Philadelphia premiere, *Queenie Pie* played a month at the Kennedy Center in Washington, D.C. A year later, George C. Wolfe, still flush with the success of *The Colored Museum,* told the *New York Times* that he was doing research on the Harlem Renaissance in preparation for bringing *Queenie Pie* to Broadway; so far, nothing has come of this. The staging and dancing still need work, to judge from the Philadelphia performance, but the music is a fine starting point. *Queenie Pie* shouldn't be allowed to die. At the very least, someone should sponsor the Ellington Orchestra in a concert presentation of the music. And perhaps it's not too late for a cast album.

But I'm begging the original question: Is *Queenie Pie* major Ellington? If Ellington were still alive, it wouldn't matter. The best numbers would go into his working repertoire, where they would undergo further revision, and the others would be forgotten. But the problem with posthumous discoveries is that they have to be masterpieces or ephemerae, with no allowance for anything in between. *Queenie Pie* is neither. Ellington came closest to integrating music and spectacle in his three concerts of sacred music, his sound track for Otto Preminger's 1959 film *Anatomy of a Murder,* and (presumably) his Cotton Club revues. Compared to these, *Queenie Pie* is Ellington Lite. But *Queenie Pie* affirmed that even minor Ellington can be pretty wonderful, and suggested that the moment was overdue for revivals of *Jump for Joy* (1941), *Beggar's Holiday* (1947), and *My People* (1963), as well as first performances of *Poussé Café* (1962) and the undated *The Man with Four Sides.*

(SEPTEMBER 1986)

Ellington's Decade

J azz scripture insists that composition is, at best, a springboard to improvisation; at worst, an obstruction to it. But jazz scripture also insists on progress, and in the past decade, as improvisers have been retracing their steps, composers have been the ones breaking new ground—writing formally ambitious works that, while not eschewing improvisation altogether, relegate it to second place and demand more rigorous self-editing by improvising soloists. Many of these composers are rejecting jazz's traditional isolationism to collaborate with poets, choreographers, and classical instrumentalists. What was unique about *X*, Anthony Davis's opera about the life of Malcolm X, which was presented by the New York City Opera in 1986, was that it actually got funded—there could he other *X*'s waiting to happen, by Dave Burrell, Ornette Coleman, Abdullah Ibrahim, and Henry Threadgill, all of whom have described similarly grand initiatives. Other contemporary composers thinking big—if only in terms of thinking orchestrally, even when they are able to hire just six or seven players—include Muhal Richard Abrams, Anthony Braxton, John Carter, Joseph Jarman, Leroy Jenkins, Steve Lacy, Roscoe Mitchell, Butch Morris, James Newton, Errol Parker, George Russell, Leo Smith, Cecil Taylor, Edward Wilkerson, and the members of the World Saxophone Quartet (Hamlet Bluiett, Julius Hemphill, Oliver Lake, and David Murray) and the String Trio of New York (Billy Bang, James Emery, and John Lindberg). But if one accepts the premise that composition has been the key element in jazz in the eighties, the decade's central figure is not any of these, but Duke Ellington, who died in 1974.

Ellington's influence has never been greater. Typed as a "jazz" composer only by circumstance of race, he spent his career chafing against the restrictions of jazz, much as his spiritual descendants are chafing now. His scope was enormous. In addition to ballads even shapelier and riffs even more propulsive than those expected of a swing-era big-band leader, his legacy of more than fifteen hundred published compositions includes tone poems, ballet suites, concertos for star sidemen, sacred music, topical revues, film scores, picture-postcard-like impressions of faraway places, and extended works unparalled in jazz until very recently and classifiable only as modern American music. (His only shortcoming was as a popular songwriter, and, in part, this was because he never found his Ira Gershwin or Lorenz Hart.) A butler's son who dared to imagine himself the lord of the manor, an experimentalist who courted and won mass acceptance, Ellington was one of America's greatest composers (regardless of idiom), and perhaps the most quintessentially American in the ease with which he navigated the distance between the dance floor and the concert hall.

IN 1984, THE JAZZ CRITIC GARY GIDDINS ESTIMATED THAT FIFTY HOURS OF new Ellington recordings had been released in the ten years following his death. More have been released since then, including long-forgotten studio sessions and concert tapes previously circulated only among collectors. Invaluable as much as this material has proved to be, it is ironic that it has generally been easier to come by than Ellington's most celebrated work—the epochal sides he recorded for RCA Victor in the early forties, for years available only on French import labels or by mail order from the Smithsonian Institution.

The 1986 release of *Duke Ellington: The Blanton-Webster Band* (RCA Bluebird 5659-1-RB, also available on cassette and compact disc) indicates that RCA is finally beginning to realize what treasures lie in its vaults. The four-record set collects the Ellington Orchestra's entire commercially released output from March, 1940, to July, 1942—arguably Ellington's most fertile period, although most of his larger-scale works, beginning with *Black, Brown, and Beige,* were still to come. By 1940, most of Ellington's sidemen had been with him a decade or longer, and he had been so important in shaping their sensibilities that he could virtually predict the content of their improvisations. (Indeed, in some cases he wrote their "improvisations" out for them beforehand.) This enabled him to take daredevil risks as a composer and arranger, and gave even his "through-composed" works an improvisatory ring. The two newcomers alluded to in the collection's title perhaps stimulated him even more. Jimmy Blanton, the first jazz bassist to phrase with a horn player's melodic fluidity, gave the Orchestra's syncopations unprecedented bite and opened Ellington up as a pianist. The arrival of Ben Webster, the Orchestra's first tenor saxophone star, gave Ellington another ace soloist to call on, as well as another color for his palette. (He acquired still another, more exotic color in 1941, when Ray Nance, who doubled on violin, replaced Cootie Williams in the trumpet section.)

The detail of Ellington's writing and the individuality of his soloists never fail to astonish, no matter how familiar one is with the tracks on *The Blanton-Webster Band.* "Concerto for Cootie," with its beautifully elongated theme and Cootie Williams's piquant variations on both muted and open horn, is a masterpiece that lost something when Ellington rounded off the main theme from ten bars to eight to accommodate Bob Russell's lyrics, and the piece became "Do Nothin' Till You Hear from Me." "Cootie" is here in its pristine form, and I envy anyone hearing it for the first time—the same goes for the surging dialogues between Blanton and the full ensemble on "Jack the Bear." "Ko-Ko" offers intimations of pedal-point modality and *Kind of Blue;* and the delight of "Cotton Tail" (based on "I Got Rhythm," in anticipation of bebop) lies in its layered sax-section riffs and Webster's sinuous choruses (which foreshadowed both the "tough" tenor style and Coltrane's "sheets of sound"). The charms of "I've Got It Bad (And That Ain't Good)" include Ellington's celeste, Paul Francis Webster's plain-spoken lyrics (the finest ever to grace an Ellington song), the lovely countermelody between choruses, and the blissful conjunction of Johnny Hodges's alto and Ivie Anderson's voice (as harmonious a union as that achieved more informally a few years earlier by Lester Young and Billie Holiday). "Main Stem" and "Harlem Air Shaft" are among the tracks that highlight Ellington's penchant for experimentation even within the conventions of the blues and the thirty-two-bar popular song format. The numerous cover versions of pop ditties of the period ("Chloe" and "You, You, Darling" are my personal favorites) demonstrate Ellington's powers of transformation, even though Herb Jeffries's ungainly warbling proves that even Ellington was human (with the exception of Anderson, he never employed a first-rate singer on a regular basis). This was also the period in which Billy Strayhorn, Ellington's protégé, blossomed into an influential composer and orchestrator under Ellington's watchful eye. Strayhorn's "Raincheck" and "Johnny Come Lately" anticipate bebop phraseology, and his "Take the 'A' Train," which ultimately became the Ellington Orchestra's signature theme, cleverly underlines the band's playful swank. But the most evocative Strayhorn piece here is "Chelsea Bridge," with its lordly Webster solo—as a successful jazz appropriation of Ravel and Debussy, this remains unsurpassed even by Ellington, a master impressionist in his own right.

It's too bad that the producers of *The Blanton-Webster Band* failed to include Ellington's 1941 duets with Blanton, or the small-group dates from the same period led by Hodges, Bigard, and the trumpeter Rex Stewart, all of which featured Ellington on piano. If it is true, as Strayhorn is said to have put it, that Ellington's real instrument was the orchestra, it's equally true that the piano became an orchestra at his urging. (*Money Jungle* [Blue Note BT-85129], a bristling encounter with the modernists Charles Mingus and Max Roach, recorded in 1962 and reissued with additional material in 1986, provides a good, long look at Ellington the dissonant stride pianist.) Although the vintage performances on *The Blanton-Webster Band* have been digitally remastered, the sound isn't as vivid as on the French reissues, nor is the pitch always accurate. If RCA intends to do justice to its Ellington catalog, its job is far from over—the Ellington Orchestra recorded masterpieces for the label before 1940 and after 1942. *The Blanton-Webster Band* is a godsend for those on a tight budget: others are advised to search the specialty shops for French RCA's increasingly difficult-to-find *The Works of Duke,* twenty-four volumes available separately or in five boxed sets. Still, music that is timeless and universal in its appeal belongs in chain stores as well as in specialty shops, which is why the reappearance of this material on a well-distributed domestic label is so welcome.*

IN THE YEARS SINCE ELLINGTON'S DEATH, ICONOCLASTIC PERFORMERS associated with the jazz avant-garde have recorded albums of his compositions. They have brought their own agendas to his music, which has proved more malleable than anyone might have imagined (though there is some justice in the complaints of those who insist that to play Ellington means playing him his way or not at all). The most striking of these revisionist homages are the flutist James Newton's *African Flower* (Blue Note Bt-85109), the pianist Ran Blake's *Duke Dreams* (Soul Note SN-1027, distributed by PolyGram Special Imports), and the World Saxophone Quartet's *World Saxophone Quartet Plays Duke Ellington* (Nonesuch 79137-1), the most recent of these entries, as well as the most wholly satisfying in terms of fealty to Ellington's tempos and the ineluctable *rightness* of its deviations from text.**

That so many performers who are generally adamant about playing their own original material would choose to interpret Ellington is eloquent testimony to his inexhaustible influence, as are the Ellingtonian flourishes (sometimes filtered through his disciple Charles Mingus) that pervade the writing of John Carter, Abdullah Ibrahim, David Murray, and Henry Threadgill. But when I call Ellington the key figure of the eighties, it's not just because modernists continue to play his tunes or to aspire to his orchestral majesty. Musicians from all stylistic camps have long done that much, and Mercer Ellington

---

*The Blanton-Webster Band ends with titles recorded on July 28, 1942, after which a musician's strike against the record companies kept the Ellington Orchestra out of the Victor studios until December 1, 1944. *Black, Brown, and Beige* (RCA Bluebird 6641-I-RB), another four-record set, released in 1988, resumes the chronology (and the sound is much better than on *The Blanton-Webster Band*). Included along with *The Perfume Suite* and excerpts from *Black, Brown, and Beige* are "Midriff" and "Esquire Swank," two 1946 performances inexplicably omitted from the otherwise complete *Works of Duke.*

**Chico Freeman's *Tales of Ellington* (Black hawk BKH-537–1) should be added to this select list.

keeps his father's most familiar music in circulation with albums like *Digital Duke* (GRP GR-1038), released in 1987. (If anything, the familiarity of the material on *Digital Duke* is a disadvantage; with so much obscure Ellington and Strayhorn still awaiting discovery, new versions of "Satin Doll" and "Take the 'A' Train" are luxuries we can live without.) Nor is it just because plungered, speechlike brass styles like the ones that Bubber Miley, Cootie Williams, Rex Stewart, and Joe Nanton patented during their years with Ellington are again all the rage, thanks to the trombonist Craig Harris and the trumpeters Lester Bowie and Olu Dara. Nor is it because Anthony Davis and many other black composers are consciously, and in some instances programmatically, giving musical expression to the goals and frustrations of black society, just as Ellington did with such mural-like works as *Harlem, The Deep South Suite,* and *Black, Brown, and Beige.* This is Ellington's decade because visionary jazz composers are taking up his unfinished task of reconciling composition and improvisation. Jazz is thought of as extemporaneous and fleeting—that's another part of its romance—but these composers are aiming for a perpetuity like that which Ellington achieved. They are mounting larger works, as lie did, without worrying whether the results strike everyone as jazz.

Of course, not everyone who listens to jazz is as sanguine about this development as I am. Some fear that jazz is recklessly heading for the same dead end that classical music arrived at earlier in this century with atonality arid serialism. And it's true that the composers I nominate as Ellington's heirs lack his common touch, his willingness to play the role of entertainer; and they will probably never find themselves in a position to develop this commendable trait. Jazz has experienced growing pains since Ellington's time, and the innocent idea of entertainment had become enslaved by the cynical science of demographics (the question no longer is whether something is entertaining, but how many, and precisely *whom,* it entertains). In its maturity—some would say its dotage—jazz has become an "art music"; because reconciliation with pop seems out of the question, a rapprochement with classical music is probably the key to its survival. Ellington gives these contemporary composers much to strive for, but his mass appeal is out of their reach. This is unfortunate, because a larger audience should be part of what a composer hopes for when he starts to think big.

(AUGUST 1987)

POSTSCRIPT

"Ellington's Decade," which was written on assignment for *The Atlantic* in January, 1987, finally ran in the August issue (as "Large-Scale Jazz"). Several readers found it curious that my piece didn't address James Lincoln Collier's

Ellington biography, which—entirely by coincidence—appeared in stores that same month. They were correct in assuming that I disliked the book.

Collier makes two serious charges against Ellington. The first—that he "stole" from his sidemen—is easily dismissed. As Gene Santoro pointed out in an article on Miles Davis in *down beat:* "Ellington set up what was essentially a closed feedback loop between himself and his band members. He kept his players on salary and used the studio and bandstand as compositional sketch pads. If during the course of a workout or jam a Johnny Hodges or a Tricky Sam Nanton or a Juan Tizol hooked a melodic idea that grabbed the Maestro, he'd seize it (sometimes with credit, sometimes not) and weave his rich orchestral tapestry around it. In the process, it would become a total composition, something living in a fully ramified way, quite apart from the scrawl or flash that had given it birth. . . . [This] helps [to] explain why so few of Duke's sidemen ever went on to become imposing bandleaders in their own right, even aside from the very real socioeconomic considerations involved." By Collier's logic, *Rhapsody in Blue* was written, not by Gershwin, but by Ross Gorman, whom Gershwin is supposed to have heard playing that famous clarinet glissando during a Paul Whiteman band rehearsal.

The second charge—that because Ellington's music depended so heavily on improvisation and so little of it was put down on paper, "we are entitled to question not just whether [he] was America's greatest composer but whether he was a composer at all"—is more difficult to debate, based as it is on an apparently un-shakeable value judgment. In applying the same highbrow standards that he elsewhere mocks Ellington for "naïvely" aspiring to, Collier is competing with his subject, and rigging the rules so that Ellington can't win. "Duke was finding ways to slide by that sounded to lay audiences a good deal better than they would to professionals," Collier muses at one point; and at another, "I am certain that Duke would not usually have been able to analyze his own scores in the way that a more formally trained arranger would." So what? Dismissing the *Sacred Concerts,* Collier notes that although "Duke's fans and the loyal jazz press always found good things to say about [them] . . . I have not been able to find support for this position among *professional* music critics" (italics mine). It takes a few readings to realize that Collier is referring to the hacks who review classical music for daily newspapers, all jazz critics presumably being well-meaning amateurs who are sometimes lucky enough to be paid for their opinions.

Only a fool would rank the *Sacred Concerts* among Ellington's greatest works, but the point is that classical reviewers generally took a patronizing tone toward Ellington when they paid him any mind at all. The goal of a biographer should be to put his subject in perspective; Collier just wants to put Ellington in his place. Although Ellington's hypochondria, superstitions, active libido, and often-callous behavior toward those closest to him provide the ammunition for what Joyce Carol Oates calls "pathography," Collier lacks the rancid eloquence and prurient curiosity of an Albert Goldman or an Arianna Stassinopolous Huffington—his *Duke Ellington* is neither as vile nor as readable as their Lennon and Picasso bios. But even when praising Ellington, Collier's tone is grudging, and some of his comments about Duke and his intimates are so mean-spirited and condescending as to be construed as unconsciously racist. "The first of Duke's rules was to break them," Collier writes, and slipping into his characteristic amateur psychoanalytical mode, adds, "He was driven to this conclusion by temperament, not by any careful process of thought," as though it made a difference. Collier's Ellington is a man-child of impulse whose disdain for formal training was a sign of "laziness" rather than the justified arrogance of the autodidact. As portrayed by Collier, Ellington's father was a silly old Kingfish whose determination to become a "gentleman" was an expression of "pretentiousness," and whose "feeling for the elegant"— food and wine and china and such—was "superficial" emulation of the wealthy white family he worked for. Why can't Collier give this self-educated black man the benefit of the doubt? The grown men in Ellington's orchestra are more than once referred to as "boys."

In subjecting Billy Strayhorn to special abuse, Collier plays off of Strayhorn's alleged homosexuality: "Ellington always evinced a tendency—weakness, if you will—toward lushness, prettiness, at the expense of the masculine leanness and strength of his best work, the most 'jazzlike' pieces. Strayhorn encouraged this tendency. . . . To be sure, Strayhorn wrote some very nice swingers . . . but in the main he was exploring a tropical rain forest thick with patches of purple orchids and heavy bunches of breadfruit. Duke's work increasingly moved in this direction." In other words, Strayhorn *feminized* Ellington's music. Collier stops short of suggesting that Strayhorn, not music, was Ellington's mistress.

This book poisons the waters for the rest of us. I doubt I am the only critic who has found himself overcompensating on Ellington's behalf. (In a review of Strayhorn homages by Art Farmer and Marian McPartland in the *Philadelphia Inquirer,* for example, I crossed out a line about Strayhorn's being Ellington's superior as an impressionist for fear that readers would conclude that I agreed with Collier that Ellington wasn't all he was cracked up to be.) Collier has already been criticized strongly by, among others, Santoro in *The Nation,* Dan Morgenstern in the *Times Book Review,* Martin Williams in the *Washington Post,* Michael Ullman in the *Boston Phoenix,* and Gary Giddins in the *Times Literary Supplement.* But the estimable Michiko Kakutani's favorable review in the *New York Times* demonstrates how tragically little America's best and brightest know about jazz, and how easily Collier's distortions could become the Official Version. Kakutani, whose specialty is minimalist fiction, can be forgiven for repeating Collier's half-truths. But what excuse is there for E. J. Hobsbawn's rave in *The New York Review of Books?* Forget that Hobsbawn used to write jazz criticism under the name of Francis Newton. As a socialist, he should be able to recognize cultural conservatism.

(AUGUST 1987/FEBRUARY 1989)

The Mystery of Herbie Nichols

In 1955, two offbeat pianists found champions at jazz record companies. One was Thelonious Monk, then a cult figure whose first two Riverside albums were collections of Duke Ellington favorites and pop standards calculated to dispel his forbidding image. Although the strategy was unsuccessful—producer Orrin Keepnews underestimated Monk's gift for reshaping any tune at hand into his own creation—Monk soon gained a sizable following willing to accept him on his own terms. Herbie Nichols wasn't as lucky. The man some consider Monk's equal as both a pianist and composer was a more willing interview subject than the intransigent Monk (Nichols wrote articles on music himself, for *Metronome* and other publications): this alone should have made him a better bet for stardom. But it didn't happen that way, and why it didn't is one of the most frustrating mysteries of jazz. Nichols recorded thirty titles (twenty-nine of his own compositions plus George Gershwin's "Mine") at five different sessions for Blue Note between May, 1955, and the following April, with Al McKibbon or Teddy Kotick on bass, and Art Blakey or Max Roach on drums. Blue Note's Alfred Lion released twenty-two of these performances—among the most imaginative ever recorded by a pianist in a conventional trio setting—on two ten-inch LPs and one twelve-inch, but forgot about the remaining eight after it became obvious that Nichols wasn't going to sell on any configuration. It's tempting, but ultimately pointless, to speculate how easily Monk's and Nichols' fates might have been reversed if Keepnews had shown less perseverance and Lion had shown more.

Among those in the know, Nichols is often invoked, along with Elmo Hope and Sonny Clark, as one of the black pianists martyred by the indifference of critics, record companies, and club owners in the 1950s. But as heroin addicts, Hope and Clark contributed to their martyrdom, unlike Nichols, who reportedly didn't even drink to excess. Though Hope and Clark were fine pianists and composers, Nichols was their superior. Yet they at least enjoyed the respect of the leading musicians of their generation—witness the many records they made as sidemen with the likes of John Coltrane, Dexter Gordon, and Sonny Rollins. By comparison, Nichols's credentials, taken at face value, were those of a blue-collar musician. Shunned by his equals, he earned his living backing gutbucket saxophonists like Hal "Cornbread" Singer, Floyd "Horsecollar" Williams, and Big Nick Nicholas in Harlem, and playing dixieland with semipros in Greenwich Village. In 1956, Billie Holiday gave Nichols what should have been his big break, when she put lyrics to his "Serenade," and retitled it "Lady Sings the Blues" (also the name of her autobiography, and her signature tunhe until her death three years later). But even this gained Nichols little notice. By the early '60s, he was reduced to a six-nights-a-week gig at the Page Three in Greenwich Village, backing three singers, a comedian, a shake dancer, and a stripper who began her act disguised as a man. Granted, one of the singers was the superb Sheila Jordan; and in addition to slumming celebrities like Tennessee Williams, Shelly Winters, and Lenny Bruce, the audience frequently included Cecil Taylor, Steve Lacy, Archie Shepp, and Roswell Rudd—key figures in the emerging jazz avant-garde, all of whom credited Nichols as an influence, but none of whom was yet in a position to do him much good.

Nichols died of leukemia in 1963 (ironically, the year that Monk made the cover of *Time*), at the age of forty-four. Two things have kept his name alive: the chapter on him in A. B. Spellman's *Four Lives in the Bebop Business*, a 1966 book used as a text in black studies as well as jazz courses; and today's mania for 1950s jazz, which makes reclamation projects like *The Complete Blue Note Recordings of Herbie Nichols* (Mosaic MR5-118) economically feasible. This five-record box set contains all thirty of Nichols's Blue Note performances, including the "missing" eight tracks (two of which first surfaced on a Japanese anthology released a few years ago), and eighteen alternate takes. The neglect that Nichols suffered in his own era works to his advantage now: vintage ceases to matter because the contemporary listener doesn't feel like an earlier generation got there first. Like Duke Ellington, Nichols was a master of the musical vignette—the out-of-step chorus girls on Nichols's "Dance Line" would be right at home in Ellington's *Harlem*. But because Nichols worked on a much smaller scale than Ellington, a better comparison is to the Charles Ives who wrote such short piano pieces as "In the Inn" and "Some Southpaw Pitching," especially given the dissonance, polyrhythmic complexity, and pianistic focus of Nichols's writing.

In "House Party Starting," for example, a frolicsome riff made to seem vaguely apprehensive through repetition eerily conveys the discomfort of being the first arrival at a party. In "The Spinning Song," a wistful, Asian-sounding scale that gradually turns harsh and staccato leaves no doubt that what's being spun is the wheel of fortune, and that it's always landing on bankrupt. The most provocative of the previously unissued performances is the aptly named "Sunday Stroll." But Nichols's masterpiece is "The Gig," a riot of clashing notes and tone clusters depicting a pickup band at odds with itself about what to play—sixty-seven oddball measures long with a fitful nine-bar opening strain that builds terrific momentum for the whiplash improvisation that follows. With its flatted fifths and echoes of "Tiger Rag," this is a "Strike Up the Band" conceived in the aftermath of the squabbles between the boppers and the figs, undoubtedly owing something to Nichols's nights of toil as the lone modernist in dixie joints. (Nichols believed in happy endings, so the jammers ultimately reach accord; just as a bevy of happy, talkative guests finally shows up in "House Party Starting.") It's significant that "The Gig" is from a session with Roach and McKibbon, a combination more in empathy than Blakey and Kotick were with Nichols's desire to tap the hidden melodic potential of walking bass lines and snare drum overtones. Nichols wanted bass and especially drums to provide melodic coloration as well as propulsion; or, as he put it, he wanted rhythm to *sound,* as it does in African music (to which he was one of the first American jazz musicians to pay serious attention). Nichols's tracks with McKibbon and Roach rival Ahmad Jamal's with Israel Crosby and Vernel Fournier as the best integrated piano-bass-and-drums performances of the 1950s, and they enjoy a big advantage over Jamal's in not being as coy or overformatted. When he wasn't experimenting with the kind of extended form represented by "The Gig," Nichols was subverting thirty-two-bar convention from within, with between-the-bar-line chromatics and arpeggios, and teasing intros and codas that were all part of the grand design but didn't count against the final tally (the best example of this is in "Steps Tempest"). As an improviser, he was strictly a theme-and-variations man, as he could well afford to be, because his compositions prefigured practically every conceivable harmonic option. (For this reason, the Mosaic box's alternate takes generally differ from the masters only in tempo. They are a justifiable luxury, however, because with the exception of a handful of sides reissued on Savoy, a 1957 Bethlehem LP, and incongruous dates as a sideman with swing trumpeters Rex Stewart and Joe Thomas, this is all the Nichols there is on record.) Nichols was like Monk in this and in many other ways, including the vestigial echoes of Harlem stride in his left hand and his uncanny ability to conjure the secret notes between the keys. In 1943, as a regular columnist for the Harlem-based periodical *The Music Dial,* Nichols had the distinction of giving Monk what was possibly his first review. After praising Monk's "rhythmical melodies," Nichols chastised him for his partiality to "certain limited harmonics" that would keep him from taking a place beside Teddy Wilson and Art Tatum. As a judgment of Monk, this was absurd. But as a statement of Nichols's own values, it was perfect: Tatumesque flourishes of the sort that Monk disdained prevented Nichols from sounding like Monk's twin brother.

In confirming Nichols's greatness, *The Complete Blue Note Recordings* leaves hanging the question of why his peers turned deaf ears to him. To say that his music was "difficult" won't suffice. So was Monk's, after all. As a result of Nichols's diverse experience, he had to be a skilled and versatile accompanist (in a liner note for an earlier reissue, Roswell Rudd likened playing with him at a sixties loft session to being "a soloist in a grand concerto, with a multitude of other voices leading, supporting, and responding"). When his own records didn't sell enough to justify keeping him under contract, why didn't Blue Note find use for him as a sideman, or commission pieces from him for others on the label's roster? Were Ike Quebec, Lou Donaldson, and Stanley Turrentine so different from the saxophonists Nichols worked with in Harlem? Lion deserves the credit he's received for recording Nichols, but he also deserves censure for not sticking with him, as the less-deified Keepnews did with Monk. In a sense, Nichols's Blue Note recordings foster what may be a misleading impression of him as a composer of flawless miniatures for piano, bass, and drums. For an inkling of what he might have sounded like with horns, you have to turn to two eighties albums featuring the Dutch pianist Misha Mengelberg: *Regeneration* (Soul Note SN-1054) with Rudd and Steve Lacy, and *Change of Season* (Soul Note SN-1104) with Lacy and George Lewis. Toward the end of his life, Nichols told Spellman that too few black instrumentalists knew what to make of musical notation: the lament of a composer who knew that his un-recorded works would survive only on score paper—which meant that they might as well never have been written.

I asked a few of Nichols's musical associates for their recollections of him, and if they had any explanation for why he was so unjustly overlooked.

Big Nick Nicholas: "When we played together in Harlem, we'd play his tunes and mine, plus standards we both liked. He was a good accompanist who played his own style no matter who he was playing with. You'd always know it was him. But he was a very dedicated musician who was willing to play any kind of music in order to make a living. He played dixieland because it was steady work. The alternative would have been to work a week every once in a while, then not work again for six months. You can't live like that. He wasn't an opportunist. There are two kinds of musicians. There are guys like Herbie Nichols and myself who don't push, and there are the guys who are out there pushing every day, which is unfortunately what does it in America. Some guys who aren't very good are very good at telling you how good they are. He wasn't one of those."

Sheila Jordan: "Jackie Howell, the owner of the Page 3, adored Herbie. He always had an attentive audience there—she made sure of that. I still have a lot of the chord changes he wrote out for me: 'Lush Life,' 'Love for Sale,' 'Lady Sings the Blues,' and a song of his that he never recorded called 'My Psychiatrist.' Most of the singers at the Page 3 didn't have their music together. They'd ask him for I'm Confessin" in D-flat, but he'd never complain. He was a very good-looking man, very tall and mysterious, and always well dressed. I remember one time he was standing outside of the club and he saw me getting out of a car driven by a man who needed a shave. He asked me what I was doing with a gangster. I said 'Herbie! That's the drummer in the trio that's here on Mondays, your night off.' He couldn't imagine a musician not being well groomed. He'd stand in the background when he wasn't playing, never saying very much, but you knew he was taking everything in—he saw the guys coming in, buying the strippers drinks, and he feared the worst about me when he saw me getting out of that car. He was such a sweet man. You know how musicians on the scene can be, always telling each other 'I have a record date coming up, and you can be on it if I can be on yours.' Herbie wasn't like that. He was very reserved—not unfriendly, but very dignified and very shy."

Archie Shepp: "When I knew him, he knew he was ill, and he was starting to become rather disillusioned. He felt that there was too much politicking in the music. He was a genius, but he got lost in the shuffle, which seems to be an unfortunate aspect of this system of ours—to lose geniuses in the shuffle. I don't know why he didn't get more work as a sideman. He could play with anybody, but I don't think he would have been comfortable as a sideman in a conventional jazz setting, any more than Monk would have been. That's a dilemma inherent in our music: should a gifted soloist and composer like Herbie be forced to bend in order to fit into a traditional sideman's role?"

The Herbie Nichols who emerges from these recollections was a quiet man disinclined to tout his own virtues, which is evidently what it took to get ahead in the competitive jazz scene of the fifties. But there must have been more to it than that. Was Nichols gay, or was something else that no one wants to talk about an alienating factor? You could argue that his two-handed attack struck his contemporaries as old-fashioned in the wake of Bud Powell. But what about Erroll Garner and Oscar Peterson? Did the period's more strung-out musicians resent Nichols for being such a straight arrow? Maybe so, but didn't they adore Clifford Brown for just that reason? If Nichols had survived, would endorsements from Rudd, Shepp, Cecil Taylor, and others associated with free jazz have won him more attention? It's debatable. Nichols complained to Spellman that a musician had to be a junkie or an Uncle Tom in order to be accepted by audiences; my guess is that he would have considered the militancy that became *de rigueur* in the wake of free jazz yet another loathsome black stereotype. Besides, with the obvious exception of Taylor, there was little call for pianists in the new music. As Shepp points out: "It isn't a question of what would have happened if Herbie Nichols had lived longer. It's a question of whether circumstances would have been any better for him than those he had lived under. If he had gone on living under the same circumstances, he might have become an extremely bitter man."

Nichols is going to remain a mystery. The twenty-four-page booklet that comes with the Mosaic box gives us as complete a picture of him as we're ever going to have. It includes Rudd's track-by-track analysis, testimonials by Rudd and others, a Nichols discography, samples of his poetry and prose (not his Monk review, though), and Francis Wolff's phantomlike snapshots of him—all this, plus his music, which is so magnificent you can't help wondering why he wasn't allowed to make more.

(APRIL 1988)

Sunshine, Too

Sheila Jordan was once the subject of an amusing exchange between D. Antoinette Handy and George Russell—a classic confrontation between an empiricist and an artist who makes his own truth. It happened during a 1984 colloquium on jazz at Temple University, in Philadelphia. Arriving a day before he was scheduled to deliver a lecture on his Lydian Concept, Russell sat unrecognized in the audience for a panel on women in jazz that included Handy, the author of a 1983 book on the International Sweethearts of Rhythm. She talked about a work in progress: a biographical dictionary of black women instrumentalists.

"You failed to mention two very important women in your talk this afternoon," Russell told Handy when the discussion was opened to the floor.

Who were they, Handy wanted to know.

"Billie Holiday, for one," Russell answered.

Handy patiently explained that her book was to be about *instrumentalists*, and Russell mumbled something about Holiday having influenced more musicians than any of the instrumentalists whom Handy had mentioned.

The second woman, Handy asked, somewhat testily.

"Sheila Jordan," Russell replied—to embarrassed laughter from the audience, because, as Handy quickly pointed out, "Sheila Jordan is white."

Russell, who is black but has often been mistaken for white (including by Wilfrid Mellers in *Music in a New Found Land* and, I would conjecture, by many in the audience that day), grinned devilishly and paused before delivering the punch line: "Well, that depends on how you define it, doesn't it?"

More than Sheila Jordan was at issue here, of course—though Russell is himself an academic and (via his adoptive parents) a product of the black bourgeoisie, the combination antagonizes him when he recognizes it in anyone else. In calling on a merit-system logic similar to the one that Lenny Bruce used in declaring Lena Horne Jewish and Sophie Tucker a Gentile, Russell was redefining the question of "authenticity" that hangs in the air whenever distinctions are made between black and white jazz performers. To Russell's way of thinking, Jordan was black because she'd paid more than anyone's share of dues: as a child of poverty, an hereditary alcoholic, the divorced white mother of a racially mixed daughter, and, perhaps most of all, as a jazz singer committed to expressing herself honestly in a society that places little value on honesty or jazz.

"Now I understand it," Jordan laughed, when I told her the story. "I was working at One Step Down [in Washington, D.C.] about a year ago, and a very nice black woman told me that my singing just blew her away. She introduced herself as D. Antoinette Handy and asked me to serve with her on a panel for the NEA [the National Endowment for the Arts]. She said that something George Russell once said about me made her feel that she had to hear me. She told me that what George said about me was absolutely right. And you know, I wondered what he could have said."

SHE WAS BORN SHEILA DAWSON, "AT HOME, ON A MURPHY BED IN A furnished room, in Detroit in 1928." (She kept the name Jordan from her brief marriage to the pianist Duke Jordan, who was Charlie Parker's pianist when she met him in the late forties.) Her parents had married earlier that day, and didn't stay together long after her birth. She was raised by her maternal grandparents in Summerhill, Pennsylvania, "in the mountains, about a mile and a half from Erenfield, a mining town that we used to call 'Scoopytown,' which is where I think the actor Charles Bronson is from."

A short woman with dark bangs, attractive moon face, and a big, toothy smile, Jordan speaks with a rural accent, dropping many of her final g's and losing some of her vowels—when she sings Hoagy Carmichael's "Baltimore Oriole," or mentions the record company she almost signed with in the early sixties, "Mercury" becomes "Merkry." She talks about her life with the same candor and lack of self-dramatization that characterizes her singing. "People used to sing a lot where I was from, because it was a very depressed area, and there was nothing else to do except go to the beer gardens and drink and sing and forget your problems. I've been singing since I was three. I'd sing when I was happy, and I'd sing when I was unhappy, which was more often. I sang just for the joy of singing. I remember I used to have to pass a graveyard on my way to the store, and, boy, I would sing my lungs out because I was so scared. In Johnstown, they sold magazines with the lyrics to all the current songs, good songs that later became the standards that the jazz people took and made into classics. That's what I grew up singing. I always felt better when I sang. Singing made life bearable. I never sang in church, because I was Catholic and only boys were allowed in the choir. But do you want to know something? I just recorded a Gregorian chant, in Latin, with George Gruntz's big band. After all these years. But I was never allowed to sing in the Catholic church.

"On Saturday afternoons, I used to walk two miles to South Fork to the movies, when I could get the money and there was a Fred Astaire movie playing there. I loved his singing, the same love I later felt for Billie. He had such a personal sound. He and Ginger Rogers—that was glamour to me. It was an escape from the poverty and unhappiness at home. I grew up in what was basically an alcoholic family. My mother died from the disease. My grandfather was an alcoholic, and my grandmother also started drinking very heavily toward the end of her life. The bills would never be paid, and the lights were always being turned off, which meant no radio. We didn't even have a library in town. I wanted to play piano so badly, and my great aunt—my grandfather's sister—was teaching me. But she hated the fact that my grandfather drank, and they had a big fight about it once. That was the end of my piano lessons. In small towns like that, people hold grudges. They never make up.

"Since my mother was the oldest of nine children, my uncles and aunts were like my brothers and sisters. Before me and one of my uncles, who was ten years younger than me, nobody in my family went past the sixth grade. The boys quit school to work in the mines, and when the mines were on strike, they would go away to the CCC camps, where they would clear fields or pave roads and send money back home. When I was about fourteen, my mother came back to visit. She was still drinking heavily, which she did up until her death in 1981, but my grandfather had temporarily stopped, which, of course, led to a big fight with me as the pawn. My mother said, 'Well, I'm taking her back to Detroit with me.' And my grandparents said, 'Sure, now that we've raised her.'

"I was terribly lost in Detroit. Here I was with my mother, who was totally out on booze—a beautiful woman, very warm and sensitive, but with a horrible drinking problem. I loved my mother, but she didn't give me anything of herself when I was a child. She was just a kid herself, in many ways. No, we never really came to an understanding before she died. She knew that I loved her, and I knew that she loved me, but she was incapable of showing her love for me the way she should have because of her disease. I never really began to understand that until I got the disease myself, and I didn't *really* understand it until around four years ago when I started going to ACOA [Adult Children of Alcoholics].

"My mother had seven husbands altogether, and when I lived with her, she was married to a creep who was a professional card shark. This guy—I refuse to call him my stepfather—was beating my mother up, and I couldn't stand to watch it. She was a little ninety-pound woman, a very attractive woman who was unable to defend herself, and he was breaking her nose and knocking all of her teeth out. Plus, he was getting fresh with me, fondling me when he thought I was asleep. It was just too much for me. I moved out when I was seventeen, got a part-time job, and rented a room in the Evangeline Home, a place for young women. That's where I was living when I finished high school. My classmates thought that was pretty cool, me being on my own like that."

Jordan is sometimes included in lists of illustrious jazz graduates from Cass Tech, the accelerated Detroit high school that produced Gerald Wilson, Milt Buckner, Paul Chambers, Tommy Flanagan, and Donald Byrd. "But I actually only went to Cass for a year, and not because I was so smart. It was just that they didn't know where to place me when I transferred from Pennsylvania. To be perfectly honest, I couldn't keep up with the work at Cass, so I transferred to Commerce, which was connected to Cass by a bridge. Commerce was where you went to learn typing and shorthand, and that was good for me because I knew I wasn't going to college and I was already thinking in terms of how I was going to support myself. The kids from Commerce ate lunch in the Cass Tech cafeteria, and took certain academic courses at Cass. It was basically one school, and we all hung out together."

She was exposed to jazz by her friends at Cass, and her love for the music was part of a larger infatuation with black culture in general. "What made me feel a bond with black people, first and foremost, was the music, which I think literally saved my life. But I remember something my grandfather once said. He was reading a story about black people in the newspaper, and he looked up and said, 'You know, those poor people get blamed for everything.' He wasn't an educated man. He was a house painter who had only gone to third grade, but he had beautiful handwriting, and he had compassion for people. I really identified with the black people I met in Detroit, maybe because I felt like I had experienced prejudice myself in Pennsylvania. There were two families that were poorer than all the others, and we were one of them. My grandfather was the town drunk, and he was considered an atheist because he wouldn't go to church. He was part Cherokee, and very much into his own way of believing. I couldn't understand why we would go to church on Sunday mornings and not eat breakfast, in preparation for receiving holy communion—I mean, not that there would have been much for breakfast anyway, but he would get mad that we couldn't eat a piece of toast or something. He wasn't a violent man. He never struck us, but we would have to sneak off to confession and communion when he wasn't looking.

"I was in an awful state in Detroit, and black people were the only ones who showed me compassion. I felt black. I wanted to be black. I used to tell people I *was* part black, because I hated the words I heard white people use to describe blacks, and I thought that maybe they wouldn't use that language around me if they thought I was black. My friends were Barry Harris, Tommy Flanagan, and Kenny Burrell, who were all around my age. The police were always harassing us. I'll never forget the last time I was taken down to the police station in Detroit. When they stopped our car, my girlfriend Jenny was in the front seat with the fella she liked, and I was in the back seat with Frank Foster [the tenor saxophonist who now leads the Count Basie Orchestra], who I had a crush on. I threw my cigarette out the window, and, don't you know, they crawled down under the car to find the butt. They thought they had us for possession, but they took us in anyway and gave us the third degree. I told the detective I was going to be leaving town soon anyway, and he made fun of me. 'Oh, sure,' he said. 'To New York, I suppose, where everyone's so *cosmopolitan* and all the white girls have black boyfriends. Let me tell you something, young lady. I have a nine-year-old daughter, and if I thought I was ever going to catch her in the situation I just found you in tonight'—he touched his holster—'I'd go home right now and shoot her in her sleep.' He gave me the chills. I knew I had to leave Detroit as soon as I finished school."

THOUGH SHE'D PERFORMED IN DETROIT WITH SKEETER SPIGHT AND LEROY Mitchell in a teenage vocal trio that improvised lyrics to bebop solos, Jordan bolted for New York with no intention of pursuing a singing career. "I was chasin' the Bird, just like everybody else in those days. I wanted to be able to hear Charlie Parker all the time, and sit in with him once in a while. The first time I met him was in Detroit, when my friends and I were trying to talk our way into the Club El Sino, where he was working. First of all, we were underage, and second, it was a black club and my girlfriend and I were white girls with two black guys. They turned us away, because they didn't want any trouble with the law. We went into the alley behind the club, and the door was open on account of the heat—they didn't have air-conditioning in those days. Bird came out and looked around. I wouldn't have thought of this then, but maybe he was coming into the alley to get high. I don't know. But he saw us and talked with us. Then when he came to town again, he let us sit in with him at the Greystone Ballroom—Skeeter, Mitch, and I.

"I took him to the Bluebird Inn, where he sat in with the house band. He drank Angel Tips—that's what he called it—crème de cocoa with cream on top. He had one and bought me one, but he never tried to come on to me. He was always a gentleman with me. He used to hang out at my loft in New York, and he turned me on to Bartók and the modern painters. He appreciated all kinds of music. He even liked Dinah Shore. He could hold an intelligent conversation on any subject. He could meet an engineer and rap about engineering with him. He was an amazing man, and that's why I'm almost afraid to see the movie about him. I feel too close."

In New York, Jordan studied briefly with Lennie Tristano, who had a reputation for insisting that his instrumental students sing. (The point was to make them realize that the music originated in them, not in their instruments.) How did he go about teaching an actual singer? "The same way. He asked if I could sing along with one of Bird's records, and I told him I already did that. He put one on, I sang along with it, and he said 'Ah, so you do.' Then he assigned me Lester Young. He also wanted me to sing along with Billie and Sarah, which I didn't want to do, great as I thought they were, because I wanted to sing my own feelings. So he didn't press it. He mostly coached me in rhythm and harmony.

"I studied with Lennie because I was looking for a place to sing, and I knew that he had sessions at his place every Friday and Saturday. I wanted to sing, but it was the same way it is to this day. My goals weren't the same as other singers'. I didn't have any aspirations of being a great jazz singer, and everybody knowin' about me and thinkin' I was wonderful. I've always sung for the sheer pleasure of it."

Though she rarely sang professionally during her early years in New York, she was always on the scene. Her loft was a hangout not only for Parker, but for countless other musicians and their camp followers. (In a *Cadence* interview, she reminisced about a time when she came home from work to find Sonny Rollins jamming in her loft; so many people were there that she couldn't squeeze in.) On the face of it, she was leading the bohemian life. But she had a daughter to provide for (Traci, from her marriage to Duke Jordan), so her situation was more complicated than it might have been for a male scene-maker. She worked as a typist and sang whenever an opportunity presented itself, even if the job paid next to nothing.

Fortunately for the rest of us, musicians appreciated her singing, and one in particular nudged her into the spotlight. In 1962, she was performing with a group that included the bassist Steve Swallow at the Page 3 in Greenwich Village. "Steve Swallow was very close to George Russell at the time," she recalled on a 1980 ECM promotional interview disc, "and George Russell came in one night to hear Swallow and to hear [the pianist] Jack Reilly [who was studying with Russell and told him] you should hear this singer. George came in, and he heard me, and he really liked me—in more ways than one, I might add. [*Laughter*] So George and I became very close, and he was a great supporter of my music. . . . If George Russell had not come into the club that night, I would never have been recorded. He took money out of his pocket and made a tape of myself and [the guitarist] Barry Galbraith, and took it to Al Lion and Mercury. Of course, I never thought anything was going to happen with that. I was just so happy there was going to be a chance for me to sing on record, whether it was going to come out or just be a tape. . . .

"Blue Note signed me immediately. . . . But before I did *Portrait of Sheila** . . . [Russell] wanted to know, 'Where do you come from to sing that way?' So I took him back to Pennsylvania and showed him the mines. A miner asked me to sing 'You Are My Sunshine.' I said, 'Oh, I don't sing that anymore.' He said, 'Well, you used to.' . . . My grandmother said, 'Well, let's all sing it.' So she played it on the piano, and we all sang it, and George got an idea, and that's how 'You Are My Sunshine' came about on *The Outer View.*"**

THE FIRST TIME YOU HEAR IT, JORDAN'S VOCAL ON "YOU ARE MY Sunshine" is so electric that the rightness of all that surrounds it—Russell's probing piano lilies (at once dissonant and folkloric); Swallow's combative, Mingus-like bass counterpoint; the quiet virtuosity of the brief horn solos (the tenor saxophonist Paul Plummer's, in particular); the sarcastic coda at double the tempo and the final negating three-horn raspberry—almost passes by unnoticed. But Jordan's vocal is what makes the track overpowering even after you know every note by heart. She enters *a capella* about five minutes in, singing the beery, unlovely melody as sweetly as a child intones a prayer—yet the words acquire an unaccountable erotic chill (her slight lisp, all the more noticeable with no instruments to mask it, works in her favor here, as I suspect Russell knew it would). After the horns reenter, a precipitous key change as the tempo quickens forces her above her natural range in a successful attempt to exploit her tendency to sing a quarter-note sharp. Although she makes the notes, it sounds like she's straining; but this helps in transforming the feckless song into a lover's needy plea and something else beside—something very close to what Michael Cimino failed to get at with the singing of "God Bless America" at the end of *The Deer Hunter* (which was set in the same part of Pennsylvania as Jordan's hometown). I once played "You Are My Sunshine" for a friend who wasn't really a jazz fan, and told him the story of how Russell and Jordan came to record it. He listened to it in silence, then said that he never before realized how symbolically charged sunshine must be to coal miners who spend their days working in darkness. Or, as Russell said about Jordan's performance in the original liner notes to *The Outer View,* "She's jazz, but she's *Sunshine,* too."

IT'S SHOCKING TO REALIZE THAT AFTER *PORTRAIT OF SHEILA,* JORDAN HAD to wait twelve years to make another record under her own name. It wasn't

---

*Just reissued on compact disc only, Blue Note CDP-7-89002-2.
**"You Are My Sunshine," which Jordan recorded with Russell in 1963 (and is still available on *Outer Thoughts,* Milestone M-47027), wasn't her first recording. Two years earlier, she sang "Yesterdays" on *Looking Out* (Wave LP-1), an album by the bassist Peter Ind.

until she became the surrogate "horn" in the pianist Steve Kuhn's quartet in 1980 that she performed with any regularity outside of New York. On the road with Kuhn, she was astonished to discover that she was something of an under-ground cult figure—the women singers of Jordan's post-bop generation whose values reflected those of jazz rather than show business could be counted on one hand (Jordan, Betty Carter, Abbey Lincoln, Jeanne Lee . . .), and of them, Jordan excited the most loyalty; in part because she had recorded so little that every note was precious. There were fans who had practically worn out their copies of her few albums, and who felt they had to tell her how much she meant to them. "Her treatment of a ballad is such that it makes me feel I'm intruding or that she knows what *my* story is," one fan wrote *Down Beat* in 1963, speaking for all of us.

Shortly before surfacing with Kuhn, she made a resolution to deal with the drinking problem she feels she inherited from her mother. "I've been sober for two and a half years now, although I stopped drinking around 1975," she explained. 'I slipped only once, when I started drinking nonalcoholic beer, which led to actual beer drinking. That lasted for about a year before I stopped again in 1977. The reason I joined a self-help group wasn't because I was afraid I would start drinking again, but because I was getting scared of my depen-dency on coke. How it started was that around 1981 people who didn't know I had an addictive personality would offer me some now and then. I switched seats on the Titanic. I never reached the point where I needed it every day, but I was never an everyday drinker, for that matter. I would have total blackouts when I drank, so I drank only on the weekends. Never during the week, because if I touched a drop, I would be off and running. It was the first drink that got me drunk.

"It was the same way with the coke. With Charlie Parker, it was the oppo-site pattern. He drank more when he wasn't using dope. Once he came to a party in my loft and drank rubbing alcohol when there was nothing else left to drink. Another time, on a Sunday morning when the bars were closed, he went to the store and bought ten bottles of lemon extract, drank them, then went back and bought and drank I don't know how many more bottles of it. I can identify with what Bird was going through. I remember one time I dropped a little brown vial of coke on my bathroom floor. It splintered into pieces, and, don't you know, I picked out the glass I could see and snorted. I mean, how sick can you get? Your habit overpowers you. It tells you what you will do and what you will not do. It's a disease, and I could sit here all night and tell you I'm over it, then slip right back into it tomorrow morning. The worst part is that knowing, hey, this stuff can kill you isn't enough to make you stop. You don't care whether it kills you because you have a death wish anyway."

EVEN AS THE PACE OF JORDAN'S CAREER QUICKENED, SHE NEVER considered giving up her nine-to-five job that she held since 1966 as a typist for Doyle Dane Bernbach, a major New York advertising company. "I was poor as a child, and I swore to myself that I would never, so long as I could help it, live like that again. I've always had a job. But you have to be careful of what you pray for, because you might get it. Every morning, I used to pray that the day would come when I could go on Social Security and devote full time to music. But last year, my company merged with another company, and they laid me off. After twenty-one years! I was devastated at first, but I guess it was the push I needed. I'm a full-time singer now, and so far it's worked out fine."

At sixty, Jordan finds herself in steady demand. When she sat down to talk, she had just returned from three months in Europe with the George Gruntz Concert Jazz Band. A few days later, she was off again, for a series of voice and bass duet concerts with Harvie Swartz. She also travels as a single, performing with local rhythm sections in each town, and she devotes much of her time to teaching (she has conducted vocal workshops in Gratz, Austria, and at City University in New York). When she was still married to Duke Jordan, "He used to ask me, 'Why can't you sing the melody just the way it is, *then* do what you feel you have to do to it after the first chorus?'" Though she declines to admit that this was good advice, she does admit offering a variation of it to her own students. "I tell them you want to approach a song melody-first, the way it's written. If I feel a kid isn't being honest with a song, I'll slow her down. I'll say, 'Sing me the song first. Until you're able to sing a song with feeling all the way through, you're not ready to scat.'"

With her severance pay from Doyle Dane Bernbach, she made a down payment on a house in Hunter's Land, New York, in the Adirondacks, where she now spends most of her free time. "I was seeing a man from there, and after we broke up, I realized how much I liked the serenity up there. I grew up in the mountains, and I never thought I'd want to live in the mountains again. But I guess that as you get older, you find yourself getting in touch with your roots. There's nothing like having someone you love and respect who loves and respects you back. But if you can't have that, you're better off alone, like I am. I don't like being alone, but I'm in no position to have a relationship. I'm away too much, and I had one that lasted sixteen years and almost did me in when it was over. I don't want to go through that again so soon.

"At this point, my daughter is a vice-president at Motown Records. She was in promotion at Arista, working on behalf of Aretha Franklin and Billy Ocean, but she was getting so many offers from other companies that she knew it was time to move on. The only bad part of it, for me, is that she had to move out to Los Angeles, so I no longer see her as much. But the title means a lot to her as a black woman. She didn't have it easy. You can imagine how proud I am of her. I'll tell you a story. Once when she was a baby, I was taking her to Coney Island, because she loved the water. A woman on the subway with two infants of her own said, 'Oh, what an adorable colored baby. Where did you get her?' I said, 'I got her the same way you got yours, lady.' The prejudice never seemed to bother Traci, but it occasionally bothered me."

CERTAIN SONGS ARE NOW ASSOCIATED WITH SHEILA JORDAN. *BODY AND Soul*, a recent Japanese release (CBS/Sony 32DP 687) was practically a Sheila Jordan retrospective, with new versions of "Baltimore Oriole," "I'm a Fool to Want You," "Falling in Love with Love," and "When the World Was Young" from *Portrait of Sheila*. She has written others that deal frankly with her life (for instance, the title track on *The Crossing*, Black Hawk BKH 50501-1-D). But if her singing has become more autobiographical, it has also become, paradoxically, less direct. It's no longer so intense, which is understandable; one suspects that singing no longer amounts to an emotional release for her, as it did when she had fewer opportunities to perform. For my taste, she now scats too much for someone with her gift for interpreting lyrics (though, in all fairness, it should be added that her scatting rivals Betty Carter's for harmonic aptitude and rhythmic acuity).

Still, at her best, there's no one else like her. Her personal integrity has made her a role model for young women singers, including some who owe nothing to her stylistically. In a 1981 *down beat* Blindfold Test, Jordan said about a record by Billie Holiday: "Billie's sound is so strong that you forget who's playing behind her. . . . All you're aware of is this wonderfully human voice with all this emotion and love in it, and pain—the whole thing, it's just right there. I mean she could sing with anybody—she could sing alone, she could sing with the guy on the street corner, she could sing with anybody and make it jazz. She *is* jazz, she still is, she's *the* jazz singer to me." When told that a younger singer had recently said much the same about her, Jordan said, "Oh, wasn't that sweet of her. I had no idea she felt that way about me. It's always wonderful when someone tells you how much they enjoy your work. Sometimes they don't, because they assume you hear it all the time. But I *don't* hear it all the time. What I sometimes hear from black singers, who aren't really putting me down or anything, you understand, is, 'Well, it isn't really Sheila's culture' whatever that's supposed to mean. Maybe it wasn't my culture to begin with. But I didn't steal from anybody. The only person I ever wanted to steal from was Charlie Parker, and I didn't have to. He gave it to me.

"I know how hard it is for women singers, and I try to give then advice if I can. First of all, if they're good lookin', they're going to have to go through a lot of B.S. with club owners and record producers. And any time anything goes wrong, the singer's always the one who gets blamed. I don't feel I'm an entertainer, but from having been with Steve Kuhn's band and doing the bass-and-voice duets with Harvie, I've learned to present my music in a way that allows the audience to become involved. Years ago when I sang, I was closed up, standing very stiff with my head down. Steve Kuhn used to say, jokingly, that when people came to hear the quartet, they left raving about me, not the band. The focus was always on me, as hard as we tried to present that group as a quartet, not just a singer with a trio. But I said, 'You gotta remember one thing, Steve. I'm the one they talk bad about, too, when they don't like us.'"

(NOVEMBER 1988)

She's Susannah McCorkle

usannah McCorkle has chosen two antithetical careers for herself, one begging for solitude, the other demanding the spotlight. "I have two literary
agents, one here and another in England, telling me not to equate my ability
to write with being unfulfilled," she says. "Before I got involved in a good relationship, I thought of myself as a solitary woman, speaking for other women
who thought of themselves the same way. But who am I now? And who am I
speaking for?" She's published several short stories, one of which—"Ramona
by the Sea," about a moody, overweight young woman's alienation from both
the middle-class values of her parents and the radical alternative of her college
classmates—was included in the 1975 O. Henry Prize collection, in the fast
company of works by Alice Adams, Harold Brodkey, Raymond Carver, E. L.
Doctorow, and Cynthia Ozick. There is an unfinished novel in her drawer,
which she plans to resume work on after recovering from what she hopes is a
temporary case of writer's block—brought on, in part, by changes for the better in her love life and success in her second career as a jazz-oriented singer.

Because McCorkle—who is guarded about her age, but is probably in her
early forties—performs standards, rarely scats, and seldom uses her voice as a
horn, there are some who dismiss what she does as gentrified pop. Her failure
to record with pacesetting black instrumentalists has hurt her credibility with
younger jazz critics, who not having much use for women singers anyway, tend
to rate them by the company they keep. (How else to explain the reams of
praise for such earnest but unconvincing young black singers as Carmen
Lundy and Cassandra Wilson?) But what distinguishes McCorkle as the outstanding female jazz singer of her generation is her unforced affinity for the
era of Billie Holiday, Lee Wiley, and Mildred Bailey, when jazz and pop shared
a repertoire, and the test of vocal improvisation was straightforward melodic
embellishment and scrupulous attention to lyrics. McCorkle recognizes that
the best older songs still have plenty of life in them: she feels no need to treat
them as faded art songs, as too many modern cabaret performers do. Nor does
she accessorize songs, like Linda Ronstadt and other rock singers who embrace
vintage pop as an excuse for period extravaganza. She merely *sings*—in a merry,

slightly throaty voice that puts itself at the service of a song, instead of the other way around.

She's had bad luck with record companies, twice signing with financially insolvent independents that hoped to make big bucks with fusion and had little notion of how to promote a quality singer. But this hasn't prevented her from recording the best composer/songbook series since Ella Fitzgerald's. McCorkle's best albums are *The Songs of Johnny Mercer* (Inner City IC-1101), *Over the Rainbow: The Songs of E. Y. "Yip" Harburg* (Inner City IC-1131), *The Music of Harry Warren* (Inner City IC-1141), and *Thanks for the Memory: The Songs of Leo Robin* (Pausa PR-7175). On none of these does she settle for just the songs that everyone remembers. She includes Mercer's "Harlem Butterfly" along with his lyric for "Blues in the Night," Harburg's lyric for "'The Begat" from *Finian's Rainbow* as well as that for "Over the Rainbow," Warren's "The Girlfriend of the Whirling Dervish" along with his "Forty-second Street," and Robin's lyric for "Hooray for Love," as well as that for "Thanks for the Memory."

But McCorkle, who is genuinely interested in songs that reflect contemporary mores, and who fears being stereotyped as an antiquarian, has also recorded three albums—*The People That You Never Get to Love* (Inner City IC-1151), *How Do You Keep the Music Playing?* (Pausa PR-7195), and *Dream* (Pausa PR-7208)—which have juxtaposed Rupert Holmes with Jerome Kern, Jimmy Webb with Irving Berlin, Paul Simon and Antonio Carlos Jobim with Cole Porter and Rodgers and Hart. "People have told me I would have been a big star if I had come along back in the thirties or forties," she says, "but I've never wished for that, because I prefer being a woman now. I would have been a band singer or a starlet—a blonde cutie. I'm not one of those people who thinks that every song from the thirties and forties is wonderful and we should bring back the big bands. I just like good songs, and I can hear right through the period trappings, including the instrumental trappings of the seventies and eighties. Recently, a friend of mine in his late thirties made a tape for me with lots of what I suppose would be called country-rock songs on it. The melodies bore me, but I can relate to some of the lyrics, and there's one song by John Hiatt that I'm thinking of doing. I don't enjoy his singing, but his lyrics are about universal themes: failing relationships, marital disappointment, coming to terms with the fact that you can be just like your parents, no matter how differently you've tried to live your life. The song I like is called 'You May Already Be a Winner,' inspired by those millionaire sweepstakes offers we all get in the mail. It's really a song about taking stock of a relationship and deciding that maybe life isn't so bad. We may already be winners, because we love each other. It's a good example of a song that couldn't have been written in another decade."

McCorkle's list of favorite singers—Billie Holiday is one, as you would expect, but so are Ray Charles, Mose Allison, and early Nat Cole—is surprising for someone whose own style is about effervescence, not grit. However much her phrasing owes to Holiday (and however much she sometimes sounds like Marilyn Monroe might have in clothing that actually fit), McCorkle's precise diction and fresh-scrubbed timbre recall nobody so much as Doris Day—an observation she accepts gracefully enough now, although it used to vex her no end.

"The owner of a gay club I worked at in London told me not to come back without spiked heels, false eyelashes, and tits out to here. He fired me for sounding too much like the girl next door. *'You sound like Doris Day!'* That hurt. As I get older, my voice is becoming deeper and darker, but it's still very sweet and youthful, and I've gone through periods of hating it, when I felt pretty battered by life and wondered why my voice didn't reflect that. I'm flattered now when someone says I sound like Doris, because I've come to realize what a wonderful singer she is. But she's still not one of my favorites, because she's not the kind of singer you hear and think, 'Who is this woman and what has she lived through?' like you do with Billie Holiday. You never wonder that about the well-brought-up white ladies. The first time I heard Billie, I felt as though there was nothing separating us. She was right there. You heard the human being, not the performer. I want people to feel that way about me."

IN MARCH 1988, MCCORKLE TAPED A LIVE CONCERT FOR WMHT, ALBANY'S PBS station, at Proctor's Theater in nearby Schenectady, the city she commutes to from New York to be with her fiancé, a reporter for Albany's CBS-TV affiliate. Called *Susannah McCorkle and Friends: Jazz Meets Pop,* the concert also featured Gerry Mulligan, Mark Murphy, the Gene Bertoncini–Michael Moore Duo, and the Eastman Jazz Ensemble.

Schenectady's evacuated factories, streets, and stores depressed me. So did the people I saw aimlessly wandering the streets—it was difficult to tell who was homeless and who was just on the way there. General Electric, which boasts of bringing good things to life, sentenced this once-thriving GE company town to death. Downtown looks like all cities will soon look in an America without the prosperity that once entitled anyone who could hold a job to think of himself as upwardly mobile. From my hotel, I could see the skyline, which was nothing but crosses and spires: there's a lot to pray for in Schenectady.

The only visual relief from this urban disintegration was Proctor's Theater, a Art Deco movie palace with quaint little shops in its arcade lobby, vaulted ceilings, ornate balconies and mezzanines, a proscenium stage, gaslights, and the pipes of a 1931 Golub Mighty Wurlitzer Organ up two walls. If Schenectady's

economy were better, Proctor's would've been sold to a movie chain and mul-
tiplexed years ago; restored in 1979 to something approaching its original
grandeur, it's an Edenic shrine. ("One summer when I was eleven or twelve, I
hitchhiked [from Amsterdam, New York] to . . . the metropolis of Schenectady,"
writes Kirk Douglas in his 1988 autobiography, *The Ragman's Son*. "How large
it was! The streets were so wide! And Proctor's movie theater was so much bigger than anything in our town. . . .") I also liked the people I met in Schenectady, especially McCorkle's beau, Dan DiNicola, a Chet Baker fan and
frustrated trumpeter who hovered around Proctor's during rehearsal, playing
stage lover—attending to the dozens of technical details every performer needs
someone to attend to (especially a female performer, who risks being thought a
bitch if *she* attends to them herself), and clearly taking vicarious pleasure in
watching McCorkle on stage. (Ironically, as a result of being on TV, he's better
known around town than she is.)

On stage at Proctor's, McCorkle cut such a trim, confident figure in a neat
pageboy and a succession of sequined gowns and belted pantsuits that it was
difficult to believe she ever had anything in common with the protagonist of
"Ramona by the Sea," whose obesity was symptomatic of a chronic lack of
self-worth. But like the unkempt Ramona, McCorkle was a compulsive
overeater as a teenager. "I'd be in the supermarket at midnight, eating cakes
and whole loaves of bread while I was still in the checkout line. It was frightening, because this was before anyone knew very much about feminine eating
disorders, and I thought I must be the strangest person in the world. It's like
being a drug addict or an alcoholic, except that you can't say you're going to
cut out food entirely, the way you might with drugs or alcohol."

Also like Ramona, McCorkle was estranged from her college peers.
Although active in the Free Speech Movement at the University of California
in her native Berkeley, she was uneasy with the liberated cultural mind-set that
went with political radicalism on college campuses in the 1960s. "My parents
were active in leftist causes before me. My father is an anthropologist, but he
worked on the waterfront during the war. I grew up with no religious training at all, knowing that you didn't cross a picket line no matter what, and
believing that this country rightly belonged to Native Americans. I was raised,
I would say, as a socialist agnostic. So political activism didn't represent the big
breakout for me that it did for some other students. It was a wonderful time
to be in college, because we really did feel we were effecting change. We were
the first generation of college students to take on adult responsibilities, instead
of acting like postgraduate high school students. But it was also very frightening to be twenty years old and see the police swarming all over campus, and
hear the people you knew from classes talking about blowing up banks. A
friend of mine from college recently asked me, 'How did you live through

those years?' I never went in for floral shirts, love beads, acid rock, sleeping around, or naming children after continents. I hated going to parties where everybody smoked dope and lolled around, not talking. I wanted to go to parties to dance, meet a boy, and fall in love. In my writing classes, I was laughed at for writing stories that everyone said belonged in women's magazines. Everybody else was writing about first sexual experiences or first acid trips, and I couldn't, because I hadn't had either."

After graduation, McCorkle worked as an interpreter and translator in Mexico, France, and Italy, and it was while living the expatriate's life that she discovered jazz. "I went to Europe in pieces, determined never to return to the U.S. I can't say that I reinvented myself while I was abroad, because I didn't even feel that I had been anyone yet. But in Europe, I found a vindication for those instincts that had been completely thwarted in college: my romanticism, my love of quality writing and beautiful melodies, as opposed to loud, screaming guitars. So what if my stories were about housewives, so long as they were thoughtful, well-written stories? The things I responded to were valued in Europe, where you could buy a book of George Gershwin songs translated into Italian, see all the classic American movies of the thirties and forties for a few francs in Paris, and buy a Billie Holiday album for what amounted to a few dollars in a drugstore or supermarket. When I discovered jazz, it felt like being reunited with a family I never knew I had. I was glad, in a way that I hadn't grown up listening to this music, because it might not have hit me so hard when I finally discovered it—I might have taken it for granted. Musicians I met lent me records by Kay Thompson, Duke Ellington, Stan Getz. It was like being accepted into a tribe. Once when I was flying from Rome to California, I had a few hours stopover in Mexico City, which I spent in a nice little café I remembered from when I had lived there for a few months. I struck up a conversation with a man who was excited to find out that I sang, and who told me that he was married to Jack Teagarden's daughter. It was an unhappy marriage, he said, 'but when you love jazz as much as I do, and you meet Jack Teagarden's daughter, of course you marry her.' Sometimes I think Dan wishes I was Chet Baker's daughter."

McCorkle made the leap from listener to performer "one, two, three," which says something about the galvanizing power of the music, because offstage I was still a very gloomy girl. As a teenager, I had sung in school plays and summer theater productions. My mother had encouraged me to try for a career on Broadway, but I didn't want to be Rose in *Bye Bye Birdie,* singing the same songs the same way every night, in the same costume, with my hair sprayed black. I didn't like singing in character. I just liked opening my mouth and singing. In Mexico City, after sitting in my room all day writing stories, I used to take walks down a traffic island during rush hour, singing where no one could hear me. It was a release from the solitude of writing, and I guess that's also how I became a performer. Getting an immediate response from an audience was very gratifying for someone like me who was used to writing a story over a period of weeks, having it published months or sometimes even years later, and maybe receiving one letter that the magazine would forward to me."

BECAUSE SHE WAS ALREADY WRITING PROSE, MCCORKLE TRIED WRITING her own material when she first began performing. "But it seemed as though every time I got a good idea for a lyric, I found an old song that expressed the sentiment much more eloquently. And I came across lyrics that Truman Capote and Dorothy Parker had written that were just okay—good, but nothing special. So I quickly realized that fiction and songwriting were different crafts. The older songs I liked had beautiful melodies like I knew I would never be able to write, and I also doubted that I could team up with anyone else my own age who could. The songwriters I knew were into rock, folk, country, and the blues. They weren't interested in writing pretty melodies, and even if they had been, could they have matched Harold Arlen or Cole Porter?"

While living in Italy, McCorkle decided that the time had come for formal training. Out of the blue, she phoned the director of an Italian opera company, and asked if he could recommend a good vocal coach. "He volunteered to coach me himself, and I didn't have the nerve to tell him that I wasn't planning to sing opera. He was short, fat, and terribly forbidding—an almost cartoon-like maestro waving his arms around in a dusty old apartment full of photographs of divas kissing him on the cheek. He kept whacking my jaw in an effort to get me to relax it, and made me buy a surgical corset because he thought I wasn't holding my stomach properly. He was very fond of me because I spoke fluent Italian and was very, very earnest. But after a few lessons, he finally told me—with regret in his voice—'I have to tell you, you will never be an opera singer. You have a tiny, tiny voice.' I told him that wasn't what I wanted anyway, and sang 'Hi Lili, Hi Lo' for him, as an example of the music I did want to sing. I chose it because it's a song about being sad, and I thought I'd be able to draw on the sadness I felt at that moment, on account of his having made me almost too self-conscious to sing. He listened to me and said, very contemptuously, 'For that kind of song, you have enough voice already.' I felt rejected, but also very relieved.

"I've never taken another lesson, although I do sing three octaves of chromatic scales every day, and try to keep in good physical shape by race-walking, exercising, and eating well. I don't read music, but I have ideas about how music should sound. I come to rehearsals with pages of notes about where I want key changes and rhythmic breaks. The musicians I work with respect that. They sometimes make fun of my imagery—when I tell them that I want a hazy, druggy feel on 'Old Devil Moon,' for example, or that I want to hear the bass sound like a heartbeat on 'If I Only Had a Heart.' But once they know the feeling I want, they have the freedom to translate it into their own terms. I'll never forget something Peter Ind, the American bass player, told me when I sang with his band in England, and confessed my feelings of inadequacy to him. He said, 'If you can let go and sing in a way that pulls the band and the audience into a song, do you really think anybody's going to care that you don't read music?'"

MCCORKLE FIRST ATTRACTED ATTENTION AS A SINGER DURING THE FIVE years she lived in London, before moving back to the U.S. in 1979 with her then-husband, the British pianist Keith Ingham. The marriage dissolved soon afterward, although the couple continued to work together in New York until 1983. "I treasure the experience of singing with Keith, but we were incompatible except musically—and even music became a problem. Keith loves Chicago jazz of the 1930s, and wanted me to be the reincarnation of Lee Wiley or Mildred Bailey, his favorite singers. I like them, too, but I wanted to expand. We would have big arguments whenever I wanted to do a contemporary song. The first time I showed him [Rupert Holmes's] 'The People That You Never Get to Love,' he crumpled up the sheet music and threw it across the room. He didn't even want to do 'There's No Business Like Show Business,' although I bet he would have if he'd known that Sonny Rollins had recorded it. He also didn't like Brazilian music, which I love, and he scoffed at the notion of having an act. A singer has to think about pacing, beginning and ending strong. You don't want to be Las Vegas, but you do have to be aware you're doing a show. I think that if Keith had enough money, he wouldn't even perform; he'd buy a magnificent piano and sit at home and play it. He defined himself as a vessel through which music passes—a very European attitude, and a good attitude to have for someone recreating classic jazz. Mine was the American attitude of 'I'm me, the performer that I am, projected through music.'"

Truth be told, I tend to side with McCorkle's ex in thinking that the contemporary tunes in her repertoire are unworthy of her. It's not that today's songs are intrinsically unworthy (though when we start talking Rupert Holmes, they are), just that the most memorable of them aren't songs *per se*, but hit records so identified with their original performers (who, in most cases, are also the composers) that they resist fresh interpretation. Which is why at Proctor's it was Paul Simon's "Still Crazy After All These Years," not George and Ira Gershwin's "'S Wonderful," that called up memories of a specific time and place. Something else was troubling. I once heard McCorkle dedicate a song to Fred Astaire, whom she said she admired "for just being a guy singing"; that's also the kind of integrity she usually projects, standing perfectly still except to rise ever so slightly to her toes for high notes. But smiling for the cameras at Proctor's, she indulged in arm-waving stagecraft and between-numbers patter that sounded over-rehearsed. (It was, at a six-hour dress rehearsal earlier that day; I thought it was amusing that Mark Murphy, a singer whose fans adore him for his alleged spontaneity, but whom I find unbearably "jazzy," did his numbers the same way every time. In the language of boxing, "meets" means "versus," and any time that *Jazz Meets Pop* on television, the smart money is never on jazz to win.)

But give McCorkle the benefit of the doubt. For her, singing Rupert Holmes and Paul Simon is an honest effort to reestablish contact with her own generation, not a desperate attempt to stay up to date, as it would be for a singer ten or twenty years older. She might not write her own songs, but she wants some of those she performs to reflect her own experiences and those of her generation, which is perfectly understandable, even commendable. She's internalized the dilemma confronting jazz in the face of rock hegemony. Besides, at Proctor's, she managed to make the tuneless "The People That You Never Get to Love" sound like the keening blues it secretly longs to be. And despite the uneasy mix of standards and what might (not uncharitably) be called substandards, her effortless version of "On the Sunny Side of the Street," with Gerry Mulligan's crooning obbligato, was a vivid illustration of the twofold pleasure McCorkle offers at her best: incomparable songs from an earlier day, and someone incomparable to sing them for us now.

(JULY 1988)

Susannah McCorkle took her own life, jumping from the window of her sixteenth-floor Manhattan apartment, on May 19, 2001.

Too Late Blues

For a jazz critic to admit to a fondness for Bobby Darin isn't as embarrassing as it sounds. After all, Darin was a *down beat* cover boy in 1960, when Gene Lees, then the magazine's editor, delivered this encomium: "Darin today is unquestionably the only young male pop singer who handles standards with something approaching the polished intensity of Sinatra." Thirteen years later, when Darin died following open heart surgery, the same magazine ran a moving obituary by the jazz critic and record producer Michael Cuscuna. Gary Giddins once told me that as a kid in New York he begged his parents to take him to hear Darin at the Copa. So I'm in good company as a fan. But I can go my distinguished colleagues one better: I used to want to *be* Bobby Darin. I still remember my junior-high glee club director's delight when I volunteered to sing "Mack the Knife" at assembly. "Oh, *Threepenny Opera!*" she exclaimed. I stared at her blankly. What did I know from Kurt Weill? I knew "Mack" from AM radio, which was where I picked up the rest of my Darin repertoire: "Splish Splash," "Queen of the Hop," "Artificial Flowers," "Clementine," "Beyond the Sea"—all his hits, in fact. I don't need to be told that I could have chosen a hipper role model. But even as a teenager, far less inhibited than I am now, I found it easier to snap my fingers and warn anyone who would listen to watch out for Miss Lolly Linner (well, that's how I heard it) than to swivel my hips and caution those who were looking for trouble that they had come to the right place. I was essentially a good kid, not a punk. Like most of us who grew up to become jazz critics, I respected my elders, and I think I sensed that Darin did, too, despite his flippant air.

Darin's Atco hits weren't included in the fourteen-record soul retrospective that Atlantic released at the end of 1985. And that was only right, because he epitomized chutzpah, not soul. Yet it's impossible (for me, anyway) to think of Atlantic without remembering Darin, who was the Atco subsidiary's biggest moneymaker between 1959 and 1961 (the period of Atlantic's greatest fiscal growth), and whose producer was none other than Ahmet Ertegun, Atlantic's head honcho. I recalled Darin even earlier last year, though, when RCA surprised us with *Sam Cooke Live at the Harlem Square Club,* the long-overdue antidote to *Sam Cooke Live at the Copa*. Comparing the posthumous concert to the one released during the great soul singer's lifetime, critics made much of the different racial make-up of the two audiences, which seemed to me only half the story. In the early sixties, before anyone in the record industry actually used the term to describe the leap from ghetto to suburb, "crossover" also meant bridging the abyss from teen to adult, from sock-hop insouciance to supper-club savoir faire. Most in the industry's upper echelons were convinced that teenagers would outgrow rock 'n' roll along with acne and wet dreams, and that rockers who wanted to last in show business would eventually have to change their tunes (which is one reason that Tin Pin Alley standards and Broadway showstoppers provided the padding on so many early rock albums). It's unlikely that Cooke's producers had to twist his arm to get him to sing for aging white Manhattanites at the Copa. Certainly, no one had to twist Darin's. Although he was Atlantic's lead entry in the Italian-American pinup sweepstakes (one of his early albums was titled *For Teenagers Only*), Darin clearly considered swooning adolescent girls a necessary evil. You need only skim the paeans from Walter Winchell, Earl Wilson, and Dorothy Kilgallen on the back of *Darin Live at the Copa* (originally released on Atco in 1961, and now reissued in a facsimile edition on Bainbridge BT-6220) to ascertain the other audience Darin and Ertegun were openly courting.

Remember the *Dick Van Dyke Show* episode in which a mobster shanghaied Alan Brady's staff writers and bullied them into donating routines for his nephew, an all-around mediocrity who sang, danced, and did impressions? On *Darin at the Copa*, Darin comes dangerously close to reminding you of that nephew: he mimics W. C. Fields, Dean Martin, Walter Brennan, Ray Charles, Jimmy Durante, and Señor Wences; he fawns over an eight-year-old girl at one of the tables as he tosses off "Dream Lover" with contemptuous dispatch; he hobnobs with Joey Ross (Officer Tootie of *Car 54, Where Are You?*) and other "celebrities"; be cheapens his own deft vibraphone solo by cracking, "Red Norvo, eat your heart out"; he introduces "Mack the Knife" as "an old Bavarian folk song"; and he refuses a request for "Splish Splash" on the grounds that "That's going back too far" (making it clear that it's regression, not nostalgia, he's avoiding). Whew! Listening to this jive, you begin to wonder what it was you ever heard in Darin, but then he reminds you. Some of his banter shows sharp wit, as when he spots the heavy-lidded singer Keely Smith in the audience and announces, "Time to wake up, Miss Smith," or when he satirizes his own unctuous delivery on an impromptu "That Old Black Magic." In pop terms, his "Mack the Knife" cuts Sting's, and even Armstrong's, though the version here is a pale hint of his studio hit. Best of all, there are four well-modulated numbers that suggest Darin's unfulfilled potential as a Sinatraesque barroom crooner: Rodgers and Hammerstein's "I Have Dreamed," Arthur

Schwartz's "By Myself," and Cole Porter's "You'd Be So Nice to Come Home To" and "Love for Sale." You come away from *Darin at the Copa* marveling at what Darin was capable of when he respected his material, and angry that his vulgar energy was never channeled positively for very long.

At its worst, *Darin at the Copa* still offers insights into the bourgeois ideals of Entertainment (gaudy) and Taste (proprietary) in the years before the Beatles. (You can almost hear the audience thinking, "Are we having fun yet?") *Two of a Kind* (Atco 90484-4-IY), an album of duets with the singer and songwriter Johnny Mercer released in 1961 to tighten Darin's grip on the adult market, doesn't even have that going for it. Think of the Mercer lyrics he and Darin *might* have sung—"Skylark," "One for My Baby," "Come Rain or Come Shine," "Something's Gotta Give"—and what novel interpretations the cheeky Darin might have given them. Instead, *Two of a Kind* is squandered on Mercer ephemerae like "If I Had My Druthers" (from *Li'l Abner*) and "Lonesome Polecat" (from *Seven Brides for Seven Brothers*), and non-Mercer inanities like "Who Takes Care of the Caretaker's Daughter?" and "Paddlin' Madeline Home." Billy May's Jimmie Lunceford–like (or Sy Oliver–like, to be more accurate) arrangements are the album's only strong point, and they become more impressive when you consider the poverty of what May was given to work with. Atlantic would have served Darin's memory better by returning to circulation *That's All,* the 1959 album of show tunes and standards that yielded "Beyond the Sea" and "Mack the Knife," arguably the two finest vehicles for his anachronistic instincts (both tracks are still available on Atco's *The Bobby Darin Story**).

Darin might have developed into one of the finest American singers; his beginnings were no more ignoble than Tony Bennett's, who was little more than a human vibrato at the beginning of his career. It's tempting but ultimately discouraging to speculate what he might be doing had he not died at thirty-five. I remember that his reemergence as a denim troubadour in the late sixties struck me as opportunistic, though not in the way you might think: it

---

*As a substitute for *That's All*, I'd recommend *As Long as I'm Singin'* (Rare 'n' Darin 1), a 1987 compilation of TV airchecks and previously unissued masters. It includes confident performances of "Minnie the Moocher," "This Nearly Was Mine" and "Just in Time," as well as a live version of Darin's own "That's the Way Love Is" (a well-crafted tune originally released as the flip side of "Beyond the Sea" and included on *Love Swings*, Darin's stab at Sinatra's *Songs for Swinging Lovers*). But *As Long as I'm Singin'*'s absolute highlight is a TV aircheck of "Mack the Knife," recorded before Darin grew tired of the song, when he was still having fun with it. On the out chorus, he stretches syllables and lags behind the beat with the freedom and sophistication of a born jazz singer.

was as if by singing his original protest songs, like "Long Line Rider" (about convicts found buried in an Arkansas prison yard), he thought he could reconcile his need to stay contemporary with his desire to transcend pop. This was not a mode he fully developed, however, and chances are that he would now be on the oldies trail or knockin' 'em dead in Vegas (consider that Wayne Newton started off with "Danke Schoen," a "Mack" clone originally offered to Darin). Having briefly studied acting at Hunter College, Darin gave gritty performances in such bleak sixties melodramas as *Too Late Blues, Pressure Point,* and *Captain Newman, M.D.* (for which he received an Oscar nomination). Although he did his share of silly romances, in film, at least, he surpassed Elvis and might have caught up with Sinatra. But by the time of his death, he'd worn out his welcome in Hollywood. The filmography at the end of Al DiOrio's well-researched but dully written biography *Borrowed Time* (Running Press, 1981) lists numerous shelved or uncompleted projects, including *The Vendors,* which Darin wrote, produced, directed, and starred in. Not magnetic enough for leads and too streaky to be a reliable character type, he would probably be thankful for *Love Boat* guest shots at this point. Darin's exuberance was pitifully wasted during his youth, but the waste might have become more flagrant once he reached middle age. Do I still endorse him in light of the evidence I've brought against him? Oddly enough, the answer is yes, though I'd be as hard put to explain why now as I would have been at fourteen. Other than muttering how nostalgia ain't what it used to be, it's tough to mouth profundities when you're busy snapping your fingers.

(MARCH 1986)

West Coast Ghost

===

The hottest new name in jazz is that of a fifty-three-year-old alto saxophonist who sacrificed his youth to heroin. Frank Morgan was one of a legion of musicians doomed to addiction by their idolatry of Charlie Parker, whose habit was as mammoth and as legendary as his genius. "I think it was 1952, when Bird came back to L.A. for an engagement," Morgan says of breaking the news to Parker that he was "a member of the club." "It broke his heart," Morgan says. "He said, 'I thought you would be the one who had sense enough to be able to look at what it's done to me.'" The sermon ended when Morgan flaunted the half ounce of heroin and the half ounce of cocaine he'd just scored. "After we got high, he talked to me about dying. In a tragic sense, I think Bird felt he could set a better example by dying."

If so, his disciples failed to heed the warning. Upon learning of Parker's death (at the age of thirty-four, in 1955), Morgan and several other participants at a Los Angeles jam session mourned him by shooting up and playing "Don't Blame Me." A few months later, *Frank Morgan* (GNP Crescendo GNPS-9041), Morgan's first album as a leader, was released, with hard-sell liner copy nominating him as the new Charlie Parker. By that point, Morgan was well on his way to a hundred-dollar-a-day habit, which he eventually supported by forging checks and fencing stolen property. First arrested in 1953, Morgan spent the better part of the next thirty-two years in California county jails and state penitentiaries, and the few critics and record collectors who remembered him assumed that he was dead.

I spoke with Morgan this spring, during his second visit to New York, a city with good associations for him. The day before his first trip East, last December, a California court lifted his parole, which was scheduled to last until 1988 and would have prevented him from accepting lucrative offers to perform in Europe this summer. During that first week-long stay, he recorded a live album at the Village Vanguard and was in constant demand for interviews for the first time in his career.

He was in perpetual motion on his return trip; going to a methadone clinic early every morning, recording an album with the pianist McCoy Tyner over the course of three long afternoons, and performing three sets a night at the Vanguard, usually not returning to his hotel until 4:00 A.M. There was a near crisis on opening night at the Vanguard. Morgan fired a veteran New York pianist who he thought was feeding him the wrong chords. This distressed Morgan, first of all because the pianist had recorded with Charlie Parker in the 1950s, and second because he worried that the New York musicians whose favor he was courting would be up in arms if an outsider found fault with one of their own. But the musicians Morgan talked to, including Cecil Taylor, assured him that they sympathized, and he basked in their approval. During his stay, he met with the *New Yorker* staff writer George W. S. Trow, who sought his collaboration on a musical drama. Trow says that the play, which depicts some incidents from Morgan's life, as well as from his own, was partly inspired by the "nobility" he perceives in Morgan, as a musician and as a man. Morgan will have both a musical and a speaking role in the play, which will have its premiere in New York next month.*

It was difficult, as I shared a taxi from the recording studio with Morgan and his entourage, not to see the city through his eyes. With rain on the way, the skyline looked even more oppressive than usual, to anyone used to looking at it. But this was the skyline Morgan had imagined from countless prison cells—a skyline with his star glittering on the horizon.

A FREE MAN AT LAST, WITH THREE HIGHLY RATED ALBUMS TO HIS CREDIT since 1985, Morgan is obviously good copy—which, one suspects, is why he has been interviewed for *Newsweek* and *CBS Sunday Morning. People* magazine even took him back to San Quentin for a photo shoot. The mass media have no great love for jazz, but they do love a success story—especially (now) one whose moral can be boiled down to the sanctimonious slogan "Just Say No."

Prison-Made Tuxedos (the title refers to Morgan's experience with the San Quentin band, which would perform every Saturday, in tuxedos made by fellow prisoners, for visitors making the grand tour of the prison) opened at St. Clement's Church in New York in November, 1987. Morgan was responsible for most of the play's poignant moments—reminiscing about how a prison sentence prevented him from attending his grandmother's funeral, for example, or about how he was attracted to Charlie Parker's erudition as well as his music. Morgan also played, and in jazz parlance, his music was saying something. In contrast, Trow was merely *trying* to say, like Benjy in *The Sound and the Fury*. Morgan's part of the show was nakedly autobiographical, but Trow hid behind satirical convention, never coming clean. The uneasy juxtaposition of their lives convinced you that Trow is one of those guilty white intellectuals who thinks of inhibition as White Man's Disease.

But Morgan has also attracted the attention of fellow musicians, who have seen far too many redeemed junkies rise from the ashes to work up much enthusiasm for another one, unless he has something else going for him. Players who emerge from oblivion to make waves are generally either prophets (like Ornette Coleman, when he introduced free improvisation in 1959) or anachronisms (like Bunk Johnson, rediscovered in Louisiana two decades earlier). Morgan is neither. He plays bebop, which is still the most prevalent form of modern jazz although it is now over forty years old and has been subject to endless permutations. But he plays it with an urgent authenticity that inspires fantasies of the Royal Roost and Minton's in the era when Parker himself held sway, before bebop splintered into hard bop, "cool" jazz, and free bop, and finally devolved into cliché—the price it paid for becoming the most prevalent form of modern jazz.

In one sense, Morgan is a West Coast Ghost—the title of a Charles Mingus composition, and Mingus's apt designation for those California-bred musicians like himself who chose New Yorkers like Parker and Dizzy Gillespie as their role models. Because jazz history is as prone to oversimplification as any other branch, jazz on the West Coast in the forties and fifties is supposed to have been mentholated and supernal—*cool* in polarity to bebop's scalding heat. Morgan's fire is a necessary reminder that bebop became a bicoastal phenomenon during the sixteen eventual months that Parker spent in California, beginning with an engagement at Billy Berg's in Hollywood in December 1945. Bop was also biracial, of course; as was cool, which was essentially a bop offshoot. But because the overwhelming majority of records issued by West Coast labels during the period featured white musicians with temperate styles, listeners in other parts of the country were given an incomplete picture of California jazz. "We weren't part of that cool scene at all," Morgan says of the Los Angeles bebop underground, which included the trumpeter Howard McGhee, the alto saxophonist Sonny Criss, the tenor saxophonists Dexter Gordon and Wardell Gray, the pianist Hampton Hawes, and others who have been forgotten. "It was a racial squeeze. Only a few of the black musicians on the West Coast were being recorded."

But despite his loyalty to Parker, Morgan's penchant for improvised counterpoint when working with another horn suggests that cool's niceties haven't been lost on him, just as the overblown notes and scalar runs that dot his up-tempo solos suggest a willingness to use techniques associated with free jazz to give bebop an unexpected modern spin. Morgan was still using heroin and wanted for parole violations when he recorded the understandably furtive *Easy Living* (Contemporary C-14013), his first album as a leader in thirty years, in June 1985. *Lament* (Contemporary C-14021), recorded almost a year later, after Morgan turned himself in and served six months, was the album that announced his resurrection. *Lament's* ballads showed that Morgan shared Parker's speechlike delivery, his courtly approach to melody, and his knack for transforming pop songs into the blues. In other words, it was clear that Morgan was blessed with what might be called "the common touch," a way of appealing to the unschooled listener on the most basic musical level even while improvising lines of baffling harmonic complexity. His passionate reading of the folk singer Buffy Sainte-Marie's "Until It's Time for You to Go" was a vivid illustration of the power of ardor to rehabilitate treacle (Morgan's two versions of "Theme from Love Story"—with George Cables on *Double Image,* Contemporary C-14035; arid with the McCoy Tyner Trio on *Major Changes* Contemporary C-14039—are even better examples of this), and Morgan's nimble choruses on Wayne Shorter's moody "Ava Maria" demonstrated his flair with non-bebop repertoire.

Despite its more conservative material, *Bebop Lives!* (Contemporary C-14026), recorded Morgan's Village Vanguard debut in 1986, is the album that captures him at his peak. The flugelhornist Johnny Coles's sidelong phrasing contrasts nicely with Morgan's more frontal attack, and they banter good-naturedly in stating the theme of Thelonious Monk's "Well, You Needn't." Morgan proves that he's capable of running the chords with the best of them on Jackie McLean's "Little Melonae" and a version of Cole Porter's "What Is This Thing Called Love" jammed with allusions to Tadd Dameron's "Hot House," one of the song's more ingenious bebop derivatives. But Morgan's unaccompanied introduction to Jerome Kern's "All the Things You Are," with its broken cadences and phantom glisses, is finally the most convincing display of his mastery. His solitary wail offers needed reassurance that bebop still holds potential for soul-searching introspection, not just breast-beating exhibitionism.

MORGAN, WHO WAS BORN IN MINNEAPOLIS IN 1933, IS A SECOND-generation musician. His father is Stanley Morgan, a guitarist who recorded with Harlan Leonard and the Rockets in 1940 and now leads one of several different groups performing as the Ink Spots. Stanley Morgan groomed his son as a musician even before he was born. "My mother recently told me that when she was pregnant with me, my father would stand behind her and reach around her with his guitar, leaning the back of it up against her stomach as he strummed, so that I would pick up the vibrations." Because his parents were frequently on the road, Morgan lived with his grandmother in Milwaukee from the age of six to fourteen, when she put him on a train for Los Angeles, where his father had opened a club. "She caught me with a joint, and felt the time had come for a father's guidance." In Los Angeles, Morgan studied at Jefferson High School with Samuel Browne, a music teacher whose other students over the years have included Don Cherry, Art Farmer, Dexter Gordon, and Wardell Gray. At fifteen, he won a TV talent-show contest, and got to record "Over the Rainbow" with the Freddy Martin Orchestra as a prize (the arranger was Ray Coniff, and the singer was Merv Griffin). By 1952, he was good enough to win a seat in Lionel Hampton's saxophone section (like most musicians who've been with Hampton, he complains that the vibraphonist paid badly, and added insult to injury by always bumming cigarettes from him). His first arrest cost him the opportunity to join the original edition of the Max Roach–Clifford Brown Quintet.

According to Morgan, it wasn't just his addiction that was responsible for his long pattern of recidivism. He was a privileged character behind bars, admired by fellow inmates for his musical prowess and his adherence to the underworld code (he once refused to lead authorities to his higher-ups in a forgery ring, despite being offered leniency if he would do so). "I went to great lengths to be a stand-up criminal that other criminals would admire. I was charged with a hundred thousand dollars' worth of forgeries, and I didn't have a dime." After his refusal to cooperate, he was sent to San Quentin, where he had everything he felt he needed, including plentiful supplies of heroin and ample opportunity to practice his horn and perform regularly with the prison band. "That was good for me, because I was the kind of junkie who would forget all about music when I was out on the street trying to score." Had he so desired, he could have even had his choice of male sexual partners. "The night I arrived in San Quentin, I had fifteen or twenty 'ladies' to choose from. Not real ladies—that's the prison vernacular for them. But that wasn't my thing, and one of the first things you're warned about in prison is to stay clear of that if you want to live. Sex is what most of the killings are about, not drugs. People actually consider themselves married, and the jealousy is intense.

"I had everything I wanted except for freedom, privacy, dignity, self-esteem—everything I value now. In San Quentin, I had a better rhythm section than I had at the Vanguard last night. Maybe not better man-for-man, but, for me, prowess isn't as important as rapport. But I couldn't fire a musician, like I did last night. I'd have been stuck with him until he got paroled, or until another stupid musician who played better went and got himself locked up. In prison now, there might be good rock rhythm sections, but they couldn't give me the guys to play with, and even if they could, I wouldn't want to go back. The prison population has changed, or maybe I've changed. The guys I just left in prison, I don't want to be around those motherfuckers. I'm not like them."

TEN YEARS AGO, THE ALTO SAXOPHONIST ART PEPPER—ANOTHER WEST Coast Ghost, and a former band mate of Morgan's at San Quentin—arrived in New York with a story much like Morgan's, but with more squalid and frightening details. Pepper also recorded during a triumphant engagement at the Village Vanguard, but later admitted (in his 1979 autobiography, *Straight Life,* co-authored by his wife, Laurie Pepper) to shooting so much cocaine that he practically had to be carried to the club on the final night. Although Pepper's solos took on awesome power in the five years between his Vanguard debut and his death in 1982, suspicion lingers that he never successfully kicked his habit.

A cynic might observe that Morgan, having blown his chance to become the new Charlie Parker, might instead become the new Art Pepper. (Contemporary is a subsidiary of Fantasy Records, as is Galaxy, Pepper's final label.) Morgan is clean, but will he able to stay that way? He has a supportive lover in Rosalinda Kolb, a painter and photographer. But he and Kolb have been a couple since the late seventies, and she admits that she wasn't able to save him then: "He would lie to me, and say that he wasn't using, and there would be an element of self-deception on my part. To be able to stay with Frank, I had to look the other way a lot. But I knew what was happening, and it made me sick to watch him."

I'm told by those who have worked with him that Morgan is capable of losing his temper if that's what it takes to get his own way. Still, he's visibly milder in temperament than Pepper, whose criminal exploits seemed to allay his early feelings of inauthenticity as a white musician in a field dominated by blacks. I suspect that Morgan relishes the newfound attention he's receiving too much to risk losing it by reverting to his old ways. Success, now that he's had a small taste of it, might prove to be the most addictive high of all. "Before, I always had excuses. I remember when Ornette Coleman came on the scene, I lost hope. I said, 'I'm not going to play this.' Same thing when Ronald Reagan was elected president. I milked that one pretty good. When I was offered a recording contract a day after I got out of prison, on April 2, 1985, it scared the shit out of me. I think it contributed to my using again. But when I walked into the studio [two months later, to record *Easy Living*] and played with Cedar Walton and Billy Higgins [a pianist and a drummer, respectively, both much better established than Morgan at the time], and found out I could do it— that, in fact, it maybe wasn't even the ideal rhythm section for what I wanted to do—everything changed. I no longer had an excuse to fail."

(NOVEMBER 1987)

Black Like Him

W ith its Victorian banquettes and pastel murals of fat wood nymphs striking fey poses (by the forgotten pseudo-Frenchman Marcel Vertes), the Café Carlyle is a dowdy relic from a time when a hotel's amenities were understood to be for the local gentry rather than for conventioneers. The Carlyle's waiters, busmen, and wine stewards are like the supercilious house servants you see in old movies: they go about their business as though invisible, demanding in return the sort of peel-me-a-grape insouciance it takes generations of inherited wealth to pull off. Anything more than that is an affront.

But which is more humiliating: to think of yourself as rude for not acknowledging services rendered, or to he thought gauche by others for not recognizing when expressions of gratitude are inappropriate? My companion and I were trying to be invisible, too, but we were making ourselves conspicuous by thanking someone each time a dish or piece of silverware was brought or removed. Our parents taught us that good manners would make us appear gracious, but what did they know of such things? When you're around people who take service for granted, you realize that good manners are a dead giveaway of humble beginnings.

What were we doing at the Carlyle if we felt so out of place? We wanted to hear Bobby Short in his natural habitat, but (speaking for myself) Short was only the half of it. I grew up believing, as many working-class Irish Catholics do, in an inverted Protestant ethic: heaven was reserved for have-nots like for me and my family, because wealth was conclusive evidence of corruption somewhere along the line. (This is still the creed I live by, and it's a good one to cling to if you plan on being a jazz critic.) But encouraged by the drawing-room musicals of the thirties and forties that I watched on television, I also grew up equating adulthood with limos, penthouses, luxury liners, and sinfully expensive supper clubs like the Café Carlyle (it didn't occur to me till later that none of the adults I knew in real life enjoyed any of these plums). Was the Carlyle as I imagined it would be? Yes and no. Remember the scene in *Hannah and Her Sisters* when Woody Allen drags Dianne Wiest to the Café Carlyle? She does coke right there at their table as they listen to Bobby Short.

"They wouldn't know the difference!" she protests when Allen scolds her. "They're embalmed!" Just my luck. I finally make it to the Carlyle and nobody who's anybody goes there anymore. The Bright Lights in the Big City are somewhere else now, panting for more lurid thrills.

The Carlyle is the sort of room in which the entertainment is generally as unobtrusive as the rest of the help. But Bobby Short, who's synonymous with the place, is the antithesis of such a whispering performer. Befitting his past as a child vaudevillian, Short is a belter who spends a surprising amount of time on his feet, away from the piano (which, given his sub–Errol Garner effusions, is just as well). lie claps his hands together *hard* every so often, as though realizing that the room itself is his competition. His extravagance transforms a bandstand tucked away against a wall into center stage.

"The audience has so much to distract their attention," Short remarked during a brief conversation I had with him in his tastefully appointed Sutton Place apartment the afternoon following my visit to the Carlyle. "They have a drink or dinner or a cigarette in front of them, and someone very important to them, either romantically or in terms of business, across the table. The idea is to go out there and grab their attention as quickly as you can and maintain it until you go off. You see, I can't give the audience a chance to resume their conversation.

"Before my arrival, the Café was a place where not only guests and residents of the hotel went for dinner, but also people from the neighborhood. The girls from Finch College would have their beaus take them there, and dine there with their parents, who would stay at the hotel when they came to visit." With his pampered moon face and rounded, townhouse diction, Short is the only man I have ever heard use the word "beaus" without sounding sarcastic. No, he wasn't wearing a monogrammed smoking jacket, but his dark blue jumpsuit looked as elegant on him. As he spoke, he sat in front of open shelves of African art objects. From time to time, his Dalmation, resting glumly on a divan, attempted to jump on his lap. "Jealous thing," he scolded, rubbing the dog's neck. "That's what he is, you know.

"The Carlyle was, and still is, that kind of upper-crust, Upper East Side hotel," he continued. "The café had always held its own financially, but it had never been that important a part of New York social life. I'm sure that many of the people who frequented the Café were unhappy with the changes that my presence brought about. On the other hand, people from all over started coming and liked me, which is why I'm still welcome there."

SHORT HAS HELD FORTH AT THE CARLYLE AT LEAST SIX MONTHS A YEAR since 1968. His current twentieth-anniversary engagement follows on the heels of his best record ever—the record that, to be frank about it, made me take him seriously. *Guess Who's in Town* (Atlantic 81778–1) is an homage to the late Andy Razaf, a prolific black lyricist best remembered for his collaborations with Fats Waller, although (as the album demonstrates) he also wrote memorable songs with Eubie Blake, James P. and J. C. Johnson, and the white transplanted Englishman Paul Denniker, among others. *Guess Who's in Town* is unusual for Short in that it exposes rather than disguises his lineage from Ethel Waters and other black vaudevillians. It's his *Black Album,* as it were.

The album's four Waller tunes are an unexpected pleasure, in light of Short's admission (to Whitney Balliett in *The New Yorker,* almost twenty years ago) that he felt "inadequate" to sing Waller. "I was probably thinking of Waller's bubble, and how impossible it would be to capture," Short said, when I reminded him of the quote. "But I feel quite comfortable singing the ballads he wrote with Razaf, because when Waller chose to sing a serious song, he often had a difficult time overcoming his comic image." A case in point is "How Can You Face Me?" one scoundrel's admonishment to another in Waller's interpretation, but a wounded reverie of seduction and abandonment in Short's.

Razaf's witty but down-to-earth lyrics rescue Short from the chi-chi that is sometimes his downfall, and he returns the favor by washing away the implied blackface that too many contemporary singers of both races seem to feel is necessary to interpret vintage black pop. He gives these songs the same respect he would Gershwin or Porter, and they deserve it. Recognizing that Waller's "Black and Blue" is as much a protest against a black pecking order based on skin color as it is against white oppression (Spike Lee thinks he discovered something new?), Short finds a poetry in Razaf's lyric that even Louis Armstrong barely touched. ("It's right there in the verse," Short told me. "'Browns and yellows, lucky fellows, ladies seem to like them light.' It's especially touching when you remember it was originally written to be sung by a woman [in the 1929 revue *Hot Chocolates*]. Coal-black women have always had a hard time of it in black society.") The late Phil Moore's arrangements frequently put a good horn section—featuring the trumpeter Harry "Sweets" Edison, the trombonist Buster Cooper, the alto saxophonist Marshall Royal, and the baritone saxophonist Bill Green—to trivial uses, most noticeably on a over-syncopated "Honeysuckle Rose," and an aimless pastiche of big band themes on Denniker's "Make Believe Ballroom." But Moore's setting for "Ain't Misbehavin'" is refreshingly modern, with moody counterpoint between Short's piano and John Collins's guitar in advance of the horns. There are sprightly arrangements of Denniker's "S'posin'" and Blake's "Tan Manhattan" (an ode to Harlem's cultural self-sufficiency, although uncharitable ears might hear it as just another darky song), and a stark reading of J. C. Johnson's "Lonesome Swallow," featuring only Short's voice and piano, in faithful evocation of the classic 1928 version by Waters and James P. Johnson. The only one of the album's eleven tracks that backfires is William Weldon's "I'm Gonna Move to the Outskirts of Town," because Short, with his dainty elocution, sounds ludicrous shouting the blues.

IN AMERICAN LEGEND, CAFÉ SOCIETY HAS ALWAYS BEEN WHERE THE WHITE and the black folk meet, but in reality, the black folk are usually there to do their jobs. In his twenty years at the Carlyle, Short has sung himself practically hoarse. His baritone is so split with phlegm that he sounds some of his low notes in two different keys. (Thankfully, *Guess Who's in Town* was recorded during one of his vacations, when he was well rested and in relatively strong voice.) But age has done Short an unintentional favor in slowing down his vibrato, and in a space as confined as the Carlyle, he has propinquity working in his favor: the lavaliere microphone he wears on a string necklace allows him to fill the room without sacrificing intimacy. His between-numbers anecdotes are charming and full of information about what year and movie or show each song is from. He lavishes attention on obscure introductory verses, not as a pedantic exercise, the way thirty-something cabaret show-offs like Michael Feinstein and Andrea Marcovicci do, but as a way of injecting suspense into overfamiliar material (and, in some cases, as a way of replicating the easy transition from narrative to song that the verses originally provided on stage or screen).

Accompanied by the bassist Beverly Peer and the drummer Robbie Scott, Short did a dozen songs the night I heard him, including two that have become unaccountably obscure—Kurt Weill's and Ira Gershwin's "You've Only One Life to Live" (from *Lady in the Dark*) and Harold Arlen's and Leo Robin's "Hooray for Love" (from the 1948 film *Casbah*). He revitalized Cole Porter's "I Get a Kick Out of You," giving it an unexpected twist by performing it as a ballad, phrasing the "You obviously don't adore me" line with genuine poignance instead of the customary Ethel Merman pizzazz. And he sang "Bye Bye Blackbird" with such feeling and style that I no longer doubted the legend that Miles Davis decided to record his classic version of this tune as a direct result of hearing Short's. (Miles voted for Short in a 1956 "Musicians' Musician" poll that Leonard Feather conducted for *The Encyclopedia Yearbook of Jazz*.)

To my regret, the set included nothing from *Guess Who's in Town*. But toward the end of the show, Short sang "Princess Poupouly Has Lovely Papaya," a piece of fluff from the public domain. With his shoulders thrown back in a characteristic pose that reflected his pride in being a self-made man, he told the audience that this was a song their parents used to hear as they drifted from nightspot to nightspot in the naughty twenties. I don't think I'm attaching too much importance to the fact that he didn't say *our* parents. For me, the key to Short's appeal is in the delirium with which he delivers the opening lines of "Make Believe Ballroom": "Away we go, by radio, to realms of sweet delight. . . ." This is a song Short has lived. Now in his sixties, he grew up wanting in on the good life he heard about on the radio and in the movies. So did I, but white boys don't have to answer to anyone for dreaming beyond their means.

A shocking number of both blacks and whites find something incongruous about a black man in bibbed shirt and cummerbund singing Cole Porter and Noel Coward to white swells, as though getting funky was what a black man had to do to certify his blackness. (And as though the race was too impoverished to accommodate variety—too isolated from the white majority to share any of its values.) Short has his own kind of soul. The ninth of ten children born to a Danville, Illinois, domestic who considered the blues too vulgar to permit in her house (and who allowed her son to enter vaudeville only because the family needed the income during the Depression), Short reminds us that black America has its own traditions of gentility and aspiration, by no means limited to its bourgeoisie. "I am a Negro who has never lived in the South," he wrote in *Black and White Baby*, his 1971 memoir, ". . . nor was I ever trapped in an urban ghetto." He's not a native of the high society he's bought into, either. But neither were the upwardly striving small-town Midwesterners and sons of Jewish immigrants (all of them black and white babies themselves, in terms of what they absorbed from jazz) who wrote the songs that have become smart-set anthems. The Republicans think that ours is a trickle-down economy, but the truth of the matter is that our culture trickles up. Like the money we slave for, these songs about the finer things in life are too valuable to be entrusted solely to the rich. Which is why it's comforting to know that the man currently doing the best job of singing them in a supperclub knows what it's like to sing for his supper.

(MAY 1988)

The Home and the World

======

Every individual in South Africa is traumatized by apartheid—the oppressors perhaps more so than the victims," said Abudullah Ibrahim, the South African pianist and composer formerly known as Dollar Brand. "At least *we* have hope for the just society to come: a South Africa that belongs to all of its peoples, regardless of color, as stated in the Freedom Charter. The oppressors' only hope is to forestall the inevitable. The only wisdom they can teach their children is to always carry a gun."

I visited Ibrahim and his wife, the singer Sathima Bea Benjamin, on June 12, 1986, the morning that South African president P. W. Botha declared a nationwide state of emergency in anticipation of the tenth anniversary of the Soweto uprising. Kneeling in front of a video monitor, Ibrahim—wearing a dashiki and corduroy jeans—tried without success to tune in C-SPAN for its live coverage of Botha's address to South Africa's parliament. "The police have rounded up all the opposition leaders," he told me in a melting-pot patois that was British in formality but African in emphasis and lilt. "What is the logic of that—to remove from circulation the only people who can say to the masses, 'Hold back'? The confrontation is near. It is just a matter of time. It will be this weekend."

TALL AND FIT, WITH LONG, GRACEFUL, ACTIVE HANDS AND THE BEARING OF a diplomat (which, in a sense, he is), Ibrahim was born in Cape Town in 1954, but has spent most of his adult life in voluntary exile in Europe and the United States. He is a cultural eclectic—no different from most global wanderers in that respect, though his being born a member of a colonialized people undoubtedly gave him a running start. (Moreover, his mixed racial heritage, which classifies him as "colored" rather than black by South African law, puts him in an assimilationist position remarkably similar to that of the New Orleans Creoles and mulattoes who played a decisive role in the gestation of jazz.) But like most political exiles, Ibrahim is also a displaced cultural nationalist whose longings for home filter his perception of new surroundings. The South African sound he once eloquently described as being a synthesis of "the

116

carnival music heard every year in Cape Town, the traditional 'colored' music, the Malayan strains, and the rural lament" remains the thread that keeps his music from seeming crazy-quilt despite its patchwork of cross-cultural borrowings. Those include West African ceremonial and popular rhythms, Moslem incantation, British military-band concord, gospel sanctimony and minstrel sanguinity, French impressionism and modal reverie, Monkian dissonance, and Ellingtonian Cotton Club panache (what's surprising about Ibrahim's music, given its origin in a troubled place, is its defiant joy). A mesmerizing pianist whose rhythms splash across the keyboard in thunderous ostinato waves, Ibrahim is "beyond category," to borrow a pet phrase from Duke Ellington, one of his earliest admirers (and the producer of his first American LP, in 1962).

Over the last twenty years, Ibrahim's solo piano recitals have evolved into lengthy, continuous medleys of his own attractive themes and those of favored composers like Ellington, Thelonious Monk, Billy Strayhorn, and Eubie Blake. The aspect of his work is best documented on *Autobiography* (Plainisphare PL-1267 6/7), a two-record set recorded live in Switzerland in 1979. In his otherwise perceptive liner notes for *Autobiography,* the musicologist Wilfrid Mellers likens Ibrahim's medleys to collage—a comparison better suited to Keith Jarrett than to Ibrahim, because what distinguishes Ibrahim from ramblers like Jarrett is his dedication to composition and his insistence on full thematic exposition. There is nothing fragmentary or episodic about Ibrahim's treatment of the myriad themes on *Autobiography,* or about the way he builds from rhapsodic, harplike glissandi to house-shaking honky-tonk, or from thick, frigid clusters to long-steepled, liturgical-sounding tremolos. (Exactly how many themes there are on *Autobiography* is difficult to say. The jacket lists eight Ibrahim originals, plus Monk's "Coming on the Hudson," Strayhorn's "Take the 'A' Train," and the standard "I Surrender, Dear." But Blake's "Memories of You" frames the homages to Monk and Strayhorn, and I hear at least five other unidentified Ibrahim pieces, in addition to Charlie Parker's "Ornithology" and Monk's "Four in One.")

Ibrahim's piano solos blueprint larger designs; as with Ellington, you can hear the colors of an orchestra bleeding together and separating in the voicing of each chord. But with the exception of *African Marketplace,* an out-of-print masterpiece from 1980 (Elektra 6E 252), Ibrahim's large group recordings haven't represented him very well. His music is holistic and horizontal, the melodies rolling steadily over and around embedded rocks of rhythm. Merely harmonizing the heads of his tunes and running their changes (as many American musicians have done), you wind up on dry, flat land or in murky swamp. Ibrahim's approach to improvisation, which arises out of a folk tradition that uses improvisation to extend melody and rhythm, puts him at odds with most

American and European jazz musicians, for whom improvisation is an end in itself. "Improvisation is not standing up there and playing twenty choruses," he once told the critic Don Palmer. "It is using what's at hand."

With Ekaya—the fluid septet that Ibrahim formed in 1983 and with which he has recorded two albums—for his and Benjamin's Ekapa label—Ibrahim found sidemen confident enough to shun chordal rhetoric and crest on his rhythms. Even though the band is a septet, it's tempting to think of its two albums—*Ekaya* (Home) (Ekapa/BlackHawk BKH 50205-1), and *Water from an Ancient Well* (Ekapa/BlackHawk BKH-50202-1)—as big-band records, because Ibrahim's voicings for trombone and three saxophones are so plump and varied in texture, and because he showcases his soloists so strategically. With Ibrahim's rhythms brewing below him, the young tenor saxophonist Ricky Ford reverts to his Sonny Rollins influence, and he's never sounded so passionate, fierce, or suave. But Ibrahim's most simpatico accomplice is the Panamanian alto saxophonist and flutist Carlos Ward, whose piercing, jubilant leads define the band's ensemble sound, and whose solos match Ford's in crackle and invention. Perhaps the truest proof of Ibrahim's genius as a bandleader, though, is his ability to coax trim, inspired improvisations from the trombonist Dick Griffin and the baritone saxophonist Charles Davis, two journeymen who are usually more prolix.

EKAYA REPRESENTS A COMPROMISE BETWEEN THE LARGE TROUPE Ibrahim desires and the small group that economics dictates. "The ideal situation would be to have as many people as possible," he told me. "The more people the better! Not just instrumentalists, but singers, painters, sculptors, poets, nutritionists, physicians, and martial artists, to show that music can provide a conducive atmosphere for all other daily activities, as it does in more traditional societies."

He likens his empathy with Ward to that which he once enjoyed with the late Kippy Moeketsi, "the Charlie Parker of South Africa," in Ibrahim's estimation, and the father figure in the Jazz Epistles, the Cape Town combo that begat Ibrahim and the trumpeter Hugh Masekela in the late 1950s. "Kippy was the first to insist that we recognize the wealth of musical influences available to us as South Africans and not look exclusively to the U.S. for inspiration. That was at a time when our sense of ourselves as a nation was being born, and Kippy's musical philosophy was a part of that. He was a pillar of strength against those who would have had us believe that we were inherently inferior as musicians."

Ibrahim remembers the seaport of Cape Town as "a cosmopolitan mixture of Xhosa, Zulu, British, Dutch, Khosian, and Malayan traditions. As musicians there, we heard everything, and we played everything. There was even a

Cape Town Symphony Orchestra and an opera company that performed *Madame Butterfly, La Traviata, La Bohème.* All of my early piano teachers were well versed in the European classical tradition. American merchant vessels would dock in the harbor, and we would run to meet these ships, because the African-American sailors on board would have American jazz records to sell to us. It was from these sailors that I received the nickname 'Dollar' Brand—my real name was Adolf. My grandmother was a founding member of the African Methodist Episcopalian church in South Africa, and my mother was the church pianist, so I was exposed to the black American tradition through the so-called Negro spirituals I sang in the choir.

"I was familiar with Islamic customs long before embracing Allah, because the Christian and Moslem communities were very close in Cape Town as a result of so much intermarriage. The Moslems would know when we were celebrating Christmas or Easter, and we would know when they were celebrating Ramadan. Many families observed all the religious holidays across the board. Ethic diversity—that's the way it is all over the world. There is no pure race. Yet in South Africa, the races that have mingled since the beginning of time are separated by law. They have this multitiered system, which is actually a class system. On top, you have the whites. The second stratum is the so-called 'colored,' the Asians, and the Indians. And at the bottom, the blacks, who are broken down further by tribe."

Ibrahim began to read from a newspaper clipping. "More than a thousand people officially changed color in South Africa last year. They were officially changed from one race to another by the government. Details of what is called The Chameleon Dance were given in Parliament: 715 coloreds turned white, 19 whites became colored, one Indian became white, 15 Indians became colored, 43 colored became Indian, 31 Indians became Malayan, 15 Malayans became Indians, 349 blacks became colored, 20 coloreds became black, 11 coloreds became Chinese, 3 coloreds became Malayan, 3 Chinese became colored, and 3 blacks were reclassified Malayan.

"No whites became black, and no blacks became white."

SATHIMA BEA BENJAMIN, WHO WAS BORN IN CAPE TOWN IN 1936, remembers it as "a beauteous place, with mountains, sea, perfect climate, flora and fauna, exotic birds, and gorgeous sunrises and sunsets. There seemed to be music in the air, always. Is that possible, or is it just the way that I remember it?"

Benjamin and Ibrahim asked to be interviewed separately. "I am Sathima, and he is Abdullah, and although we love each other very much, we have separate careers." Whereas her husband tends to express himself in parables, Benjamin speaks in the down-to-earth fashion of a woman who has spent a good deal of her life preparing meals and caring for children. "I don't perform as often as I would like, because I cannot. I have three roles, the most important of which is running the house and looking after our children [son Tsawke, fifteen, and daughter Tsidi, ten]" she said during a conversation she crammed in between picking Tsidi up from school and keeping an appointment with a tax lawyer. "Second, there is my music, and third, Ekapa, the record company. My life is simpler now that we've turned over Ekapa's distribution to BlackHawk Records. I spend much less time at the post office. I guess I actually have four jobs, because Abdullah and I act as our own agents. When he's away, which he is much of the time, his phone still rings, and someone has to answer it.

"I was raised to be a dutiful sort of person. My parents were separated by the time I was five, and I was raised by my paternal grandmother, who was very strict, very proper, very British in her ways, although she was quite African-looking. I was a lonely child, and along with my daydreaming, which I indulged in constantly, music was my only solace. I listened to American singers on the radio: Ella Fitzgerald, Nat 'King' Cole, Joni James, Doris Day. I was very attracted to the music of Victor Herbert, songs like 'Indian Summer' and 'Ah! Sweet Mystery of Life,' which I still perform. Musicians ask me, 'How do you know those songs? You weren't around in the 1920s.' And I tell them, 'No, but my grandmother was.' When I joined the choir in high school, I noticed that the director never assigned me solo parts, even though I had a very strong voice. I asked him why, and he said, 'Because you sweep. You slide up and down the note, instead of staying directly on it.' That meant nothing to me at the time, but, in retrospect, it shows that I was unconsciously trying to imitate the black American singers I heard on the radio.

"After completing college, I taught school. But on the weekends, I sang in the nightclubs in the white areas, where black and so-called 'colored' entertainers were allowed to perform but were not allowed to mix with the customers. We had to sit in the kitchen during intermissions, just as black musicians were having to do in the American South. There wasn't such a strong ban on U.S. literature then, so I was able to read a good deal about black Americans, and I felt a bond with them, with their longing to be free." Lighter in complexion than her husband, she, too, was classified as colored. "Sometimes people ask me, 'Oh, Sathima, why do you call yourself black? I have to be careful not to overreact, but *inside* I overreact. Black is not a color, it's an experience. And in South Africa, there are only two possible experiences. I was never privileged to know what the white one was. That makes me black."

She and Ibrahim first left South Africa to live in Zurich in 1962, and it was there that they encountered Ellington, "the first American that either of us had ever met—and thank God it was him. Abdullah and I had been brought together by our mutual love for his music, so to actually meet him was like a fairy tale. I still marvel at how truly *grand* he was." In addition to producing *Duke Ellington Presents the Dollar Brand Trio* for Reprise, Ellington also supervised Benjamin's never-released debut. "Duke and Billy took turns accompanying me at the piano. I remember Duke standing in the control room at one point and saying to Billy, 'Can I hear some birdies?'—meaning could he play something sweeter than the wild things he was playing behind me. And Strayhorn answered, 'I am playing birdies—condors.' Fortunately, from having sung with Abdullah, I was used to heavy, dissonant chords."

Benjamin told me she was contemplating an album of Strayhorn compositions as a companion piece to her 1979 album, *Sathima Sings Ellington* (Ekapa/BlackHawk BKH-50201-1). About ten years ago, relatively late in her career, she began to write her own material. "At first, I was hesitant even to show my songs to musicians, because I know I'm not a trained composer like Abdullah. But the musicians I work with—Kenny Barron, Buster Williams, Billy Higgins—encourage me. 'Remember, Sathima, music isn't just the notes.' they tell me. 'It's the feeling, too.'" She still "sweeps": there's a catch in her voice that would be easy to mistake for coquettish affectation if not for the sob it barely holds in check.

"THE REASON I LIKE LIVING IN NEW YORK IS THAT I DON'T FEEL THAT different from anybody else," Benjamin said. "There are people from so many different countries here, so many different nationalities of people you encounter just riding the bus. It helps me to accommodate myself to the fact that I've been uprooted." Despite living in the Hotel Chelsea for almost a decade, Benjamin took the oath of U.S. citizenship only last year. "For most of those at the swearing-in ceremony, it was a joyous occasion. And it was for me, as well. But I went through a period of soul-searching that I can't begin to describe, because South Africa will always exert such a pull."

"I am still a citizen of South Africa," declared Ibrahim, who nonetheless said he intends to apply for U.S. citizenship eventually. "I always will be. Sathima and I are in strategic retreat, but we expect to return. We used to say that our music was our home. For years, we were free to go and return as we pleased, so long as we didn't make any overt political statements. Soweto changed all that. The struggle had reached another level, and it was important for us as artists to play a more visible role." He and Benjamin were last in South Africa in 1976, and cannot return there even to make final amends to the mother Benjamin barely knew, now seventy-five and gravely ill. If they were to risk a visit, it isn't likely that they would be permitted to leave: the Botha government, in retaliation for their fund-raising for the outlawed African National Congress and the forthright political tone of much of their recent work, last year refused to renew their passports. "Our children were born in

Africa—I insisted on that much," Benjamin said. "But New York is where their memories of growing up will be, and memory is a very powerful force."

Unlike their parents, Tswake and Tsidi consider themselves New Yorkers, not South Africans. The home that Benjamin and Ibrahim knew as children no longer exists—at least, not as they remember it. "Perhaps the most notorious of all the government removals in the urban areas was the destruction of District Six, home of 30,000 people classified as 'colored' in the heart of Cape Town," writes Francis Wilson in the preface to *The Cordoned Heart,* a collection of photographs from South Africa.

District Six was a diverse society established over a period of two hundred years. Its inhabitants prayed in mosques and churches and synagogues. . . . There were sounds of fruit vendors, homemade banjos, muezzin calling the faithful to prayer, the laughter of children, Hindu funerals and Muslim weddings. . . . It was a cultural centre. At one time or another, it had been home to musicians like Abdullah Ebrahim [*sic*], writers like Richard Reve, political leaders like Cissie Gool. . . .

In 1966, the district was proclaimed white. The order setting in motion the removal of the citizens there and of the destruction of their homes was signed by the then-Minister of the Department of Community Development, P. W. Botha. . . . Virtually every building was broken up by bulldozers. Hundreds of strong brick houses, some of them over a century old, were reduced to rubble. The vibrant world of District Six became an empty wasteland. It was as if there had been war.

"District Six is synonymous with what happened all over South Africa as a result of the Group Area Act," Ibrahim said when I read him the passage. Behind him, I noticed a Moslem prayer calendar tacked to the living-room bulletin board, alongside more earthly reminders about piano pupils and furniture in storage. "Allah says, 'Fight injustice wherever you find it, or you will become one of the unjust.' I am homesick for South Africa, but not for the home that is there. Even people still living in the houses they were born in South Africa are homesick for another home, the spiritual home. Allah says, 'I do not burden a soul with more than it can bear. Those who leave their homes for my sake, I will provide for them a better home.'"

(JUNE/NOVEMBER 1986)

Streams of Consciousness

Sporadically throughout his life, the fifty-one-year-old pianist Ran Blake has kept a bedside diary of his nightmares—"usually only for six months or so at a time," he says, "until I begin to feel ashamed of my self-indulgence. Besides, I'm so in touch with that state, so able to recall the imagery during waking hours, that keeping a journal is a bit superfluous. Sometimes, following a particularly disturbing dream, I rush to the piano to recapture the mood in composition; the notes are already there in my subconscious. I had a real lulu the other night. I was at my own funeral, but I wasn't in my grave. I was there as an observer, watching the mourners interact with a group of strangers enjoying themselves around a bowl of punch that someone had brought out to the cemetery. I became very caught in this, almost the way I do in certain films."

Blake's dreams are in black and white, like the keyboard at which he labors, like the racially checkerboard jazz subculture he inhabits for lack of a more suitable niche, like the *noir* films (those of Alfred Hitchcock, Fritz Lang, and Robert Siodmak, in particular) that rescued him from loneliness as a child in New England in the 1940s. "As a teenager, I spent a few hours a day practicing the obligatory scales, hating every second. But I would sneak off to the movies two or three times a week, and then creep down to the living room piano in the dead of night—careful not to play all the dynamics, so as not to wake my parents—and attempt to convey my impressions of the films while the memory of them was still vivid.

"I started collecting soundtracks, but soon realized that it wasn't film music that gripped my imagination—it was the films themselves, and their ambiance more than their plots: Dana Andrews slowly falling in love with the painting of Gene Tierney in *Laura,* for example. Except for some scores by Bernard Herrmann, the music generally wasn't rich enough for me, unless there was the implication of violence or foul play, or unless the characters were experiencing sensations of fear, guilt, anxiety, or dread, which the music had to establish. Then there might be a few dissonant chords that appealed to me, but nothing that Bartók and Stravinsky hadn't already done better. If I had only known about them, I could have been studying twentieth-century composers instead. But I spent every spare moment as an adolescent in movie houses and black churches.

"One Sunday morning when we were still living in Springfield [Massachusetts], my parents sent me off to services, and I took a wrong turn and wound up at a black Pentecostal church, beckoned there by those pounding rhythms. I went back every Sunday after that. When my folks asked me how church was, I'd say I loved it, and not be lying—exactly. This was my first exposure to black music, and it lasted for months—until my parents ran into our pastor. When we moved to Suffield [Connecticut], which was lily white at the time, I would travel to the Holy Trinity Church of God in Christ, in Hartford, where I wound up making my professional debut, playing for the gospel choir. I remember they said they like my rhythmic feel, though they had some qualms about my dissonant voicings.

"So there you have it: *film noir,* Mahalia Jackson's moan, and the midnight world of dreams. Those have been the chief influences on my music."

DESPITE WINNING THE APPROVAL OF THE CONGREGATION IN HARTFORD— to say nothing of the skeptical audience at Harlem's Apollo Theater, where, in 1961, he and the black singer Jeanne Lee won an amateur-night competition with their nubby, decelerated interpretations of such pop standards as "Laura" and "Summertime"—Blake felt out of place in black jazz circles. "White jazz was Stan Kenton and Gerry Mulligan; black jazz was Thelonious Monk, Charles Mingus, Max Roach, and Abbey Lincoln. You can guess which I gravitated to," says Blake. Shortly after arriving in New York, he took a job as a waiter at the Jazz Gallery, but was demoted to the kitchen after he "became so involved in what was going on in the bandstand that I fell over people's legs and dropped a tray of drinks on James Baldwin's lap. The Baroness Nica de Koenigswarter saved my job, and I was eventually made her private waiter. The music I wanted to play had black roots, but I was approaching it from a white-intellectual perspective, which put me at too great a distance from the source. All the same, I had no desire to become one of the hip young white boys sitting in at Birdland every Monday night. I wasn't interested in blowing twenty choruses on the chord changes of 'All the Things You Are,' even if I could have—and, believe me, I couldn't, because I would grow bored, start to daydream, and miss the turnarounds. I didn't much like playing with bassists and drummers, and they absolutely dreaded playing with me. I didn't read well enough to become a classical pianist, and much as I loved singers, my chord choices were all wrong for vocal accompaniment. I was forever running to Bill Evans, Oscar Peterson, and Mal Waldron for lessons and career counseling, and at one point, in the late sixties, I almost called it quits. I never stopped playing, but, from 1971 to '76, I stopped hustling for gigs, though I did take what few gigs were offered me. Oddly enough, the few musicians who thought I had something new and provocative to offer were black, but their approval never reached the point of hiring me for their bands. They knew that what I was playing wasn't compatible with what they were doing."

Blake credits the composer, conductor, critic, and educator Gunther Schuller with "saving my life by suggesting that there was more than one way to approach improvisation. Maybe my music wasn't jazz at all, he said. Maybe it was 'Third Stream,'"—the phrase Schuller had coined in the fifties to describe the confluence of jazz and classical musics. Schuller, appointed dean of the New England Conservatory of Music in Boston in 1967, named Blake to the extension faculty a year later. Initially Blake was in charge of the school's community outreach program (in the inner city, prisons, senior citizens' homes), but in 1973, Schuller created a degree program around him. As chairman of the Department of Third Stream Studies, Blake has gradually broadened Schuller's original definition of "Third Stream" to include temporary alliances of Western and ethnic musics—"sometimes bypassing jazz and classical altogether," Blake notes. Indeed, the best-known group to emerge from Blake's classroom is the Klezmer Conservatory Band, which usually plays Jewish community centers and synagogues rather than concert halls or nightclubs. (Hancus Netsky, the band's director, is now chairman of the New England Conservatory's jazz department.) "There's streaming in Mingus—hard jazz, lush balladry, church music. But he'd probably have punched you in the nose if you were to call his music Third Stream," says Blake, who teaches "by ear, as in the African aural tradition," and whose students are known around Boston as "Also-Rans."

"Students in the Third Stream Department learn to create a highly individual music," reads the Conservatory's course guide, "a music they feel in themselves but do not hear around them"—which is precisely what Blake has done in his own music, in making Third Stream a stream of consciousness. The records of his that count are those he's made since turning forty (although it would be a mistake to dismiss his earlier work out of hand, as an Italian critic recently did, in a burst of enthusiasm for his output since 1976). These later records include *Duke Dreams* (Soul Note SN-1027: dark reflections on the corpus of Ellington and Strayhorn), *Suffield Gothic* (Soul SN-1077: a meditation on New England as repository of personal memory and national myth), and *Film Noir* (Arista Novus AN-3019) and *Vertigo* (Owl 041)—companion attempts to retrieve the frisson of cinematic melodrama from the flicker of memory).

MUSICALLY, BLAKE IS CONTENT TO TRAVEL HIS OWN PATH AND LET THE world catch up with him when and if it chooses. But he seems beset by

insecurities of a more personal nature. When I spoke with him before a concert in Philadelphia in April, he told me that several thousand had turned out
to hear him in Greece a few months earlier. "But I doubt it was me who drew
them," he said, scrunching his face. "They were just curious to see an American musician." In Philadelphia, the crowd was in the dozens, and Blake feared
that the promoters were losing money by indulging their personal enthusiasm
for him. Told that Sun Ra and Cecil Taylor were scheduled to play in the same
solo piano series, he was more alarmed than flattered: "I feel a bit like an
imposter, because their music is much closer to jazz than mine is." And
although he is a tireless recruiter for the New England Conservatory (the Third
Stream Department is allowed to continue only so long as enrollment demonstrates a need for it), he voiced doubts about the value of jazz education, pointing out that "Monk and Bix Beiderbecke did pretty well without it."

I asked Blake if he still considers himself a political artist (in 1969, he
released *The Blue Potato and Other Outrages* . . . [Milestone M-9021), an
album of dedications to Eldridge Cleaver, Malcolm X, Che Guevera, and
Régis Debray, combined with standards whose titles commented ironically on
Southern racism and the military coup in Greece). "No," he said. "I may be
an impressionist, but my music is not programmatic. Audiences have no way
of knowing if a thundering cluster is supposed to represent police brutality in
South Africa or the dishes falling off my table as I attempted to prepare a curry
the night before. Maybe if I were famous, it would be different. Nobody much
cares what I think, and it's too easy for a white man to exploit black issues for
his own self-aggrandizement. I guess I feel more impotent against injustice
than I used to. At a certain point, I realized that listening to Billie Holiday,
enjoying a reasonably good dinner, and reading a stimulating book an hour
before bedtime to facilitate entry into the dream world are the activities that
have the most bearing on my music. I know that sounds selfish, but I don't
want to pass myself off as better than I really am."

For his Philadelphia concert, Blake played Monk, Fletcher Henderson,
Shorty Rogers, Pete Rugolo, John Philip Sousa, Bernard Herrmann's score for
Vertigo enfolded with Blake's own variations, adaptations of traditional
Sephardic music inspired by the recent film *Shoah,* and impressions of *Rebecca,
The Wild One,* and *The Wrong Man*—a characteristic program for a performer
who has raised eclecticism to a discipline. The surprises were Rogers and
Rugolo, palefaces associated with West Coast jazz and the top-heavy Stan Ken-
ton Orchestra of the forties and fifties (but, significantly, the most obvious pre-
cursors to the Third Steam movement, aside from Ellington and Mingus).

Blake will teach a course on Monk this fall, which should prove interesting, because Monk is the jazz pianist he most resembles, if only in the emphasis he places on the nuances of touch, an aspect of pianistics criminally

overlooked in most assessments of technique. "It's funny. I once wrote an article on Thelonious for one of the keyboard magazines, and never even mentioned his touch, though I certainly should have," says Blake, who was once the jazz critic for *The Bay State Banner,* a black-owned newspaper in Maine. "It's also something I've never given much thought to in my own playing, though I do remember one of my first teachers telling me not to bang the keyboard, and me thinking that there were instances when banging was called for. I play fewer notes than most pianists, and perhaps that's Thelonious's influence. But I think it has more to do with a subconscious desire to imitate a vocal line. I'm probably the only pianist of my generation more in debt to Billie Holiday, Mahalia Jackson, Abbey Lincoln, Chris Connor, Stevie Wonder, and Victoria de los Angeles than to Bud Powell."

(AUGUST 1986)

Circles, Whirls, and Eights

=

had this incredible vision when I was younger," the pianist Borah Bergman said recently. "As I'm playing, everyone is running out of the hall, and this is making me very, very happy. I had a friend around that time who sometimes played drums with me, and I once asked him, 'What do you think I do best?' He looked at me and said, 'Borah, the thing you do best is make tumult.'"

Bergman is an outcat. The hipster pianist Paul Knopf, who released two excellent but overlooked albums in the late fifties, coined the word, in a mood of flippant defiance, to celebrate himself as "an outcast and a far-out cat combined." By popular stereotype, all jazz musicians are outcats. But those of us within music recognize the outcat as a specific type too self-absorbed to be part of any movement (and too idiosyncratic to spearhead one, even posthumously), and too self-reliant to seek audience or peer approval (and too marginal in the larger scheme of things to elicit much). The word conveys undertones of exile, rootlessness, alienation, despair. Thelonious Monk? Maybe. Herbie Nichols? Definitely.

Outcats tend to be pianists, which seems only fitting, because the keyboard—a complete orchestra within hand's reach, as most outcats, including Bergman, think of it—is just the instrument for a musician determined to keep his own counsel. Though they seldom play jazz, there are outcats in movies (Frank Sinatra in *Young at Heart* and Harvey Keitel in *Fingers*) and in literature (Eddie Leen, the doomy, on-the-lam-from-life hero of David Goodis's *Down Here,* a.k.a. *Shoot the Piano Player*—and Earl Morgan, the father of Virgil Morgan, the narrator of Scott Spencer's *Preservation Hall*).

Spencer's description of Earl Morgan's "lurching, pouncing, halting, racing experiments in pure sound," and Virgil Morgan's alienated response to them, suggest the similar trials that Bergman can put even an experienced listener through when he leans bodily into the piano, with his left hand moving furiously, independent of his right and ultimately usurping, in devil's crossed-hands motion, the right hand's domain at the top of the keyboard: "There was something grand and assertive about (his) compositions and you felt at once lonely and besieged when you heard them. They were pieces to take the color out of stained glass, something to remind you that there is no afterlife."

"A GIRL WHO WAS UP HERE ONCE TOLD ME 'BORAH, YOUR MUSIC ISN'T *nice.*' But I don't think you have to *like* art. You have to respond to it," says Bergman, fifty-two, who makes his living teaching music in the New York public school system. Originally from Brooklyn, he now lives alone near Central Park, in a studio apartment at once spartan in furnishing and cluttered because of the piano in the middle of the floor and the clavier (a soundless keyboard good for improving finger dexterity) beneath the one row of windows. During a three-hour conversation, Bergman (who looks something like Dick Miller, the bristly comic lead in Roger Corman's *Bucket of Blood*) ran his fingers through his thick black hair so often that it stood up above his forehead in a rooster's comb. He speaks in a hectoring whine, with a crescendo somewhere in each sentence—a speech pattern that shrieks "Brooklyn" to New Yorkers, but shouts "New York" to everybody else. He talks about himself incessantly, revealing insecurity rather than a surfeit of ego; you get the impression that at any moment he might say, 'But enough about me. What don't *you* like about my music?'"

When talking about music, Bergman's thoughts keep veering off to subjects that at first seem irrelevant, until one realizes that the novelists he read as an English major at New York University ("I was always drawn to the expressionistic writers like Thomas Wolfe—it's like Henry Miller said, the important thing is to get it all out") and the abstract expressionist school of painters he admires ("someone once accused me of putting Fats Waller and Cecil Taylor into a shredder and coming out with a solid block of sound—which is a perfect description of a Jackson Pollack painting, by the way") have shaped his music as much as other musicians have. As musical influences, he cites the boogie-woogie and stride pianists, Thelonious Monk, Ornette Coleman, Bud Powell ("I loved his purposeful fumbles"), and Lennie Tristano ("the father of free piano, but he drew back; he never learned to play those lines he created by overdubbing in real time").

Bergman played clarinet as a child, and didn't start piano seriously until he was in his twenties, "when I already knew a good deal about jazz, which was both good and bad. I knew there was no point in sounding *almost* as good as Bud Powell. I said if you're going to play piano, you have to get something of your own; otherwise, quit." He decided to play as fast and hard as he could, for as long as he could. His inspiration was John Coltrane's "Chasin' the Trane": "There may have been sexual innuendoes to it; wanting, unconsciously, to have intercourse that lasted twenty minutes. I don't know. But if you want to think of it in those terms, most pianists, including Cecil Taylor, were limiting themselves to foreplay. . . .

"I felt something going on when I was playing fast. But sometimes, after awhile, I felt nothing. It was all worked out in my mind so I knew what was coming next, and I was *bored*. But I found that if I broke it up, and shot both hands this way and that way, it would revive me." He resolved to learn to play everything he could play with his right hand with the left. Eventually, he began to execute improvised passages and conceive entire pieces for the left hand alone.

Although numerous classical composers, including Ravel and Scriabin, have written pieces for the left hand, the strength and independence of Bergman's left hand makes him unique among improvising pianists. If his music resembles that of any of his contemporaries, it is Cecil Taylor's but only in terms of sound mass and his fondness for recurring motifs. "When the left hand is playing one thing and the right hand another, there are two things going on simultaneously," Bergman says. "So I don't see the comparison to the one very beautiful thing going on in Cecil's parallel-hands playing. I'm right-handed, but I intentionally developed my left hand because I get a completely different feeling in my body from playing with my left hand. I don't know if it's neurological or the nature of the piano, where the left hand is always playing in the darker-sounding areas. There are also cultural implications for me. The left hand has traditionally been the bastard, the stooge, the devil, but also the dreamer. It sounds corny, but I associated the left hand with the oppressed. I'm from a very left-wing background. My parents, who were Russian Jewish immigrants, were socialists, and we were surrounded by anarchists, Trotskyites, and Zionists. I grew up thinking that there was nothing like having a good fight for your rights on your hands. Something to fight for was something to live for. I've always been inclined to go the opposite way. If somebody else had been doing what I was doing with my left hand, I wouldn't have done it. For me, the left hand was the great equalizer. It didn't matter anymore whether I was young or old, or black or white, because I had something of my own."

In choosing such an odd and physically strenuous style, Bergman has sometimes been guilty—much like Norman Mailer, another of his favorite writers—of bidding the will to do the work of the imagination (will is sometimes also required in reading Mailer and in listening to Bergman). But beginning with "Poignant Dreams" and "Ballad of a Child," two suspended-animation ballads on his 1985 album, *Upside Down Visions* (Soul Note SN-1080), his work has undergone a thaw similar to the one that Virgil Morgan notices in his father's music toward the end of *Preservation Hall:* "It was different from the kind of music I associated with him. The jittery rhythms had been smoothed out and though the chords were stuffed with notes they seemed remarkably agreeable, almost placid, unlike his usual chords in which the notes blindly warred . . . the music sounded natural, strong, and, as lovely melodies always sound to people who don't understand music, unbearably sad. I had always thought of the great composers brushing teardrops from the score as they worked and now, for the first time, I thought of (him) composing the same way."

There is more breathing room between phrases in *Upside Down Vision's* ballads (and in the title track, taken at an only slightly faster tempo that Bergman describes as "atos," all tempos at once)—they convey more of a sense that somebody might be out there listening. These ballads are almost tactile in their intimacy. Although their cragginess and tension save them from meditative prettiness, they'd sound like something on Windham Hill or ECM with just a little more reverb.

"God forbid I should be on ECM!" Bergman said in mock horror when I told him I was glad he wasn't. "I might sell more records and make some money. People have always asked me how I can play so fast, and now I can play slower than anyone else, too. I always wrote ballads, and maybe I would have played them if I had a little neo-bebop quartet. But playing them solo, they made me feel depressed, vulnerable. The problem was that I couldn't play them with as much drive as the faster pieces. Now I can, because I can now do something I couldn't do before, or at least not with ease, which is to play crossed hands continually, sometimes with the left hand in the treble and the right hand in the bass. Since the hands are mirror images, all the chords are inverted. Playing a ballad now, I feel exquisite, a little depressed, out of this world. When I play fast, my brain is working, along with my desire for identity or survival or whatever. When I play a ballad, I feel the sense of elegance you get when expressing a complete thought.

"So I have a serious dilemma, and I don't know what to do about it. My ballads I know I have an audience for. Not a mass audience, but a certain number of people who wouldn't like anything else I do. People *like* my ballads. But once you start seeking acceptance, you become less rambunctious. You take smaller steps."

A FEW DAYS AFTER I INTERVIEWED HIM, BERGMAN CALLED ME TO ASK ME to recommend duet partners. This surprised me, because I think of him as a solo performer, hammering away at the keyboard and his thoughts ("making the silence answer," as he once put it). He also dropped me several notes, handwritten on unlined white paper, with parenthetical thoughts written vertically in the margins. These are examples of what he had to say:

"Francis, the hands are merely stooges now for my *ideas*." [underlined]

"My next step will be MEDIUM TEMPO and 'swinging' pulse—but now the left hand can go like a right—relaxed—THIS MAY enable me to BEAT THE ODDS—it's not Wynton Kelly, Red Garland, etc. but thinking of them playing 'Upside Down' _____ or Bill Evans, etc."

"I'll be able to play Albert Ayler with my left hand—that pathos."

"If someone asked me I'm playing BLACK and WHITE music: of course the piano has BLACK and WHITE keys—joke."

"The concept of dialogue will be based on the ability of each hand to play (alone) conceptions such as Circles, Whirl + Figure 8s, Swift River, Webs and Whirlpools, Uncharted Rivers, etc."

"I'm on to some kind of 'ecstacy'—it started with the voicings on 'Poignant Dream' (the improvisation) and 'Child Alone.'"

"I've always liked the Chicago players—there's a record on Columbia Bud Freeman, Condon, Kaminsky, Teagarden, Russell?, "After Awhile" "Muskrat Ramble" and others. The record you gave me [of Steve Lacy's early adventures in dixieland with the trumpeter Dick Sutton], fun, but diluted dixieland—fun, but not like the depth, poignancy, 'pain' + 'joy' of the earlier stuff."

[On the telephone] "I think those white Chicago musicians will eventually be considered significant for epitomizing a consciousness that existed at the time. It wasn't the robust, ebullient, wonderful thing that came from New Orleans. It was different: to be alive and drinking and playing jazz. I must start listening to the thirties again."

"I don't know what I'll do now—I'm at a crossroads—in two weeks I'll know—I'm getting out of teaching in June, if I keep the Steinway B—if I sell it I can get out now."

"Someday I'll tell you the REAL story of my life—I TRUST you'll be amazed."
(OCTOBER 1987)

from

BEBOP AND NOTHINGNESS

Pres and His Discontents

"There are men who stir the imagination deeply and uncomfortably, around whom swirl unplaceable discontents, men self-damned to difference, and Edgar Pool was one of these," wrote John Clellon Holmes, the most conventionally "literary" of the postwar American beats, in *The Horn,* his jazz roman-à-clef:

> Once an obscure tenor in a brace of road bands, now only memories to those who had heard their crude, up-tempo riffs . . . Edgar Pool had emerged from an undistinguished and uncertain musical background by word of mouth. He went his own way, and from the beginning (whenever it had been, and something in his face belied the murky facts) he was unaccountable. Middling tall, sometimes even lanky then, the thin mustache of the city Negro accenting the droop of a mouth at once determined and mournful, he managed to cut an insolently jaunty figure, leaning toward prominent stripes, knit ties, soft shirts, and suede shoes . . . Edgar had been as stubbornly out of place [in the swing era], when everyone tried to ride the drums instead of elude them, as he was stubbornly unchanged when bop became an architecture on the foundation he had laid.

Pool holds his saxophone "almost horizontally extended from his mouth," with his head at a "childishly fey" angle. He addresses everyone, male as well as female, as "Lady," and has had an ambiguous relationship with a singer resembling Billie Holiday. Having already achieved immortality, he drifts through his days and nights in an alcoholic haze, as though the only thing left for him to do is to die. Though named for Edgar Allen Poe, a morbid ideal for all American artists driven to madness, Pool is a fictional double for Lester Young, the tenor saxophonist who died five months short of his fiftieth birthday, in 1959, the same year that *The Horn* was published.

Young, the key figure in jazz evolution between Louis Armstrong and Charlie Parker, first appeared on the scene in the late 1930s as the most compelling soloist in the big band that Count Basie brought east from Kansas City—

hardly "an undistinguished and uncertain musical environment," although Young's comings and goings to that point must have indeed seemed "murky" to jazz listeners of Holmes's generation. Born in Woodville, Mississippi, and on the road with his father and two younger siblings in their family vaudeville band for much of his childhood and adolescence, Young was twenty-seven and already in possession of his mature style when he made his first recordings with Basie in 1936.

Jazz lore maintains that each of the leading soloists of the 1920s and 1930s gained an edge over his competition by developing an unmistakable "sound"—a tone that amounted to a personal signature that could not be forged. Black musicians may have felt especially challenged to do so. "Everybody knows that the ofay's playing is clean," the late trombonist Dicky Wells, a bandmate of Young's with Basie and a trailblazing soloist in his own right, observed in *The Night People,* his 1971 memoir, which has just been republished by the Smithsonian Institution Press. (It's an "as told to" book, to which Wells's collaborator, the critic Stanley Dance, selflessly refrained from adding "writerly" touches.) "No other way he knew. And deep down in, he's the master when it comes to cutting something, when you put the music up there. The Oxford Gray [a term for a black musician, coined by Young] was noted for his fuzz and just swinging."

Fuzz or no fuzz, by the time that Young arrived in New York from out of the blue—at what was then considered to be a ripe old age for a jazzman, with an almost imperceptible vibrato and an airy sonority influenced to some extent by Frankie Traumbauer's on C-melody saxophone—Coleman Hawkins's big, robust tone had been codified as a just and proper voice for the tenor saxophone. The story goes that in 1934, when Young briefly replaced Hawkins in Fletcher Henderson's orchestra, his arrival resulted in so much dissension that Mrs. Henderson sat him down at a record player for a crash course in Hawkins—luckily, to no avail.

What soon became clear was that in Young's case, no less than in Hawkins's, sound was determined by conception. Hawkins needed an ample, vigorous tone in order to accent two beats in each measure and meet each upcoming chord change head on (as did Herschel Evans, Young's opposite number in the Basie saxophone section). Young, whose approach was more elliptical, did not. The consternation over his light timbre initially deflected attention from the most innovative aspect of his style, gracefully described by Whitney Balliett as "Young's absolute mastery of broken-field rhythm and phrasing—the ability to emphasize the beat simply by eluding it." Balliett's comment occurs in one of the most perceptive of the thirty-seven pieces collected in *A Lester Young Reader,* the first in the Smithsonian Institution Press's planned series of anthologies devoted to major jazz musicians.

A case could be made for Young, who was nicknamed "Pres" (short for "The President"), as the first jazz modernist, based solely on his refusal to let bar lines dictate the length or destination of his phrases. If only in terms of their rhythmic flexibility, his earliest recorded solos with Basie anticipated bebop by a good ten years. And though he was essentially a "linear" (or melodic) improviser, his sophistication in implying, rather than spelling out, most of the notes in a chord (rhythm wasn't the only area in which he practiced sleight-of-hand) provided a model for developments after bop, including "cool" jazz, Lennie Tristano's harmonic extrapolations of popular standards, and Miles Davis's investigation of modes and scales.

YOUNG SET THE STAGE FOR CHARLIE PARKER IN YET ANOTHER WAY. HE WAS probably the first black instrumentalist to be publicly recognized not as a happy-go-lucky entertainer, à la Armstrong, but as an artist of the demimonde whose discontents magnified those felt by his race in general.

Here's Holmes's Edgar Pool on the bandstand, alienated from his workplace in the manner of most laborers, but overcome by a disgust presumably unique to black performers resentful of their status as nightclub entertainers rather than as concert artists:

> Almost gagging, he hated everything there—the smell of bad breath and dried saliva that filled his nose from the microphone, and the smell of melted Italian cheese and dishwater that came out of the kitchen each time the door swung, and the smell of his own liquored sweat and damp clothes, and most of all the *feel* of the impatient crowd out there who could see every stain down his tie, and every sleepless hour on his face, but whom he could not see. He had never cared before that a jazz musician was condemned to utter his truth in the half-dark of dangerous, thronged rooms where every-one's breath tasted of alcohol and cigarettes, and everyone left something of the day behind him at the door. But suddenly he saw that he had spent his life a moody fugitive among sensation hunters, enunciating what seemed to him just then . . . a rare and holy truth in the pits of hell.

Race undoubtedly contributed to Young's alienation, as it did, in a quite different way, to that of the very earliest white jazz musicians, who had to be estranged from white bourgeois values even to *know* about jazz. (A number of them adopted what they imagined to be Negro modes of behavior, Mezz Mezzrow being the extreme example.) But the potential for alienation can be found in the lives of most black musicians of Young's era—certainly in the life of Dicky Wells, who was forced to go to work as a Wall Street messenger (his first day job) at the age of sixty, and whose memoir (among the most intimate and unselfconsciously lyrical accounts we have of life on the road as a big band sideman in the 1930s) ends with an account of three muggings at the hands of "soul brothers in action—no grays [slang for white people], so I am still for the cat who treats me as I treat him—black, green, white, or blue." Aside from complaints about jazz having evolved into a different sort of music than what he played in his youth ("It's a kind of imaginary thing when there are no people dancing," he notes wistfully, at one point), Wells's narrative is loquacious and engagingly lighthearted from start to finish, like his best recorded solos.

The only possible criticism of *The Night People* in the present context is that it tells us little we don't already know about Lester Young, who must have struck even fellow musicians as strange. Young wasn't "part of the family, if that's what it was," writes the late Bobby Scott, in one of the remembrances included in *A Lester Young Reader.* A pianist and singer who first hooked up with Young on a 1955 tour of Norman Granz's Jazz at the Philharmonic (JATP), Scott manages to draw a lifelike portrait of Young despite two dozen or so superfluous references to Nietzsche, St. Augustine, and Padraic Pearse, among others. A friend of mine who attended many JATP concerts recalls Young standing aloof from the other horns and not playing exaggeratedly "hot," as they did, in an attempt to win the crowd. On tour with JATP, Young usually booked a room in a black hotel, rather than stay in integrated lodgings with the rest of Granz's troupe. Was he keeping his distance from whites, or just keeping his distance?

Although heterosexual, Young affected effeminate mannerisms, including what a "psychosomaticist" quoted in a 1959 *Down Beat* essay republished here describes as a "mincing" walk. (Others say he "sidled"—perhaps as a result of a degenerate case of syphilis diagnosed on his induction into the U.S. Army in 1943, suggests Frank Buchmann-Moller, in an addendum of sorts to *You Just Fight for Your Life,* his meticulous 1990 Young biography.) Young wore his hair unconventionally long in back and (we learn from Nat Hentoff) planned at one point to put ribbons in it. (He tells the aforementioned physician that photographs of Victorian-era women in their ribboned skimmers gave him the idea for his trademark wide-brimmed porkpie hat.) He imagined that people were looking at him in restaurants (they probably were) and, toward the end of his life, could only sleep with the lights on and the radio at full blast.

Despite his dissolute way of life (gin and marijuana, but nothing harder, perhaps due to his terror of needles), Young prided himself on always being on time for his engagements, often going to absurd lengths to avoid being late. And as if to compound the enigma, many of the musicians quoted in the *Reader* insist that he was religious—or, as Scott puts it, that he at least believed that the existence of a Deity "was to be taken for granted." Calling on him in a New York residence hotel for a *Melody Maker* interview in 1950, Leonard Feather noticed "soiled plates" and bottles of gin and sherry on a night table, and "innumerable figurines, many of them religious," on the mantelpiece.

JUST AS YOUNG WAS MEASURED AGAINST COLEMAN HAWKINS AND WAS
found wanting by some in the late 1930s, his unyielding rival after World War
II was the memory of his former self. Critics usually trace his artistic decline
to the ten months he spent in a Georgia detention compound following his
1945 court martial for possession of marijuana and barbiturates. The problem with this "broken man" theory is that it makes no allowance for his innumerable total recoveries of form. Young's vibrato grew sluggish and his tone
steadily darkened in the last fourteen years of his life, and, especially toward
the end, some of his recorded solos were so wobbly that you can practically
smell the whiskey on his breath. But sprinkled among his postwar discography are performances so graceful in execution and so powerful in their emotional range (his 1956 *Jazz Giants* session with Roy Eldridge and Teddy
Wilson, for example) that they alone would guarantee him a ranking as one
of the greatest of all jazz improvisers; they are at least as memorable as his early
records with Basie and Billie Holiday.

Lewis Porter, the editor of *A Lester Young Reader* and the author of a previous book on Young that (for the most part) confined itself to musicology, has
established himself as the leading defender of the "late" Lester Young among
American jazz academics. Given this advocacy, it's not surprising that many
of the essays included in the *Reader's* third and final section (devoted to musical analysis) support his position. Graham Columbe is persuasive in extolling
"the mature tragic awareness" of Young's 1950s recordings, and there are lucid
points made along the same lines by Erik Wiedeman and Henry Woodfin,
though (disappointingly) nothing from the editor himself.

Porter demonstrates evenhandedness by including both a 1953 *Melody
Maker* review dismissive of Young at that point, as well as several appreciations
of the 1930s Pres that adhere to conventional wisdom in assuming that the
postwar Pres is hardly worth mentioning. But in giving this cross-section of
musings on Young something resembling a point of view, Porter's revisionist
zeal also gives it value beyond its obvious handiness as a library time-saver. It's
readable straight through, in a way that anthologies primarily intended for reference use seldom are. Combining old magazine clippings and previously
unpublished oral history, Phil Schaap's opening essay traces Young's life more
or less chronologically, the representation of so many different and often con-
tradictory voices achieving a complexity in keeping with the book's enigmatic
subject. The middle section is subtitled "Young in His Own Words," which is
something of a misnomer in that it mostly consists of brief profiles whose
authors bowed to 1950s jazz-magazine conventions in putting a happy spin
on Young's malaise. But this section also includes the first complete transcription in English of the much-excerpted interview that François Postif
conducted with Young in a Paris hotel room a month before Young's death—

testimony so haunting that one American saxophonist is said to have obtained a dub of the original tape and to have memorized every word of it, as musicians have traditionally memorized recorded improvisations.

With so much of interest included, to chide Porter for what's missing smacks of ingratitude. Nevertheless, the lengthy passages quoted by Hentoff from Ross Russell's incisive 1949 *Record Changer* study of Young's work do raise the question of why Russell's essay isn't here its entirety. I wish that Porter had included John McDonough's 1981 *Down Beat* article on Young's court martial, or better still, Buchmann-Moller's chapter on it, which includes three full pages of Young under cross-examination. And at risk of seeming not to appreciate Porter's exemplary dedication in separating fact from fiction regarding his subject, I wish he had seen fit to include a chapter, or at least a few paragraphs, of Holmes's overwritten and factually suspect novel, which I think belongs here for the same reason that excerpts from Dorothy Baker's *Young Man with a Horn* would belong in a Bix Beiderbecke reader and that posthumous supermarket sightings of Elvis Presley would belong in a biography of Presley. The ability to stir the imagination "deeply and uncomfortably" is, after all, a large part of what makes an artist major.

(JUNE 1992)

Apple Pie

==

I was sick, but I'm getting better," Art Blakey told me without naming a specific ailment when I visited him in his Greenwich Village penthouse apartment this summer. In 1964, when Blakey was still in his mid-forties but already regarded as a hard bop father figure, Blue Note titled one of his albums *Indestructible*. For decades, the word fit the man known in jazz circles as the world's healthiest (and most discreet) junkie. But now, at the age of seventy—white-haired, stooped, and with a weak handshake—Blakey no longer seems impervious to time.

In his right ear he wore the hearing aid he was fitted with a few years ago, but which he eschews onstage. "I feel the vibrations through the floor, just like Beethoven," he said, gingerly lowering himself into a stuffed chair in his spacious living room. "That's all music is, anyway. Vibrations."

He spoke in a phlegmy rumble that made me recall Dan Morgenstern's description of a Blakey press roll as "the sound of a giant clearing his throat."

Blakey's physical deterioration shocked me into asking formulaic questions, most of which I was forced to repeat several times, and several of which I finally had to yell. He laughed frequently—not by making a sound, but by throwing back his head and showing his teeth—as though self-amused by the disingenuous ring of some of his answers, as when I asked him why drummers make such good bandleaders (think not only of him, but of Chick Webb, Gene Krupa, Max Roach, Mel Lewis, Ronald Shannon Jackson, Jack DeJohnette).

"I just play and try to make a showcase for the youngsters, so they can hone their art."

Asked if he considers himself a teacher (he's usually spoken of that way), he protested, "Hell, no. How can I be, if I don't tell them what to play?" On the other hand, he answered a question about whether, for the sake of camaraderie, he ever wished that his sidemen were closer to his own age, "Can't teach old dogs new tricks."

And when I pointed out to him that so many of the musicians who have joined his band in the last two decades have been graduates of college music programs (in contrast to their predecessors, who, like Blakey himself, were

self-taught), he joked, "When I came along, you couldn't mention jazz in colleges. So there's been progress. Youngsters today go, learn theory, learn harmony. Then they graduate, join the Messengers, and start their real
education." But he pointed with an autodidact's vindication to his own hon-
orary degrees from the New England Conservatory of Music and the Berklee
School of Music. "They're over there, bound in leather, on top of the piano,
if you want to look at them."

Blakey's relationship with his young sidemen has been one of tough love,
though—the painful truth—for the last few years, they've been carrying *him*.
"I tell them what *not* to play. They're not youngsters. They're young men, old
enough to make babies. I treat 'em that way." He admits to nudging them out
of the Messengers when he feels they're overdue to start their own bands.

The position of music director (held over the years by Horace Silver, Benny
Golson, Wayne Shorter, and Bobby Watson, among others) is strictly titular,
Blakey told me when I asked him what the qualifications for the job were.

"I'm the real music director back there. I'm the one directing the traffic,"
he said, suddenly adamant. "But I like to give each of my men some responsibility, and the ones you named were good composers."

How come Blakey himself hasn't composed more?

"I compose," he protested. "Don't you think I don't. I'm composing on
drums up there."

But composition in the formal sense?

"Give them the chance to do it," he shrugged.

"WANT SOME APPLE PIE?" BLAKEY ASKED ME, PUTTING OUR CONVERSA-
tion on a different footing. "Best in New York! From Balducci's!" he said
temptingly, naming a well-known Village gourmet shop. "You know what
they say about Balduccis. Spend a hundred dollars there and you can fit what
you buy in the glove compartment of your car. Daniel, bring him some pie.
And bring me a cigarette."

What the hell, the interview wasn't going anywhere anyway.

The strapping German fellow who handles Blakey's bookings from an office
just off the kitchen brought pie for me and an ashtray with a Marlboro Light
already burning in it for Blakey. In the background, the radio was tuned to
WBGO-FM. The disc jockey gave details of a public memorial service for the
pianist Walter Davis, Jr., a two-term Messenger who'd died of liver and kid-
ney failure three days earlier, at the age of fifty-seven.

Taking shallow drags on the cigarette, Blakey started bitching about his
most recent ex-wife, who had left him two years earlier, fleeing to her native
Canada with their two adopted children and (Blakey says) a large sum of
money that was supposed to have been set aside for his taxes.

"I've had four wives, all jealous of me," he rasped conspiratorially, balling his fingers into a fist and adding, "They weren't interested in Art Blakey *as a man*. The last one told me 'You make more money in one night than my father made in a year.' Well, whose fault was that? He could have been prime minister of Canada, couldn't he? Wasn't nothing stopping him. He was Caucasian.

"I miss Buddy Rich," he suddenly exclaimed, apropos of nothing in particular, as the radio played something by Freddie Hubbard. "The year before he died, I saw him at a festival in Europe. I asked him, 'Why don't you go somewhere and retire, old man? All those heart bypass operations you had.' You know what he said to me? He pointed to that stage and said, 'There's no place else I want to be.'"

Taking advantage of his reflective mood, I asked Blakey about his days as a teenage singer and pianist in Pittsburgh (the story goes that he switched to drums after being intimidated by the young Erroll Garner).

"Hell, I wasn't no piano player," he protested. "I just sat at the piano and knocked out a few chords. It was a means of escape. There was child labor in my day. I started work in the coal mines when I was eleven. I was by myself, no brothers or sisters. It was tough, but I had to be tougher. My mother died when I was five months old. I never even saw a picture of her. Her best friend took care of me. They got married in the church, my mother and my father. He sat my mother in a carriage, said wait here while I go to the drug store and buy a cigar. They told me she sat there nine hours waiting for him to come back. He ran off to Chicago with some other chick, because my mother was too dark for him. He was a mulatto. Lived to be a hundred-and-three. Must have been a hell of a man. He loved me but couldn't accept me as his own, because of the times. When I met him later on, I wouldn't even talk with him, because he wouldn't act like a man.

"My first child was born when I was thirteen. I never abandoned my kids. I love children. I fathered seven. I adopted seven more. That makes fourteen. I don't remember how many grandchildren I have. I haven't met them all yet. But I'm a great, great grandfather," he said, coughing between the "great"s. "So that's my life. I have no regrets. I've had a ball. I've outlived some of my children. I've outlived some of my grandchildren. I've outlived most of my contemporaries. And I've been fortunate to be an American. This is the greatest country in the world. Nobody's going to tell me that it's not! You got the freedom to do anything you want.

"Somebody dies—crocodile tears! Liars!" he fairly seethed, perhaps thinking of the upcoming services for Walter Davis, Jr. "I didn't go to Monk's funeral. I loved him. He and I were like brothers, birthdays one day apart in October. But I didn't go to his funeral. People asked me why. I said the day somebody comes back from the dead and says to me, 'Oh, what a beautiful funeral they gave me,' that's the day I'll start going to them. Nature takes its course. Slowing up, retiring. You're born, you die. It's what you do in between."

IN PARTING, I ASKED BLAKEY IF HE'D READ MILES DAVIS'S AUTOBIOGRAPHY (in which Miles accuses Blakey of once having fingered him to narcotics agents, back when both of them were using).

"I ain't got time to read that. That's garbage. I read books I can get knowledge from, the Koran, the Torah, the Bible from Genesis to Exodus," he said, sweeping his arms toward a shelf full of what appeared to be books on World War II.

I told him what Miles had said about him.

"Did he spell my name right? Then, good."

Downstairs in the lobby, the security guard was listening to a vibrant uptempo tune on the radio. It could have passed for something by the Messengers, circa 1978, except for an element that was missing. Call it the crust. It turned out to be the Harper Brothers, the band co-led by drummer Winard and trumpeter Philip Harper (a recent Messenger).

Thanks to the many successive generations he's sired, there will always be bands that sound like Blakey's. But will there ever be anybody else like him?

(NOVEMBER 1990)

Art Blakey died on October 16, 1990—about four months after my visit, and five days after his seventy-first birthday.

Real Stuff in Life to Cling To

I f it's possible to seem unpretentious dressed in black tie and surrounded by a chamber symphony onstage at Carnegie Hall, Tony Bennett did when I heard him there last spring. The show began without announcement: Bennett just walked onstage, where the pianist Ralph Sharon, his longtime music director, sat waiting for him, and sang "Taking a Chance on Love." On the line "I walk around with a horseshoe," he pointed a thumb at his chest and lifted one foot off the ground, as though proud enough to strut. He followed with "My Foolish Heart," slowly shaking his head "no" on the line, "For this time it isn't *fascination*," turning palms down on the offending word for good measure. He and Sharon were then joined by the bassist Paul Langosch and the drummer Joe LaBarbera, and eventually by the horns and strings. But in keeping with his self-image as a glorified saloon singer, Bennett stayed close to the piano, sometimes unselfconsciously resting an elbow on it. (Now and then Sharon would play something that let you imagine sawdust and peanut shells under Bennett's feet.)

This expert but understated stagecraft goes along with Bennett's reputation as a consummate entertainer who also happens to be the decent sort of man you'd be happy to find on the next barstool. Frank Sinatra might own the patent on that persona, but Bennett gives the impression of being that way for real (with his jutting nose and jawline, he even looks the part of best friend, not leading man). He was in good voice at Carnegie, despite what sounded to me like an inadvertent key change on the fortissimo ending of "I Left My Heart in San Francisco," at the climax of a far-from-perfunctory medley of his greatest hits. The evening's only real clinker was promotional, not musical. The concert, which also featured songs from *Astoria: Portrait of the Artist* (Columbia), Bennett's ninety-first album in a career dating back to 1950, was being subsidized by the Gitano Group, Inc., which meant that Bennett had to sing his 1963 hit "The Good Life" to footage of young marrieds and their children romping outdoors in the sponsor's sportswear.

I know that corporate underwriting of live music is a necessary evil at this point (chamber symphonies cost money), but by presenting what amounted to a TV commercial onstage, Gitano was crossing one of the few remaining lines. (In ending with the printed slogan THE SPIRIT OF FAMILY, the ad was politically objectionable, too. Doesn't anyone at Gitano know or care that the fundamentalist right has corrupted "family" into a buzzword in its war on sexual and procreative choice?) The whole thing was unworthy of Bennett, and I was glad that he seemed a little embarrassed by it. "This is my commercial," he said in introducing "Lost in the Stars"—his third and final encore, after "Fly Me to the Moon" and "How Do You Keep the Music Playing?"—and then explained to the audience that the song was from a 1949 Broadway adaptation of the South African novel *Cry, the Beloved Country*, and that he found its message of brotherhood still timely.

But Bennett had already given the audience something to think about with "Fly Me to the Moon." He often does this song as his encore (probably because it allows him to exit after singing the final words, "I love you," and pointing to the front rows), and he frequently asks that his microphone be turned off when he does it in nightclubs. Still, it was a surprise to hear him make the same request in a hall as large as Carnegie.

"Musicians' shoulders go back when they walk onstage there," he told me a few days later, during an interview in his business office, a few floors down from his apartment in a midtown Manhattan hotel. He meant that he had wanted to prove himself still worthy of Carnegie Hall, at sixty-three, by bouncing his unamplified voice off its walls.

Actually, there were moments during the song when you could barely hear him, but his lung power wasn't what made the stunt remarkable. Bennett was breaking down pop's fourth wall (how often these days, even in concert, do we hear a singer's actual *voice*, minus echo, reverb, and artificial sibilance), and thus exposing his style to closer scrutiny. I was finally able to put my finger on something I had always thought of as curious: his way of elongating the final words of certain phrases and assigning each of them several different notes, a melismatic touch that I (perhaps owing to my own ethnic background) associate with Irish crooners, not with an Italian-American singer like Bennett.

"Ah, that's Crosby," Bennett said when I mentioned this. "You see, my uncle was married to an Irish lady, and they both adored Bing." Then, indirectly, Bennett pinpointed one of the secrets of his own appeal. "He loved to sing and you could hear it. That's something that you can't buy. Either you have it or you don't. It had nothing to do with the money he made. He had a natural love for it. Just like a guy in a barroom. You say, 'Come on, sing us a tune.' And he sings."

IN A 1965 ARTICLE FOR *LIFE* MAGAZINE IN WHICH HE FOUND MOST vocalists wanting in one way or another (the piece bruised as many egos in show business as Norman Mailer's "Evaluations: Some Quick and Expensive Comments on the Talent in the Room" had in literary circles when published in *Esquire* six years earlier), Frank Sinatra called Bennett "the best in the business . . . the singer who gets across what the composer had in mind and probably a little more." These words from on high have since acquired the air of prophecy, no matter how dubious they must have sounded at a time when Sinatra himself was still very active.

To gain a measure of Bennett's musical growth over the decades, all you need to do is compare the new version of "The Boulevard of Broken Dreams" on *Astoria* with the 1956 version included on *16 Most Requested Songs* (Columbia), a CD-only compilation of Bennett's hits of the 1950s and early 1960s. The original version's Apache dance of an arrangement, for which Bennett can't be held accountable, isn't the only problem. There's also Bennett's vibrato, which doesn't know when to stop, and his overzealousness in punching up each note, even at the expense of lyrical message and rhythmic flow.

The new version, with spare but effectively atmospheric accompaniment by just Sharon, Langosch, and LaBarbera, demonstrates Bennett's mature willingness to let a song breathe. The lower key, though obviously dictated by Bennett's diminished range, amounts to an advantage: it's more in keeping with the rueful mood of Al Dubin's lyrics, which Bennett manages to make seem almost worthy of Harry Warren's lovely melody, virtually sighing that silly but delightful line about "gigolo and gigolette." *16 Most Requested Songs* also includes Bennett's back-to-back Number 1 hits from 1951, the quasi-aria "Because of You" and his clueless pop crossover version of Hank Williams's country hit "Cold, Cold Heart."

On the albums of standards he made with jazz musicians in the 1950s and 1960s, you can hear Bennett on his way to becoming the singer he is today. A reissue from this period worth seeking out is *Basie/Bennett* (Capitol/Roulette). Although Basie plays piano on only two tracks, his band is present throughout. Sharon did the arrangements, including an especially lovely version of Lerner and Lowe's "I've Grown Accustomed to Her Face," from *My Fair Lady.*

But I think that Bennett reached a turning point in 1972, when he was dropped by Columbia Records after twenty-two years on the label, his departure hastened by his reluctance to do more albums like *Tony Sings the Hits of Today,* from 1970, on which he sang cover versions of rock 'n' roll tunes for which he had no genuine feeling. At least Bennett was assigned songs by Stevie Wonder, Burt Bacharach, and Lennon and McCartney—unlike his labelmate Mel Tormé, who was given "If I Had a Hammer," "Red Rubber Ball," and "Secret Agent Man." When I spoke with Bennett in March, he likened his disgust at being pressured to do "contemporary" material to that of his mother, a seamstress, when she was forced to work on a cheap dress.

Although Bennett was off the hit parade, appealing mostly to listeners beyond record-buying age, he continued to fill nightclubs and concert halls. The confidence that he was going "to make a buck no matter what" seems to have encouraged him to strengthen his relationship with jazz, recording an album of voice-and-piano duets with Bill Evans for Fantasy and two collections of Rodgers and Hart with the guitarist George Barnes and the cornetist Ruby Braff for his own label, significantly named Improv (for which he also recorded another album with Evans). On the road constantly, he became a kind of traveling salesman for American popular song. He also began to enjoy success in his second career, as a painter, signing his works "Anthony Benedetto" (his real name) and selling them for as much as $40,000 each (though you have to wonder if collectors are paying for the paintings or his signature).

It was during his banishment from Columbia that Bennett developed what's since become his most endearing vocal trait: bearing down on the key words of a lyric and sometimes delivering them in what's practically a stage whisper or a shout, like a man thinking out loud while singing con brio. The effect is too fleeting—too intimate and too much Bennett's own—to be characterized as sprechsteme or parlando. In addition to making a virtue of the slight huskiness that's crept into his voice with age, it gives his performances an autobiographical depth comparable to that which Sinatra achieved in his late prime, in the 1950s. The most striking instance of this is on Bennett's recording of "Make Someone Happy" with Evans. "Fame if you win it, comes and goes in a minute. Where's the *real stuff* in life to cling to?" Bennett sings, and you sense that the real stuff to which he's holding fast includes the song itself and others like it.

AFTER GOING NINE YEARS WITHOUT A NEW RELEASE, BENNETT RESIGNED with Columbia in 1986. His three new albums since then have been produced by his son, Danny, and delivered to the label as finished products. *The Art of Excellence* featured mostly newer, nonrock songs of Bennett's own choosing; although the emphasis was on such dolorous, overblown ballads as "How Do You Keep the Music Playing?" and "Why Do People Fall in Love," Bennett sang them beautifully. On *Bennett/Berlin,* Bennett did with "White Christmas" what might have seemed impossible, putting the song across with gentle barroom yearning in place of the family-around-the-fireplace smugness with which it's usually sung. *Bennett/Berlin* captured Bennett at his absolute best, with flawless support from his trio and cameo appearances by George Benson, Dizzy Gillespie, and Dexter Gordon.

Astoria, with Bennett's trio, plus an orchestra conducted by the arranger Jorge Calandrelli on all but two of the fourteen tracks, is what used to be called a concept album: a musical "autobiography" (though Bennett wrote none of the songs) and a celebration of the working-class section of Queens in which the singer grew up and for which the album is named. (Given this, *Astoria* bears a superficial resemblance to Bennett's long out-of-print 1958 album *Hometown, My Town*, whose unifying, extramusical subject was Manhattan's exhilarating pace.)

Although a song from the 1930s called "Just a Little Street Where Old Friends Meet" ("and greet you in the same old way") successfully evokes the front-stoop culture that Bennett remembers, *Astoria* finally amounts to an uneven collection of vintage and recent songs. The older songs are fine: aside from "The Boulevard of Broken Dreams," the best performance here might be "Body and Soul," if only for the pleading edge with which Bennett renders the line (which most singers find nearly unsingable) "My life a wreck you're making." Bennett also fares well with "Speak Low," "The Folks That Live on the Hill," "A Weaver of Dreams" (interpolating it with "There Will Never Be Another You"), "The Man I Love" (which Bennett sings as "The Girl I Love," using Ira Gershwin's alternate lyrics), and the Billie Holiday-associated "It's Like Reaching for the Moon."

The problem is that whereas these older songs are about love, friendship, ambition, heartbreak—the works—*Astoria's* newer songs tend to be about little more than older songs. This is true usually only in terms of mood but quite literally in the case of P. J. Erickson and Buddy Weed's "Where Did the Magic Go?" whose lyrics pine for "Francis Albert," "The King of Swing," and the "Dorseys' sound," as well as "Spencer playing Katherine's beau" and "Fred and Ginger dancing slow." (The lyrics also rhyme "Hemingway" and "Courvoisier," reducing educated taste in literature, movies, and song to consumerism with class.) Bennett puts the infernal song across with such snap that I find myself humming along despite myself. I suppose that what really bothers me is that songs like this (and the cultural conservatism presumed to go along with them) provide ammunition for those who would dismiss Bennett and the songs he does best as irrelevant to contemporary life.

"All this music is written and sung in the style that dominated popular song before rock & roll—which means before the '60s, before what we've come to accept as the dawn of modern life," Greg Sandow complained in his review of *Astoria* in *Entertainment Weekly*.

Men, in those days, were men; marriage was forever; women comforted men and cooked their meals. No, Bennett never explicitly sings that here. But every time he does sing about marriage . . . the very sound of his music drags me back to an age when wives were expected to spend their time keeping house. And that, I'm afraid, tells me why the classic American popular song might be going out of style.

To spot the illogic in Sandow's argument, you don't need to know that he's a former classical music critic (arguably the best ever on the subject of the classical avant-garde) who now writes with a convert's zeal about rap and heavy metal, genres whose lyrics hardly tend to be enlightened in their view of women. Sandow is forgetting that music and the emotions it calls into play don't have to be raw in order to be real. He's also not giving Bennett—who's twice divorced and (like so many of the singers and songwriters now associated with pop's disdainful upper crust) a product of the ethnic working class—credit for realizing that life doesn't always work out the way it did in the great old songs, and for knowing that might be the best reason to go on singing them.

Some of Bennett's supporters wind up hurting his cause. "All of this only two years ago, right out there, front and center, on a Bruce Springsteen planet," Jonathan Schwartz, a writer and New York radio personality with a past as a progressive-rock disc jockey to recant, wrote in praise of *Bennett/ Berlin* in *Wigwag* last year. Bennett's own pronouncements often don't help, either. In summing up the difference between rock and his kind of pop, he smugly told me, "One is marketing, the other is good music."

But why should it be necessary to choose between Tony Bennett and Bruce Springsteen? Bennett conveys as much urgency as Springsteen does, though it's of a different sort. Often written about as though he were Sinatra's exact contemporary, he's eleven years younger, the difference of at least a generation in pop. The lost magic that Bennett mourns on *Astoria* was already vanishing by the time he began his career: jazz and pop were no longer close kin, Broadway and Hollywood were entering what everybody must have sensed would be their last decade of providing durable new songs, and rock 'n' roll was just around the corner. Forty years later, Bennett has become the best singer of his kind, but he must sometimes feel like an ambassador from a country that's fallen off the map.

(AUGUST 1990)

This was written a few years before MTV adopted Bennett as its token adult. (I don't think, by the way, that his audiences have gotten any younger; it's just that the people who've always liked him now feel better about themselves.) I keep waiting for him to make a fool of himself; to break an egg on his head and crow "Cock-a-doodle-doo," like Emil Jennings in The Blue Angel—*but so far he hasn't. I guess class tells.*

"Zorn" for "Anger"

John Zorn, whom John Rockwell of *The New York Times* has called "the single most interesting, important and influential composer to arise from the Manhattan 'downtown' avant-garde scene since Steve Reich and Philip Glass," is the only musician I've ever considered suing. I'm not entirely joking. In 1989, when Zorn (whose name in German means "anger"), wearing a T-shirt that read DIE YUPPIE SCUM!, was playing Ornette Coleman tunes on alto saxophone with his band Spy vs. Spy at the Painted Bride Art Center in Philadelphia, he put me and everyone else in the small auditorium at risk of permanent hearing loss by recklessly turning the volume up as high as it would go.

I'm not ordinarily squeamish about loud music, but Spy vs. Spy's opening downbeat was so brutal that I thought I felt my eardrums break. Thirty seconds into the first tune my head was spinning as though I had been drunk and awake for days on end, and my stomach began to churn in reaction to the music's velocity, which I decided was almost as senseless as the volume. Zorn and Spy vs. Spy—the alto saxophonist Tim Berne, the bassist Mark Dresser, and the drummers Joey Baron and Michael Vatcher—were grinding Coleman's music down into a feelingless, monochromatic din. They treated his compositions, which are benchmarks of free jazz, as though they were speed metal (bohemianized heavy metal, without the oversized stage accoutrements) or hardcore (the most dystopian contemporary mutation of what used to be called punk). Although intended as homage, the concert amounted to heresy, presenting Ornette Coleman without swing, sensuality, and blues-based joie de vivre that make even his own forays into rock and funk recognizable as jazz and identifiable as his.

All around me people were fleeing with hands over their ears, while a handful of mostly younger audience members, there for the duration, sneered. I should have fled, too, but a combination of shell shock and journalistic instinct kept me glued to my seat. (Someone, maybe an infuriated Ornette Coleman fan, overturned a sales table of Zorn albums and compact discs on his way out.) Who would have thought that a quintet without a single electric instrument could inflict such pain? As though to add insult to injury, the band members

151

chatted among themselves between salvos but didn't address the audience until about twenty minutes and nine or ten numbers had passed. When Baron glanced up from his drums (rather dazed-looking himself, I thought) and asked, "How ya doin' out there?" I didn't hear anybody answer him.

This nightmare was still on my mind when I spoke with Zorn in New York last spring. "A lot of people were outraged when they first heard Ornette play his music in the fifties and sixties," he said, in defense of his similar junking of Coleman on his 1989 album *Spy vs. Spy* (Elektra Musician). "The speed and the power and the volume, those are elements that admittedly were not part of Ornette's original conception. But those are essential elements in bringing it up to date, in giving it the same impact it had then. Volume is an important parameter. It's visceral. Physical."

Granted, with practically anything now permissible in the name of music, the threat of physical damage posed by unreasonable volume might be the last remaining shock. But shouldn't a musician be wary of longtime effects on his own hearing? "Forget about it," said Zorn, a mild-looking New Yorker in his late thirties with a long, narrow face, stylish eyeglasses, and, when I last saw him, the beginnings of a ponytail. "My ears are blown already. I've been playing loud music for a long time." But he admitted that some of his sidemen wear earplugs. "That's the loudest situation they've ever been in," he said, referring to Naked City, yet another of his bands, which, in addition to jazz tunes and movie themes, also plays old surf hits and Zorn's own hardcore originals—a repertoire for which, I told him, top volume does seem appropriate. When I heard Naked City perform live, they were less painfully noisy than Spy vs. Spy.

That observation brought a hoot. "We probably weren't loud enough then," Zorn said.

BY ZORN'S CURRENT STANDARDS, PROBABLY NOT. ONE OF THOSE NEW Yorkers who gives the impression of being as proud of that city's murder rate as Iowans are of their corn (the cover of Naked City's eponymous debut, released earlier this year, is Weegee's famous photograph of a corpse face down on the sidewalk with his revolver a few feet away), Zorn delights in his self-cast role as the bad boy of Manhattan's eclectic fringe. By this point, it's part of the identity he brings onstage with him.

In 1989 when the Brooklyn Philharmonic performed his "For Your Eyes Only" as part of New Music America (NMA), an annual showcase for avant-garde music that is staged in a different city each year, he used the space allotted to him for a biography in the festival brochure to attack NMA for annually sponsoring "the same tired names [and] pompous, overblown projects." (Most reviewers lambasted Zorn for taking the money if he felt that way, but—in all fairness—his piece had been commissioned by the Brooklyn Philharmonic, which considered the piece its own to perform whenever it wished.)

Zorn once wrote a piece for the Kronos Quartet that called on the members of that resolutely with-it but essentially straitlaced string ensemble to bark and growl like dogs. This was an example of his humor at its most lighthearted, but it can be heavy-handed, too. He once faxed a message to an Austrian concert promoter requesting that his trio be billed as ZOG—an acronym for Zionist-Occupied Government, which is a rallying cry for The Order, the Aryan supremacist group that murdered the Denver talk show host Alan Berg in 1984. The trio, which Zorn describes as "the world's first all-Jewish heavy metal band," and whose other members are guitarist Elliott Sharp, a veteran free improviser, and drummer Ted Epstein, from Blind Idiot God, Zorn's favorite speed metal group, ultimately decided on the name Slan, after a monster in a 1950s science fiction novel.

Zorn, in short, is exactly the sort of rude, overgrown adolescent you would go out of your way to avoid, if only he weren't so . . . well, interesting, important, and influential (at least potentially). A decade ago he seemed just a minor figure in the New York avant-garde—not innovative, just eccentric. At the time his work consisted mostly of his "games" pieces: prankish, discontinuous, Zorn-"cued" group improvisations with titles like "Archery," "Rugby," and "Soccer." These sounded like frat-house Stockhausen and qualified as Zorn "compositions" only in the sense that a party can be said to belong to the person who throws it.

Then Zorn sprang a delightful surprise with *The Big Gundown* (Nonesuch/Icon), a 1986 album on which he "covered" the film music of Ennio Morricone, an Italian composer best known in this country for his soundtracks to Sergio Leone's spaghetti westerns. But Morricone has a much greater range than that, as Zorn showed. The album would have been notable if only for rounding up a veritable subterranean Manhattan who's who, including the keyboard player Wayne Horvitz and the guitarists Bill Frisell and Fred Frith, all of whom subsequently joined Naked City. With its kinesthetic mix of musical styles and its equivalent of jump cuts, wipes, fades, and dissolves, *The Big Gundown* played like a witty essay on the relationship of music and film—the perfect salute to its subject. In an obvious parallel with contemporary painting, the album established Zorn as a composer by acquisition, capable of altering a work's meaning by shifting its context. He gave new significance to the word "cover," traditional record business parlance for slavish emulation of another artist in an attempt to tap a new audience (in the 1950s, for instance, Pat Boone and other white artists "covered" Fats Domino and Little Richard). In Zorn's terms, reinterpretation in another style is simultaneously transgressive and the ultimate act of homage.

A year later, he followed up with *Spillane,* an album whose lengthy title track so successfully evoked the testosterone-and-bile ethos of its pulp-novel-ist namesake that, as Zorn complained to me, it was accepted as another of his covers rather than as an original work. With these back-to-back releases, Zorn helped to clarify a previously murky new aesthetic: "avant-garde" as an *attitude* toward music and as an eclectic, self-contained genre, rather than sim-ply a vanguard movement in classical, jazz, or pop.

ZORN ALSO CALLED ATTENTION TO AN AUDIENCE WHOSE VALUES WERE identical to his as a performer, and that had just been waiting for someone like him to come along—something usually true of only the biggest pop stars, and almost never true of avant-gardists. "In general, my generation and younger, this is how we grew up," Zorn, who was born in Manhattan and raised in Queens, told me. "We had an unprecedented variety of music available to us, because of the availability of everything on LP."

Zorn's mother, a professor of education, liked classical music and world eth-nic recordings; his father, a hairdresser, listened to jazz, country, and French chansons. "And through my brother, who's seven years older and wanted to be a greaser in the fifties, I was exposed to doo wop and the Silhouettes, groups like that." Around the age of fourteen, Zorn says, he immersed himself in Stravinsky, Webern, Ives, Varese, and such contemporary experimental com-posers as Stockhausen and Mauricio Kagel. "But all through that period, I was listening to the Doors and playing bass in a surf band." As a high school stu-dent commuting daily from Queens to Manhattan, he also spent a lot of time in Manhattan's repertory movie houses, sometimes staring at the screen so long that he had to sleep at a schoolmate's apartment in Manhattan to avoid taking a subway home at a dangerous hour.

By practically living at the movies, he says, he was avoiding his squabbling parents, who are still together today, though not on very good terms with their son. But Zorn also found himself spellbound by film music—"the many [dif-ferent] styles a film composer has to know in order to complement the images. In that sense I think the great film composers are the precursors of what my generation is doing today." In addition to Morricone, Zorn's pantheon includes Bernard Herrmann, John Barry, Dimitri Tiomkin, Jerry Goldsmith, and Henry Mancini. His biggest formative influence of all, though, was Carl Stalling, whose music for Warner Bros. cartoons he worshiped, he realized later, for its discontinuity and use of Stockhausen-like "sound blocks"—not to mention the antic sound effects.

Stalling is suddenly in vogue. Last fall, in New York, *Bugs on Broadway* featured Bugs Bunny cartoons accompanied by a live orchestra playing Stalling's original music. The best of his soundtracks for Bugs, Daffy Duck,

Road Runner, and others in the animated menagerie have now been collected on *The Carl Stalling Project: Music from Warner Bros. Cartoons* 1936–1958 (Warner Bros.). Zorn, in the liner notes, praises Stalling for "following the visual logic of screen action rather than the traditional rules of musical form," thus creating "a radical compositional arc unprecedented in the history of music."

After high school Zorn briefly attended Webster College, in St. Louis, "a very small hippie liberal arts school that let you study whatever you wanted to and was the only college that would accept me." It was there that he "got turned on to the jazz scene seriously," through live exposure to Julius Hemphill, Oliver Lake, Hamiet Bluiett, and other then-local musicians who had bonded in a collective called BAG, for Black Artists Group. "I knew I didn't have a place in that, but I didn't really want a place. Jazz was just another kind of music I studied and learned from, like classical or rock."

When trying his hand at straight jazz, Zorn can be controversial without even trying. On *News for Lulu* (Hat Art), a 1987 trio session with Frisell and the trombonist George Lewis, Zorn plays compositions by Sonny Clark, Kenny Dorham, Hank Mobley, and Freddie Redd—unsung jazzmen associated with Blue Note Records in the late 1950s and early 1960s, a period and sound also favored by hard boppers Zorn's age and younger. But Zorn's approach is the antithesis of that of these neoconservatives. To begin with, his instrumentation is unorthodox (no rhythm section), and his choice of tunes is noncanonical. And instead of merely zipping through the chord changes of the tunes, he pays careful attention to their melodies and rhythms, finding in them improvisational possibilities that even their composers overlooked.

Not everyone appreciates Zorn's fresh slant on hard bop. Some reviewers dismiss it as his desperate attempt to mask his lack of conventional musicianship. Such criticism irks Zorn, although he swears it doesn't. "Some people say I can't play the changes, some people say I can't play in tune, and some people say I can't play the saxophone," he told me. "My basic response is I'm doing the best I can. You can spend your whole life, like Frisell has, learning to get inside the chords. I don't do it that way."

ZORN'S WAY STILL INCLUDES FREE IMPROVISATION. LAST MAY HE GAVE A three-night retrospective of his "games" pieces—each involving a different group of improvisers—at the Knitting Factory, in lower Manhattan, a few blocks from his apartment. I was in the audience the first night, sitting behind two musicians awaiting their turn to go onstage. "Which piece is this?" one asked the other during Zorn's "Rugby." "I don't know. Don't they all sound alike?" the second musician replied. I had the feeling that they'd had this conversation many times before.

A truism about free improvisation is that it's fun to play but murder to sit through. Another truism is that you gotta be there: it doesn't work on disc. At the Knitting Factory the rowdy fraternity of Zorn's music won me over, especially the trio piece "Rugby," performed by the cellist Tom Cora and the violinist Polly Bradford, with Zorn on saxophone and duck calls. (Apparently more considerate of audiences on his home turf than of those on the road, he warned that "Rugby" would be "excruciatingly loud," though it wasn't.) But I hesitate to recommend even *Cobra* (Hat Art), arguably Zorn's most successful record in this genre, which I listened to immediately upon receiving it in 1987, and have had no interest in listening to since.

Along with *The Big Gundown* and *Spillane,* the best introduction to Zorn's work is *Naked City* (Elektra/Nonesuch), on which he takes genre-bending to delicious new extremes. Zorn being Zorn, *Naked City* tries your patience with a cluster of eight ear-numbing rants by the band and the screaming singer Yamatsuka Eye, none lasting more than thirty-eight seconds. My advice is to skip selections ten through seventeen when programming the CD, because the other eighteen tracks justify the effort. Zorn atones for *Spy vs. Spy* with a crafty reinterpretation of Ornette Coleman's "Lonely Woman" loaded with verbatim Coleman quotes over a this-means-business bass line appropriated from John Barry's "The James Bond Theme" (which is itself transformed into a Jimi Hendrix-style rave-up a few tracks later). It shouldn't work, but it does. The most satisfying of the disc's several movie themes are Georges Delarue's "Contempt" (done as an art-rock symphony, à la Glenn Branca) and Morricone's "The Sicilian Clan," on which Zorn's improvisation takes the form of a edgy but apposite countermelody.

Of the Zorn originals the one that stays with you the longest is "Saigon Pickup." Just under five minutes long, it comes at you in sections (as Fred Astaire said of a femme fatale in the Mickey Spillane parody-sequence in the movie *The Bandwagon*): a minimalistic, almost Philip Glass-like piano theme; then Zorn squalling over an Asian-sounding scale; then a country and western pastiche; then back to the piano theme, this time reinforced by string synthesizer; then more squalling, followed by more C&W; then some lounge jazz; then some psychedelic organ and reggae drumming; then a gleeful, Ornette Coleman-like melody; then more country, more squalling, more minimalism, and the final fade. The miracle is that it isn't a hopeless audio collage. You never feel as though you're being given a smug demonstration of what's currently hot in music, as you sometimes do with Zorn (on this album's "Graveyard Shift," for example).

Zorn's breadth is such that he tends to fragment the intrepid audience he already has, which would seem to put mass cult adulation out of the question. But on tracks like *Naked City's* "Latin Quarter," "Reanimator," and "Batman" (a Zorn original, not Prince's movie or Neal Hefti's TV show theme), the group rocks out so hard that some of his fans have begun to think of it as Zorn's "boogie" band—his ticket to commercial success. Guess again. *Naked City's* second release, due later this year, will consist of what Zorn calls "classical covers" of works by Debussy, Ives, Scriabin, and others. It's all part of Zorn's effort to take listeners by surprise. Let's hope this one doesn't hurt.

(JANUARY 1991)

Grand Guignol, Naked City's album of classical "covers," was eventually released by Avant, a subsidiary of the Japanese label DIW, after Zorn severed his ties with Elektra/Nonesuch. Zorn, who no longer gives interviews, now lives part of the year in Japan and seems to have reembraced Judaism, to judge from such recent works as Krystallnacht and Masada.

Bagels and Dreadlocks

======

"Y" ou wanna hear the tune of Mickey's that's the hardest of 'em all to play?"
Don Byron asked, fast-forwarding the home cassette of *Mickey Katz Plays Music for Weddings, Bar Mitzvahs, and Brisses* he said I could take with me when we left.

"This is it," he said, landing on the beginning of something he identified as "Frailach Jamboree." It was one of the tunes he'd taught his band in preparation for a tribute to Katz at the Knitting Factory a few nights later.

"Listen to them motherfuckers! They're puttin' some *swing* on the *thing!*" he shouted over the woofing clarinet, the hot-as-salsa trumpet, the Schlomo Grappelli violin. "You hear that tempo, B.?"

"B." was short for "Homeboy," which is what Byron calls you once he decides you're OK. I said that such a lickety-split tempo must be difficult not to screw up.

"Don't say that, man," he pleaded, looking at me as though I was hopeless. "Don't put the jinx on me."

DON BYRON IS PROBABLY SICK AND TIRED OF PEOPLE JOKING THAT HE doesn't *look* Jewish. Maybe it's the dreadlocks, har, har, har.

Klezmer, a Yiddish word borrowed from Hebrew, literally means "instrument or vessel of music," or just "musician." But it was also the name for the *kind* of music—party music, really—that Eastern European Jews brought with them to this country from the shtetls about a hundred years ago. Musicologists say that it was an instrumental secularization of medieval cantorial singing, a theory that makes sense once you've heard Byron or any of the older klezmer clarinetists he admires uvulating fervently up and down a note.

As one of very few klezmers of color (the only others I can think of offhand are Al Patterson and J. D. Parran, both of whom are in Byron's band), Byron might seem to be in a position analogous to that of a white bluesman. There are obvious differences, though, beginning with the fact that it's par for the course for whites to perpetuate fading black styles, but virtually unheard of for a young black musician to revive a white ethnic minority's rara avis. And unlike some of the white boys who play that funky music, Byron isn't on a race-switching trip. "I'm not Mezz Mezzrow in reverse," he told me, referring to the fabled Jewish clarinetist and drug dealer of the 1930s, who convinced himself and the French jazz critics (if nobody in Harlem) that he was black underneath the skin. "It's not like when I play Yiddish music, I close my eyes and forget that I'm a black man, not a Jew. And I'm not pretending that I'm in the middle of a field somewhere in Poland in the nineteenth century, like a lot of the Jewish kids who're playing klezmer."

Even when jamming with their idols, white bluesmen usually wind up doing their stuff for fellow white blues fans. But Byron regularly faces audiences who think of klezmer as theirs, not his. "A few weeks ago, we were doing Mickey Katz's 'Trombenik,'" he told me on the afternoon that I took the number six local up to Elder Avenue in the South Bronx, where he met me on his bicycle and escorted me over to his place on 187th Street. "The title is Yiddish for a no-good-nik, and you pronounce it 'TrumBENIK.' I know that. But as a joke, I announced it as 'Trum-BONE-nik,' because it features the trombonist. Do you know, about a dozen Jewish cats yelled out '*Trum-BENIK! trum-BENIK!*'"

This wasn't at a synagogue or Jewish recreation center, mind you. It was at the Knitting Factory, a nondenominational temple where, as *The New Yorker* never tires of pointing out, "beat and melody are optional [and] 'music' and 'noise' [are] relative terms." Actually, the joke was on the pedants who yelled out, as though correcting a bar mitzvah boy. According to Leo Rosten, a *trombenik* is somebody who blows his own horn. So Katz, in featuring his trombonist, was making a pun.

Even so, Byron isn't taking any more chances. "You all can rate me on my pronunciations," he announced the last time I heard him perform "Trombenik." "Like the Olympics. 'Five-point-five from the Rumanian judge.'"

"DO YOU MIND IF I PUT THE TV ON IN THE OTHER ROOM AND LET IT BLAST while we talk?" Byron asked, after pouring me a glass of cherry seltzer. "*Video Music Box* is on, and you can never tell when they might play 'Big Ol' Butt' by L. L. Cool J. I wanna tape it if they do."

Byron's one-bedroom apartment is on the second floor of a three-story walk-up owned by his parents, who live across the hall "and who first turned the key in that door downstairs the day my mother's water broke." The apartment is indifferently furnished and littered with *tchotchkes*—movie posters ("That describes my current relationships," he said, pointing to one for something called *Three Murderesses*), Sports Flix baseball cards ("This one of Tom Seaver in a Red Sox uniform is going to be worth money someday"), rare LPs by both Mickey Katz and James Brown, toy footballs, and a 1950s viewmaster Byron clinked absentmindedly as he talked.

Byron, who's thirty-one and doubles on baritone saxophone, is a postmodern eclectic in good standing: one of Marc Ribot's Rootless Cosmopolitans, and the leader of a strings-and-woodwinds, Schoenberg-and-beyond chamber group called Semaphore. He's interpreted Scott Joplin with Gunther Schuller's New England Conservatory Ragtime Ensemble, and Duke Ellington with the ghost band led by Ellington's son, Mercer (in which he took the part of the mighty Harry Carney—"an Arnold Schwarzenegger gig").

But he keeps coming back to klezmer. Eleven years ago, as an undergraduate at the New England Conservatory of Music in Boston, he was a charter member of (and one of a handful of non-Jews in) the Klezmer Conservatory Band (KCB), the brainchild of Hankus Netsky, and just one of several Yiddische revival ensembles formed around that time in various parts of the country. He stayed with the KCB until 1986, by which time he'd begun to make a noise in jazz as a sideman with such younger eminences as Hamiet Bluiett, Craig Harris, and David Murray.

In fact, it was right after Byron had been fired by Bluiett, at a New York club called Carlos I in 1988, that I first introduced myself to him. Bluiett's Telepathic Orchestra (Leaving Too Much to Telepathy would have been more fitting) had just finished murdering Wayne Shorter's "Footsteps," and a frustrated Bluiett had waved Byron and another member of the reed section off of the bandstand, throwing a stool in their general direction for good measure. Byron said that this was a typical night with Bluiett—including the firing, which didn't necessarily mean that he was excused from playing the second set.

I learned something else from him that night. I assumed that the KCB had been just a gig for him—a way of getting his chops together for the big time. But he told me that he was now working Jewish affairs with his *own* band.

"Yeah, even though I was playing with all the heavy cats," Byron said, when I reminded him of that first conversation. "See, I left the KCB because it's difficult to be in a band with fourteen other people and get along with everybody year after year. But I was afraid that I would never play klezmer again, and I didn't want to lose that skill. I felt like one of those track-and-field cats who has nowhere to go after the Olympics. Ingrid Monson, one of the trumpeters in the band, who's Swedish, was leaving, too, and she felt the same way. I mean, it wasn't like the rabbis I met with the KCB were going to be calling *me* up and asking if I could make a gig at their synagogue. So Ingrid and I made a band together. No concert gigs, just weddings. She did the bookings, and I took care of the music.

"Nobody had a book like us. In fact, you gotta take a look at it, B." Byron said, fetching a bound volume of arrangements from the other room. He leafed past the klezmer transcriptions and the Israeli material to the Motown tunes. "I had twenty, maybe twenty-five Motown transcriptions, with those bad James Jamerson bass lines that bring the sound right out to the people on the dance floor. Plus things like 'Downtown,' 'Judy's Turn to Cry,' 'Cold Sweat, Part 2' . . ."

What about the Jewish stuff?

He flipped back to "Ayhar Nach Mein Chassene." "You know that one? It means 'a year after our wedding.' Let's hear *you* pronounce it, B."

I admitted that my Yiddish wasn't so good.

"Mine, neither," he said. "But when *I* say it wrong, it's supposed to be cute," he added in a dour voice, revealing just the proper amount of cynicism toward those audiences who find the idea of a black man doing that old yi-diddle-diddle just too adorable for words.

"I HEARD ALL SORTS OF MUSIC AROUND HERE WHEN I WAS GROWING UP," Byron said. "Now the neighborhood is mostly black and Hispanic, but there used to be a lot of Jewish families. That church on the corner," he said, gesturing toward the window, "used to be a synagogue. If you look close, you can still see the star above the door. I used to hear Jewish music on the radio, on *Bagels and Lox: Art Raymond's Sunday Simcha,* on WEVD, 'the station that speaks all languages.' My folks were almost militant about me checking out all different kinds of music, whether it was Dizzy at the Village Gate or Leonard Bernstein's Young Person's Concerts. You used to watch them on TV? Well, I was in the audience for some of them."

Byron's father is a retired mailman who, though not Jamaican, once played bass in New York calypso bands. "My mother's not a musician, but she's likely to sit down and play 'Clair de Lune' on that piano over there whenever the mood strikes her. She worked for the phone company, as one of the first generation of Adam Clayton Powell-installed blacks hired to do more than just sweep up the floors. She's retired now, but you still can't say anything bad about the phone company around her.

"Before clarinet, I played little knickknacky instruments, like recorder. What happened, we had a dog that I was allergic to, and the allergy developed into asthma. So the doctor recommended as therapy either swimming or a wind instrument. I have a phobia about going into the water, so I inherited a clarinet from the family pool of instruments."

Byron pointed to a copy of Lawrence Welk's *Save the Last Dance for Me* thumbtacked to the wall. "He had the only TV show where you ever saw anyone playing clarinet. That was my ambition—to play in his band and with the Conservatory Ragtime Ensemble, which I must have seen on PBS." Because I wanted to give Byron the benefit of the doubt by chalking some things up to camp, I had restrained myself from asking about Welk—and about the Neil Diamond song on his answering machine. But I did ask about the color poster of a dignified gentleman identified as Guy Deplus.

"Guy Deplus!" Byron exclaimed, and began to read the legend under the photo. "*Professeur de Clarinette du Conservatoire National Supérior de Musique de Paris!* My idol! Mister New Music. The clarinetist on the original recording of Messiaen's 'Quartet for the End of Time'!"

Jimmy Hamilton, Tony Scott, and Artie Shaw were Byron's favorites among jazz clarinetists. "Until Paul Gonsalves joined Duke, nobody in that band was playing any hipper shit than Hamilton. He was the hippest cat in a section of hip cats. Artie Shaw was bad, man. He was a better legit player than Benny Goodman, whose classical recordings are a joke among people who know that music—whether or not they'd want to say that in print. But it's not like I can steal lines from Artie or any other jazz clarinetist, because we're talking about an instrument that's been dead in the water since 1960, as far as jazz is concerned. I listen to saxophonists and pianists. Joe Henderson is really my man.

"You know, even before I started playing jazz, people in school had me stereotyped as a jazz player because I didn't look or talk Bryant Gumbel-ish, the way that most brothers in classical music tend to do. When I got into jazz, my friends were [the alto saxophonists] Greg Osby and Donald Harrison, from the Berklee School of Music. They were the baddest young cats in Boston at that time. For a while I wanted to do what they were doin'—get in front of a too-loud drummer and sound like Coltrane. But I was also running down to New York every chance I got to hear punked-out bands like Defunkt and James White and the Blacks.

"Klezmer was the first old music I ever responded to. Before that, I was one of those guys who wouldn't even watch silent movies, because I started thinking how most of the actors in them were probably dead and that would depress me. Hankus Netsky recruited me for this band he put together to play three klezmer tunes for a NEC faculty concert called 'Contemporary Dimensions of Twentieth-Century Jewish Music,' or something like that—the other faculty members played stuff by Leonard Bernstein and George Rochberg, but Hankus wanted to do something different. That was the beginning of the Klezmer Conservatory Band.

"At first, my attitude was, OK, you put a piece of music in front of me and I can deal with it. But I responded immediately to the *mischief* in that music: the place on each of the old records where the clarinetist would play the most *out* thing he could think of. It's not like in jazz, where a guy gets hot and takes another chorus. There might be just one exciting trill, but that's where the creativity was. Most of the young cats playing klezmer are just trying to sound like the old 78s. But those guys on the records were taking risks. That's what

I think I brought to klezmer that excited the rest of the band. Maybe some of the stuff I played was inappropriate, especially in the beginning. But at least I was doing something new. And as time went by, I developed my own voice in that language."

LATELY BYRON HAS CHANNELED HIS INTEREST IN KLEZMER INTO THE MUSIC of Mickey Katz, a clarinetist, singer, and noveltymeister of the 1950s, for whom indigestion was the ultimate Jewish experience—or so you might think from his "Bagle Call Rag," "Don't Let the Schmaltz Get in Your Eyes," "How Much Is That Pickle in the Window," and his devastating Mel Brooks-ian *schlemielization* of Tennessee Ernie's "Sixteen Tons":

> *To eat a piece* kishke,
> *you must have* koyech.
> *Just like a* shtayn,
> *it lays in your* boyech.

I knew that Katz, who died in 1985, once was an arranger for Spike Jones, and that he was Joel Grey's father and Jennifer's grandfather. What I wanted Byron to tell me, as he walked me back to Elder Avenue, was (a) whether he got all of Katz's Yiddish and Yinglish jokes, and (b) whether it was true what other klezmers had told me, that there were two Mickey Katzes: the *tumler* of the parodies and the maestro responsible for the scintillating *Music for Weddings, Bar Mitzvahs, and Brisses.*

"Nobody gets all the jokes, man, because nobody knows that much Yiddish anymore," claimed Byron, whose Mickey Katz band includes Patterson on trombone, Parran on reeds, Tony Barrera on trumpet, Mark Feldman on violin, Lee Musiker or Uri Caine on piano, Mark Dresser on bass, Richie Schwarz on drums and Mr. Bones xylophone, and Loren Sklamberg on vocals—sidemen whose collective credentials range from Ellington, Basie, and *Black and Blue* to Anthony Braxton, Steve Reich, Frank Zappa, and John Zorn.

"And no, you can't say there were two different Mickey Katzes, because that's one of the few instrumental albums he made like that, with just incidental vocals and patter. The rest of his stuff is the parodies which are very, very funny, including one called 'Paisach in Portugal' that I won't do in concert because it's got an awful *faygelah* joke. But on almost every record he ever made, that instrumental genius bursts through, usually when the band goes into that hora thing in the middle of the parody.

"The first time I heard him, it was 'Mickey's Dreidel,' one of the records from Hankus's collection, and I thought 'What is this? This stuff is *bad*. And whoever that is on clarinet sounds a little bit like *me*.' Because his playing had that athleticism I like. Getting a band together to play his music is something I've wanted to do for a long time, but I didn't know where I was going to find the musicians to do Mickey justice until I was on the road with Mercer Ellington. The lead trumpeter was Tony Barrera. Big, macho, Latino cat. We became running buddies. I asked him if he ever heard of Mickey's trumpeter, Mannie Klein. And he yelled, '*Mannie Klein!* That's my *man!*'"

SOMEBODY RECENTLY ASKED ME IF BYRON WAS IN KLEZMER'S "MAIN-stream." What a foolish question. Counting his there are perhaps only about half a dozen active klezmer bands, and the question worth asking about the rest of them isn't "mainstream or fringe"? but "Orthodox, Conservative, or Reform"? Klezmer is resolutely secular: for dancing, not davening. As Byron points out, "if religion is mentioned at all in the lyrics, it's usually to say, 'Oh, look at the rabbi. He's making a fool of himself by eating too much,' or something like that." But for many younger Jewish musicians, including those in the KCB, klezmer has become a source of cultural identity, growing desecularized in the process. These days, if you don't lock arms for the hora at the end of a KCB concert, you're worse than a spoilsport—you're probably a gentile (which I, in fact, *am,* though I know Jews who feel the same way). These bands make klezmer mirthless fun.

Byron doesn't have a sanctimonious bone in his body. As a non-Jew he responds to klezmer strictly as music (significantly, a style of music in which clarinet is undisputed king) and asks that his listeners do the same. Does his brand of klezmer smack of opportunism, all the same? Not at all. It's not as though there's much demand for this music even at catered affairs, where you're more likely to hear a mix of Motown, current Top 40, *Fiddler on the Roof* ("Sabbath Prayer" has become a favorite of with-it cantors who accompany themselves on electric guitar), and Israeli folk tunes (Hebrew is where the action is now). Besides which nobody—black or white—is going to make a bundle performing Mickey Katz, full appreciation of whose lampoons requires not only some fluency in Yiddish, but also some familiarity with (and maybe a peculiar affection for) that dreck-filled period of popular music between the demise of the big bands and the official birth of rock 'n' roll—a period so forgettable that not even Casey Kasem has a name for it.

Even so, Byron commands a loyal following, at least in New York. In April, he filled the Knitting Factory to at least twice its fire capacity (standing room only, and not much of that): the people you think you always see there (guys with ponytails dating from the *last* time men wore them) rubbing elbows with people who looked as though they had metaphorically crossed Delancey just for this. I suspected that word had leaked out that Joel Grey was going to be singing three of his father's parodies with Byron that night. The bartender said the club was always like this when Byron did Mickey Katz.

At any rate, unlike most klezmer audiences, this one was hip enough not to throw off the musicians' timing by attempting to clap along. My own entourage included a friend from Boston, a music critic specializing in rock and world beat who knew nothing about Byron and even less about Katz. We were curious to see his reaction. "This is delightful," he said over the amen ending of "Mazeltov Dances," echoing my sentiments exactly, but surprising me with his word choice (he usually indicates approval with words like *feral*). The music hooked him, as it had me, with its contrapuntal oomph. It was like the MJQ, but with wailing horns, ethnic charm, and a dab or two of Jelly Roll Morton and John Philip Sousa. Delightful was the word for it, all right.

"This is Jewish hip hop," Byron deadpanned in introducing Katz's "Litvak Square Dance." "Hope it's klezmer def and klezmer fresh enough for you. Know what I'm sayin'?" In addition to Katz's originals, parodies, and traditional arrangements, Byron also played a piece of his own called "Tears," accompanied by just Mark Dresser's bowed bass and Uri Caine's tolling piano-in-octaves. It was a lament for Katz combining elements of traditional Yiddish *doyne* and a cool meditation on the overtone series, with a slowed-down and deliciously extended quote from "Kiss of Meyer" (Katz's send up of Georgia Gibbs's "Kiss of Fire") toward the end.

"My father would have loved you!" Joel Grey told Byron when he joined him to sing "Tickle Tickle" ("Tico Tico"), "Geshray of de Vilde Kotcke" ("Cry of the Wild Goose"), and "Haim affen Range" (you shouldn't have to ask). Joel Grey at the Knitting Factory? I had seen Grey perform live once before, in a road show of *Cabaret.* And I do mean *seen,* not heard: suffering from laryngitis, he'd lipsynced his numbers while a backstage stand-in did the actual singing. But hearing him with Byron's band was like hearing *Cabaret* for real, if only because it revealed how much of his father's mocking delivery Grey had borrowed for his role as the Kit Kat Klub's master of ceremonies—especially for the S.S. favorite, "If You Could See Her Through My Eyes (She Wouldn't Look Jewish At All)." Grey exuded the right sort of theatricality, milking the laughs without overdoing it, pausing just long enough between jokes for the punch lines to sink in and not a second more. Between him and Byron, you had no doubt that you were hearing the definitive reinterpretation of Mickey Katz.

On the way home, I listened to the Mickey Katz tape that Byron had given me and found myself thinking about how Byron's musical ecumenism made him a kin of sorts to the first American klezmers. Like most professional musicians, then as now, klezmers were naturally curious about other ways of making music and prided themselves on their ability to deal with anything put in front of them. Take Mannie Klein, for example. In addition to working with Katz, he also played with Goodman and Dorsey, backed Frankie Laine on "That's My Desire," and dubbed bugle for Montgomery Clift in *From Here to Eternity.*

I remembered something Byron said about klezmer à la Mickey Katz: "It wasn't folk music, man. It was some *nasty, urban, ethnic* shit, B." Then I flipped over his cassette to find that he'd recorded King Curtis and Champion Jack Dupree on the other side.

(JULY 1990)

Out There

===

I'd left word with a friend of Charles Gayle's that I was looking for him, and he'd surprised me with a phone call. He was waiting for me, as promised, on the corner of Broadway and 10th, with his saxophone case by his feet. Even though I knew what he looked like from having seen him play, it took me a minute or two to spot him standing there by the curb away from the lunchtime crowd, completely inside himself, unnoticed and unnoticing. Maybe I was surprised just that he had shown up.

Although lunch was on *The Village Voice,* Gayle wasn't eating. He ordered just a muffin, then hardly touched it as we lingered in a coffeeshop on Astor Place, across from where the wretched of the earth dump old rags, shoes, and rained-on reading material on the sidewalk as though waiting for somebody to come along and bargain. (Who says capitalism no longer works?)

"Can I ask *you* a question?" Gayle wondered at one point, after I'd turned off my portable cassette player at his request.

No actual question was forthcoming.

"A lot of people are working and I'm not. I don't know why, and I don't know what to do about it," he finally said, after a pause, pointing a finger to his forehead and fixing me with a wary eye. "See, sometimes you can't get no work, you begin to think you must be terrible. Don't misunderstand me. I don't even know if I'm interested in that—the music business. It's just that I wouldn't mind working every once in a while. That's all."

This sudden plea caught me by surprise. Earlier in our conversation, after revealing that he earned just enough money for one meal a day by playing on the streets (his own music, he assured me, though he does take requests), he'd characterized that unprofitable form of self-enterprise as "the only honest alternative" for a black musician opposed to the almost exclusively white ownership of jazz venues.

Somehow, what he was saying now didn't strike me as a contradiction. What difference was one night at the Knitting Factory—or, for that matter, three nights there, like he said he had coming up on consecutive Sundays in December—going to make in the way he lived? I took a good look at him, noticing the gold cap over one of his bottom incisors and the string tied around his right pinkie. If he hadn't mentioned that he would be fifty-two in a few weeks, I would have taken him to be at least five years younger, despite the gray on his chin. Gaunt, with long, expressive fingers more like those of a pianist than a tenor saxophonist, he was neatly dressed in layers, with a blue denim jacket over a green plaid flannel shirt and a dark green T-shirt, and nobody was giving him a second glance.

"See, I still haven't solved the mystery of why anybody would want to listen to me," he'd said when we first sat down, trying to convince me that he wasn't going to be a very compelling interview subject, especially since questions pertaining directly to his past were understood to be off limits. "Wynton Marsalis can probably tell you who *he* is as a musician, and Sonny Rollins can tell you who he is, but I don't know who *I* am, because I'm not part of the music world, so I don't know how I'm regarded or if what I do even counts. I know there are some people who can hear themselves and evaluate whether they're good or bad. But I can't do that.

"I'm not trying to be modest. I just can't. I'm just a street person. I mean, I live in a squat in Bed Stuy. But I'm practically in the street. I will be again, soon."

After overhearing the part about the squat, our waiter rushed to refill our cups and assure us that the table was ours for as long as we liked.

I THINK THAT THE FIRST MENTION I EVER SAW OF CHARLES GAYLE WAS IN Bob Rusch's interview with Buell Neidlinger, in a 1986 issue of *Cadence.* Neidlinger, who played bass with Cecil Taylor before joining the Buffalo Philharmonic in 1962 and eventually becoming a first-call L.A. session man, remembered Gayle "pushing televisions around in the Westinghouse factory" in Buffalo. "I brought him down to New York [for a concert] in '67 or something like that . . . Pharaoh Sanders had his band, and Archie Shepp was playing. He blew them all off the face of the earth," Neidlinger said. According to Neidlinger, this mystery man had "stayed one day and went right back to Buffalo, [because] he couldn't deal with New York."

Rusch passed along the tantalizing information that Gayle was back in New York, "playing like a mother."

I heard no more about him until two years later, when Marty Kahn, whose Outward Visions handles Steve Reich, the Art Ensemble of Chicago, the World Saxophone Quartet, and other avant-garde fixtures, left me a phone message urging me to hear Gayle at the Knitting Factory. The gist of the message was that Gayle blew tenor with an intensity unmatched since Albert Ayler. What made the call different from any other I'd ever gotten from a bizzer was that it wasn't made on behalf of a client. Although circumstances prevented me from being there for Gayle's Knitting Factory debut, the euphoric word from friends who went was that Gayle's trio played unrepentant free jazz—that his music was "out there," as we used to say, way back when.

I sensed the beginning of a genuine, street-level buzz, maybe the first for an unrecorded performer since Wynton broke in with the Messengers in 1980, or since David Murray started to make a name for himself in the lofts a few years earlier. But unlike Murray and Marsalis, both of whom were then teenagers, Gayle was a middle-aged man (roughly the age that Ayler himself would have been, in fact) with an element of uncorrupted Bunk Johnsonism enhancing his credibility—though not for me.

In its own era free jazz (nonchordal improvisation after Ornette Coleman, but especially the winged multiphonics and glossolalia that followed Ayler's *Spiritual Unity* in 1965) and the militant nationalistic rhetoric that usually accompanied it were blamed for scaring away what little had remained of the jazz audience. In punishment free has been banished from most academic histories and magazine trend pieces tracing the evolution of modern jazz from bop to fusion to bop again. In jazz the 1960s have become the decade that never happened—or that never should have.

Yet I know (and so do you, if you get around enough) a type of romantic first-generation free jazz fan, now in his (always his) middle forties and usually (though not always) white, for whom free like it was in the 1960s, with indignant black men raising heaven's floor for hours at a stretch, is the only music that does the trick. Being first-generation myself (with the ESP Discs to prove it), I sympathize. But only to a point, because I suspect that this is my generation's moldy-fig primitivism.

I finally heard Gayle in Philadelphia, about a month after Kahn's phone call. As reported, Gayle's yawp was fierce enough to pin anybody's ears back. But as yawps go, it was a lot like Ayler's, though lacking both his melodic lurch and his thematic continuity. The concert was like somebody's foggy notion of a typical night at Slug's, circa 1966, with Dave Pleasant splintering drumsticks on his stripped-down kit, Hilliard Green plucking and bowing his bass with such force that it rocked, and Gayle scooping for high notes and bending from his waist for low ones. For its part, the audience got into the act by whooping and bowing forward rapidly as though davening, just like folks were said to do back when soloists measured their phrases by the breath, not the bar.

SAY WHAT YOU WILL ABOUT THE SUPERIORITY OF LIVE MUSIC, TAKE-HOME is sometimes preferable for sparing you the inevitably misanthropic exercise of comparing your reaction to that of everyone else in the room. In the early spring of 1988, just weeks after I'd dismissed him as a shuck, Gayle recorded *Homeless, Spirits Before,* and *Always Born,* the three Silkheart CDs that, when finally released earlier this year, forced me to reverse that judgment. Both *Homeless* and *Spirits Before* feature Gayle's trio, with Sirone (of Phalanx, The Group, and the Revolutionary Ensemble) on bass in place of Green. Sirone is also on hand, along with AACM drummer Reggie Nicholson, on *Always Born,* on which Gayle faces off against John Tchicai (who played alto on Coltrane's *Ascension,* but sticks to tenor and soprano here).

In other words Silkheart's Keith Knox, perhaps hedging just a bit, surrounded Gayle and Pleasant, both virtual unknowns, with impressively credentialed sidemen. Sirone, in particular, merits raves for his miniature symphonies of slurs, strums, and artfully timed double stops. But Tchicai frequently gets hung up on repeated phrases, never quite entering Gayle's orbit. And though Nicholson does fine, Pleasant is terrific. A heedless basher in concert, or so I thought (Sunny Murray taught him drumming in a hurry), he heats up *Homeless* and *Spirits Before* with a personal amalgam of vintage free drumming styles, ranging from Milford Graves's tabla patterns behind Giuseppi Logan to Sunny Murray's unmetered cymbal synapses behind Ayler and Cecil Taylor.

Gayle himself is the mind-bender, though. His longer solos are crap shoots, sometimes testing your patience along with his endurance (*Spirits Before*'s title cut, for example). But others—typified by *Homeless*'s "Then Creations," almost Monk-like in its gradual enlargement of a three-note theme—rivet you with their energy, control, and endless ripple of ideas. Gayle at his most impressive is Gayle at his most "accessible"—nothing wrong with that. The track I keep returning to is "Lift Ev'ry Voice and Sing," J. Rosamond Johnson's "black national anthem," here mistitled "Lift Every Voice" and consigned to the public domain. Fortified by Pleasant's lashing cymbals and Sirone's rolling bass, Gayle ravages the song, subjecting it to about six minutes of convulsive variations before allowing the melody to emerge in all its hardscrabble dignity, then brings it to a prolonged climax that's simultaneously turbulent and serene.

Published in 1900, with lyrics by James Weldon Johnson, the composer's brother, "Lift Ev'ry Voice" was a popular sign-off theme on black radio stations in the 1970s, which is probably how Gayle knows it. The only non-original on the three CDs, it begs comparison as an anthem to many of Ayler's humble little themes, and Gayle underscores the similarity by stretching his intervals and fluttering melismatically at the end of phrases. But the resemblance to Ayler is flattering enough to Gayle to seem circumstantial rather than the result of direct influence. "We must have been drinking from Lake Erie around the same time," Gayle quipped when I asked him about the Ayler connection. "He was from Cleveland, you know, and I'm from Buffalo."

"DID CHARLES GIVE YOU HIS POLITICAL RAP?" A FELLOW CRITIC ASKED ME alluding to the strange night at the Knitting Factory last June when Gayle spent most of a set haranguing whites for attempting to play jazz, pretending to appreciate it, and controlling its presentation. (Remember, Amiri Baraka's preferred term for "free jazz" was "the new black music.") That night has since become part of Gayle's legend, along with the time he supposedly requested a jar of baby food as his preconcert dinner.

The rap I got—maybe by virtue of facing Gayle across a table rather than being one white face among many in a darkened room—was softer and sadder. He told me that he was part Cherokee and that he had grown up in a Buffalo neighborhood in which all of the stores were black-owned-and-operated. "You could walk all over the city and feel that you were coming home to something that belonged to you," he said.

This was as autobiographical as he got. A friend of mine, who once worked as a graduate assistant in the Department of Adult Education at SUNY Buffalo, had told me that one of her co-workers there had been involved in a stormy relationship with Gayle. "That was my wife's name," he said when I mentioned the woman my friend remembered. But the silence that followed made it clear that he wasn't going to open the door any wider.

From talking with a few current and former upstate musicians, I did find out that Gayle himself once taught at the university, inheriting the jazz course from Charles Mingus in 1969. Somehow that piece of information wasn't as surprising as the news that one of his students was Jay Beckenstein, who later founded the wretchedly successful fusion group Spyro Gyra.

"I recall a funny scene with Charles trying to teach Jay how to play the blues," said the saxophonist Paul Gresham, another of Gayle's students, and later a member of his band. Gresham, who's still active around Buffalo, remembered Gayle as "the kind of musician who could pick up any instrument and play it well. When I was in his band, with both of us playing saxophone, he would often play piano behind my solos."

On the other hand, another Buffalo musician who requested anonymity told me that he thought Gayle "played free from start to finish, with no tonal center" because he was a late starter who never mastered chord changes or saxophone technique—an accusation that dogs every free musician. But according to Gresham, Gayle was "like Eric Dolphy in that respect. He would play inside the changes, but so fast and so completely that it might go right by you. It was inside, but it sounded outside."

Did Gayle have an audience upstate? This also depends on whom you ask. Gresham remembers him always packing the house, "whether it was some hole-in-the-wall club or a concert at the university." Then again, how often would a free player like Gayle have worked? Buffalo was a hotbed of avant-gardism in the early 1970s, with Robert Longo showing at Hall Walls; an experimental video scene forming around Steina and Woody Vasulka; Lukas

Foss conducting the Buffalo Philharmonic and commissioning works by John Cage, Morton Feldman, Lejaren Hillyer, and others; John Barth and Robert Creeley on the university faculty; and Allen Ginsberg in town for a drug symposium every other month or so. "But jazz was never included in that," says the drummer Bobby Previte, who grew up in nearby Niagara Falls. "The jazz scene was owned by the boppers. It must have been brutal for someone like Charles Gayle, coming out of late Coltrane and Albert Ayler. It was for me. That's why I'm in New York."

"IT WASN'T JUST BUFFALO. THERE WAS NO AUDIENCE FOR THAT KIND OF music all over, except maybe New York," Gayle told me, visibly considering but finally unable to answer the question of when he moved to New York, "because I was going back and forth for a long time."

Gresham remembers hearing Gayle in Greenwich Village with the drummer Rashied Ali's band around 1973. Otherwise, the years between Buffalo and now are a mystery.

As a general rule of thumb, neglected geniuses bear some complicity for their neglect. But I don't know what skeletons Gayle has in his closet, and he wasn't about to tell me. Still, we could talk about music. As we walked east on St. Mark's Place, I asked him why hardly anybody else was still playing free. I have my own pet theories, of course, one of which is that many of the style's originators are now too waddled in middle age to take many risks anymore, and another of which is that they grew so weary of hearing not just their musicianship but their sanity questioned that they themselves must have begun to wonder how many times they could go to the edge before forgetting their way back (Ayler wound up in the East River, after seeing flying saucers).

"It was just a fad," Gayle said, surprising me. "It didn't start off to be, but you know very well that it became that. They couldn't continue because it wasn't in them to continue. It was just the *time*."

What about him?

"It's just something in me. It's a fate that challenges you until it becomes very natural. You have to dig inside your soul and keep creating. You have to fight your memory, because it's easy to recapitulate. You keep pushing, because it's there, and you don't know what it is. You just keep going."

I asked him if he needed anything—a taxi to where he was going next, maybe?—but he wouldn't take my money.

TWO DAYS AFTER OUR MEETING, GAYLE FLEW TO AMSTERDAM ON A ONE-way ticket bought for him by one of his admirers. He'd heard that a musician could make a decent living playing in the streets there. A few weeks later I heard that he was back in New York again, inclement weather having prevented him from earning very much money. This bit of hearsay was from someone who knows someone else in New York so passionate about Gayle (the ultimate jazz cult hero, famous for longer than fifteen minutes, but known to only fifteen people) that she kept track of the weather in Amsterdam the whole time he was there. Again, I left word for him to call me, but he never did. In the library a few weeks ago, while researching another story, I considered looking up "Gayle" in the Buffalo telephone directory, to see if he still had relatives there. But I didn't have the heart.

Gayle showed up at the Knitting Factory for his gig the Sunday before Christmas, along with Dave Pleasant, Hilliard Green, and about two dozen late niters, including me. Thirty years ago Ornette Coleman, just in from California (some said the moon), confounded New Yorkers by not counting off his tunes. Gayle doesn't count off, either. He announced his presence with a sustained renal shriek, the first of many during the next forty-five minutes, which ended with him jackknifing into oblique staccato phrases that, given a different rhythmic underpinning, could have passed for R&B. Remember when reviewers used to complain that the problem with free jazz was that you could drop the needle down anywhere on the record and hear the same thing? To anyone ducking in and out of the club every five or ten minutes, Gayle's performance might have sounded as monomaniacal. But if you stuck with him, he overpowered you with his soaking emotionalism, his flying dynamics, his lovely and unexpected sobs of melody. It was free jazz not just like you remembered it, but like you always wished it could be.

(JANUARY 1991)

Gayle now works frequently enough to rent a small apartment.

White Anglo-Saxon Pythagorean

═══

Roswell Rudd, a trombonist now in his late fifties, will, regardless of what he accomplishes or fails to in his remaining years, always be identified with the jazz avant-garde of the 1960s, so indelible was his mark on it and its on him. Last summer I heard him sing "The Beer-Barrel Polka" as a member of a show band in a Borscht Belt resort and sound as though he was having a good time doing it. It would heighten the incongruity if I could say that I walked in on this by chance. But I didn't. I was looking for Rudd, and I knew exactly where to find him, thanks to an item in *Down Beat*.

Toward the back of each issue the magazine runs a feature called "Pro Session," in which a recorded improvisation is transcribed and analyzed for the edification of those readers who are themselves musicians. The subject of "Pro Session" in December 1990 was the pianist Herbie Nichols's 1955 recording of his own "Furthermore." The transcription and analysis were supplied by Rudd, who was identified as "a trombonist currently working in the Catskill Mountains at the Granit Hotel [in] Kerhonkson, N.Y.":

> He has recorded with Archie Shepp,
> Carla Bley, Gato Barbieri, Charlie
> Haden, and John Tchicai, and his
> recording, *Regeneration* (Soul Note)[,]
> with Steve Lacy and Han Bennink,
> included a number of Nichols'
> compositions.

No mention of Rudd's having thrice been voted best trombonist in the magazine's own International Jazz Critics Poll (in 1975, 1978, and 1979), or of his having finished no worse than seventh as recently as 1987, strictly on reputation (his last New York concert had been in 1983, and he hadn't been featured on a new jazz release since his appearance on one track of *That's the Way I Feel Now,* the auteur record producer Hal Wilner's 1984 double album of novel Thelonious Monk interpretations). Nor was there any hint of how

174

long Rudd had been in the Catskills—the last I'd heard, he was teaching in Augusta, Maine, at a branch of the state university—or of what on earth he was doing there.

Much of the romance of jazz improvisation is in its evanescence, and as if in keeping with this quality, jazz musicians themselves tend to disappear. Years ago when a musician vanished from the scene, it was usually for one of two reasons: drugs, or steady work either making TV-ad soundtracks ("jingles") in the recording studio or playing in the orchestras for films or Broadway shows, depending on which coast the person in question called home. Today when someone goes a few years between records or concerts, it's assumed that he's grown weary of improvising an income for himself and his dependents and has accepted a university teaching position or taken a day job. Or that he's become homeless.

But few musicians ever disappear completely or put away their horns for good, even after learning the hard way that there's very little chance for a big payoff in jazz. Pop musicians and their fans are often puzzled by this, for the same reason that screenwriters—even unproduced screenwriters—are puzzled by novelists, and even more so by poets (at least a novel is of some potential value as a "property"). Publication is almost anticlimactic for most poets. They just *write*. It's the same with most jazz musicians. Jazz isn't just a craft; it's a calling, and one that they can never completely stop heeding.

What about those of us who merely listen to jazz? Like serial monogamists, most of us find ourselves drawn to a certain type. Mine seems to be the Missing Person—the great player who drops out of sight. Browsing in record stores these days, or listening to many of the bland new releases sent to me to review, I feel as many voters say they do when forced to choose between equally unqualified candidates: there must be something better than this. That's when I begin to think of musicians like Roswell Rudd, unforgettable but apparently forgotten, and wonder what on earth has become of them.

IT WAS STICKY EVEN IN THE MOUNTAINS ON THE SATURDAY AFTERNOON last summer that my girlfriend and I drove to Kerhonkson, about twenty miles south of Woodstock. When we pulled into the parking lot of the Granit Hotel and Country Club, at around three o'clock in the afternoon, a band we later found out was the Sherri Orchestra—*not* the band with Rudd—was playing "Tea for Two" as a cha-cha next to the outdoor swimming pool. This was my first time in the Catskills, and I felt terribly out of place, despite having been briefed on Borscht Belt do's and don'ts by my companion, a Brooklyn native who had summered here with her parents when the Catskills were really something (what she meant was, before her parents and a massive number of Jews of their generation retired to Florida, for summer all-year-round). My alienation wasn't entirely due to my not being Jewish (the activities sheet we picked up in the lobby on checking in listed bocci, and where there's bocci there must be Italians), nor to my companion and I being among a distinct minority of guests under retirement age. The problem was my aversion to group activities and my bewilderment at other people's enthusiasm for them. Fortunately for me, participation in the Granit's daily shuffleboard tournament was optional, as it was in the basketball free throw contest, the isometric exercises with Sam, the financial seminar with George Kimmel, the class in skin care and "hi" fashion with Miss Jeri of Estelle Durant Cosmetics, and the open discussion (presumably on the day's burning issues) with Trudy Berlin. By virtue of our late arrival we'd missed all of these events anyway. But if we hurried, we could still compete in the daily ping pong tournament, take a lesson in ballroom dancing from the Tiktins, and mingle at the happy hour in the Mystic Lounge (to the music of somebody calling himself Ralph Mellow).

Such an industrious approach to leisure struck me as Protestant, not Jewish. But my companion said that the old adage about the devil finding work for idle hands had nothing to do with it. Keeping yourself occupied from morning on was a way of ensuring that you were getting your money's worth, since most of the activities were *included,* as they say in the Catskills. So were meals and anything in between, she added, which meant never saying no to that second helping or dessert, regardless of what restrictive diet your doctor might have you on back home. To hear her tell it, food was to the Catskills as slots were to Atlantic City, the difference being that here you played games with your cholesterol, instead of with quarters. Shuffleboard and the rest of it were just something to do between feedings.

The day's most looked-forward-to activity was dinner, which she said was going to remind me of one of her family's catered affairs without the bar mitzvah boy or the bride and groom. Were we staying at the Granit for a month or the entire season, the maitre d' would call on his knowledge of human nature to seat us at a table with couples just like ourselves, with whom we would make friends for life, perhaps even planning to meet here again in coming summers. As things stood, however, we'd probably be put wherever there were two empty seats. Even so, she warned, small talk would be expected of me.

As we rounded the lobby into the Golden Tiara Nite Club for predinner cocktails (another excuse for noshing, because everybody knows it isn't wise to drink on an empty stomach), we heard an innocuous bossa nova above the chatter of those already helping themselves to hors d'oeuvres. It was Burt Bacharach's "The Look of Love," being played (we surmised) by David Winograd and the Granit Orchestra, the seven-piece combo that would be backing the comedian Nipsey Russell and the singer Karen Saunders at the Tiara's "Broadway Showtime" in just a few hours. Before we could spot the musicians, a trombonist broke free of the ensemble just long enough to let loose three staccato blats. He then smeared Bacharach's melody into a lopsided glissando before blending into the other horns.

I think I would have recognized that sound anywhere, and the absurdity of the setting only intensified my delight. I jokingly asked my friend what she thought our chances were of being seated for dinner with others like us who were here just to listen to the band. It should have bothered me that nobody else was paying Rudd much attention. But sometimes it's better that way—anybody who loves jazz so much that he's become somewhat possessive about it (and somewhat resigned to other people's hearing it as background music) will know what I mean. I didn't even mind it when, during the band's version of Kool and the Gang's "Celebration," an *alter kocker* doing an arthritic lindy hop in front of the tuxedoed musicians admonished "No, no, rock-and-roll," clapping his hands on the wrong beat as Rudd stretched the funk rhythm deliriously out of shape. More important, Rudd didn't seem to mind either.

THIRTY YEARS AGO WHEN RUDD WAS A NEW FACE IN JAZZ, THE CRITIC Martin Williams praised him for combining "the robust earthiness of a Kid Ory plus all the refinements jazz trombone has been through since, including some of the latest developments in [jazz] as a whole." The comparison to Ory—the trombonist in Louis Armstrong's Hot Five and Jelly Roll Morton's Red Hot Peppers, and a rallied-around figure in the Dixieland revival of the 1940s—was no idle hyperbole. Rudd, while still an undergraduate at Yale, had recorded two albums of Dixieland as a member of a ragtag collegiate outfit called Eli's Chosen Six. This was before he obtained citizenship in the New York avant-garde through his association with Steve Lacy, Archie Shepp, Bill Dixon, and Cecil Taylor. An ironic consequence of Rudd's apprenticeship as an Ivy Leaguer playing Dixieland, a style that demands a vocalized approach from its horn players, was that he became the first (and, until the emergence of George Lewis, Ray Anderson, Craig Harris, and several Europeans in the 1970s and 1980s, the only) trombonist capable of matching split tones and glossal outbursts with saxophonists who were bidding their horns to speak in tongues.

This is how innovation usually spreads in jazz: one or two or as many as three or four players make breakthroughs on their horns, and the rank and file play catch-up. In that fashion J. J. Johnson became the ne plus ultra of bebop trombonists by negotiating Charlie Parker's and Dizzy Gillespie's harmonic abstractions and fleet eighth-note runs with his slide. (His West Coast counterpart was the sadly overlooked Frank Rosolino.) In the case of many of Johnson's followers, though, as in the case of those who sought to emulate Tommy Dorsey's unperturbed lyricism, this meant ignoring the trombone's potential for mirth. Zipping around on their horn as though the instrument were a darker-toned and only slightly unwieldy trumpet, they sounded like fat men running up stairs with huge bundles. They were ill suited to free improvisation, though many of them tried their hand at it.

Rudd achieved his primacy among free trombonists without emulating Ornette Coleman, John Coltrane, Albert Ayler, Archie Shepp, or any of the other pacesetting saxophonists of the 1960s. He simply reversed the process begun by Johnson, reacquainting the horn with the whoops and hollers, the slow-motion horse laughs and elephant snorts, that had been part of its jocular vocabulary before bop.

Thanks to his sprung time and his knack for locating dissonances between positions on his slide, he was able to do this without sounding like an old-timer who had wandered into the wrong gig. Even on dirges (his forte, as such composers as Michael Mantler and Carla Bley quickly realized), he often sounded as if he were shouting or laughing or cursing into his mouthpiece, with or without a plunger stuck in the bell of his horn to facilitate such vocal effects.

The other keepsake of his Dixieland experience that made Rudd such a valuable asset in free jazz was his commitment to collective improvisation. The problem with much bebop is that the musicians playing it are simply blowing on chord changes rather than taking full advantage of the melody and rhythm. The problem with free jazz is that even though the chord changes have been dispensed with, the musicians are frequently still just blowing. The New York Art Quartet, the band that Rudd co-led with the alto saxophonist John Tchicai for a short time in the 1960s, was notable for many virtues, not the least of them the contrapuntal chatter that Rudd and Tchicai kept up behind each other's solos. Rudd's presence in a band of more than four or five pieces practically guaranteed attention to color and dynamics. It also guaranteed levity. He brought a touch of John Philip Sousa to one of Archie Shepp's best small groups of the late 1960s, and, a decade or so later, gleefully played the ham in the midsize ensemble led by Carla Bley, a composer who doesn't so much select sidemen as cast them to type.

Rudd's sense of himself as first and foremost an ensemble member was so unshakable that when an Italian label invited him to make a solo album, he chose instead to overdub himself singing and playing piano, bass, drums, and even extra trombone parts. That was in 1979, on *The Definitive Roswell Rudd* (Horo), an eccentric tour de force that proved to be his last opportunity to date to record an album of his own compositions. Three years later, he made *Regeneration,* featuring three pieces by Thelonious Monk as well as three by Herbie Nichols, for Soul Note, another Italian label. It was his last complete album.

THE PEOPLE SEATED NEXT TO US AT DINNER TURNED OUT TO BE CATSKILLS regulars, a couple in their early fifties, who informed us that the Granit was strictly Grade B, right down to the entertainment. "The Concord gets Paul Anka, the Granit gets Robert Merrill," the wife complained. "If you don't have to ask if somebody's still alive, they're too big for the Granit."

Maybe so, but I doubt that any other Catskills resort boasts a band capable of jamming so euphorically on "Mack the Knife." To my surprise Rudd wasn't the only band member with impressive professional credentials: the lineup also included Bobby Johnson, about whose trumpet solo on Erskine Hawkins's 1945 recording of "Tippin' In" Gunther Schuller wrote (in his landmark book, *The Swing Era*) that it was "so admirably conceived and executed" that "one assumes the presence of one of the great trumpet stars of the period, not the well-nigh forgotten Bobby Johnson." This missing person sang a few numbers in a swaggering voice reminiscent of Jimmy Rushing's and still played with effortless grace, despite appearing to be in his early seventies.

I actually enjoyed the show. Karen Saunders, a fine young singer whom I had never heard of, delivered a convincing "The Man I Love," with Rudd supplying a virile plunger obbligato on the slow intro. And Nipsey Russell broke up the band with a joke about a bygone Harlem jazz club where "they had an intermission every twenty minutes, to wheel out the dead and injured."

"I don't think Nipsey was having a good night, though," Rudd said, on joining us later in the Mystic Lounge. (The ivory tickler there *now* was Irving Fields, the composer of "The Miami Beach Rhumba," practically a Borscht Belt anthem, "Managua, Nicaragua," a number one hit for both Guy Lombardo and Freddie Martin in 1947, and "Chantez, Chantez," a ditty popularized by Dinah Shore in 1957. And can you think of a better name for a songwriter than Irving Fields?) "He wasn't working the audience the way I've seen him do. He stuck to the usual order of his routines.

"Comedians are like the jazz musicians of the Borscht Belt," continued Rudd, who's closer to average in height and build than the yawp of his horn would lead you to expect. A caricature of him would emphasize his watery hazel eyes and his auburn and gray beard, which his wife says she would leave him if he ever shaved. "The high priest of comics here—the most original and articulate—is Mal Z. Lawrence. Then there's Ralph Pope, Jay Jason, Lenny Rush, and Mickey Marvin. I don't know if you've ever heard of any of them, but they're incredible. And they *do* improvise, within a set form. They work with a set number of variables—like a musician would with, say, twelve tones—and they shift the order of things according to how the audience is reacting. They usually start out the same and have a big thing they do at the end that brings it to a peak and lets them bow out gracefully. Like a final coda or cadenza. But in the middle, you never know where they're going next. That's the exciting part."

The following afternoon my companion and I drove to Accord, a few miles east, for brunch with Rudd and his wife, Moselle Galbraith. They live on a secluded dirt road, in a one-story house as narrow as a trailer and laid out like a railroad flat. The house, though less crowded than when the couple's son, Christopher, and Moselle's two daughters from a previous marriage still lived with them, is so small that Rudd wouldn't be able to extend his slide in it without poking a hole in the ceiling or knocking Galbraith's knickknacks off the mantelpiece. (Counting Rudd's grown son from his first marriage, he and his wife have four children—"his, hers, and theirs," as Galbraith puts it.) There wouldn't be room in the house for a piano. In order to practice or to compose music, Rudd has to go deep into the nearby woods, where he says he sings and chants and dances the notes out, in addition to "just letting it burn on my horn, which I have to be careful *not* to do on the job."

It soon became apparent that the house wasn't the proper site for an interview. Galbraith, who suffers from various respiratory and intestinal ailments, was having a bad day on account of the heat (she was unable even to lift her weight out of her chair in front of the air-conditioner to change from her nightgown and to comb her matted hair). So Rudd and I spoke at length on the phone a few nights later, interrupted only when Moselle had him hunt for their shih tzu, the smallest of their four dogs, who had crawled underneath the sofa.

Rudd was born in Sharon, Connecticut, in 1935. Despite his Hotchkiss and Yale education, he doesn't come from money. A small inheritance long since spent was all that enabled him and his wife to relocate to the Catskills in 1982, two years after Rudd was denied tenure by the University of Maine. Both Rudd's parents were teachers in private schools, and his father—a record collector and avocational drummer—introduced him to jazz. One of his father's records that made an especially vivid impression on him was the Woody Herman Orchestra's recording of "Everywhere," featuring the tune's composer, Bill Harris, on trombone.

"It just killed me," Rudd told me. "I think a lot of it had to do with it being his own composition. It wasn't like he had to bring his musical personality to bear on somebody else's form. The song was *his,* and it was like I could tell that right away." (Rudd later reinterpreted Harris's ballad—half smoldering romantic reverie, half drunken army reveille—as the title track on his first LP in 1966). The other family member who helped to steer Rudd into music was his grandmother, "a Methodist church lady who was the director of her choir and who, on the out chorus of the hymns, would improvise a descant super libre in a high, pneumatic voice and just soar over the entire choir."

Rudd spoke with excitement about his grandmother (whom he once compared to the trumpeter Cat Anderson, the high-note specialist in Duke Ellington's band) and a number of other musical topics, including the marching bands in which he played French horn in as a teenager ("Your section was integrated into the other sections: a post-Industrial Revolution, urban hierarchical, almost Wagnerian kind of thing"); Greenwich Village jam sessions in the early 1960s ("There would be as many as ten horns up there, and as a guy would be soloing, the other horns would be riffing behind him, harmonizing the riffs, and it would be like Duke Ellington used to do, only happening spontaneously"); and a love for battered upright pianos, with their weird overtones, which he inherited from Herbie Nichols, the maverick pianist who was mentor of sorts to him ("The last one I had, in Maine in 1982, just collapsed from the tension of the strings on a rotten frame").

Rudd's talk about music—which is probably all he would ever talk about if given a choice—made it obvious that he wasn't burned out on jazz and just going through the motions at the Granit. After talking with him, I still don't know the complete answer to how he got where he is. The long and the short of it might be that jazz brought him little fortune and only marginal fame. As tastes in jazz became more conservative, he found himself stigmatized, despite his consummate musicianship, as someone supposedly incapable of doing anything but making noise on his horn. He was already teaching part-time at Bard and working on and off for the folklorist Alan Lomax when the offer came along to join the faculty at Maine in 1976. In Augusta his efforts to integrate raga and other improvisational world music forms into a jazz curriculum displeased his department head, who, one assumes, wanted a real teacher, not a gifted eccentric. After relocating to the Catskills, where a friend had a handyman's special for sale, he worked sporadically in area clubs for a few years before successfully auditioning for David Winograd at the Granit in 1986.

RUDD'S WIFE, A NATIVE NEW YORKER OFTEN MISTAKEN AS JEWISH, LIKES to joke that he's too "white bread" for the Catskills. But even though the only stretch of green visible from the Granit's lobby is the golf course, Kerhonkson itself is rural, and Rudd says he's always more at home in rural settings (his fondest memory of Maine is its green summers, which he says "just *raged* with life"). A self-described "White Anglo-Saxon Pythagorean," Rudd is the sort of easygoing bohemian unassuming fellow who gets along just fine with everyone. My girlfriend didn't even mind his addressing her as "Doll," though I'd like to see anyone else try to get away with it. Rudd was one of very few whites welcomed into the inner circle of militant black musicians amid the tumult of the 1960s. "At the time, in New York, a major topic of discussion was the reality of being black and playing this music versus the reality of being white and attempting to play it from a black perspective," Bill Dixon, a trumpeter and composer now tenured at Bennington, recalled during a recent conversation we had about Rudd. "But Roz fit right in because of his musicianship and, I would have to say, his personality."

Told how Rudd was now making his living, Dixon said, "It just proves that being a wonderful musician isn't enough anymore. But you know, in one sense, he's fortunate." Rudd could be driving a taxi or painting houses or working as a plumber, a carpenter, or a camp counselor—all jobs that he has held at one time or another. (His most interesting day job was with Lomax, helping to analyze "Cantometrics," which can be roughly defined as the measure of "song" in various ethnic musics.) Rudd's hotel job pays family health benefits, which were a blessing when he still had teenagers living at home, and are perhaps even more of a blessing now, given his wife's poor health. The job also gets him out of the house and lets him take pride in his craft. In some ways he's a better musician now than he was before. His sight-reading has improved, and he and his six bandmates have had a lot of practice in paring down big-band arrangements that some of the Granit's headliners bring along with them. He's come to place a higher value on showmanship. "No matter how tired they might be or how few people are in the audience, the performers here go onstage and deliver," he told me, admiringly. After speaking with Rudd, I saw his beloved Mal Z. Lawrence in a video excerpt from the show *Catskills on Broadway,* and thought he was nothing special. But even though Rudd might be giving run-of-the-mill Borscht Belt tummlers too much credit in comparing them to jazz improvisers, his enthusiasm for them suggests that he is one of those artists on whom nothing is wasted.

The drawbacks to the job at the Granit begin with the nagging feeling that a musician of Rudd's stature belongs somewhere else, doing something better. As the last member of Winograd's band to have been hired, he's the first to be laid off when business at the hotel is slow, as it was this past winter. Even when on full-time salary at the hotel, he has to drive a bread truck five mornings a week in order to make ends meet. A number of prominent jazz musicians live in Woodstock or nearby towns, but there's no local jazz scene to speak of—unfortunately for Rudd, whose essentially passive nature makes him one of those musicians able to blend easily into an existing scene but unable to start one around themselves. Bandleaders he worked with years ago still call him occasionally with offers to go to Europe for a few weeks, but because he's reluctant to leave his job unprotected and his wife uncared for, he routinely turns them down. He's said no so often that some musicians have wrongly concluded that he's just not interested anymore.

This June, however, Rudd surprised everybody—possibly including himself—by accepting an offer to bring a quintet to Italy, for the Verona Jazz Festival. (His travel costs were defrayed by Arts International, an organization that provides assistance to American performers invited to participate in festivals overseas.) Rudd was scheduled to play outdoors, but rain forced his concert into an auditorium with no amplification. Nevertheless, Rudd returned in excellent spirits. "It was beautiful to play some music," he told me, implying a distinction between what he had performed at the festival—several of his own recent compositions, plus his arrangements of a few of Herbie Nichols's tunes and Kid Ory's "Creole Trombone"—and his nightly fare at the hotel.

He also said something that struck me as inconsequential at first but that I later realized summed up the unaccustomed elbow room the trip had afforded him. "At the hotel I'm sitting behind a music stand all night. It felt good to stand up, to do my little dance as I played. They'll be sending me a video of my set. It'll be a chance for me to see myself in flight."

One gig hardly amounts to a comeback, but there might soon be others, including a foreign tour by the reassembled New York Art Quartet, featuring Rudd, John Tchicai, the drummer Milford Graves, and the bassist Reggie Workman. In the meantime Rudd is at least playing music, even if it's only "The Look of Love."

(SEPTEMBER 1992)

Rudd has subsequently recorded with Steve Lacy, Archie Shepp, the New York Art Quartet, and under his own name. An example of interventionist criticism, this piece played some small part in bringing him back into circulation.

RECURRING CHARACTERS

The Unsure Egoist
Is Not Good for Himself

====

Although it's beset with galling inconsistencies, *Star People* (Columbia) finally delivers the testimony his more optimistic fans have been anticipating from Miles Davis ever since the tarnished trumpet idol broke his long silence two summers ago. The wait has been painful. The gameness of Davis's solos on 1981's *The Man with the Horn* (Columbia) compensated neither for a puffy tone symptomatic of six years of inactivity nor for the numbing clamor of the two electric guitarists he had taken under his wing. And 1982's live double *We Want Miles* (Columbia), which reeked of the stale odors of sports-arena fusion and heavy-metal exertion, sounded especially ponderous compared with the sleeker, friskier, funk-influenced jazz of Ornette Coleman, Ronald Shannon Jackson, and James Blood Ulmer. Of course, many listeners who felt exactly as I did about *We Want Miles* bought it anyway. And I should talk—I bought it, too, which only goes to prove that the Miles we want and the Miles we're willing to settle for are often entirely different creatures. The set did have its moments, though they were few and far between. "Jean Pierre's doddering nursery-rhyme theme was oddly contagious, even if the leader was the only soloist who really seemed to "catch" it either time around (his "Lullaby of Broadway" quote on take one was especially wry). There was a boldly phrased, going-for-the-limit trumpet solo on "Back Seat Betty," and the soprano saxophonist Bill Evans (not to be confused with Yusef Lateef) tried valiantly to sustain the mood of Davis's improvisations, though the effect wasn't always pleasurable when he succeeded. (It's impossible to say at this point whether Evans is a player of rare sensitivity or just Fashionable Mr. Hybrid.) What was most distressing about both *The Man with the Horn* and *We Want Miles* was how dated their licks sounded in light of all that happened in jazz and pop during Davis's withdrawal—no wonder he had Ulmer's group bumped from the bill at his 1981 Kool Jazz Festival comeback concert, and no wonder that wags were suggesting he title his next LP *The Unsure Egoist Is Not Good for Himself,* from a line by the poet Robert Creeley.

With *Star People,* though, Davis has partially regained his confidence and his knack for telling understatement. The centerpiece of the album is the title track, a 19-minute slow blues as basic and as savoury as any Davis has ever recorded and a proving ground for his continued eloquence with Harmon mute. "Star People" gathers power as Davis and his resourceful drummer Al Foster (whose shadings gave both *The Man with the Horn* and *We Want Miles* the illusion of swing) up the improvisational ante on each of the trumpeter's three solo turns, until the suspense is its own payoff. Parceling out notes in a conversational mid-range, Davis stirs excitement not with blinding speed or stratospheric bolts but with mounting rhythmic complexity and tensile-strength in his ever-lengthening phrases; all the while, Foster's terse (post-dubbed?) afterbeat, distant at first, is encircling wider areas of rhythm, growing denser and more combustible. As "Star People" opens, Davis is spraying notes on the Oberheim organ, a ploy he repeats to dramatic effect following an edit 12 minutes into the cut; along the way Evans preaches briefly on tenor, and the guitarist Mike Stern boomerangs BB King-like blue notes so grand you hardly notice how derivative they are.

The title cut dwarfs the rest of the album, but there are two other notable workouts. Davis and Evans supply lightly dancing horn solos on the engaging "U 'n' I," a breezy melody bumping along on the fat bottom of Marcus Miller's Fender bass lines. "It Gets Better" is another slow blues, with sly Davis choruses and savvy fills by John Scofield, the subtler, warmer-toned guitarist who alternates with Stern. The rest is uneven. "Come Get It" boasts a fine Davis solo based on the fanfare from Otis Redding's "Can't Turn You Loose," but the band vamps endlessly before sliding in gear behind the leader and thunders off track completely once he has spoken his piece. "Speak" is an elephantine dance riff that stumbles under its own weight, and "Star on Cicely" fails to exploit a misterioso guitar-and-soprano-saxophone voicing contributed by Gil Evans, who attended the recording session in a troubleshooting capacity, according to the liner notes (another full-scale Davis/Evans collaboration is always rumored to be on the drawing board, but don't hold your breath).

Davis's reign as an avatar might be over; jazz has splintered into so many factions that no single album can reverberate the way *The Birth of the Cool* did in 1949, or *Kind of Blue* in 1959, or *Bitches Brew* in 1970. Still, *Star People* reassures us that one of the greatest living improvisers is still committed to and capable of making soul-nourishing music—something that didn't seem at all certain just a few months ago.

(MAY 1983)

II

In jazz circles, *You're under Arrest* (Columbia) has gained instant notoriety as the album on which Miles Davis plays, among other things, tunes associated with D Train, Cyndi Lauper, and Michael Jackson. The Jackson hit "Human Nature" is little more than glorified filler, but D Train's "Something's on Your Mind" is the album's most spirited workout, and Lauper's "Time after Time," with its pellucid melody and mournful harmonic suspensions, proves to be a surprisingly effective vehicle for Davis, who, come to think of it, has long nurtured an affection for slow-motion ballads of just this sort. But unlike his classic showtune interpretations of the 1950s, which begged comparison to nothing save one another, "Time after Time" is essentially a jazz instrumental cover of a recent pop vocal smash—Cyndi Lauper, not Miles Davis, supplies the context, and it's ominous to realize that the most cocksure of jazz musicians no longer feels he is in a position to call his own tune, at least not when radio programmers might be listening in.

You're under Arrest's original material (by Davis, the guitarist John Scofield, and the synthesizer player Robert Irving III) also tilts in the direction of pop—more specifically, what the trade papers call urban contemporary—with reinforced guitar and synthesizer licks which suggest that, like the rest of us, Miles spent last summer listening to *Purple Rain*. It's tempting to dub this music post-fusion: though it might seem like one more permutation of the jazz/rock synthesis Miles presaged with *Bitches Brew*, it's slinkier, brighter, and infinitely more enticing—only "Katia," with its keynote John McLaughlin guitar hyperbole echoes the murk and tumult of Davis's mid-'70s concert LPs and last year's wretched *Decoy* (Columbia). There are a number of attractive melodies here—most notably Davis and Irving's hooky "Ms. Morrisine"—and Davis plays superbly. Still, though his solos wound deeply, their pensive melancholy is frequently out of whack with the orgiastic bumping on the rhythm tracks, and the contrast is jarring in ways that seem unintentional. This is party music for stay-at-homes: it might be good dance music, but it's hardly likely to get anyone up on the dance floor.

Poor Miles. As a thinking man's pop star, he's unbankable in a market that increasingly depends on conditioned reflex. As a jazz panjandrum, he's been trading on credit for far too long. To judge from the leather and embroidery and mascara he affects in the cover photograph, even his fashion sense has deserted him: fine Italian silk is in again, thanks to his anointed heir and label mate Wynton Marsalis. It's easy to say that music is music and categories don't count—the standard line of Miles apologists—but it's difficult to imagine either a jazz or pop audience being thrilled with *You're under Arrest*, modestly diverting though it may be.

(JULY 1984)

Talking with Miles

===

You talk to me like I was just born with a trumpet in my mouth and that was it. Man, I *studied*," scolded Miles Davis, the only musician I ever phoned on behalf of *The Philadelphia Inquirer* who sounded disappointed when he found out it wasn't *The National Enquirer.* "I'm a musician, right?" he asked rhetorically, in that raspy whisper. "I deal in styles. I play different styles, you understand? When I'm in a Chinese restaurant, I eat Chinese food. When I'm in a Japanese restaurant, I eat Japanese. When it's a ballad, I play a ballad. If it's funky, I do that. The same way I treated *Sketches of Spain,* I treated *Tutu.* I treat all music the same. Respect it, and do your best. If you can't do it, don't even try. I don't *try* anything, I do it."

Davis, enduring the interview in his Central Park apartment, said he'd just come back from Los Angeles, where he spent the better part of a month laying down tracks for a new album, his second for Warner Brothers after thirty years with CBS. Although he'd reveal only that it would contain "more music," his current listening preferences—"everybody on the black stations: Cameo, Prince, Jimmy Jam, Colonel Abrams, the Time, Michael, Janet, everybody," he said, turning the radio up full blast and holding it against the phone, becoming annoyed when I couldn't make out what was playing—indicate that his next LP will be another attempt to get on the good foot, just like last year's *Tutu* (Warner Brothers).*

---

*Not exactly. Davis's next release was *Music from Siesta* (Warner Brothers), the soundtrack from a pretentious 1987 film directed by Mary Lambert and starring Ellen Barken. If this was the album that Davis had just come back from recording when I spoke with him, no wonder he mentioned *Sketches of Spain.* In addition to boasting the most haunting solos that Davis had recorded since 1983's *Star People,* the soundtrack was also fascinating as the composer and producer Marcus Miller's homage to Gil Evans—a synthetic *Sketches of Spain,* as it were. This was ironic, given that Miller was prematurely praised by some critics for evoking Evans on the deplorable *Tutu.* *Music from Siesta* had more orchestral verisimilitude, though it sounded like a stunt.

190

That'll strike some people as good news. After all, *Tutu* won Davis a Grammy for the best performance by a jazz soloist. But here's what puzzles many of his longtime admirers, myself included. If, as Davis seems to believe, music is music, and staying contemporary isn't the issue, why doesn't he surprise everyone with an acoustic jazz album?

"You know people who think that? I don't think they think that. You don't know the public. The public is a lot hipper than you think they are. You don't know what the fuck you're talking about, Francis." Miles is notorious for not granting many interviews and not being especially cooperative when he does. Yet like many public figures who have been interviewed thousands of times over the years, he's mastered the trick of remembering and periodically using his interrogator's name—the difference is that he uses your name when he's cussing you out. This should add insult to injury, but it's actually pretty charming. It does make exact quotation in a paper like the *Inquirer* difficult, however, and yet to bowdlerize him does him an obvious disservice, because his profanity gives his speech its rhythmic thrust, much the way Philly Joe Jones's rim shots once propelled his solos. Once an interviewer demonstrates that he can withstand Davis's rancor, he becomes surprisingly open, answering the questions he thinks he *should* have been asked.

DAVIS IS ONE OF THE HALF DOZEN OR SO MOST IMPORTANT FIGURES IN jazz history, and the only musician active in the bop era whose work still incites controversy. Only Duke Ellington has had as far-ranging and as long-lasting an influence on other musicians, and only Louis Armstrong, Charlie Parker, and Ornette Coleman have altered the course of jazz more abruptly. In the forties and fifties, when bop and cool were still regarded as antithetical, Davis played a large role in the gestation of each, going straight from an apprenticeship with Charlie Parker to collaborations with Gil Evans, Lee Konitz, and Gerry Mulligan. *Kind of Blue,* recorded in 1959, with John Coltrane, Cannonball Adderley, and Bill Evans, anticipated nearly every significant development of the next decade, including free form, modal impressionism, and soul. The harmonically spacious, metrically suspended music he played with Wayne Shorter, Herbie Hancock, Ron Carter, and Tony Williams in reaction to Coleman in the mid-sixties remains the dominant style of jazz two decades later, although no one has yet put a satisfactory label on it. In 1969, Davis became an avatar of jazz-rock fusion when he hired the guitarist John McLaughlin and recorded *In a Silent Way* and *Bitches Brew.* Ironically, just as his defection to electric music alienated many of his older fans, there are now younger listeners who mourn Davis's rejection of fusion for a slicker brand of funk.

For twenty-five years, beginning in the late forties, Davis's music was a sure index of progress in jazz, and one cannot attach too much significance to the fact that jazz took a nearly fatal commercial dive during the six-year period (1975–81) that Davis withdrew from recording and live performance. But since his comeback five years ago, Davis has no longer been setting trends, just following them. In attempting to crack urban contemporary radio, he isn't selling out so much as buying in—the baddest horn in jazz gamely trying to impress his badness on younger black listeners for whom a horn is merely a prop for puttin' on the hits. Still, the hit single that Davis needs to establish contemporary relevance continues to elude him. At this point, following his Honda commercials and his guest shots on *Crime Story* and *Miami Vice,* he's in danger of becoming a celebrity, one of those people famous for being famous.

On stage, he remains the most electrifying figure in jazz. He has his best band in years, with the tenor saxophonist Gary Thomas and the percussionist Marilyn Mazur prominently featured. Thomas plays dark, slow-building solos that match Davis's own for lyrical intensity, and Mazur—caged in by her various floor drums and overhanging rhythm tubes on an elevated perch at stage right—is fun to watch crawling around even before she leaps down alongside Miles to shake the bells on her ankles and hips ("Miles' percussion slave," a friend of mine described her). Miles himself has become a kind of roving conductor, walking from musician to musician, describing the rhythms he wants from them with a pump of his shoulders, blowing riffs in their faces and letting them pick it up from there. He still spends a good deal of each set with his back turned to the audience, like he was scolded for doing in the fifties and sixties. The difference now is that he has a microphone attached to his horn that allows him to be heard with his back turned—and, at this point, audiences would be disappointed if he failed to strike this iconic pose. The last time I saw him, he was in an uncharacteristically accommodating mood, even introducing the band members by name (first names only, granted—but that's more than he ever did for Cannonball and Coltrane). Though the show was never boring, I wasn't sure how I felt about it afterwards, and I'm still not. Is Miles admirable, as his apologists would have it, for refusing to rest on his laurels, for keeping up with the latest black musical and sartorial trends? Or is there something pathetic about the sight of a sixty-year-old man in jheri curls and platform heels shaking his ass to a young man's beat? Musicians from earlier generations also prided themselves on keeping up, but they also kept some perspective on what was for kids and what was for keeps. Does Miles know the difference anymore? Does anyone these days?

TUTU, WITH DAVIS SULKING AND ATTITUDINIZING (MINUS HIS BAND) above synthesized, assembly-line arrangements of the clock-punching funksters Marcus Miller and George Duke, was noteworthy only for Irving

Penn's cover photos, which transformed Davis's handsomely creased face into something like an African mask. Everything else about the album was generic, save for Davis's wraithlike solos, which, though venturing nothing substantive, were instantly identifiable as his, if only by their timbre. Miller's "Splatch" and Duke's "Backyard Ritual" were marginally more palatable than the other tracks, but only because they were bouncier, not necessarily more involving. And if Miller's "Full Nelson" and the cover version of Scritti Politti's "Perfect Way" were slightly unsavory, it was because they found Davis contemptuously alluding to better days, with throwaway snippets of "Fran Dance" and "Half Nelson." As a result of Davis's self-reflexiveness, *Tutu* sounded like nothing else released in 1986—but not from lack of trying. If not for its reggae-*cum*-hip hop afterbeat and slight existential twist, *Tutu* could have been a new release by Herb Alpert or Chuck Mangione.

Which is not to say that Davis no longer wields influence. In fact, "Keep Your Eyes on Me," Alpert's current smash, sounds suspiciously similar to the tracks on *Tutu,* albeit with a hotter rhythm mix (courtesy Jimmy Jam and Terry Lewis, who also produce Janet Jackson) and without the foreboding that rescued *Tutu* from complete frivolity but doomed it as a dance groove.

"If that's what it sounds like to you, that's what it sounds like to you," Davis said, when asked if he heard the similarity. "I like Herb. I don't like that record. I like it when he does *his* thing, He's not black. . . .

"You thinking for me now? You don't know what the fuck I think. Don't put words in my mouth," he warned, when I asked him if his well-publicized hatred for the word "jazz" stems from the false expectations the word creates in the minds of listeners who prefer his music from twenty or thirty years ago. "I don't like the word because the record companies don't push it when it's called that, because white people want to protect their daughters' ass. They think all jazz musicians want to seduce their daughters—and white people have told me that. That word has been worn out and never been used right anyway. It meant, 'Let's get these people to march for us and entertain us the way they did in New Orleans.' Nobody paid attention to the music. It was just the smiling and the shining of teeth. Now they're trying to clean it up, build monuments to jazz and all of that shit, but it's too fucking late, man.

"I went down to Washington for Ray Charles', what do you call it; [Kennedy Center) Lifetime Achievement Award, and, Francis, it was sad. Cicely [Tyson, the actress, his third wife] started crying because all these black kids were there to honor Ray. It was touching, man, but the white people there, politicians and their wives, didn't feel nothing. They didn't know what to feel. I felt sorry for them, damn. They act so sophisticated, and they don't know nothing.

"Come on, what else. I gotta go," Davis said impatiently, abruptly changing mood. He confided that, yes, his long-rumored collaboration with Prince might yet take place, boasting of just having spent a few days with Prince on the West Coast. (Shouldn't Prince be the one boasting?) And, yes, he intended to do more TV—in fact, he has just completed a pilot for a series called *Shake and Bake,* in which he plays private eye Tom Skerritt's wheelchair-bound, ex-gangster sidekick.

Just one more thing, Miles: Do you agree with the people who say that a player's tone is an accurate projection of his character?

"What? You gotta ask a white psychiatrist about that, not me," he said, perhaps sensing that the next question would have been what his sound—the juxtaposition of his vulnerable trumpet style and his curt, self-aggrandizing manner—revealed about him.

I wanted to ask him if he still listened to singers like Frank Sinatra and Tony Bennett, as he reportedly used to, or if he had rejected them for not being "contemporary" enough. But it was clear that he wasn't going to indulge any more of my foolish questions. In exchanging goodbyes, I remarked that, in light of the autobiography he was working on with the writer Quincy Troupe, I was surprised that he was still granting interviews. Wouldn't most musicians in that situation figure they'd save it for the book?

"Including me. But I don't mind just talking, you know? But a lot of the shit you ask me, I just don't know. You ask me questions an analyst would ask." In that case, maybe I should send him a bill.

"That's right," he said, laughing. "I'll pay you back when I play." Then he hung up.

(MAY 1987)

Miles Agonistes

In *Miles: The Autobiography* (Simon and Schuster) the trumpeter Miles Davis remembers his excitement at hearing the Billy Eckstine Orchestra, with Charlie Parker and Dizzy Gillespie, in a St. Louis nightclub in 1944. "It was a motherfucker," Davis writes (notorious for his profanity, he hasn't toned himself down for publication) of his first in-person exposure to bebop, and also his baptism by fire as a musician—just eighteen at the time, he was pressed into service as an emergency fill-in. "The way that band was playing music— that was *all* I wanted to hear."

Davis's reaction was typical of that of most young musicians in the 1940s. What thrilled them about bebop was its impossible combination of the break-neck and the Byzantine. It was all they wanted to hear and all that they wanted to play. But an early mark of Davis's singularity was that soon after becoming Gillespie's protégé and Parker's sideman, he also became their loyal opposi-tion. "Diz and Bird played a lot of real fast notes and chord changes because that's the way they heard everything; that's the way their voices were: fast, up in the upper register," Davis observes in *Miles,* which was written in collabo-ration with the poet and journalist Quincy Troupe. "Their concept of music was *more* rather than *less.* I personally wanted to cut the notes down."

Davis's entire career can be seen as an ongoing critique of bop: the origins of "cool" jazz (his collaborations with Gil Evans in the late 1940s), hard bop or "funky" (his 1954 recording of "Walkin"), modal improvisation (the track "Milestones" in 1958 and the 1959 album *Kind of Blue*), and jazz-rock fusion (*In a Silent Way* and *Bitches Brew,* both recorded in 1969) can be traced to his efforts to pare bop to its essentials. His decision, in 1969, to court a younger audience by playing rock venues, adding amplified instruments to his ensem-ble, and cranking up both the volume and the beat, also amounted to a cri-tique of modern jazz, which he felt had become tired and inbred. So, in effect, did his withdrawal from recording studios and public performance from 1975 to 1980, years in which "sex and drugs took the place that music had occu-pied in my life until then, and I did both of them around the clock." He barely touched his horn in these years, but he haunted jazz with his silence.

TWO GENERATIONS OF LISTENERS NOW FEEL THAT DAVIS HAS SOLD THEM out: jazz fans of a certain age who have never forgiven him for going electric, and the rock audience that discovered him with *Bitches Brew* and—try as it might—can't get with the slick techno-funk he's been recording since *The Man with the Horn,* in 1981. The audience he has his sights on now, though he's unlikely to reach it without a hit single, is the audience that grooves to Prince and Michael Jackson, and commercial survival doesn't seem to be his only motivation—ego, racial identity, and a desire for eternal youth (or continuing relevance) all seem to be mixed up in it.

For many of his more worshipful fans, of all ages and races, Davis's music has always been just one component of a mystique that also involves his beautiful women, his up-to-the-minute wardrobe, his expensive taste in sports cars, and his scowling black anger: his celebrity boils down to an insider's lifestyle and an outsider's stance. (Or as Ornette Coleman once put it, Miles is a black man who lives like a white man.) His magnetism is so powerful that fans who haven't liked anything he's done in years continue to buy his records and attend his concerts, irrationally hoping for a reversal of form.

Onstage he remains an electrifying presence, though you wonder now (as you do with Dizzy Gillespie, but for a different reason) not how well he'll play, but how *much.* He's become a kind of roving conductor, walking from sideman to sideman, describing what he wants from them with a pump of his shoulders or a wiggle of his hips, blowing riffs into their faces and letting them pick it up from there. He still turns his back on the audience for much of the show, as he was infamous for doing in the 1950s and 1960s. The difference is that now he has a wireless microphone on his horn that allows him to be heard clearly with his back turned—and that audiences would be disappointed, at this point, if he failed to strike his iconic pose. Though his shows are never boring, you're not quite sure how you feel about them afterward. Is Davis admirable, as his apologists would have it, for refusing to rest on his laurels— for keeping up with the latest black musical and sartorial fashions? Or is there something pathetic about the sight of a sixty-three-year-old man in clogs, parachute pants, and jheri curls shaking his fanny to a younger generation's beat?

"When I hear jazz musicians today playing all those same licks we used to play so long ago, I feel sad for them," he writes.

Most people my age like old, stuffy furniture. I like the new Memphis style of sleek high-tech stuff . . . Bold colors and long, sleek, spare lines. I don't like a lot of clutter or a lot of furniture either. I like the contemporary stuff. I have to always be on the cutting edge of things because that's just the way I am and have always been.

Anyone this vigilant about staying on "the cutting edge" is chasing trends—
not starting them, as Davis did in jazz from the late 1940s to the early 1970s
(*Bitches Brew* and most of the double albums that followed it, though turbid
in retrospect, were undeniably influential at the time).

DAVIS HAS TWO NEW RELEASES IN THE STORES, ONE OF WHICH IS SO
shockingly good that you're slightly disappointed in it for not being perfect.
Aura (Columbia), recorded in 1985, is an ten-part orchestral work by the
Danish composer Palle Mikkelborg (who is also a Davis-influenced trumpeter,
though he doesn't solo here); it bears the influence of certain pieces from the
early 1970s by George Russell, an American composer who was then living in
Denmark. More boldly than Russell's works of that period, *Aura* attempts to
reconcile electronically generated and acoustically produced sonorities,
advanced harmonies, and a big, crunching beat. The work sags in places: Davis
and the bassist Niels-Henning Orsted Pedersen's duet has too much New Age
gloss surrounding it, as do the passages dominated by woodwinds. But a number of the ten sections cagily evoke Davis's landmark collaborations with Gil
Evans, and three sections—subtitled "Red," "Blue," and "Electric Red"—are
spectacular in their endless permutations of the work's initial ten-note theme
and static but oddly compelling 7/8 rhythm. On these three sections in particular, Davis responds to the orchestra with ecstatic, sustained improvisations
that give an idea of what he's still capable of when challenged.

Amandla (Warner Brothers) is more current and more typical of Davis's
1980s output. It has its virtues, not least among them its yeasty rhythms; Davis
and his producer, the multi-instrumentalist Marcus Miller (who wrote most
of the tunes), have obviously been listening to *zouk* and other African dance
music. But too much of *Amandla* sounds like generic instrumental funk, with
Davis playing sound stylist rather than improviser—in contrast to the alto saxophonist Kenny Garrett, whose brief solos inventively harmonize the signature attributes of two of his predecessors in Davis's group: Wayne Shorter's
ascetic spatial sense and Cannonball Adderley's preacherly bonhomie. Davis,
in a rare act of noblesse oblige, guest-stars on two tracks of Garrett's *Prisoner
of Love* (Atlantic), a disappointing exercise in saxophone smooch-and-groove
à la Kenny G. Even without consulting the personnel, you'd recognize Miles
by that hornet-like middle-register buzz of his. He exudes presence, but puts
so little of himself into his solos that he sounds like he's being sampled.

AURA NOTWITHSTANDING, DAVIS'S MAJOR ACCOMPLISHMENT OF RECENT
years is *Miles,* which enjoys an obvious advantage over the Davis biographies
by Ian Carr, Jack Chambers, Eric Nisenson, and Bill Cole. Without the full
involvement of their subject, these were essentially turntable companions—

critical guides to Davis's work within a biographical framework. But with *Miles,* Davis proves to be his own most perceptive critic (at least about his music before 1969), and the book is so successful in capturing Davis's voice (including his incessant, if tonally varied, use of profanity) that the odd line that sounds like the doing of Troupe (as when, for example, Davis supposedly resorts to quoting a jazz critic to describe the dramatic contrast between his style and that of his former sideman John Coltrane) calls for a double take.

"The challenge . . . is to see how melodically inventive you can become," Davis writes, giving the most succinct explanation I've ever read of the advantages of improvising on modes or scales rather than chord changes. "It's not like when you base stuff on chords, and you know at the end of thirty-two bars that the chords have run out and there's nothing to do but repeat what you've done with variations." *Kind of Blue,* which popularized modal improvisation, was the most influential jazz album of its period, but it was a disappointment of sorts for Davis, he writes. The sound he wanted on *Kind of Blue,* and feels he didn't quite achieve, was that of the "finger piano" (probably an African thumb piano) that accompanied a performance he saw by an African ballet troupe. Though Davis himself doesn't make the connection, what an unexpected rationale this provides for the three electric pianos that phase in and out behind the horns on *In a Silent Way!*

He writes about fellow musicians with an eye for detail that brings them into photograph-like focus. On Gil Evans, for example:

> When I first met him, he used to come to listen to Bird when I was in the band. He come in with a whole bag of "horseradishes"—that's what we used to call radishes—that he'd be eating with salt. Here was this tall, thin, white guy from Canada who was hipper than hip . . . But bringing "horseradishes" to nightclubs and eating them out of a bag with salt, and a white boy? Here was Gil on fast 52nd Street with all these super hip black musicians wearing peg legs and zoot suits, and here he was dressed in a cap. Man, he was something else.

Though acknowledging Charlie Parker's genius, Davis characterizes him as "a greedy motherfucker," who "was always trying to con or beat you out of something to support his drug habit."

> Bird always said he hated the idea of being thought of as just an entertainer, but . . . he was becoming a spectacle. I didn't like whites walking into the club where we were playing just to see Bird act a fool, thinking he might do something stupid.

Miles's considerable value as jazz history isn't what makes it such a page-turner. Autobiography is a problematical literary form, because it's never clear which is being submitted for the reader's approval, a book or its author. Davis writes that he loved Parker as a musician, but "maybe not as a person," and the Miles Davis who emerges from *Miles*—as complex as any character in recent fiction—elicits a similar ambivalence from the reader.

His treatment of women is contemptible: it seems like he's slugging another one every twenty pages or so. It isn't bad enough that he talks with unconvincing remorse of hitting his own women; a story intended to establish Billy Eckstine's tough-guy credentials has Eckstine slapping a would-be girlfriend while Davis looks on admiringly. He's spiteful toward the actress Cicely Tyson, the most recent of his ex-wives, whom he professes not to have felt "the sex thing" for after their marriage

> Cicely has done movie and TV roles where she played an activist or something like that, a person who cared a lot about black people. Well, she ain't nothing like that. She loves to sit up with white people, loves to listen to their advice about everything and believes everything they tell her.

Davis's fame and his relatively privileged upbringing (his father was a dentist and an unsuccessful candidate for the Illinois state legislature) haven't spared him from injustice, such as being clubbed over the head by a white policeman after he was ordered to move on from the entrance of a New York City nightclub in which he was performing in 1959. But much of what Davis interprets as racism is his own hubris, as when he speculates that white jazz critics of the 1960s wrote as much as they did about such black avant-gardists as Ornette Coleman, Cecil Taylor, and Archie Shepp in an effort to deflect attention from *him*. (Never mind that the critics most identified with what was then called "The New Thing" were Amiri Baraka and A. B. Spellman, both of whom are black.) He's peacock vain. He tells of admiring himself in a mirror in 1956, when his star was on the rise. He wasn't yet making as much money as he thought he should be, but he was looking "clean" in Brooks Brothers and custom-made Italian suits. "I felt so good that I walked to the door and forgot my trumpet."

He writes of getting together every so often with the late James Baldwin in France and "lying our asses off." You have to wonder, as you do with all autobiographies, how much lying is being done here. Probably not a lot, because for a man this caught up in his own mystique—a man fully aware that his art and life are already the stuff of legend—just telling the truth about himself as he sees it amounts to a form of self-aggrandizement.

(JANUARY 1990)

Miles Davis died in 1991, at the age of sixty-five.

Hottentot Potentate

What distinguishes American heroes of this kind [those of Cooper, Melville, and James] . . . is that there is nothing in the real world, or in the systems which dominate it, that can possibly satisfy their aspirations. Their imagination of the self . . . has no economic or social or sexual objectification; they tend to substitute themselves for the world. Initially and finally at odds with "system," perhaps their best definition is Henry James Sr.'s description of the artist as hero . . . "the man of whatsoever function, who in fulfilling it obeys his own inspiration and taste, uncontrolled either by his physical necessities or his social obligations." The artist-hero may be, as he often is in American literature, an athlete, a detective, or a cowboy. . . .

Or an autotheistic bandleader in his early- to mid-seventies who lords it over his sidemen (many of whom are themselves getting up in years) in a Philadelphia rowhouse. The quote from Richard Poirier's *A World Elsewhere: The Place of Style in American Literature* describes not only Sun Ra's indifference to temporal realities (he says he wasn't born of a woman, and, according to what his tenor saxophonist John Gilmore told Bob Rusch in *Cadence,* he doesn't plan on dying, either), but also his independence from any jazz movement or school.

Ra is obviously a major figure in jazz, even if it is difficult to pinpoint why. He's often assumed to have been the spiritual father of the Association for the Advancement of Creative Musicians, given the circumstantial evidence of his Chicago roots, his theatricality, and the multi-instrumentalism he demands of his musicians. But Ra and true believers kept to themselves in Chicago in the fifties, and to my knowledge, no AACM charter member has ever cited him as a progenitor. His relationship to free jazz was provisional, if not antagonistic—the Arkestra's group-gropes were meant to represent the chaos that would ensue on earth without Ra's divine intervention. Despite his prescient use of electronics, his music bears little resemblance to fusion or Ornette Coleman's harmolodics. He's frequently hailed as the last of the great big-band leaders, but despite the Duke Ellington and Fletcher Henderson tunes in his repertoire, his loyalty to that tradition is theoretical. Even when able to afford a full horn section, he hasn't exploited its potential—a big-band *sound* is less important to him than the blueprint for black solidarity he understands big bands to embody.

Decades from now, Ra's career might be divided into three tidy phases on the basis of his albums (most likely excluding the hundreds he's released on his own now-you-see-them, now-you-don't, Saturn label). It will seem as though the Sun Ra Arkestra started off as an anomalous, hard-bop big band with regrettable exotic trimmings in the no-nonsense fifties, mutated into an avant-garde stunt troupe in the freaked-out sixties, and finally hit its stride as a ragtag repertory orchestra in the time-warped eighties. But records are deceptive, especially in Ra's case. At Sweet Basil or the Bottom Line, you never know which Arkestra you'll get: with luck, you'll get all three. In substituting his panoramic overview for whatever happens to be in fashion at any given moment, Sun Ra has become doggedly *sui generis,* and part of the fun in hearing him is the recognition that there has never been anyone so intransigent or bizarre. In terms of the marketplace, he is a lowly cult figure, but his avid following is surprisingly broad-based. In addition to jazz buffs, he appeals to new-music types looking for their own crackpot-genius *à la* the art world's Howard Finster; to the metallists, iron men, and Lester Bangs wanna-be's who write for the *Village Voice;* and to his own equivalent of the Deadheads—pot smokers old enough to remember when the Arkestra travelled with a light show, who still feel free to light up at Ra's concerts. (Given the camp extravaganza of his stage presentation and rumors about his sexual preference, it's only surprising he doesn't have an identifiably gay following.)

The only jazz musician assured of a gig every Halloween, Ra sports a planet-dotted tunic, sequined knit hat, tie-dyed goatee, and a patriarchal smile on the cover of *Reflections in Blue* (Soul Note). As the first album to justify claims for Ra as a latter-day Fletcher Henderson, *Reflections in Blue* is noteworthy for more than Ra's iconic cover pose. The program includes no Henderson, just Irving Berlin and Jerome Kern as Henderson might have played them, and originals with reed voicings as luxurious as Henderson's or Don Redman's, but with enough personal twists to let you know this is Sun Ra.

The swing arrangements that began to dominate Ra's sets around ten years ago confirmed suspicions that he was as much showman as shaman, that his love of pomp had more to do with race memory of hot jazz and hokum, the Cotton Club and the TOBA circuit, than with ancient Egypt and outer space, his cosmological mumbo-jumbo notwithstanding. But the benefits of those all night drills that Ra is rumored to put his men through aren't always evident, and once the shock of hearing the Arkestra tear into "Queer Notions" or "Yeah, Man" wears off, the band's chancy intonation becomes a problem.

What's intended as sincere homage frequently sours into parody. Yet it was difficult to condemn Ra for this shortcoming, because his willingness to present virtuosos and rank amateurs side by side was what validated him as an avantgardist in the sixties and early seventies, when a desire for cultural identity, rather than a fascination with chords and scales, motivated many black musicians to pick up horns relatively late in life. (One agenda of most postwar avant-garde movements, including free jazz, has been to show that master craftsmen have an awful lot to learn from motivated beginners.)

Still, it comes as something of a relief that the pros have regained the upper hand on *Reflections in Blue.* The best of the new recruits are the guitarist Carl LeBlanc, the trombonist Tyrone Hill, and the trumpeter Randall Murray, all of whom solo energetically and add spark to the pep sections below the solos. But the album's MVP is homecoming alumnus Pat Patrick, once the Arkestra's baritone saxophonist and now its lead altoist (assuming it's he and not Marshall Allen lofting those gorgeous lines). Patrick's swiftly articulated solos on "Yesterdays," Ra's "State Street Chicago," and his own "Nothin' from Nothin'" (the album's catchiest theme) are delightful for laying anachronistic bop licks over Ra's charleston, shuffle, and two-beat rhythms. Allen turns in leaping choruses on the title track (more a modified boogie-woogie than a blues, and one of Ra's earliest numbers). John Gilmore, the Arkestra's star soloist from the beginning, although not featured as prominently as one might wish, performs his usual chordal prestidigitation on several tracks. Ra, playing synthesizer as well as piano, evokes Ellington, Basie, Garner, Monk, and Meade Lux Lewis, often simultaneously. He sings "I Dream Too Much," taking his cue from the oneiric title rather than the lovelorn lyrics, and giving a whole new meaning to the word *atonal,* although the result is very endearing.

Clearly recorded and well distributed (by PolyGram), *Reflections in Blue* is as definitive as Sun Ra albums get. Manny Farber, the film critic, once made a distinction between two kinds of art: "white elephant," which lavishes "overripe technique" on hammy, self-aggrandizing pseudo-masterworks; and "termite," the subversive Farber's own preference, characterized by "buglike immersion in a small area without point or aim, and . . . concentration on nailing down one moment without glamorizing it, but forgetting this accomplishment as soon as it has been passed; the feeling that all is expendable, that it can be chopped up and flung down in a different arrangement without ruin." Sun Ra, Hottentot Potentate of a World Elsewhere, is his own white elephant, but most of his carelessly produced concert albums are those of a termite artist. *A Night in East Berlin,* originally released as a Saturn cassette but now available on Leo (from New Music Distribution Service) fades in on what sounds like the middle of a number. Without visual cues, it's impossible to make sense of what's going on on the remainder of side one, especially after Ra brings things to a standstill with his Phantom of the Opera synthesizer.

But despite dismal sound quality, side two is a reminder of how much fun Ra can be. After the processional "Interstellar Loways" (a cross between "Tenderly" and Ra's own "Fate in a Pleasant Mood," with an elegant piano intro and a fluent alto solo), Ra paces the Arkestra and the June Tyson Dancers through a medley of his greatest hits, including "Space Is the Place," "We Travel the Spaceways," "Rocket Number Nine," "Next Stop Jupiter," and "Shadow World" (the ultimate showpiece for Gilmore's sustained upper-register squeals—a "Flying Home" for moderns). What's surprising is how much of the rollick of Ra's swing-era adaptations has rubbed off on his own vintage material. Either that, or this stuff is now old enough to inspire its own nostalgia.

No survey of Ra's recent output would be complete without mention of *John Cage Meets Sun Ra* (Meltdown). Recorded live at Sideshows by the Seashore in Coney Island in 1986, the album is damned near unlistenable, but fascinating as hell for what it reveals about the differences between the jazz and classical avant-gardes (the title is something of a misnomer; Cage and Ra perform together only briefly). Cage is so important a thinker that it no longer matters what his music sounds like, or whether he bothers to make music at all: the idea is what really counts. As putative entertainers, jazz musicians are denied such luxury, which might be as good an explanation as any for why Ra's sloppy, melodramatic synthesizer solos possess a vitality lacking in Cage's rigorous, empty words (from *Roaratorio: An Irish Circus on Finnegan's Wake*? I can't tell, and Howard Mandel's otherwise informative liner notes don't say). Jazz demands that even its stargazers keep both feet firmly planted when showtime rolls around. For Sun Ra, the show never ends. The audience just goes home.

(FEBRUARY 1988)

Sun Ra, Himself

===

Like most musical road warriors, Sun Ra and the entourage of instrumentalists, singers, and dancers he calls his Arkestra (sometimes the Myth Science Arkestra, sometimes the Cosmo Jet Set Arkestra, but always the Arkestra) often find themselves carbound in the middle of the night, when traffic is light but nobody's as wide awake as he should be. Bessie Smith, Scott LaFaro, and Clifford Brown, among others, died from injuries sustained in car accidents, and practically every musician you ask—including Sun Ra—can tell you about a close call. But not surprisingly, Sun Ra's recollection detours into the preternatural.

The Arkestra was recently was on its way to the airport after a gig in San Francisco, Ra explained as we sat in the front room of his three-story home on Morton Street, in the Germantown section of Philadelphia. The since-banished Danny Thompson, then one of the Arkestra's saxophonists and Ra's de facto public relations man, who was driving, assured Ra that he wasn't tired, even though he'd already racked up considerable mileage driving to Los Angeles and back to see relatives earlier in the day.

"We were on the highway, right up on the car in front of us, with another car right behind us," Ra said in his Southern-accented monotone. His hair was tinted copper around the chin and temples, and he was wearing a black, knee-length, glitter-dusted tunic over shirt and trousers, with a matching scarf knotted in a point above the crown of his head—an eye-catching outfit, but prim compared with his onstage motley. "All at once, I heard June [Tyson], the vocalist with us, say 'Danny!,'" because he was asleep with his eyes wide open, and he was goin' to hit that car in front. He woke up, but if he put the brakes on, the car behind was going to hit us.

"That was the situation, very dangerous," Ra continued, in a matter-of-fact voice. "But we was saved because the car ahead of us shot straight up in the air and got into the next lane."

Wait a minute. The car *levitated?*

Ra smiled and nodded in affirmation. "You need a lot of protection on this planet."

SUN RA PIONEERED THE USE OF AFRICAN PERCUSSION AND ELECTRONIC instruments in jazz. He showed that a big band could play hard bop and free, footloose styles supposedly exclusive to small groups. An innovative force in jazz for over thirty years as a keyboard player, bandleader, and composer, he rivals John Cage as America's most venerable avant-gardist.

But all of this is like saying that a rhinoceros is pointed at one end and round at the other: it doesn't begin to describe what's so peculiar about the beast. This is a man who once said "knowledge is laughable when attributed to a human being," and who, when asked if he considered himself human, answered, "No. As a man thinketh, so shall he be."

The New Grove Dictionary of Jazz says that Ra was born Herman "Sonny" Blount in Birmingham, Alabama, in May, 1914. But the name and date are guesswork. According to Ra, he wasn't born, but "arrived on earth," presumably from somewhere else, on an unspecified date "outside the division of time that man has." He's forthcoming about his early life, albeit in his own fashion. He first evinced musical talent, he says, when his mother bought him a piano for his "so-called birthday" and he began transposing—by ear—the violin sonatas a school chum who lived next door would bring to him.

After studying music in high school under Professor John Tuggle Whatley, whose other students included Erskine Hawkins and Jo Jones, Ra won a scholarship to Alabama A&M, where he led the student band and majored in education, until, he says, he was kidnapped by extraterrestrials who took him to Saturn.

"I had to go up like this," he explained, demonstrating with his elbows meeting over his paunch and his fingertips clasping his shoulders, "because if I touched anything outside my body, I wouldn't be able to return.

"Did you ever see *Star Wars?*" Ra asked me. "It was very accurate."

After showing Ra around the galaxy and commanding him to alert mankind "there was goin' to be great trouble from the teenagers in high schools," they convinced him that a great destiny was in store for him: "When the world was in complete chaos, then I could speak and the world would listen, but not until then."

Asked if that moment had yet arrived, Ra smiled and said, "Well, I just got back from a jazz festival in Russia, and they declared me an international citizen, because they said I represent friendship." Also, while still in college, he decided to "try to reach God," who told him that "He wanted to find one pure-hearted person on this planet—just one." And that was Sun Ra? "Must have been." He said he once had "proof" of these experiences in a diary he was forced to "abolish" when he found his college bandmates "havin' a real good time readin' [it] on my bed. But I still retain the memory."

After college, Ra landed first in Nashville, where he recorded with the archetypal rhythm and blues singer and guitarist Wynonie Harris, and then in Chicago, where he worked with Fletcher Henderson, Stuff Smith, and an obscure blues singer named JoJo Adams, "a Chuck Berry type who had this knock-kneed dance that he would do," and performed what Ra describes as "X-rated" blues in top hat and tails, sometimes dressing his sidemen as Revolutionary soldiers. Chicago's jazz musicians nicknamed Ra "the moon man," not merely for predicting that man would one day go to the moon, but also in puzzled admiration of his far-out chords.

"They didn't understand what I was doin'," but they were fascinated by it," he explained, with no false modesty.

Those musicians who were especially fascinated became the nucleus of his Arkestra, which he formed in the early 1950s. But Ra began to attract widespread attention only after relocating the Arkestra to New York in 1961, and recording collective improvisations and pure "sound" pieces that demonstrated his kinship with John Coltrane, Albert Ayler, Cecil Taylor, and others involved in what was then called "free" jazz. Ra, however, has never marched in step with any movement, and in response to the question of how much he thought his music of that period had in common with theirs, his answer was typically expansive but cryptic.

"That was when I was having my argument with God, because I didn't want to have to be the one to have to save the world," he explained. "I told him 'Let a minister do it! Let an intellectual do it! Let a millionaire do it! Let a Muslim do it!'"

In 1969, he moved his headquarters to Philadelphia, because "to save the planet, I had to go to the worst spot on earth, and that was Philadelphia, which is death's headquarters. This is where liberty started, but the bell cracked on them, because liberty wasn't what it's cracked up to be. And that's why you have so many teenagers here smoking crack."

Actually the Arkestra seems to have moved here because member Marshall Allen's family signed over the deed to the house. These negative sentiments about his adopted hometown might have given pause to the mayor's representatives, who were planning to award Ra with a Liberty Bell before one of his performances a few nights hence. Then again, much of what Sun Ra says seems designed to give someone pause.

He blames Jesus Christ for "the reign of death" on earth. "Jesus said, 'I come to cast fire on the earth.' It's happenin' everyday, atomic bombs, people trapped in fires, can't get out. They don't believe nice, meek Jesus would do that. But He is." Ra's distrust of Christianity dates from childhood. His mother wasn't a churchgoer, but his grandmother was devout, "and I never could understand why if Jesus died to save people, why people still had to die. That seemed ignorant to me. I couldn't equate that. That's how I felt as a child, and I never changed." He also blames Jesus for introducing mankind to drugs, "on account of Him asking for drugs on the cross." (He expanded on this with something I couldn't quite follow, about how the legend "IHS" nailed above Christ's head was "shit" spelled backward. It does if the cross was the "T," I guess.)

A case could be made for Ra as jazz's first Afrocentric. The rhymes chanted by his musicians during his shows from the late 1950s on proselytized about the wonders of ancient Egypt and foretold a future in outer space. In a sense, the songs about rocket ships taking off for Saturn were as Afrocentric as those about mythic sunsets on the Nile. Both came across as expressions of his conviction that he was from somewhere else and had little in common with most of those around him—a sense of cultural displacement shared by many African Americans, but taken to extremes by Ra.

Yet though Ra was among the first American jazz musicians to perform in African regalia, he scoffs at the concept of black pride, observing that "pride goeth before the fall." He also criticizes African Americans for being too materialistic: "Black folks too close to slavery. They worked four hundred years, don't have nothin' to show for it. They tryin' to make up for that. It's about money, money, money.

"Black power, black pride. Actually, I prefer the word 'dark.' Black folks used to be darkies. 'A darky's born, he ain't no good no how, without a song,' I take that as my song. God didn't give the black man anything but his music."

On the other hand, Ra believes—as do an increasing number of academics, both black and white—that the fundaments of Western thought, usually credited to the Greek philosophers, in fact stem from ancient Egypt. (The case was argued most persuasively by Martin Bernal, a white professor at Cornell University, in his *Black Athena: The Afro-Asiatic Roots of Classical Civilization,* which was published in 1987. But it was first argued in *Stolen Legacy: The Greeks Were Not the Authors of Greek Philosophy, but the People of North Africa, Commonly Called the Egyptians,* a crackpot text published by the renegade black scholar George G. M. James in 1954. Ignored by the white academic establishment, James's book reached an avid black readership, possibly including Ra.) According to Ra, "the black races were in touch with the real creators of the universe at one time, in perfect communication with them, but they lost it. So they go to church, take dope, do all sort of things to try to regain that state. The white man never had it."

In West Germany recently, Sun Ra, who cautions his band members "to never leave me alone with any nation," was "kidnapped" by an interviewer and a photographer, who took him to a planetarium and asked him questions that even he thought were strange. "Like how did I intend to get black people off of this planet. What kind of ship was I going to use. What kind of rocket fuel. I told them I wasn't using any gasoline. I'm usin' sound. Scientists haven't reached that stage yet, where you can run your car or heat your home with a cassette. But it will happen—with the right kind of music, of course." (Ra isn't the only one who's proposed tapping his music for the greater good: Norman Mailer, after being blown away by the Arkestra in Chicago thirty years ago, speculated that Ra's music could probably cure cancer.)

Ra likes to give the impression that he's deliberately been withholding his most visionary music from a species not yet prepared for it. "For years, I been tellin' John [tenor saxophonist John Gilmore, who joined the Arkestra in Chicago in 1963 and remains with it to this day], 'play and don't play. Play your best, but retain something the world has never heard before. And one day, I will tell you, John, OK, play it.'" For whatever reason, after orbiting the outer limits for much of the 1960s, Ra's music has returned to earth in the decades since. An entire set might now be given over to his offbeat arrangements of jazz and pop standards, or even to numbers from the Walt Disney songbook (the Arkestra now sometimes takes its traditional march around the auditorium to the tune of "Hi Ho, Hi Ho, It's Off to Work We Go"). In Philadelphia recently, he says, a fan recently thanked him for playing "that sixth-grade music," meaning music that even someone with only an elementary school education could follow. Thanks to an outrageous persona more befitting a rock 'n' roller than a jazzman, he's even begun to attract an audience on the edges of pop: last year's *Blue Delight,* his first major-label release after close to two hundred independent albums (counting those on his own Saturn label) was played on college alternative rock stations, alongside Camper Van Beethoven and REM.

The most common misconception about Ra's music—the only one that irks him—is that its dissonances are a matter of happenstance. "They say, 'Does the band have music or do they just play?'" he said mockingly, rummaging around on the top of his piano and producing a densely notated page of sheet music for my inspection. This score-in-progress was about the only thing that Ra wanted to show me that he was able to put his hands on quickly. He wobbled around his workshop trying to find newspaper clippings and books of his poetry amid the clutter of record albums, hand drums, and artworks given to him by admirers (the most striking of these were a vibrant painting of him as a Pharaoh, with a headdress of piano keys, and a metal sculpture of the Egyptian sun god in which Ra had stuck his phone bill for safe keeping). He apologized for the funky asceticism of his digs by way of an analogy: "If there's no sawdust in the carpenter's workshop, no work is gettin' done."

The Ra house, on Morton Street, is weather-beaten, but not an eyesore by neighborhood standards, despite the blue paint on the window frames and the thick strips of plastic hung to keep out the cold. (Twenty-one years ago, when Ra and his men moved here, their black neighbors were frightened of them.

Now Ra and his men are becoming increasingly frightened of their younger neighbors.) Ra, who also maintains a nearby apartment for business purposes, lives here with a fluctuating number of his most devoted sidemen. The house ban on drugs and alcohol also applies to female cohabitation, which is unfortunate, because the place could use what my mother refers to as a woman's touch.

"It's more than one man can do," Sun Ra complained at one point. "I got to write my music and take care of the bookings, plus worry about the men's health, make sure they eat properly and everything."

Ra's sidemen, who were studying their sheet music and warming up on their horns as they waited for him to begin rehearsal, chatted happily about the Super Bowl and the Publisher's Clearing House Millionaire Sweepstakes notification that one of them had received in the morning mail, as Sun Ra gabbed just as casually about interplanetary travel and the secrets of antiquity. It seemed like a good time to ask him about his earthly needs. "I have to eat properly," he said. "But I sometimes forget to. I have to cook for myself, because I have to have everything just so. I like my food real done. Everybody likes my moon soup. I have to choose the vegetables real carefully—the corn, the tomatoes, the ochre—and heat it at just the right temperature, so you taste each vegetable individually. Not a soup where you can't taste none of the ingredients in it."

I asked him something I was dying to know: Had he ever gone, during his years in Philadelphia, to watch the mummers strut up Broad Street in their feathered capes and sequined headdresses on New Year's Day? The annual parade is Philly's version of Mardi Gras, and it, too, is African-derived, right down to that fluid, hips-and-shoulders strut the mummers do to "Oh, That Golden Slipper" (composed, it just so happens, by James Bland, a black man, though the parade itself, which dates to the turn of the century, has traditionally been lily-white; in addition to carrying banjos, its participants wore minstrel's blackface in the parade's early days, around the turn of the century).

He sure had, Sun Ra said: many times, in fact. "All that work for one day, and competitive, too," he said, admiringly.

But don't look for Sun Ra to show up in costume on Broad Street on New Year's Day any time soon, even if invited to. "I have to keep something of a low profile," he said, "because what I'm doin' is earth shaking. I don't want to panic anyone."

(FEBRUARY 1990)

Sun Ra left this planet, as he might put it, in 1993.

The Right Stuff

L ike most other fields of endeavor these days, jazz is governed by a rigid code of attitudes embraced as just and proper by performers and onlookers alike, and Wynton Marsalis would thus seem to be cut from all the right stuff. Consider his credentials: youthful idealism enflamed by personal ambition, brassy self-assurance muted by a gentleman's decorum in dress and behavior, a genuine reverence toward the music's history equaled by a machismo drive toward furthering its propagation. And as the offspring of the neglected New Orleans pianist Ellis Marsalis, the trumpeter is a certified second-generation jazz musician, which gives him quite a boost in a period when much of what passes for jazz criticism romanticizes the bonds between figurative fathers and sons. Scornful of pop, funk, fusion, free jazz, and anything else that strikes him as compromise or sham, Marsalis is as infuriating a paradox as Tom Wolff's astronauts—a rugged individualist out to restore traditional values with little tolerance for those who play by a looser set of rules; a straight arrow who talks like a rebel, though what he's rebelling against is non-conformity. According to Marsalis, jazz went crazy in the 1960s for the same reason the rest of the world did: no one was tough enough, dedicated enough, *man* enough, to live up to responsibilities. Although it's difficult to fault Marsalis as a trumpeter or bandleader, I sometimes wonder what it says about this era in jazz that so resolutely conservative a young musician has become its cynosure.

Marsalis came to Philadelphia one day in the summer of 1983 to do advance publicity for an upcoming concert, and a tiring round of interviews and tapings had put him in a salty, contentious mood by evening, when I caught up with him. He conceded that he had been the beneficiary of the kind of build-up seldom lavished on jazz musicians anymore. "But you know why I've gotten all that publicity?" he asked. "Not just because I was so young when people first heard of me. This music has a long history of prodigies, and nobody thought it was unusual when Lee Morgan went on the road with Dizzy Gillespie when he was 17 or 18, or Paul Chambers went out with Miles Davis at around the same age. No, see, when I first came to New York in 1979, everybody was talking about fusion. Everybody was saying that jazz was dead because no young black musicians wanted to play it anymore, and because the established cats who should have been setting an example were *bull*shittin,' wearing dresses* and trying to act like rock stars. So when people heard me, they knew it was time to start takin' care of business again. I wasn't playing shit no one had ever heard before, but at least I was playing some real music."

Marsalis, who was born in 1961, over-dramatizes the plight of jazz before his coming, but let it pass—it is indisputable that he has had a rejuvenating effect on jazz, if only in terms of winning it more media coverage. I asked him why he had stipulated to CBS that he also be recorded as a classical artist. "Because I like that kind of music, and it's important that people know I can play it," he said. "That way, what I have to say about jazz will carry more weight. I intimidate people because I know what I'm talking about. People try to say I'm arrogant, but I never said I could play. Hell, man, I'm still learning . . . I still have astronomical amounts of shit to learn, and that's not just false modesty either. That's the attitude you have to have. When Miles Davis was my age, he wasn't shit, either. He was still imitating Fats Navarro on some of those early sides he cut with Bird in the 1940s."

Asked to name the trumpeters who most influenced him personally, Marsalis rattled off what might just as well have been a litany of Great Trumpeters recited from memory—Davis, Navarro, Louis Armstrong, Dizzy Gillespie, Freddie Hubbard, Don Cherry, and Woody Shaw. Cherry is the only surprise on the list, and Marsalis is begrudging in his praise of the former Ornette Coleman sideman. "I think Cherry brought the trumpet to its furthest point conceptually—him and Miles. But Cherry has never bothered to learn to play his instrument. He doesn't project—sometimes you can't even hear what he's playing. That's why fellow musicians don't show him the respect he deserves. Every musician who has been a jazz innovator has also been a master technician—every single one. So you can't include Cherry among the innovators. But he and Ornette Coleman did some things every other musician picked up on—with Coltrane, the debt to Ornette was publicized; all the other cats tried to pretend it was just something they thought of themselves by coincidence. Miles is a prime example of that."

I noticed that Marsalis's conversation kept drifting back to Miles Davis, which seemed fitting, since the Prince of Darkness also casts a long shadow over Marsalis's solos, particularly those at slow and medium tempos. And significantly, Marsalis happened along in jazz at a time when Davis's comeback had dashed all hopes that he would return to his style of the mid-'60s—and when many listeners for whom mid-'60s Miles was still the quintessence of jazz were desperately

---

*It later dawned on me that by dresses, Marsalis meant the dashikis many black musicians wore in the nationalistic '70s. At least I hope that's what he meant.

casting about for a new idol. "People are always coming up to me and saying, 'You hear what Miles said about you?'" Marsalis complained, "I say, 'I don't care what Miles has to say about me.' I love Miles. He's one of the greatest musicians this century has produced, but you wouldn't know that from listening to the crap he's trying to peddle to the public now. The only thing I wanna hear Miles talk about is what he thinks he's doing. Let him explain that."

Davis was present the night that Marsalis received his first trumpet. "I was about five or six, and Miles, Clark Terry, Al Hirt, and my father were all sitting around a table in Al's club in New Orleans—this was when my father was still working in Al's band. My father, just joking around because there were so many trumpeters sitting there, said, 'I better buy Wynton a trumpet.' And Al said 'Ellis, let me give your boy one of mine.' It's ironic looking back on it, because Miles said, 'Don't give it to him. Trumpet's too difficult an instrument for him to learn.' Ha!"

That trumpet sat in its case untouched until Marsalis was twelve. In high school, he played it in funk bands "that did cover versions of Earth Wind & Fire and the Commodores—all that bullshit." At fourteen he performed the demanding Haydn Trumpet Concerto with the New Orleans Philharmonic. But it wasn't until 1979, when he dropped out of Juilliard School to join Art Blakey's Jazz Messengers that Marsalis began to play jazz in earnest. "I sat in with Blakey, and he was impressed with my technique, so he hired me on the spot. But I was still pretty raw. There were things I would have had together by that age if I had been born back in another period, if I had been able to hear the giants of jazz like Coltrane and Miles and Jackie McLean and Kenny Dorham on the radio when I was coming up, the way earlier generations were able to. But I'm telling you, things will be that way again real soon."

Marsalis was implying that there are plenty more where he came from, and his words already have the ring of fulfilled prophecy. Terence Blanchard, the New Orleans trumpeter who replaced Marsalis with the Jazz Messengers, was nineteen and looked about twelve but he knew his way around his horn. And the young saxophonists Donald Harrison and Jean Touissaint have also followed the Marsalises up the pipeline from the Crescent City to the Big Apple, with the requisite stopover in the Jazz Messengers. According to Marsalis, still more upstarts are on the way, not all of them from New Orleans. "We're entering a period now when there are young kids fourteen and fifteen years old all over the country who can really play. They'll all be emerging four or five years from now, and they'll insist on being heard. I don't think people are going to try to sound like me, but you are going to see young cats getting serious about their music, and I definitely think I have something to do with that."

(JUNE 1983)

Born Out of Time

J ust eighteen when he made his debut with Art Blakey and the Jazz Messengers, the trumpeter Wynton Marsalis answered the prayers of those who feared that the clock was running out on jazz, as it clearly already had on the blues. Most of the surviving heroes of swing and bebop were in decline, and the prevailing wisdom was that no successors were in the wings. But here was an immensely gifted musician still in his teens who played straight-ahead jazz, not fusion or funk. That he was a black second-generation jazzman (the son of the obscure pianist Ellis Marsalis) from New Orleans, the city generally acknowledged to be the birthplace of jazz, was taken as an especially good omen. This was in 1980, and Marsalis has since achieved a celebrity rare for a contemporary jazz musician, partly as a result of his parallel career in classical music, partly as a result of the novelty value of his youth. But at twenty-six, he's no longer a prodigy. He's already three years older than Miles Davis was when he recorded the first of his classic nonet sessions, two years older than Clifford Brown was when he recorded "Jordu" and "Joy Spring." It's time to ask if Marsalis has fulfilled his potential, what his influence has been on musicians his own age and younger, and whether he's expanded the audience for jazz, as many hoped he would.

The answer to the first part of the question is a qualified yes. With his chill tone and jabbing attack, Marsalis still echoes Miles Davis, just as he did eight years ago with Blakey. Moreover, now that Marsalis leads his own band, he takes his cues from the quintet that Davis led from 1964 to 1967, which included the pianist Herbie Hancock, the bassist Ron Carter, the drummer Tony Williams, and the tenor and soprano saxophonist Wayne Shorter (still the primary role model for Marsalis's brother, Branford, Wynton's elder by one year and a former member of his group). So Marsalis is still feeling the Anxiety of Influence, but he's making progress toward ridding himself of it. There's a sly wit to his half-valve work that owes nothing to Davis, although it does recall the veteran trumpeter Clark Terry, one of Davis's early influences. Another sign of Marsalis's enhanced individuality is the way he's zeroed in on the most provocative aspect of the Davis Quintet's music from the middle six-ties: its circling, now-you-hear-it-now-you-don't approach to the beat.

At this point, Marsalis is one of very few musicians able to line up enough work to keep a band together fulltime, and his rapport with his rhythm sec-tion on the recent *Marsalis Standard Time—Volume I* (Columbia FC-40461) attests to the virtues of stability. There are moments when Marsalis, the pianist Marcus Roberts, the bassist Robert Leslie Hurst, and the drummer Jeff Watts sound as though they're playing in four different time signatures. Actually, they're stretching a basic quadruple meter four different ways, accenting dif-ferent beats in every measure, and trusting that the listener will feel the down-beat in his bones. That the listener generally does is a tribute to Watts's zesty drumming, which, like that of Tony Williams with Davis, imparts a sensation of four/four swing while scrupulously avoiding anything so simple as a sounded beat. The effect is mesmerizing, and it would be beyond the ken of a group hastily assembled for a recording date.

Discounting a best-forgotten 1984 encounter with strings, *Marsalis Stan-dard Time—Volume I* is the first of Marsalis's albums mostly given over to vin-tage pop songs of the sort that provided excellent springboards for improvisers from Louis Armstrong to John Coltrane, but that too many subsequent musi-cians have rejected in favor of their own compositions. The album is a reminder of the outstretched hand that such songs have long offered to audi-ences trying to find a point of entry into jazz. Although the greased tempos frequently reduce the melodies to unrecognizable blurs, the hint of familiar-ity left in the standards "Caravan," "April in Paris," "A Foggy Day," "The Song Is You," and "Autumn Leaves" brings the quartet's rhythmic cunning into a sharp focus lacking in his other albums.

Marsalis Standard Time—Volume One has its minor flaws. Two Marsalis originals—a fleet blues and an almost motionless ballad—seem out of place, because, surprisingly, they're not subjected to as many rhythmic variations as the standards. "Memories of You," a solo feature for Roberts, begins promisingly, with wrinkled blues shadings and Monk-like rhythmic hesitations, but falters as a result of Roberts's attempt to cram the entire history of jazz piano, from stride to Tyner, into one three-minute perfor-mance. There are two versions of "Cherokee," both taken at a tempo consid-erably less punishing than the one that Charlie Parker set when he reharmonized the song as "Ko Ko," in 1945, but punishing enough to tongue-tie Marsalis. He redeems himself, though, with a lovely interpretation of Benny Goodman's old sign-off theme, "Goodbye," and a straightforward reading of "New Orleans" that comes across as a modernist's heartfelt tribute to Louis Armstrong.

THE QUESTION OF MARSALIS'S INFLUENCE IS TRICKY. EVEN WITHOUT HIS example, musicians in their twenties might be looking back two decades for inspiration, to the period before John Coltrane's death in 1967, and the gradual defection of Miles Davis and his sidemen to high-tech funk—the last time when there was anything approaching general agreement on what constituted the state of the art. But inasmuch as Marsalis's emergence identified this anachronistic impulse as a movement, such subsequent arrivals as Branford Marsalis, the alto saxophonist Donald Harrison, the drummer Marvin "Smutty" Smith, and the trumpeters Terence Blanchard and Wallace Roney are Wynton's Children.

Despite his large stylistic debt to Wayne Shorter, Branford Marsalis once seemed the most promising of these young musicians, but he's failed to deliver. His mastery of his instrument is impressive, and so is his grasp of jazz history. Called on to evoke Ben Webster's burly savoir faire on "Take the 'A' Train," on Mercer Ellington's *Digital Duke* (GRP GR-1038), Marsalis performs the task with admirable conviction. But *Renaissance* (Columbia FC-40711), his own most recent album, suggests that his ability to mimic different styles isn't necessarily an asset. Each of his phrases seems to be enclosed in quotation marks: not only "Wayne Shorter" but "John Coltrane," "Sonny Rollins," and "Joe Henderson," too. What's missing is "Branford Marsalis."

Donald Harrison and Terence Blanchard are from New Orleans, like the Marsalis brothers, whom they succeeded in the Jazz Messengers. The recent *Crystal Stair* (Columbia FC-40830) is typical of the four albums they've made as leaders of their own group since 1983. The level of musicianship is high, and there's as much rhythmic detail and acceleration of tempo as on *Marsalis Standard Time—Volume 1,* but Harrison and Blanchard lack Wynton Marsalis's command of dynamics, and the result is that each track is indistinguishable from the one before it. The Marsalis brothers are the models for Harrison and Blanchard, which means that *Crystal Stair* sounds like the 1965 Miles Davis Quintet, once removed. On *Eric Dolphy and Booker Little Remembered Live at Sweet Basil* (ProJazz CDJ-640, available only as a compact disc with a companion cassette of the same material), Harrison and Blanchard are miscast in the roles of two late musicians who were among the most individualistic in jazz. The other participants in this 1986 New York club session are the pianist Mal Waldron, the bassist Richard Davis, and the drummer Ed Blackwell, all reprising the roles they played on the original Dolphy and Little recordings, recorded at the Five Spot in New York in 1961. Although Blanchard is beyond his depth trying to capture Little's melancholy, Harrison surprises the listener with searing improvisations that are satisfying in their own right, even if a little too conventional in pitch to evoke Dolphy.

Marvin "Smitty" Smith, once the drummer in the Harrison–Blanchard group, makes his debut as a leader with *Keeper of the Drums* (Concord Jazz CJ-325), an album that owes much of its vibrancy to Smith's smarts in recognizing the individual abilities of the members of his ensemble—Roney, the trombonist Robin Eubanks, the pianist Mulgrew Miller, the bassist Lonnie Plaxico, and the saxophonists Steve Coleman and Ralph Moore—and allocating solo space in a way that shows each off to best advantage. Coleman's angular phrasing is well suited to the Dolphyesque "Miss Ann," for example, and the sanctified call-and-response patterns of "The Creeper" are custom-made for the blues-based styles of Roney and Miller. Roney's *Verses* (Muse MR-5335), which benefits from Tony Williams's tidal-wave drumming, is more of a blowing date, and this proves to be an advantage on "Slaves" and the title track, two themeless blues with crescendoing solos by Roney, Miller, and the tenor saxophonist Gary Thomas. But on the remaining tracks, including Miles Davis's and Bill Evans' "Blue in Green," the soloists adhere too timidly to the guidelines set by Davis, Evans, and Coltrane on *Kind of Blue.*

ON ALL THESE RECENT ALBUMS, RHYTHM IS SECONDARY TO PULSATION, and harmony is frequently suspended in the interest of mood. In that sense, these albums recall those Miles Davis made for Columbia in the middle sixties, and those his sidemen made for Blue Note during the same period, with a stable of likeminded musicians that included the vibraphonist Bobby Hutcherson, the trumpeter Freddie Hubbard, and the tenor saxophonist Joe Henderson. What gave those Blue Note albums urgency was their insistence on moderation at a time when a revolution was going on elsewhere in jazz, in the more iconoclastic music of Coltrane, Ornette Coleman, Cecil Taylor, Albert Ayler, Sun Ra, and Archie Shepp.

These newer records convey urgency, too, but it's the urgency of fighting the clock, of insisting that adventure can still be found in a twenty-year-old style of jazz that represented moderation even when new. It's not surprising these musicians in their twenties are finding a ready audience among lifelong jazz fans at least a decade older. Nostalgia for the recent past is a widespread vice, catered to by the very technology that was supposed to hurl us into a future from which there would be no looking back—the new ghosts in the machine include oldies radio, television reruns, vintage films on videocassette, and Beatles and Motown reissues on compact disc (a format still so expensive that consumers feel safer sticking with the tried and true). But nostalgia is a vice to which jazz fans are especially susceptible. In the late 1960s, Bob Dylan and the Beatles won for rock 'n' roll more intellectual cachet than jazz had ever enjoyed, and both rock and rhythm 'n' blues supplanted jazz as music for hedonistic release. For many listeners, New Age music now serves as the backdrop for meditation that Coltrane and Pharoah Sanders once provided (which is why New Age has been replacing jazz as late-night fare on public radio). It's been a long time, in other words, since a passion for jazz was regarded as hip rather than quaint. So a yearning for a time when Miles Davis was a trend-setter both musically and sartorially is understandable, even among those too young to remember such a time firsthand.

The underside of this nostalgia is a widely felt anger that discounts the onslaught of rock in order to blame jazz's fall on its own excesses after 1965. Wynton Marsalis gives voice to this animosity in statements like the following, from a recent interview with the critic Leonard Feather: "When you come to New York, there's a whole school of musicians who are called the avant-garde, and you don't really [need] any craft requirements to join their ranks. All you have to do is be black and have an African name. . . ." Were it not for the fact that he himself has no past deeds to recant, Marsalis could be the spokesman for the jazz auxiliary of Second Thought, the coterie of *mea culpa-ing* former radicals turned neoconservatives, who blame all of America's current problems on the presumed moral laxity of 1960s. Although Marsalis has expressed admiration for Ornette Coleman, the avant-garde's erosion of standards is a recurring theme in his interviews, and because he neglects to name names, he tars all of Coleman's progeny with the same brush. "You have young musicians who don't know how to play the blues, who don't care about being in tune, who can't get through any of the music that Monk wrote but try to pretend that they're what's going on because they're playing right now," he complained to Feather. And to Stanley Crouch, once an avant-garde drummer and firebrand poet, but now the jazz critic most in sympathy with Marsalis's reactionary aesthetic, Marsalis said, "It's much, much easier to whip up this hasty, fast-food version of innovation than to humble yourself to the musical logics that were thoroughly investigated by [the] masters." To Marsalis and Crouch, free jazz was as costly a mistake as black English; the code of professionalism they espouse is cousin to the rhetoric of the neo-con academics who blame open admissions for the closing of the American mind.

A good many jazz listeners agree with Marsalis, and much of what he says has the ring of truth. "Just to think of the arrogance behind a statement like, 'I play world music . . .'" he told Feather. "You're admitting that you're giving non-specific, second-hand treatment to different types of music. . . ." The avant-garde's naïve fascination with ethnic music is worthy of Marsalis's ridicule. But it's good to remember that in addition to African thumb piano and doussn' gouni and didjeridoo, the avant-garde restored clarinet and tuba to the jazz ensemble, to say nothing of importing such suspect "concert" instruments as violin and cello, thus relieving the inherent monotony of trumpet, saxophone, piano, bass, and drums (the lineup still generally favored by

Marsalis and his followers). It was also such nominal avant-gardists of the 1970s as Roscoe Mitchell, Joseph Jarman, Muhal Richard Abrams, Anthony Braxton, Anthony Davis, and Henry Threadgill who rekindled interest in composition (and thus weeded out the amateurs) by avoiding theme-solos-theme formats, and who put jazz back in touch with its pre–Charlie Parker heritage by reinvestigating ragtime, marches, Duke Ellington, Fletcher Henderson, and Jelly Roll Morton.

There's no way to turn back the clock on all that's happened in jazz over the last two decades, nor should we want to. To his credit, Marsalis *has* brought new audiences to jazz, although the critic Steve Futterman isn't the only one wondering if all that Marsalis has accomplished is to persuade "his upscale audiences that jazz could be as boring as they'd always secretly feared." Those of us who are more familiar with the rich diversity of contemporary jazz know that boredom isn't a danger so long as the music keeps evolving. Still, it gives me pause to consider that all of the most intrepid jazz experimentalists are now in their forties or older, while the leading musicians under thirty see themselves as craftsmen making small refinements on a time-tested art. Progress is frequently a myth in jazz, as in most other aspects of contemporary life. But it's a myth so central to the romance of jazz that the cost of relinquishing it might be giving up on jazz altogether.

(APRIL 1988)

Wynton's Ellington Jones

Duke Ellington's "Portrait of Louis Armstrong," from his *New Orleans Suite* and the last in what was actually a series of concertos for Cootie Williams, becomes a veritable hall of mirrors on the Lincoln Center Jazz Orchestra's *Portraits by Ellington* (Columbia): Wynton reflecting Cootie reflecting Pops. On the lips of another trumpeter his age or younger, Marsalis's whole-notes and squeezed exclamations might amount to nothing more than a sound check of brass techniques, or a modernist's condescending attempt to go old-timey. What enlivens Marsalis's choruses here (and on "Second Line," another of the album's selections from *New Orleans Suite*) is the orchestral sophistication he's acquired as a result of his immersion in Ellingtonia: his con-figuration of Duke's countermelodies (themselves buoyantly Armstrong-like) even during his stoptime diminuendo over just bass and drums.

Such thematic ingenuity would have been unimaginable from Marsalis a decade ago, during his recapitulating-Miles phase, or even five years ago, when he first discovered his horn could growl. No longer sharing much in common with his tadbop progeny, he's evolved in surprising directions, beginning with his embrace of New Orleans polyphony on *The Majesty of the Blues* in 1989. He might be uninterested in, even hostile to, innovation, but he's helped to widen this era's bebop status quo by lending his name to jazz rep. And though his Ellington jones has yet to result in a major composition (this year's *Blue Interlude,* modeled on Duke's "Pretty and the Wolf," showed him trying to display a sense of whimsy without first developing a sense of humor), it's stim-ulated his growth as a soloist. Whatever impropriety might be involved in Lin-coln Center awarding its first jazz commission to its own artistic director, Marsalis can hardly be accused of monopolizing the spotlight on the LCJO's first album, or at its Ellington tribute at Avery Fisher Hall last week (a home-coming for the band after a month touring the hinterlands). Marsalis seems to relish submerging himself in ensemble tasks, much the way that Kenneth Branagh and Emma Thompson do while returning to the Royal Shakespeare Company.

Reinterpreting Ellington can be tricky, not just because his pieces seldom suggest a stylistic era, but also because of his unusual covenant with his soloists (whose contributions were so integral to his scores that a repertory bandleader can't afford to allow *his* musicians much elbow room), and finally because we're talking about an impressionist whose music was seldom "pure." To do justice to Ellington requires doing justice to his inspiration, whether that be Bert Williams, Bill Robinson, a happy-go-lucky local, or a daybreak express. The beauty of the LCJO's conductor David Berger's transcriptions of late and/or seldom done Duke on *Portraits* (including the complete *The Liberian Suite*) lies in capturing more than just Ellington's textures and inflections; something approaching the Ellington Orchestra's irresistible surge takes over, thanks in no small part to Kenny Washington's authoritative rim-shots and willingness to let the tempos occasionally race ahead of themselves. Along with Washington and Marsalis, the album's heroes are Sir Roland Hanna, cast in the most difficult role of all, as the band's pianist; and Todd Williams, its youngest saxophonist, who—though unable to convey Coleman Hawkins's elder statesmanship (as opposed to just his harmonic buzz) on "Self Portrait of the Bean"—thrives in the near-modal climate of "Thanks for the Beautiful Land on the Delta" and amid the mock-pandemonium of "Total Jazz." On *The Liberian Suite*, the guest violinist Andy Stein strings as whimsically as Ray Nance on the 1947 Carnegie Hall premiere, even if Milt Grayson's proper, Eckstine-like enunciation is no substitute for Al Hibbler's relaxed and delightfully unaccountable cockney.

Herlin Riley, only slightly less dynamic than Washington, was the drummer at Avery Fisher, where the band was robbed of some of its sensuality by the hall's colorless acoustics and management's (or somebody's) decision to keep the houselights up, as though this were an evening with the Philharmonic. Still, the LCJO showed the benefits of its road work on a snarling "Ko-Ko" and a "Jack the Bear" properly assembled from the bottom up, with telling contributions by the bassist Reginald Veal, the baritone saxophonist Joe Temperley, and the plunger-trombone specialist Art Baron (a regular Son of Tricky Sam).

People used to wonder when jazz would finally be welcomed in bastions of high culture and if big bands stood a chance of surviving, little realizing that the answer to both questions would turn out to be the same—that the future of big bands would one day rest with monied institutions such as Lincoln Center, whose sponsorship would dictate a curatorial approach similar to that in highbrow music. Like it or not, concerts such as last week's now generate as much controversy as the taken-for-granted avant-garde once did. That's one of many ironies attending this curious period in jazz evolution, and although the ultimate outcome of this retrospective trend is anybody's guess, mine is that jazz as a side effect of its official sanction as "art" will splinter (or arguably already has) into two camps resembling those in classical music, with its own entrenched rebel elite as well as its own preservationist establishment. My other hunch is that Marsalis will continue to surprise us, though never leaving any doubt about which camp he's in.

(OCTOBER 1992)

BONUS TRACKS

My Worthy Constituents

1. The Dicty Glide

"Audiences are rarely on the same wavelength as performers," the pianist Dick Wellstood notes in *American Musicians,* a complete collection of Whitney Balliett's profiles of musicians for *The New Yorker* (excluding those of singers, which were published together in an earlier volume).

> The musician is wondering how to get from the second eight bars into the bridge, and the audience is in pursuit of emotional energy. The musician is struggling, and the audience is making up dreamlike opinions about the music that may have nothing at all to do with what the musician is thinking or doing musically.

Given that a critic's place is in the audience, it's ironic to find Wellstood's observation included in a book by the jazz writer who most clearly demonstrates the vices of impressionistic criticism, as well as the virtues. The virtues are self-evident when Balliett describes Bobby Hackett's "baronial, walk-in" tone; when he likens all great blues solos to "seizures" that "possess both the player and listener"; when he characterizes the "alarming shrieks and cries" played by Coleman Hawkins toward the end of his life as "Lear sounds." No other journalist has ever recorded his reactions to music in language so fanciful yet so oddly precise. But much of the imagery for which Balliett is celebrated is hallucinatory and overly synaesthetic (the drummer Elvin Jones's cymbals remind him of game birds "flushed" from cover, and he tells us that although Marian McPartland's slow ballads are like "rain forests," "her foliage is thinner at faster tempos"). It can also be absurdly genteel: "[Jess Stacy's playing] suggests many things: a maiden aunt summoning up her childhood, moonlight blowing through green trees, a lemon slice sliding over hot tea."

In the first chapter of *American Musicians,* on the pioneering French jazz critics Hugues Panassie and Charles Delaunay, Balliett observes that all first-rate criticism *defines;* this, of course, is what he does when his metaphors and similes hit the mark. When they miss, he merely describes—relying on imagery that projects his own leisure-class sensibility onto a music that hasn't yet fully emerged from its origins in hardship and oppression. One suspects that the pleasures of reading Balliett are strictly vicarious for a good many of *The New Yorker's* high-demographic subscribers. When he describes the view of the New York skyline from Marian McPartland's seventeenth-floor apartment—"the Empire State and the Chrysler Building and New York Hospital . . . knee-deep in brownstones," you feel as though you've been there. But when he charts out a "typical" Art Hodes blues solo, with its orderly succession of "descending right-hand tremolos, irregular left-hand tenths," "short, wobbly right-hand run[s]," "brief ascending five-note figures," "thunderous left-hand chords," "quick, right-handed glissandos," "clump[s] of single notes above middle C," and "snatches of Jimmy Yancey bass," the effect is the same—it's hardly necessary to hear Hodes on record or in the flesh, because it's unlikely that he could play a solo that would measure up to Balliett's idealized specimen.

The dicty glide of Balliett's prose (as Duke Ellington might have it) isn't the only problem with *American Musicians.* "[These pieces] form a gapped history . . . a series of close accounts of how a beautiful music grew, flourished, and (perhaps) began the long trek back to its native silence," Balliett writes in an introductory note—a requiem that admits it might be premature, but a requiem all the same. His "gapped" chronology begins more or less where it should, with Panassie and Delaunay, King Oliver, Jelly Roll Morton, and Sidney Bechet. But it ends with Ornette Coleman and Cecil Taylor, both well into the middle stages of their careers. The only contemporary musicians under the age of fifty included among these "56 portraits in jazz" are the guitarist Gene Bertoncini and the bassist Michael Moore, minor figures in chamber jazz who are in no way indicative of current directions. Bebop, much less all that has followed it, receives only token notice. Increasingly in recent years, Balliett has gone back in time to profile dead musicians, presumably because there are so few living instrumentalists for whom he can summon up much enthusiasm. (Posthumous portraits of Oliver, Morton, Bechet, Fats Waller, Coleman Hawkins, Dave Tough, Jack Teagarden, Sid Catlett, Art Tatum, Lester Young, Erroll Garner, and Zoot Sims are among the most lyrical pieces in the book.)

Given the stylistic diversity of contemporary jazz, critical specialization is inevitable, and Balliett is under no obligation to produce dutiful copy on musicians about whom he has nothing to say. But there are numerous young musicians worthy of comparison to all but their most illustrious elders, and the pity is that *The New Yorker's* readers are unlikely to discover them—unless Balliett has an unexpected change of heart.

In fairness to Balliett, he's hardly the only veteran jazz critic pining for the days when giants (supposedly) huddled on the bandstand. Among his fellow writers, there's widespread speculation that Balliett "cooks" his quotes—his subjects frequently come off sounding as eloquent as he does, and many of them are forced to shoulder so much historical exposition that they sound as though they're dictating their entries in John Chilton's *Who's Who in Jazz.*

But much of this is envious sniping. No other writer on jazz so successfully combines criticism and oral history, or elicits such revealing information from his subjects. The chapters on Wellstood, the alto saxophonist Lee Konitz, and the guitarist Jim Hall are invaluable for illuminating the anxieties that can trouble even the most accomplished improvisers. It's fascinating to hear Earl Hines speculate about how his and other black bands on tour in the American South in the 1930s might have been the first freedom riders, and Balliett lets us participate in the drama of hearing Elvin Jones tell of his decision to swear off heroin after sleepless nights listening for rats in his cell at Riker's Island (where he was briefly imprisoned after being convicted of possession). The musicians Balliett lavishes his attentions on emerge as unique, and one suspects that this is what drew him to them. One is drawn to Balliett for much the same reason. Say what you will about his profiles, there's no mistaking them for the work of anyone else.

(APRIL 1988)

2. He Thinks It's About Him

What's happened to Amiri Baraka? As LeRoi Jones, Baraka was arguably the most influential black poet and playwright of the 1960s. But his influence on younger black writers extended far beyond his books, and so did his notoriety. He was a man of words who became a man of action, a revolutionary in deed as well as in rhetoric. For a period in the early to mid-1960s, he was also an influential jazz critic, a proselytizer for the new music of Ornette Coleman, John Coltrane, and Cecil Taylor whose word carried considerable weight because he was the first black author of any literary renown to write regularly about improvised music. As a critic Baraka was strident in his enthusiasms and overly harsh in his denunciations. But his tone conveyed the rising black consciousness within the music itself, and his judgments have proved sound. Most jazz critics, regardless of race, would now accept as gospel Baraka's contention that it's impossible to discuss black music without discussing its matrix in black society (one of the central themes of his *Blues People,* published in 1963).

The Music, Baraka's first book on jazz in almost twenty years, is a messy collection of essays, speeches, poems, and an "anti-nuclear jazz musical." The book is hardly likely to enhance his reputation as a jazz journalist. Part of his appeal used to be his receptivity to the new, the feeling that he would always be within shouting distance of the men with the horns as they shook off their chains. But time has a way of catching up with all of us, and it appears to have finally caught up with Baraka, who thinks he sniffs the taint of European refinement in recent developments: "now within the music, a struggle is going on . . . between the legitimate tradition made new of Afro-American music, called jazz, and middle-class elements who think the music needs to be defunked and deblacked and creep around as an exotic tail of European concert music."

Accusations that jazz is becoming "too European" (that is, too white) are almost as old as the music itself (older, if one counts Scott Joplin and W. C. Handy). More specifically, Baraka seems to object to the jazz vanguard's increasing preoccupation with composition (and, presumably, its concomitant regard for improvisational form). But it could be argued that these developments, which have already resulted in thrilling music firmly rooted in jazz traditions, have less to do with the middle-class leanings of Baraka's favorite whipping boys than with the delayed influence of such black jazz composers as Duke Ellington, Thelonious Monk, Jelly Roll Morton, and Charles Mingus. I suspect that what causes Baraka to turn a deaf ear to this vibrant music—to yearn for the days when men were men and took forty-minute solos—is his callow brand of Marxism, which is more like bohemianism in its naive assumptions that class struggle is somehow about taste and revolution, about testing the bounds of middle-class propriety (you can take the poet out of Greenwich Village, but not Greenwich Village out of the poet). Even during the high 1960s, when nobody was faster than Baraka to spot new talent and recognize progressive trends, his self-dramatic proclamations sometimes overshadowed the music he was championing. "He thinks it's about him," the tenor saxophonist Albert Ayler used to say.

Baraka's poetry has become an exercise in hollow sloganeering ("DEATH TO ALLIGATOR EATING CAPITALISM / DEATH TO BIG TEETH BLOOD DRIPPING IMPERIALISM"), bartering its taut voice in futile simulation of jazz improvisation. *The Music* also includes a selection of likable if inconsequential poems by Baraka's wife, Amina (how can you resist someone who declares "I love the Working Class of all Nationalities" in the same litany of favorites with fried dumplings, antique rocking chairs, and Henry Fonda in *The Grapes of Wrath?*). But the poetry in this miscellany is secondary to the critical essays, the overwhelming majority of which shouldn't have been included, since they were commissioned by record companies as liner notes, a financial arrangement that can compromise a writer's independence, if he lets it. Is it a coincidence that Baraka refrains from voicing his distaste for the pianist Anthony Davis (one of the black musicians he castigates elsewhere in the book as a not-black or -proletariat enough "Tail European") in his notes for the vibraphonist Jay Hoggard's *Mystic Wind,* an album on which Davis performs as a sideman?

Baraka is still capable, if fleetingly, of incisive musical and social commentary. In his lengthy appreciation of Miles Davis, for example, he traces free-form and soul jazz (musical correlatives to the Black Panthers and the Southern Christian Leadership Conference, he argues persuasively) to Coltrane and Cannonball Adderley, the saxophonists in Davis's late-1950s sextet. And commenting on white objectification of black style—the blackening of white culture—he accurately observes that "the significant change in minstrelsy is that it more and more purports to be *real* white life." But the Davis chapter is pointlessly digressive and self-referential, and Baraka now writes as though too distracted by dogma to develop his most trenchant thoughts beyond the length of flippant asides. It's doubtful that *The Music* would have been published if its author didn't used to be somebody.

(JUNE 1987)

Jim Hall Has It Made

⸻

Jim Hall, the guitarist, is the sort of man who feels guilty about reading *The New York Times Book Review* because it means he's not using the time to read a book. His wife, Jane Herbert, is a psychoanalyst (as well as a singer and the composer of some of the prettiest songs that Hall has recorded), so his social circle includes professionals who don't consider jazz a proper career for a well-adjusted, middle-age white man. This ruffles Hall, even though he tries to let nothing ruffle him. "We recently spent a day in the country with two of Janey's colleagues, a husband and wife," he told me. "The wife asked me if I've ever thought of settling down and doing something 'meaningful' with my life. She meant it as a compliment, I guess—I was sober and reasonably articulate and not at all what she expected of a jazz musician. But it was like she was asking me what I wanted to be when I grew up. I tried to give her a sociable answer, but inside I was *seething*. I *wanted* to say, 'How about you, lady? Have you ever considered giving up your practice to become a hooker?' I'll be a jazz musician till I die. Being in the same profession as Duke Ellington and Charlie Parker isn't exactly slumming."

No one looks less like a jazz musician than Jim Hall—not even Bud Freeman, who prided himself on not looking like one. The celebrity panelists on the old *What's My Line?* would have had an awful time trying to guess the occupation of the bespectacled, prematurely bald young man who glances out from the cover of Hall's 1957 album *Jazz Guitar,* his first as a leader. Hall was the only white member of the tenor saxophonist Sonny Rollins's band in the early 1960s. On the road, when the band checked into hotels, desk clerks would mistake him for the band's manager, and the musicians often went along with the joke. Even now that middle age has combined with cosmetic improvements—wirerims, a tufty moustache—to give him a looser, more unbuttoned appearance, it's still easier to picture him holding a ledger, a stethoscope, or a rosary than a pick.

But Hall is without peer among living jazz guitarists—the only one, as Whitney Balliett once put it, "within touching distance of the two grand masters—Charlie Christian and Django Reinhardt." The late Paul Desmond, a close friend of his who had a way with words, once described Hall as "the favorite guitarist of many people who agree on little else in music," referring to musicians as different from one another as himself, Rollins, Bill Evans, Ella Fitzgerald, John Lewis, Ornette Coleman, Pat Metheny, and Itzak Perlman—all of whom have enlisted Hall's services at one time or other. He is an electric guitarist who's often commended by purists for treating amplification as a necessary evil. This misses the point. "Being amplified lets me play more *quietly* and still project," Hall explains, "and hopefully, at that lower decibel level, I can achieve a subtler range of dynamics and colors." His soft attack and veiled, underwater vibrato indeed make for contemplative listening. But only the most decibel-jaded listener could mistake Hall's lack of volume for a lack of intensity. Few soloists are as unambiguous in their relationship to the beat. He's a selfless accompanist, a sensitive interpreter of ballads, and a driving uptempo blues player. Though he's learned to accept praise graciously, it still seems to mystify him: a conversation with him suggests that even accomplished improvisers can suffer from insecurity. "I've never thought of myself as much of a blues player," he protests. "But if I am, maybe it's because you sound convincing on a blues only if you have something personal to say, and that's what I try to do all the time. It just comes out more on the blues, I guess."

WHERE HALL'S SPACIOUS BLUES FEELING COMES FROM IS ANYBODY'S guess, because he's both urban born (Buffalo, 1930) and bred (Cleveland). The first guitar he cradled in his arms, when he was ten years old, belonged to an uncle. "I've always fantasized that if he'd lived longer, my Uncle Ed would've become a famous country-and-western singer, like Willie Nelson. I adored him, but he was just my drinking uncle, like every family has. I must have shown some aptitude on his guitar, because one Christmas my parents bought me one that had to be paid off a dollar-seventy-five a week—the seventy-five cents was for the weekly lesson you had to sign up for if you bought the guitar on the installment plan. Fortunately I liked the teacher.

"By the time I was twelve or thirteen, I was playing in this junior high-school quartet—clarinet, accordion, drums, and guitar. The clarinetist owned some Benny Goodman records, and that's how I first heard Charlie Christian. I went out and bought a Goodman record with Christian on it, even though I didn't own a record player yet. I just carried the record with me everywhere I went, I guess hoping for osmosis."

Even now, an old magazine cover photo of Christian occupies a place of honor alongside the sheet music on the piano in Hall's workroom. "From hearing Christian, I got caught up in what I soon found out was called jazz, and without knowing how bad I sounded, I kept twanging away in little groups around Cleveland. I was leading a double life. In high school, I was class president and always making speeches in assembly, about citizenship and school spirit and all of that, but on the weekends I was playing saloons and running around with musicians nine or ten years older than me, which is a big difference when you're fifteen or sixteen, like I was.

"Gradually, I found other musical influences, most of whom were not guitarists. I liked Art Tatum's fearlessness about chords, and I was drawn to Coleman Hawkins, Lester Young, Chu Berry, and the men in Duke Ellington's saxophone section, possibly because I sensed that Christian had been influenced by saxophonists too."

Hall earned a bachelor's in music theory at the Cleveland Institute of Music and had begun work toward a master's in composition when "it dawned on me that everyone I knew was a perpetual student. You went to school as long as you could, then got a job teaching and avoided the real world altogether. Part of me was content to go that way, but another part of me wanted to see if I could cut it as a player. I would hear guitar players on the radio and think that could be me, but I wondered if I was really that good. Also, I had a paper due to this Viennese composition teacher who intimidated the hell out of me. So when a musician friend of mine told me that he had a job driving a Cadillac out to Los Angeles for delivery, I decided to go along for the ride, with the idea of maybe staying out there and trying my luck. I had an aunt there, so I figured I would at least have a couch to sleep on if nothing else came through. Then I wound up moving to New York around 1960 because it seemed like I was coming here all the time anyway with the groups I was joining on the West Coast."

Hall's New York baptism was as a member of the Chico Hamilton Quintet in 1956. "It was pretty frightening. We played Basin Street opposite Max Roach and Clifford Brown, and people like Bud Powell and Erroll Garner were in the audience. But everyone was very encouraging, and I felt like I had been accepted into this secret fraternity. The emphasis on strings in Chico's group [which also included cello and bass] meant that I wasn't buried underneath piano or horns, the way guitarists generally were at the time. I was always fortunate to be in groups where it was possible to hear everything the guitar was doing."

The next showcase for Hall was the Jimmy Giuffre 3, a monastic ensemble that at one point consisted of Hall's guitar, Bob Brookmeyer's valve trombone, and Giuffre's clarinet and saxophones. "Jimmy thought in terms of getting three independent melody lines going at once," Hall says, "with the rhythm taking care of itself." In practice, though, Hall functioned as a one-man rhythm section, "tuning the guitar down a fourth to get that rhythm guitar sound that would cover the bottom spectrum, and trying to play the sort of little fills that pianists like Jimmy Jones and Tommy Flanagan might when they were accompanying singers."

An even greater challenge was playing in Sonny Rollins's group for a year and a half, beginning in 1962. "The man's imagination is staggering. You stand next to him as he plays his solo, and you can't believe what you're hearing. Then it's your turn to play, and you think, 'Jesus, what's left?' It made me come to grips with the fact that there were things I'd never be able to play if I practiced for the rest of my life. But it also started me thinking about form. I still sometimes approach a solo the way I think Sonny might, taking a simple motif and expanding it until it's not so simple anymore—trying to do that without sounding studied or mechanical, because Lord knows, Sonny never sounds studied or mechanical.

"Sonny also had a profound effect on me personally. I was going through a heavy drinking period then, and though Sonny never said 'shape up' in so many words, he set an example by being completely straight and still playing all those outrageous solos. I think I was chemically disposed to becoming an alcoholic. Being on the go all the time, I needed liquor to help me concentrate and relax and increase my feelings of camaraderie with other musicians. I was very shy, very unsure of my ability, and I know that my shyness and uncertainty were sometimes misinterpreted as standoffishness, even racism— I grew up idolizing Coleman Hawkins, and when I found myself on a record date with him, it was difficult for me to put my arm around him and say, 'Hey, Hawk, what's happening, baby?' I finally reached the point where I believed I couldn't play my best without drinking, but the opposite was true. I was getting so drunk I couldn't play at all."

Hall's drinking problem drove him off the road for a few years in the mid-1960s. "After joining AA, I was afraid to walk into a nightclub for several years. I started to wonder what else I could do to make a living, so I started taking students. I taught privately for a while until it became obvious that . . . well, I don't want to say that I was a bad teacher, because I'm sure I helped the people who came to me already possessed of all the gifts and just needed encouragement. But I couldn't teach someone *how* to play guitar or *how* to improvise if my life depended on it. I had no system. Plus, I never knew what to charge for a lesson, and the people who were really good, who I enjoyed playing with, I felt funny about charging at all. Even now, I'm uncomfortable in the few clinic situations I let people talk me into doing. You know how it is: the students are all excited and start asking questions, and I have to tell them that on the subject of music I still have nothing but questions myself."

THE ANSWERS THAT HALL WAS SEEKING WEREN'T IN TEACHING OR IN THE staff position he took with *The Merv Griffin Show* in 1967—a job whose regular hours at least enabled him to put his personal life in order. When the show relocated to Hollywood in 1971, Hall stayed east. He's been back on the international club and festival circuit since then, though not at the grueling pace that once nearly did him in. He generally travels with a trio: he has used Don Thompson, Harvie Swartz, and Steve LaSpina on bass; and Terry Clarke, Ben Riley, and Akira Tana on drums. In New York, he occasionally plays duets with Brookmeyer and the bassists Ron Carter and Red Mitchell. The gigs that Hall enjoys most are those within walking distance of his Greenwich Village apartment. "I only travel two, three, or four weeks at a time, and only once or twice a year. The rest of the time I'm home with Janey, and she'll tell you I'm underfoot much more than a pediatrician husband would be." Tennis is a passion for him, fishing merely a hobby. "Bill Finegan, the arranger, is the fisherman. I'm distraught whenever I actually *catch* a fish, because I hate the idea of killing anything. For me, going out on the boat is a nice excuse to spend the day gabbing with Bill. It occasionally hits me that I've lost touch with so many of my old musician buddies. Paul [Desmond] was an old bachelor, and before his death, he used to come over for dinner once in a while and stay to play Scrabble with me and Janey and Debbie [Hall's stepdaughter, now in law school]. But most of the guys I know are on the move, out there working all the time, and I've become an old stay-at-home."

Hall is too self-effacing to acknowledge his role in shaping the values of such younger guitarists as Pat Metheny, Jack Wilkins, John Scofield, and Bill Frisell. "I hear a lot of young guys striving for some of the same things I'm after, but I think that's just the direction that the instrument is headed in now—it had nothing to do with me. One time I had the television on, going past all the channels with the sound off, and I saw someone with long hair, who I assumed was a rock guitarist. I went past that channel again, and noticed a stand-up bass in the group. So I turned up the volume and really liked what I heard. It turned out to be Pat Metheny."

In 1983, Hall wound up sharing the stage with Metheny. "Some friends of mine who teach at City College are also friends of Pat's, and they arranged for us to play a concert—my trio, Pat's group, then a little bit of us fooling around together for the encore. Some of Pat's fans were hearing me for the first time and had no idea of who on earth I was supposed to be. Janey was in the audience, and she says that two kids behind her started giggling when I came on. 'God, who's that? He looks like my father!' You know. But I think I made some converts that night. It was a very emotional experience, almost like a father-and-son reunion, though Pat and I had never met before. He was very deferential toward me, telling me how nervous he was to be playing with someone he's always admired, and I was pretty shaken up myself, hearing him talk like that. I think I embarrassed him when I asked him what all his equipment was for. I mean, Jesus, it looked like mission control up there.

"I'm not talking about Pat, but something I don't understand is the obsession that young guitar players have with hardware. I play tennis every chance I get, and one night I gave Ille Nastashe a lift home from uptown. Naturally, I was thrilled to have him in my car, and like a fool, I kept badgering him with questions about what kind of racquet he uses, what kind of strings, and so forth. The next morning, I realized that he was probably sitting there thinking, 'This guy knows *nothing* about tennis, or he'd know that stuff has nothing to do with it. If he knew anything, he'd ask me about my court sense or my backhand.' I feel the same way when I'm interviewed for a music magazine, and they ask me about my gear for the equipment box they run alongside the story. I want to caution the kids who read those magazines that the sound they're looking for has to come from inside of them, and they're only going to find it after years of hard work. Owning the right tools isn't going to do the trick, because there are no right tools."

Nevertheless, if pressed, Hall will admit to owning "two new guitars that Jimmy D'Aquisto made for me, one a regular acoustic, the other a classical guitar with a smaller neck—some people would call it a 'jazz' neck. Jimmy custom-made it for me because I don't have the long, graceful fingers you need to wrap around a classical neck. He also made me a new electric guitar that played like butter but didn't have a gutsy enough rhythm sound. So I sent it back, and he's making me another one. In the meantime, I'm still playing the old Gibson electric I've had for ages, and the two acoustics just sit there in my workroom, because I'm an electric guitarist at heart. I use soft, light-gauge flat-wound strings that allow me to do things with my left hand to get the guitar to sound more like a wind instrument. I can be expressive with softer strings because they offer less resistance and it's easier to wiggle 'em around, which is important when you play as quietly as I do. I use a standard pick—almost anything will do. I have a Polytone solid state amp that I don't like very much but which I take on the road with me because it's practically indestructible. Here in New York, I use either of the two old Gibson GA-50s that I've had forever. I like that warmer sound of the tubes. Warmth is one of the things I strive for. The other is clarity. I want a picture in my mind of the way a solo looks as I'm playing it. If I try to visualize its shape, I don't get bored. I get bored with my playing very easily, but that's a blessing in a way, because it helps me to avoid clichés."

Hall voices alarm over the emphasis younger players put on *"making it—* by which they mean making it big. I hope I don't come off sounding like one of those old geezers moaning about kids today, but I meet so many twenty-one-year-old guitar players who make demo tapes then want to get out of music and try something else when nothing happens for them *right away.* When I was a kid, 'making it' meant playing a solo that you could be proud of when it was your turn to play. Then you'd have to come back and 'make it' all over again on the next tune. Music isn't the stock market, or at least it shouldn't be. When you decide to become a musician, you're not tossing the dice to see if you'll get a hit record and make a killing. You start off with an ideal. Mine was to one day be able to play a solo that sounded as good to me as one by Charlie Christian. That's still my goal. I haven't done it yet, and I know I'm never going to, but I'll go on trying."

(JULY 1983)

OTHER FOLKS' MUSIC

Full of Foolish Song

≡

M iles Davis, on his first visit to London, in the late 1950s, supposedly remarked that he wasn't much enjoying himself, because it pained him to hear English spoken that way. It sometimes pains me, on listening to a show album, to hear Jerome Kern, Cole Porter, George and Ira Gershwin, Irving Berlin, or Richard Rodgers and Lorenz Hart performed "that way"—by which I mean as show tunes rather than as jazz. I feel this even though I realize that the fusty sopranos and rhythmless baritones making me cringe were usually the very singers for whom these songs were crafted. Insofar as Broadway was the point of origin for most of the songs now regarded as standards, musical theater is American popular song's mother tongue. But Broadway's most recognizable dialects are those of vaudeville and Viennese operetta, turn-of-the-century idioms that sound stilted to ears used to the relaxed pulsation of a Frank Sinatra or Ella Fitzgerald.

By virtue of removing songs from their theatrical context, these and other superior jazz and pop singers gain the further advantage of needing to project only themselves, not scripted characters. The fact that in practically every instance I happened to hear their interpretations first probably explains my preference for them. But another possible explanation is my having entered adolescence in the early 1960s, as part of the first rock 'n' roll generation—a generation convinced (and not unreasonably so, on the basis of *My Fair Lady, The Music Man,* and *The Sound of Music*) that Lerner and Loewe, Meredith Willson, and Rodgers and Hammerstein were synonyms for "square." A decade or so later, Broadway attempted to woo us by turning up the decibels with such frizzy monstrosities as *Godspell* and *Hair,* but this only succeeded in widening the breach. And though a soft spot for show tunes is an enduring gay stereotype, most of the gay men my own age I knew in the 1970s were more inclined to spend their weekends in discos than singing along in piano bars.

Things have changed since then. Broadway musicals are no longer categorically dismissed by arbiters of hip as bourgeois self-indulgence at its most ostentatious. Over lunch one day last year in New York, a journalist friend of mine in his late thirties who can always be counted on to know the latest buzz (as a staffer at one of the slicks, he usually has a hand in starting it) asked my companion and me if we planned to see any of the new shows while we were in town. This is a question he might once have asked only of an aunt and uncle in from the burbs for the proverbial Rotary convention. Also last year, in an edition of his *Village Voice Consumer Guide,* Robert Christgau—the rock critic most closely read by others in the field—wrote that only his preference for the original Guys and Dolls prevented him from choosing *Guys and Dolls: The New Broadway Cast Recording* (RCA Victor) as one of his Pick Hits. Studio restorations of George and Ira Gershwin's shows of the 1920s, such as the recent *Lady, Be Good!* (Elektra/Nonesuch), are accorded the same respect as new recordings of Beethoven and Stravinsky, and greeted with only slightly less curiosity than greets collections of previously unissued Bob Dylan. And people who see George C. Wolfe's *Jelly's Last Jam,* about the life of Jelly Roll Morton, leave the theater debating the show's racial politics, just as they do after seeing a movie by Spike Lee.

My generation's belated embrace of musicals past and present (and of singers such as Tony Bennett, Chet Baker, and Jimmy Scott) is generally taken to be evidence that we now require a roomier fit in our music as well as in our jeans. Maybe so, though as someone who has always held Elvis and Sinatra in more or less equal esteem and who enjoys much of the rap and alternative rock that's supposed to baffle people my age, I can hardly offer myself as living proof. My own experience is probably atypical, but one aspect of it is probably typical enough. Until persuaded otherwise by *Sweeney Todd,* massive doses of Kurt Weill and *West Side Story,* and a revival of *Oklahoma* that somebody dragged me to in the late 1970s, I had no use for Broadway. At around the time I discovered that there were musicals I enjoyed as complete scores (not just as mulch for the Fitzgeralds and Sinatras), I also realized that what had spoiled Broadway for me—along with rock 'n' roll's frank adrenal pitch—were those awful film adaptations of the hit shows of the 1950s and 1960s.

These movies, which amounted to the only exposure to Broadway that many of us had, tended to be implausibly cast (*Oklahoma,* with Rod Steiger as an ethnicized Jud who'd apparently read *An Actor Prepares,* is one example among many), and to overextend the big production numbers to the point of tedium. Much worse, in order to "open up" a show for the screen and thus prevent it from being perceived as uncinematic, its producer or director would often change into matter-of-fact dialogue talk that was originally used only to telegraph songs.

The point lost on these filmmakers was that musicals are inherently stylized, not naturalistic. The musical-theater scene that most persuasively sums up the medium's reason for being—and best reveals its capacity for magic— might be the one in Frank Loesser's *Guys and Dolls* in which Sky Masterson and Sister Sarah, just back from Havana and strolling through a quiet and nearly empty Times Square a few hours before dawn, serenade each other (and us) with "I've Never Been in Love Before," as luminous a song as any written for the stage. The crapshooter and the Salvation Army worker, tipsy with lust and unembarrassed to be "full of foolish song," could be singing this duet for all of Broadway's brimming-over couples, all the Curlys and Lauries and Tonys and Marias likewise so full of foolish song that giving voice to it becomes their only practical recourse. In drama as in life, crapshooters, street gang members, and ranchers and farmers who should be friends don't celebrate falling in love by bursting into song. In musicals they do, and when the songs are as seductive as the best of those in *Guys and Dolls*, we happily buy into the make-believe—an opportunity not offered to us by even the greatest recorded performances of Sinatra and Fitzgerald, who always are exactly who they are.

NATURALLY, "I'VE NEVER BEEN IN LOVE BEFORE" WAS OMITTED FROM Joseph L. Mankiewicz's 1955 movie of *Guys and Dolls*. So was "My Time of Day," the ode to nightlife that in Loesser's score amounted to the introductory verse to "I've Never Been in Love Before," and whose wide intervals were presumably too great a stretch for Marlon Brando, Mankiewicz's improbable Sky. But though hardly equal to the numbers he actually does warble, Brando manages to use his shy whisper of a singing voice to externalize the flamboyant Sky's hidden softness and decency, the qualities that prevent him from taking advantage of Sister Sarah after getting her soused on rum in Havana. Legend has it that Brando, once he found himself in a position to demand script approval, would insist on being shot or beaten up at least once in every movie, in order to enlist sympathy for his character. You can't help feeling sympathy for his Sky, whose wavering intonation and puzzled relationship to the beat are the aural equivalents of a bloodied nose or an arm in a sling.

Besides, there's never been an entirely satisfying stage production of *Guys and Dolls*, either—at least not in terms of the singers chosen to interpret Loesser's songs. In saying this, I realize that many will think me guilty of heresy. The LP of the original 1950 production (now available as an MCA compact disc) is one of the most cherished artifacts of the early original-cast-album era. Robert Alda and Isabel Bigley as the romantic leads, and Sam Levene and Vivian Blaine as their comic counterparts, the floating-craps-game operator Nathan Detroit and the showgirl Miss Adelaide, are generally believed to have set a standard to which the cast of the current Broadway revival can only aspire. But this lofty reputation strikes me as borrowed magic, a side effect of the realization that the unapologetic contemporary-American accent of Loesser's melodies and lyrics represented a real breakthrough for Broadway.

From the vantage point of four decades later, Bigley is nondescript, Blaine a little brassier than her role calls for, Alda close to tone-deaf, and Levene phlegmatic in the laryngological as well as the dispositional sense (a singing postnasal drip). The only performer from the original cast who gives a performance that you sense in your bones couldn't possibly be bettered is the inimitable Stubby Kaye, as Nicely-Nicely Johnson, the tinhorn who's so good at conning himself that his nag can't lose that he cons himself into believing his dream about needing to change his wicked ways. This, of course, is in "Sit Down, You're Rockin' the Boat," the biggest of the show's production numbers, delivered by Kaye in a voice as stout and unmannered as Jimmy Rushing's and preserved in the film version. (Seemingly wider than he is tall and therefore just made for Cinemascope, Kaye steals the movie; you can see the look of preternatural bliss on his face as he sings.) There's never going to be a comparable Nicely-Nicely, but on the cast album of the new *Guys and Dolls,* an eager beaver named Walter Bobbie sets the nerves on edge by whining "Sit Down, You're Rockin' the Boat" instead of singing it. I wish the role had been given to J. K. Simmons, who joins Bobbie on "Fugue for Tinhorns" and the title song, and whose voice is similar to Kaye's in amplitude as well as timbre.

In nearly every other instance, however, the new cast members outshine their predecessors, with Faith Prince and Josie de Guzman scoring especially high marks as Adelaide and Sarah, and Edward Strauss's orchestrations bringing out a jazzy shimmer in Loesser's melodies that wasn't always apparent on the first-cast album. Prince's skills as both singer and actress are such that what for once comes across in "Adelaide's Lament" is the wit of Loesser's lyrics about the perils of a girl remaining single, instead of just the character's Brooklynese. The challenge in singing the role of Sarah is that it demands two completely different voices—a prim and yearning soprano for "I'll Know," and a horny, openly amazed-at-itself slur for "If I Were a Bell." De Guzman is believable at both, perhaps because she has the wisdom not to overdo either.

As his gambler namesake, Nathan Lane relies more on comic timing than on vocal prowess, which is okay, because no role originated by Sam Levene requires much in the way of vocal prowess anyway. The role of Sky does, and Peter Gallagher isn't always up to the task, though his voice does curve handsomely under de Guzman's on their two love duets. A studious actor for whom singing is an acquired skill, as it was for Alda and Brando, Gallagher isn't bad, just unsure of himself. He's a Sky lacking in self-confidence, and this cannot be. The RCA CD includes a few of the spoken interludes leading up to the songs, and Gallagher frequently seems determined not to speak in his natural voice, much less sing in it. Just when he seems to be doing fine, he becomes Gordon MacRae.

GALLAGHER IS SAID TO HAVE DEVELOPED A COLD (AS MISS ADELAIDE MIGHT put it) just before the recording session, and this could be the reason he sounds so strained. But friends who've seen this new production tell me that Gallagher failed to live up to their mental image of Sky. One friend quipped that Gallagher comes across as so much the 1980s yuppie that the show's producers should have updated the book and had him beseeching Lady Luck to favor him in a leveraged buyout, rather than at craps.

My friend's unkind remark reminds us that actors who sing on Broadway are seldom cast for their singing abilities alone. They also have to look the part, and it helps if they're able to move and to deliver their spoken lines with some amount of grace. In a way, cast albums are no more than one-dimensional souvenirs of the shows they allegedly preserve. The exceptions are those albums on which a cast was assembled for the sole purpose of recording. These are usually not just revivals, but anthropological digs restoring to status quo ante songs discarded at one point or another during a show's early run. The masterpiece of this genre is John McGlynn's 1988 restoration of Jerome Kern and Oscar Hammerstein II's *Show Boat*—a more "theatrical" experience than most stage productions of the show, largely owing to the chill provided by Teresa Stratas as the mulatto Julie and McGlynn's retrieval of an ominous, quasi-gospel number called "Mis'ry's Comin' Aroun'."

Not every vintage show benefits from, or even justifies, this archival approach. A case in point is *Lady, Be Good*! (Elektra/Nonesuch), the latest in Tommy Krasker's series of Gershwin restorations, following *Strike Up the Band* and *Girl Crazy*. As presented on Broadway in 1924, *Lady, Be Good!*— the Gershwins' first smash—was less an organic whole than a series of star turns for a variety of the period's top performers, including Fred and Adele Astaire and the vaudevillian Ukulele Ike. In addition to the title song, the score introduced "Fascinating Rhythm" and "The Half of It, Dearie, Blues." It also introduced a number of period novelties there seems little point in recording now, especially with performers lacking the charisma of the Astaires. (An actual stage revival, with the songs complementing the action and vice versa, might be another matter.) On "Fascinating Rhythm" and "Little Jazz Bird," the singer and guitarist John Pizzarelli, this production's Ukulele Ike, exudes a carefree swing that six decades of jazz interpretations of the Gershwin brothers have conditioned us to expect from all performers of their songs. But Lara Teeter and Ann Morrison, though faithful to the composer's intentions, sound hopelessly dated in the roles originated by the Astaires.

There have been studio recordings of *Guys and Dolls,* but nothing like today's meticulous, carefully cast restorations. My own dream-cast recording of *Guys and Dolls,* featuring singers past and present, would include Stubby

Kaye and Faith Prince. My choice for Nathan would be none other than Frank Loesser, whose singing voice resembled Gene Kelly's in its regular-guy-ness, though his phrasing was far more relaxed than Kelly's—like a jazz instrumentalist singing a few choruses for his own enjoyment. I base this judgment on *An Evening with Frank Loesser* (DRG), a CD-collection of recently discovered "demonstration" versions of songs from *Guys and Dolls, The Most Happy Fella,* and *How to Succeed in Business Without Really Trying.* No one else has delivered Nathan's lines (from "Sue Me") "All right already, I'm just a no-good-nik . . . it's true / So *nu?*" with as much charm as the composer himself.

Frank Sinatra as he was in 1955 is the only man fit to play Sky, his credibility as a high roller enhanced by his long-alleged links to organized crime. Wasted in the role of Nathan in the movie of that year, presumably because Hollywood still considered him too much of a toothpick to woo a leading lady, Sinatra got his revenge eight years later as first among equals on an album of songs from *Guys and Dolls* by the Reprise Repertory Theatre (actually an ad hoc gathering of Rat Packers and their fellow travelers). This *Guys and Dolls,* reissued last year on a Reprise CD, is truly a crapshoot. Sinatra sings "I've Never Been in Love Before" so beautifully that you're willing to forget that the song is supposed to be a duet, and his bravura "Luck Be a Lady" (with Billy May's punching high brass taking the place of a chorus of crapshooters urging Sky to "Roll the dice!") has since become one of his trademark numbers. It's such a definitive performance that many of us now think of the song as Sinatra's, not Broadway's. Sammy Davis Jr.'s "Sit Down, You're Rockin' the Boat" is brash fun, and Jo Stafford's "I'll Know" is just about perfect (harmonizing with the orchestra where Sarah usually does with Sky, she interpolates the male response into the bridge). On the other hand, the McGuire Sisters' "A Bushel and a Peck" is sheer torture, as are Debbie Reynolds and Allan Sherman as Adelaide and Nathan. Your affection for Sinatra's half-juiced sing-alongs with Dean Martin and Bing Crosby depends on your sociological interest in the bonding habits of affluent middle-aged males of the early 1960s.

YOU COULD DO WORSE THAN JO STAFFORD OR JOSIE DE GUZMAN AS SARAH. But if we decide to go for shock value (and the guarantee of friction between the romantic leads), the choice would be Sinèad O'Connor, the Irish bristle-head who Sinatra said deserved "a kick in the ass" for refusing to allow "The Star Spangled Banner" to be played before one of her concerts a few years ago. Who better to play Sarah as a woman of spiritual conviction than O'Connor, a "recovering Catholic" who has likened herself to St. Joan, and who epitomizes as much as anyone on the fundamentalist right the intolerance of the pious? O'Connor's *Am I Not Your Girl?* (Chrysalis F2-21952) is hardly the first album of standards and show tunes by a rocker, nor is it the most novel. But it's the first to end with a whispered attack on "the Holy Roman Empire" for the "assassination" of Jesus Christ.

In light of which you might expect O'Connor to trash the eleven numbers she does here—an eccentric assortment including "Secret Love," "Bewitched, Bothered, and Bewildered," "Scarlet Ribbons," and "How Insensitive." And it wouldn't necessarily be a bad thing if she did; it might remind us that they're just songs, not the sacred texts that bookish young cabaret performers tend to treat them as. But O'Connor sings them straight, with no real distinction, braying only occasionally and never for very long. *Am I Not Your Girl?* is too awkwardly sincere to be enjoyable as camp, even on the Betty Boop-ish "I Want to Be Loved by You," where O'Connor sounds as though she's still wearing the platinum wig and temptress gown she donned to sing "You Do Something to Me" in the video for *Red, Hot and Blue*, the 1990 various-artists anthology that postmodernized Cole Porter in the name of AIDS (and outed him in the bargain). Like most of the rock performers who've attempted vintage pop, she doesn't have a clue how these songs are supposed to be phrased. What's surprising, in light of rock's pride in its big beat, is that rhythm is usually the area in which its singers come up short. Swing is a foreign language to them, and O'Connor is no exception.

So what do her fans hear in her? The answer's on "Success Has Made a Failure of Our Home," an anomaly for being an old Loretta Lynn hit, not something from Broadway or Tin Pan Alley. This is the only song on which O'Connor blares like she means it, as an army of dissonant horns blares right along with her. It shows how rock obviates the need for musical theater by creating lavish theater in listeners' imaginations. (Rock concerts at their most outlandish *are* musical theater, replete with sets.)

AM I NOT YOUR GIRL? ALSO INCLUDES TWO VERSIONS OF ANDREW Lloyd Webber and Tim Rice's "Don't Cry for Me, Argentina," one of them a "swinging" big-band instrumental. This mawkish number from *Evita* might seem as out of place here as the Loretta Lynn cover, except for the fact that O'Connor is twenty-five. Broadway has changed so much in the past two decades that Webber's rather than those of Rodgers and Hammerstein or Lerner and Loewe is probably the name that most people under the age of thirty now most associate with it. Webber's vulgar spectacles at least kept Broadway afloat through some lean times; that's about all that can be said in their favor. Along with British imports, the other new trend on Broadway in the past twenty years has been the "jazz" musical, usually featuring an all-black cast and built around the songs of an iconic performer of another era: Fats Waller in the case of *Ain't Misbehavin','* and Duke Ellington in that of *Sophisticated Ladies*.

Two such shows had their Broadway premieres in 1992, and there's a cast album for each. Essentially a revue, *Five Guys Named Moe* (Columbia) celebrates—or lamely attempts to—the influence of Louis Jordan, a singer and alto saxophonist whose hit records of the 1940s, which included "Is You Is or Is You Ain't (Ma' Baby)" and "Choo Choo Ch' Boogie," hilariously translated country homilies into urban jive and laid the groundwork for rhythm and blues in the process. Jordan's songs are as evocative of their period as a zoot suit, but they also represent superior musicianship of a kind that's timeless. You'd never guess this from *Five Guys Named Moe.* The title song was written for Jordan by Larry Wynn, who explains in the liner notes that the phrase "five guys named Moe" popped into his head one day as he was trying to remember the names of the lesser-known musicians on a recording date with Billie Holiday, Roy Eldridge, Teddy Wilson, Don Redman, and Georgie Auld. The five nonentities in this Broadway revue might as well all be named Moe, so indistinguishable are they in their cheery oversell of two dozen of Jordan's slyest numbers.

Jelly's Last Jam (Mercury) is something else altogether: more ambitious and more effective as theater, but mean-spirited and manipulative in its portrayal of its subject. Written and directed by George C. Wolfe, and starring Gregory Hines, the show tells the story of Jelly Roll Morton, the New Orleans "Creole of color" who claimed to have "invented" jazz—and whose tangos, stomps, and variations on ragtime and the blues practically originated jazz composition. Unfolding mostly in flashbacks after having deposited Morton and his immortal soul in the Jungle Inn, "a lowdown club somewheres 'tween Heaven and Hell," *Jelly's Last Jam* is simultaneously the most lavish of Broadway's black musicals and a withering critique of the genre. It breaks new ground in acknowledging the social disorder its subject's music evolved from, and in incorporating lighting and staging techniques associated with the shoestring avant-garde into what's essentially a mainstream, big-bucks extravaganza. But it plays Morton for a sucker, putting him on trial for being a light-skinned opportunist who formulated his music from the experiences of people darker and lower on the social ladder than himself, whom he persisted in thinking of as his inferiors. Some of the charges might be true, but you get the feeling that Wolfe, by changing the rules on Morton and questioning whether he was "black" enough by today's standards, is using Morton to work out his own conflicts regarding color and class. The most unforgivable part of it is that *Jelly's Last Jam* stacks the cards against Morton by never letting us hear his music in anything resembling its original form. The titles of his pieces have been changed to conform to Susan Birkenhead's didactic lyrics, and Luther Henderson's unsympathetic arrangements reduce Morton's idiosyncratic rhythms to generic 1920s doo-wacka-doo.

JAZZ ONCE DERIVED MUCH OF ITS REPERTOIRE FROM BROADWAY, BUT owing as much to changes within jazz as to a decline in the quality of Broadway songwriting, the process has been reversed, with shows such as *Jelly's Last Jam* and *Five Guys Named Moe* the unhappy result. In addition to the pleasures it affords in its own right, the current revival of *Guys and Dolls* is a reminder of a time when Broadway wasn't only more robust but also more autonomous.

The alto and soprano saxophonist Michael Hashim's album *Guys and Dolls* (Stash) is likewise a reminder of a time, this one approximately three decades past, when "jazz version of" LPs used to follow on the heels of the original cast recordings of most hit Broadway shows. Albums of this sort used to be plentiful: in the jazz section of used-record stores you're likely to find Teddy Wilson's *Gypsy*, Cannonball Adderley's *Fiddler on the Roof*, even (with some luck) Eddie Costa's *Guys and Dolls Like Vibes*. The target audience for such albums was presumably a little baffled by modern jazz but willing to make the effort to understand it if musicians obliged by playing familiar songs of recent vintage. This secondary market for jazz no longer exists, and such albums have disappeared along with it.

All of which might make Hashim's *Guys and Dolls* merely an irresistible anachronism. But it's also vital contemporary jazz. Thanks to their challenging harmonic structures, Loesser's melodies lend themselves as readily to chordal improvisation as they do to singing. Hashim and his sidemen—the drummer Kenny Washington, the bassist Peter Washington, and the pianist Mike LeDonne, who worked out most of the arrangements—do justice to the melodies even while taking such liberties with them as voicing "I'll Know" slightly sharp, slowing "Fugue for Tinhorns" to a saunter, and putting the drummer's brushstrokes up front on "If I Were a Bell." "My Time of Day" becomes a lonely blues wail, and "Marry the Man Today" is transformed into a semi-modal march, replete with Phil Woods-like puckers at the end of Hashim's lengthier and more excited phrases. In exercising their own improvisational flair, these four musicians also demonstrate the amenability of Loesser's songs to such novel approaches. A song-based improviser could hardly ask for better material.

They don't make albums like this anymore, in part because they don't stage shows like *Guys and Dolls* anymore, either. But did they ever? *Guys and Dolls* isn't just a Broadway musical. It's a down-to-earth platonic ideal of what a Broadway musical ought to be.

(MARCH 1993)

Infection

===

I'm so happy
I'm afraid I'll die
Here in your arms

What would you do
If I died
Like this—
Right now
Here in your arms?

So begins the first of many songs of love and death in *Passion,* the composer and lyricist Stephen Sondheim's third collaboration with the writer and director James Lapine, following *Sunday in the Park with George* (1984) and *Into the Woods* (1987). The show, which closed on Broadway last January after 280 performances (including previews) was based on the Italian director Ettore Scola's 1981 film *Passione d'Amore,* although Sondheim and Lapine also drew from Scola's original source—Iginio Ugo Tarchetti's *Fosca,* an autobiographical gothic published in 1869, the year of Tarchetti's death from tuberculosis and typhus at the age of twenty-nine. All three versions of the tale, which is as much a vampire story without a caped antichrist as it is a meditation on the nature of romantic love, take place toward the tail end of the Risorgimento, in a newly unified Italy at peace after two decades of war.

Passion survives on CD, the format in which it will inspire arguments for years to come, although there will surely be many other productions. On stage, the musical begins with a handsome young soldier and his beautiful mistress in bed together nude, tangled in post-coital bliss as they sing the duet quoted above (untitled on stage, as are all of *Passion's* individual songs, but called "Happiness" on the Angel cast album). Clara, who in the New York production was played by Marin Mazzie, is so happy she could die; Giorgio, played by Jere Shea, agrees that theirs isn't "another simple love story." Neither is the show, despite starting off like one.

On CD as on the stage, *Passion* includes no overture, nor is one needed. Military drumming followed by a stab of dissonance—what I think of as a "blood" chord—and a creeping three-note vamp reminiscent of Sondheim's music for *Sweeney Todd* blend into Giorgio and Clara's mutual declaration of love, which, with its harmonic deviations and sudden changes of tempo, foreshadows practically every subsequent number. That vamp—technically a "pedal point," or sustained notes in the bass register that remain the same as the harmonies around them change—is as sure a sign of unrest as the second S in *Passion's* elegant red logo, which is reversed and joined to the first at the down curve. The tops of the letters form both a valentine heart and a mirror image, suggestive of love as something potentially aberrant, twisted, narcissistic. The lyric to this opening number works in much the same way as the music—as a sort of premonition. This will be the last song in which an allusion to death is understood to be figurative.

We find out later (too much later, perhaps) that Clara is unhappily married but unwilling to leave her husband, because (under nineteenth-century Italian law) to do so would mean relinquishing custody of her little boy. This isn't the only thing keeping her and Giorgio apart. The luckless Giorgio, a captain decorated for saving the life of a fellow soldier on the battlefield, has received orders transferring him from Milan to a no-longer-threatened garrison in a provincial town in the northern mountains. This is where he falls prey to Fosca, his commanding officer's plain and sickly cousin, a hysteric already half in the grave. Giorgio's imagination and sensitivity set him apart from the camp's other soldiers, and Fosca recognizes him as a kindred spirit on the basis of these very qualities "They hear drums, we hear music," she sings to him at one point; and though her outburst alludes to those military cadences that open the show, the fevered rhythmic pattern to which her words are set echoes Giorgio's earlier declaration of his and Clara's "love that fuses two into one."

Fosca clutches at Giorgio, so obsessed with him that she pursues him without fear of humiliation. As many in the audience were, Giorgio is appalled by her manipulativeness and self-pity. Even so, he finds himself drawn to her, eventually concluding that her love for him—love "as pure as breath, as permanent as death, implacable as stone," in the words of the show's most haunting song—is superior in kind to any he's ever known: specifically, Clara's.

Fosca wins Giorgio's heart by convincing him that she would die for him. Someone hearing the CD for the first time, and unfamiliar with Tarchetti's novel or Scola's movie, might sneer that this isn't much of a sacrifice, given that Fosca is near death anyway. You need to read *Fosca* (available in English as *Passion,* in a new translation by Lawrence Venuti) in order to comprehend that a night of abandoned lovemaking will kill her.

CONTEMPORARY DRAMA CAN BE A TEACHER AND HIS FEMALE STUDENT ON opposite sides of a desk (David Mamet's *Oleanna*) or three men chained to a wall (Frank McGuinness's *Someone Who'll Watch Over Me*), but musicals are now admired for leaving nothing to the imagination. The most popular of them are feasts of conspicuous consumption, with the salient talking point for audiences being the cost of tickets in proportion to the size of the chorus lines and the immensity of the sets and special effects.

Passion wasn't only an anomaly by these standards, but as deliberate an affront as Sondheim and George Furth's *Merrily We Roll Along* (1981), which in lieu of costumes featured its young cast in sweatshirts that said who their characters were supposed to be. The newer show's only chorus line was a Greek chorus of uniformed soldiers who, marching in tight formation, misinterpreted Giorgio's motives in being kind to Fosca. Its primary sets were Adrianne Lobel's muted backdrops and scrims, which, an art historian friend of mine pointed out, were possibly intended to evoke the Macchiaioli, a school of mid-nineteenth-century Italian impressionists familiar only to art historians. This is a chamber musical in which a voluptuous actress who bares her breasts in the opening scene and thereafter strolls across stage reading her lover's letters in a succession of elaborate and brightly colored period hoopskirts and bustles is upstaged by another actress in drab, colorless dresses to her ankles, with a large wart glued to her face and her hair drawn back in a spinster's bun. Tarchetti's real-life model for Fosca was an epileptic. Skin and bones in an era in which obesity was a badge of both prosperity and health, the novel's Fosca might today be diagnosed as anorectic. What ails the musical's Fosca is never specified: described by the camp physician as "a kind of medical phenomenon, a collection of many ills," she seems to be suffering from generic nineteenth-century woman's disease—she faints a lot and is given to emotional outbursts. She's supposed to be hideously ugly, but the woman onstage in the New York production was no worse than homely. If this had been Andrew Lloyd Weber, there might at least be a show-stopping prosthesis.

Passion opened last May to mixed reviews, some of them frankly antipathetic. It received four Tony Awards, including one as the season's best new musical, though many in the theatrical community gossiped that this top honor was bestowed grudgingly and against not much competition. The show was a "hit" only in that it enjoyed a fairly long run, in part because it was relatively inexpensive to stage (it broke even at two-thirds capacity, and did better than that only occasionally).

Sondheim has described his score for *Passion* as "one long love song, one long rhapsody," and the show in its entirety—two hours long, with no intermission, no breaks for applause between numbers, and no postmodernist winking by the actors at the expense of their characters—as "a large one-act," "an opera in attitude," and "the world's first humorless musical." Ten years ago, when *Sunday in the Park with George* was new, Sondheim was frequently likened to the painter Georges Seurat, the show's protagonist, whose immersion in his canvases distanced him from the other characters in much the same way that Sondheim has increasingly distanced himself from Broadway audiences. Such are the demands that *Passion* makes on an audience—not just willing suspension of disbelief, but undivided attention to a score that circles back on itself endlessly—that Sondheim could also be likened to Fosca, who unreasonably demands Giorgio's love. To judge from the audiences I saw it with last summer, there could be a sign dangling from that reversed S on the Plymouth Theatre's marquee trumpeting Passion as THE NEW HIT MUSICAL NOBODY LIKES!

THIS WOULDN'T BE COMPLETELY TRUE, OF COURSE, BECAUSE THERE ARE many who admire the show immensely, including me. Sondheim's champions see him as Broadway's last remaining link to the grand songwriting traditions of George Gershwin and Jerome Kern. Some of us, again including me, regard him as this country's greatest active composer, regardless of genre. I'm not one of those people who adore everything he does, and *Passion* hardly strikes me as his richest score. It lacks *Company's* satiric vitality, *Sweeney Todd's* bigness and wicked cackle, the ill-fated *Merrily We Roll Along's* bounty of memorable songs. But coming as it does after the ostentatious *Sunday in the Park with George* and the trivial *Into the Woods* and *Assassins,* it marks a return to form. A double paradox in that it's a period music whose characters express opera-size emotions conversationally, in lyrics as spare and direct as any its composer has ever set to music, *Passion* also achieves an ideal Sondheim has been pursuing with varying success at least since *Company*—that of the Broadway score as a kind of symphony of voices, an integrated work in which individual songs are anagramatic movements.

Sondheim has said as much. "To me, it's important that a score be not just a series of songs—that it should in some way be developed, just the way [a show's] book is," he told Stephen Schiff, the author of a *New Yorker* profile published in 1993, when *Passion* was in the planning stages. The most frequent complaint against Sondheim is that audiences don't leave the theater humming his melodies, the way they did Gershwin's and Kern's. Sondheim— who was Oscar Hammerstein II's protégé but also studied with the "serious" composer Milton Babbitt, the author of a 1958 article variously published as "The Composer as Specialist" and "Who Cares If You Listen?"—often goes to perverse lengths to ensure that audiences won't hum the show on their way to the exits. The loveliest song in *Merrily We Roll Along,* for example, was "Good Thing Going," a love song that (in context) also becomes a song about the widening rupture between two men, a theatrical composer and his lyricist, who also happens to be his best friend. First sung by the lyricist accompanied by the composer on piano at a party for potential backers, the song is touted as a real beaut by the team's hostess (this is Sondheim setting a dare for himself). The most foolproof way to get an audience humming, as Sondheim has caustically observed in more than one interview, is to reprise ad infinitum throughout your show. "Good Thing Going" is instantly reprised by popular demand of those at the party—but the second time around the lyricist, reluctant to sing it again so soon, is joined by his hammy partner, and their voices are eventually drowned out by the jabbering partygoers (this is after the only partygoer so moved by the song that he hums along with it is shushed). Because the show moves backward in time, when we next hear "Good Thing Going," it's offered as an example of the songwriting team's juvenilia, taken at a nervous uptempo and saddled with awkward lyrics about the drawbacks of living in New York. The song received yet another trouncing in a wonderful revival of *Merrily We Roll Along* staged with Sondheim's blessing off-Broadway earlier this year (a cast recording is now available on Varese Saraband). It was sung as a teasing bump-and-grind by a sequined actress flanked by chorus boys in suspenders and derbies, in a devilish send-up of Bob Fosse. For that matter, the first time we heard "Good Thing Going" in this new production, Frank Sinatra was singing it. His 1981 recording was pressed into service to set up a TV interview with the song's "composers," who, in the show's present tense, are as sick of their hit song as they are of each other.

THE ORIGINAL PRODUCTION OF *MERRILY WE ROLL ALONG*, WHICH CLOSED after just sixteen performances in 1981, flopped, I think, because Sondheim incorrectly assumed that audiences were becoming as disenchanted with Broadway's excesses as he was. The songs in *Passion* don't have similar alienation devices built into them, but they discourage humming along in quite another way. John Simon in a review in *New York magazine* complained that all of the score's songs sound alike. Heard on CD, they do; but therein lies both their integrity and the root of the problem that theatergoers and reviewers had with them.

The songs are so much of a piece thematically that it's difficult even for someone like me, who saw the show more than once and has practically memorized the CD, to sing a few bars of one of them—literally or in the mind's ear—without another two or three intruding. Not that it's ever easy to extract a Sondheim melody from its harmonic crisscross, anyway—melody is his equivalent of Henry James's figure in the carpet. Sondheim is the first important American songwriter untouched by the blues, which might explain why so few jazz musicians have chosen to interpret his songs. Yet he might also be the only contemporary Broadway composer who writes songs much the way the typical jazz musician does, starting off with the chords and letting the melody emerge from them, instead of the other way around. His body of work has enormous jazz potential, but it goes unfulfilled on the new *Color and Light: Jazz Sketches of Sondheim,* a misguided all-star affair produced by Miles Goodwin and Oscar Castro Neves for Sony Classical. It also went unfulfilled on the Trotter Trio's chichi *A Passion for Jazz,* on Varese Saraband. No matter how taken you might be with them on first hearing, these songs don't replay themselves in your head for the next few hours. They're part of a score that gets under your skin and that could almost be a metaphor for a show in which one of the characters virtually infects another with her love: Giorgio's attitude toward Fosca softens only after he contracts a fever as a result of carrying her unconscious body back to the garrison in the rain, when he could have left her to die.

SONDHEIM'S MELODIES, NO LESS THAN HIS LYRICS, EVOLVE OUT OF situation and character. Yet in his shows, music clearly takes precedence over everything else, including story. He tends to be the favorite Broadway composer of those who feel that a show is finally only as good as its score, and because he's such an effective dramatist in his own right, his shows lose remarkably little on their cast albums. The *Passion* compact disc differs from most in not having a few seconds of silence encoded between bands; as in the theater, where applause after songs was actively discouraged, nothing is permitted to disrupt the show's alternating moods of intellectual contemplation and romantic swoon.

The disc actually improves on the show in one way: Jonathan Tunick's orchestration of Sondheim's score is fuller and more vibrant as a result of two dozen additional strings. Yet the moment on the disk that best captures the show's peculiar, dreamlike visual atmosphere features just woodwinds—what sounds like a trio of them—playing gaunt and wishful triads to begin a song titled "I Wish I Could Forget You." This figure, heard fleetingly throughout the score, often underneath and in counterpoint to another melody, serves as Fosca's theme

In its utter simplicity more like film music than a Broadway underscore, the theme here suggests a candle in a curtained room—burning brilliantly but close to the wick's bottom. Weakened by Giorgio's rejection of her, Fosca takes to bed with a fever. At the request of the camp physician, who's conducting what turns out to be a premature death watch, Giorgio spends the night in Fosca's room, hoping to comfort her by humoring her. She asks him to take down a letter, and though Giorgio blanches when she starts to dictate and he realizes that it's to be a letter from him to her, he reluctantly obeys. The song that follows begins as if it's going to be a duet, but as Fosca sings of what she would have Giorgio feel for her, the only line of hers he echoes is "that doesn't mean I love you"—not the next line, in which Fosca has him wishing he could.

Onstage, this scene fuses the score's most arresting song to an especially imaginative gambit by Lapine. Faithful to its sources, *Passion* is an epistolary musical: much of the time its three major characters sing letters they're writing or have just received, often in duet or trio and at a physical remove from one another. But this particular letter isn't in Tarchetti, and though Giorgio does write such a letter at Fosca's bidding in the movie, its contents aren't revealed and nothing more is made of it. In *Passion,* the letter assumes tremendous importance. Implying a physical intimacy Giorgio and Fosca haven't yet shared, it winds up in the hands of Fosca's cousin, who challenges Giorgio to a duel. Giorgio is too much the gentleman, too much the man of honor, to tell the colonel the truth, because to do so would confirm that the unlovely Fosca was incapable of arousing such deep and protective feelings in a man.

This is the stuff of melodrama, nothing more. But the song that sets these events in motion lends them resonance, if only because an epistolary musical is quite another matter from an epistolary novel. *Passion*'s stage characters literally give *voice* to one another's thoughts. The letter is an emotional forgery, an utter fabrication. Yet when Fosca—putting words in Giorgio's mouth, though we hear them from hers—has Giorgio realize that her love for him is deeper than any he has ever known, she's displaying an element of telepathy: he'll eventually decide this for himself.

Nothing short of beautiful in its melodic descent, "I Wish I Could Forget You" requires Donna Murphy, as Fosca, to swoop below the staff—a strategy by which Murphy and Sondheim manage to convey the character's shortness of breath while aligning her with Grabo's Camille and other seductive, sepulchral-voiced movie vamps. The first time I saw *Passion,* I left the theater thinking that there was a bit too much of the Broadway Baby in Murphy's singing—an excess of pizzazz at odds with her frail and gasping character. Listening to the CD, I think I was wrong: the song is Murphy's finest moment. In an earlier song, Fosca tells the captain that, unlike him, she doesn't read to learn—she reads to live. Fosca is a woman who's experienced most pleasures vicariously, and Sondheim gives her songs that, more than most, require Murphy to merge acting and singing. She portrays Fosca as a woman with a blazing inner life—someone who, in this context, *sings* to live.

THIRTY-FOUR YEARS AGO IN FRANK LOESSER'S *HOW TO SUCCEED IN* *Business Without Really Trying,* Robert Morse cunningly performed "I Believe in You" while staring at himself in a mirror. The song, extolling the virtues of "a seeker of wisdom and truth," has enjoyed a life outside its show; it's usually interpreted as an uptempo love song, an ode to an irresistible idealist. Nobody remembers that mirror.

One of the songs Barbra Streisand performed during her HBO special last summer was Sondheim's "Not While I'm Around," which she dedicated to her grown son, who was in the audience. In *Sweeney Todd,* this odd lullaby, which begins "Nothing's gonna harm you," was sung to Angela Lansbury by a street urchin powerless to prevent her death or his own. Yet there was nothing amiss in Streisand's motherly reinterpretation, because this is another song removable from its original context. Though it would make a good torch song, I can't imagine Streisand or anybody else singing "I Wish I Could Forget You" away from its show. The problem wouldn't be the lyric's indeterminate point of view. It would be those lines I quoted earlier about a love "as permanent as death," and a final verse that begins "and if you die tomorrow," which couldn't withstand a pronoun change on account of its rhyme scheme.

The song is inextricable from the show; it's what the show's about. Fosca tells Giorgio that her sickness "is as normal to me as health is to you." A few days after seeing *Passion* for the second time, I was hospitalized with a 104-degree temperature, a symptom of what was ultimately diagnosed as a serious bacterial infection. In a situation in which part of my role as a good patient was to monitor my moods and bodily functions and dutifully report even the slightest change, I no longer saw Fosca's morbid self-absorption as quite so absurd. Fosca's love for Giorgio is supposed to be superior to Clara's by virtue of not being carnal. At least that was what Sondheim and Lapine said in interviews. But I don't think they know what their show is about. One thing that works against their interpretation is that Clara is portrayed much too sympathetically for us to assume that her love is only skin-deep. (Besides which, it would be impossible to find someone who sings Sondheim as gorgeously as Marin Mazzie does wanting in any respect.) And at the end, when Giorgio sings of having recognized in Fosca "love without reason, love without mercy, love without pride or shame," you want to shake him and remind him of his earlier question to Fosca: "Is this what you call love? This endless and insatiable smothering . . ." He's merely submitting to Fosca's dementia, and neither he nor the show's creators seem to recognize the difference. Regardless of Sondheim and Lapine's original intentions, the dichotomy represented onstage wasn't between body love and soul love, but between health and infirmity, the pang of happiness and the unaccountable lure of death. On Broadway, the pink of Clara's nude flesh in the opening scene contrasted as dramatically with Fosca's coffin pallor as the two women's songs did in major and minor keys.

Passion takes place in the world of the sick—not a place Broadway audiences in the mood for uplift particularly want to go. They still want to be told they'll never walk alone. As drama, the show will always be something of a muddle, but it's moving because the score is. New York audiences had trouble accepting Giorgio's final change of heart. It struck them as illogical, and it is— but that wasn't why they left the theater unsatisfied (who goes to the theater for logic?).

The problem isn't confined to a stage production. It's musical. The song with which Giorgio expresses his love for Fosca isn't ablaze with the rest of the score's sixteenth-note rhythms and sustained chords. It's inorganic. So is "Loving You," the show's big take-out ballad, in which Fosca tells Giorgio that he's become her reason for living. This song, which has Barbra Streisand written all over it, was added to the score at the last minute, in order to make Fosca more sympathetic. It's a pretty song, but it doesn't belong in this score.

IF ONE RESPONDS TO *PASSION* AT ALL, IT'S BECAUSE OF SONDHEIM'S MUSIC, which is what newcomers will find on CD. Robert Brustein, in his favorable review of the show in *The New Republic,* said that he found himself "sobbing uncontrollably" at the end. I think the implausible story got to him only because the music did. I was similarly shaken by the new production of *Merrily We Roll Along* last summer. By the final curtain I realized that, quite without meaning to, I had conducted my personal life and my career in such a way as to betray both my closest friends and my highest ideals. Then I realized that I had done nothing of the sort; Sondheim's recurring bass figures had rubbed me raw, making me an easy mark for the book's burned-out, middle-aged blues.

More than any of Sondheim's previous shows, *Passion* embraces the concept of the "integrated" or "organic" stage musical—one like *Oklahoma!,* in which songs illuminate character and advance the plot—and takes the next logical step, to the Broadway score as a feat of extended composition. This is the sense in which Sondheim is the greatest heir of Jerome Kern, who attempted something of the same thing in his score for *Show Boat,* although this is often overlooked amid the praise for it as the first show in which music and book served a unified end.

Sondheim's dilemma is that such musical innovation is generally lost on today's Broadway audiences, who ask for nothing more from a show (and nothing less!) than vulgar spectacle and a few sentimental melodies; a patina of social consciousness is optional. In "Who Cares If You Listen?" Milton Babbitt recommended as the ideal strategy for the serious composer "voluntary withdrawal from [the] public world to one of private performance and electronic media with its very real possibility of the complete elimination of the social aspects of musical composition." As a composer of vocal music with

little taste for grand opera—however much his best scores approximate it—
Sondheim is in no position to heed his former mentor's advice. He needs
Broadway. What I wonder is if Broadway, which often seems to tolerate him
only because it needs the occasional *succès d'estime* in order to go on thinking
of itself as a thriving artistic medium, will ever realize how much it needs him.
Sondheim and Broadway isn't another simple love story, that's for sure.

(MARCH 1995)

Black Faces, Black Masks

$\equiv$

Rock 'n' roll has outlived its usefulness to most of us who grew up with it. The current hits aren't about us anymore, but that's all right—we're no longer the ones crowding the clubs and record stores. Pop has always existed primarily for the young, the only ones who have time for it. The source of our disenchantment is in realizing that the songs of our high school and college years are no longer about us either—they reflect where we were in our lives then, not where we are now.

This may be why so many of my friends have developed a sudden interest in country, a style of pop whose subject matter is less often adolescent sensuality than adult wreckage. And unless you buy the argument that Cole Porter is one of the finer things you develop a taste for in your forties, along with cognac and cigars, it may also explain why so many aging rock singers, on finding themselves in a reflective mood, have turned to songs given their definitive interpretations by Frank Sinatra in the 1950s, when our parents were our current age. With notable exceptions, including Neil Young, Richard Thompson, and Loudon Wainwright III, the pop singers of our own generation have given us no clue how grown-ups of our day are supposed to feel and behave as they enter middle age. This is because these pop singers know no better than we do. Bob Dylan sings to us now in the voice of a grizzled old prospector—not his voice but that of a unconvincing fictional character. And Bruce Springsteen's operas on the turnpike no longer give the illusion of having an unseen cast of thousands; they could now be taking place in the driveway of his and his fashion-model wife's Hollywood mansion.

I sense, too, that the first full generation after ours—the grandchildren of Marx and Coca-Cola, to extend something Jean-Luc Godard said about us in *Masculine Feminine* to its logical conclusion—might be more disenchanted with rock than we are: between their favorites and ours exists no clear line of demarcation like the one that existed between the crooners our parents had enjoyed and our yowling idols. (Not that today's kids haven't come up with an alternative to rock. It's called . . . alternative rock. Not even the flannel shirts are new.) Pop today, in other words, has something to alienate everyone: people in their late thirties and older, that it's not just theirs anymore; younger people because it never was just theirs.

No other subgenre of pop alienates as many people as deeply as rap does, despite what I sense to be a suspicion—even on the part of those who profess to find rap indistinguishable from random gunfire—that rap is the only thing happening right now, the only kind of pop with the sort of larger cultural significance taken for granted of pop since Woodstock.

BY THE TIME A RAP SONG FIRST MADE THE NATIONAL CHARTS—"RAPPER'S Delight," by the Sugar Hill Gang, in 1979—rap was already something of an old story, having started about five years earlier as an underground offshoot of disco. Its origins as a dance music are hinted at in its other name, "hip-hop," which is preferred by those for whom it's not just music but a look, an attitude, and a lifestyle, although even they frequently use the terms interchangeably. The "rap" is the lead vocal or vocals; "hip-hop" is the vocal plus everything else on the record—the background chants and disjunct instrumental sounds that initiates call "the beats," which are sometimes supplied by live singers and musicians but are more frequently the result of a disc jockey's sampling or tape-looping bits and pieces of other records.

In the beginning, the rap was optional. Hip-hop's first heroes, in Harlem and Bronx dance clubs in the early 1970s, were its DJs, turntable artists who provided a nonstop groove for dancers by isolating, electronically boosting, and repeating ad infinitum bass lines and drum breaks from 1970s funk and glam-rock hits. Although vilified by some as plagiarists and scavengers, these hip-hop DJs (Grandmaster Flash and Afrika Bambaataa became the most famous of them) were essentially grassroots successors to Phil Spector, Brian Wilson, and George Martin, the 1960s rock producers who pioneered the use of the recording studio as an instrument in its own right. A sociological study that attempted to link the rise of hip-hop to the decreased availability of musical instruments in public schools since the 1970s would be right on target. In the meantime, what needs to be acknowledged about hip-hop, apart from its paradoxical origins as a roots music dependent on electronic technology, is its remarkable staying power. It's outlasted graffiti, break-dancing, and every other manifestation of the black-teen Zeitgeist of what it was initially seen as only one component.

Rap remains dance music, despite the diminished role of DJs, increased public scrutiny of its lyrical content, and the distrust that some hardcore rappers seem to have of contemporary dance culture. ("It represents the gay scene, it's separating blacks from their past and their culture, it's upwardly mobile," Chuck D, of the group Public Enemy, says of the dance music called "house," pretty much echoing the complaints of rock 'n' rollers and soul fans about disco in the 1970s. Needless to say, Chuck D is a homophobe who can't dance.) On the most basic level, a catchy rap song wins you over in much the same manner any good pop song does: by virtue of its hooks—those vocal refrains and stupid instrumental riffs you can't get out of your head, no matter how chagrined you are to find them there. The most imaginative of the record producers who have succeeded the DJs—Teddy Riley (Wreckx-N-Effects, Kool Moe Dee, and Heavy D. and the Boys), Prince Paul (Queen Latifah, Big Daddy Kane, 3rd Base, and De La Soul) and Hank Shocklee (Ice Cube and Public Enemy)—are responsible for the only formal innovation in pop since the punk minimalism of Talking Heads and the Ramones in the late 1970s.

The controversy surrounding rap, however, usually concerns its lyrics, not its hooks or its merits as dance music. In Michael Small's informative 1992 rap scrapbook, *Break It Down* (Citadel Press), Afrika Bambaataa includes on his list of rap's possible antecedents African call and response, the insult game called the dozens, Cab Calloway, chitlin-circuit comedians, bebop scat singing, black nationalist oratory, Jamaican dance-hall "toasts," and the "political awareness rap" of the Last Poets, a spoken-word group popular in the 1970s. Others have mentioned jive-talking black radio disc jockeys, the singing poet Gil Scott-Heron, and the jump-rope game double dutch.

Rap can also be compared to 1950s a cappella or doo wop, with which it shares a street-corner male ethic, a delight in onomatopoeia, and an ingenuity in making do with very little. The difference is that doo wop's young singers were forever trying on courtly feelings much too large for them, on already popular songs such as "Red Sails in the Sunset" and "A Sunday Kind of Love." Rap has no dreamy side—unless you accept, as an indication of how times have changed, a song like Ice Cube's "It Was a Good Day," from his recent CD *The Predator,* in which Ice Cube enjoys marathon sex, gets drunk without throwing up, doesn't get stopped and searched by the police, doesn't have to attend the funeral of any of his homies, and goes the entire day without having to fire his AK-47. As if to show us what a fantasy all this is, the video for the song ends with Ice Cube in a Los Angeles SWAT team's crosshairs.

Ice Cube, a founding member of a group called N.W.A. ("Niggas With Attitude"), epitomizes "gangsta," probably the most popular style of rap right now, and certainly the most truculent and ghettocentric—the style people have in mind when they condemn rap for its comic-book Afrocentrism, its monotonous profanity, its Uzi-brandishing, its anti-Semitism and intolerance of Asians, its homophobia and crotch-grabbing misogyny, its nigger-this and nigger-that, and the seeming determination of many of its performers to fulfill every negative black stereotype. According to gangsta's apologists in the music press, these objectionable characteristics are symptoms of black disempowerment. It's difficult to argue with this at face value—difficult not to feel, on being subjected to a musical drive-by from a Jeep whose back seat has been torn out and replaced with speakers, that what one is hearing is the death rattle of Martin Luther King Jr.'s dream.

Usually it's just some kid letting the world know that he's alive and has a car. Just as there's something called alternative rock, which nobody in the music business seems quite able to define except by example, there's something called alternative rap—perhaps best exemplified by the group Arrested Development. Musically, the difference between gangsta and alternative is that alternative tends to be more playful, both in its rhymes and in its sampling. But the *perceived* difference between the two styles has almost nothing to do with music. One gains a sense of what both gangsta and alternative have come to stand for by listening to "People Everyday," a song from Arrested Development's platinum debut album, *3 Years, 5 Months & 2 Days in the Life of . . .* Speech, Arrested Development's leader, is spending the afternoon in the park with his girlfriend, when along comes "a group of brothers" swigging forty-ounce bottles of malt liquor, "goin' the nigga route" and "disrespecting my black queen." Speech at first ignores them, but after they make fun of his "colorful" garb (an Afrocentric variation on thrift-shop chic, to judge from the album cover) and start "squeezing parts of my date's anatomy," he springs into action. "I ain't Ice Cube," Speech tells us, "but I had to take the brother out for bein' rude."

It takes "three or four" cops to pull Speech off of the gangsta (who evidently survives the encounter), and the story becomes one of "a black man, acting like a nigga and [getting] stomped by an African." But Speech, who tells us on another of the album's songs that he's "a bit shorter than the average man," and on yet another that "brothers" in possession of automatic weapons "need to learn how to correctly shoot them, [to] save those rounds for a revolution," has more in common with Ice Cube than he may care to admit. A machismo fantasy's still a machismo fantasy, even if it takes the form of an appeal to black pride rather than a call for retribution against the police. And shouldn't a songwriter praised for leading one of the few sexually integrated rap groups know better than to put a woman on a pedestal as his "black queen"? At least she's not his "bitch" or his "ho," as she might be on a gangsta record. And at least Speech's politics are slightly more sophisticated than those of the gangstas, many of whom claim Malcolm X as their role model, although what they seem to find most admirable about him is that he was once a thug with the gift of gab, just like them.

BEYOND COMPLAINING THAT RAP ISN'T REALLY MUSIC BECAUSE SO FEW of its performers play instruments or "sing" in the conventional sense of the word, middle-class whites who grew up dancing to Motown's three-minute integration fantasies seem to be most alienated by what they take to be rap's black-separatist agenda. (During Reconstruction, before they switched to hooded robes, Klansmen used to wear white facemasks on midnight raids. Rap is a form of blackface in much the same way: an attempt not to overcome or disguise one's race but to idealize and exaggerate it—to do battle with it.)

A deeper source of frustration might be a sense on the part of middle-aged whites that rap's tacit off-limits sign is generational, not racial. But at whose young is rap aimed? In a nasty little cover story on rap in a 1991 issue of *The New Republic,* David Samuels argued that the audience for rap now consists in large measure of white middle-class teenagers turned on by rap's "evocation of an age-old image of blackness: a foreign, sexually charged, and criminal underworld against which the norms of white society are defined and, by extension, through which they may be defiled." The cover of Ice-T's recent *Home Invasion,* which depicts a white tousle-top surrounded by the books of Malcolm X, Donald Goines, and Iceberg Slim, listening to music (this very album?) on headphones as he fantasizes that his mother is being ravished and his father is being beaten to death by muscular black intruders, suggests that there's some merit to Samuel's argument. As does L. L. Cool J's observation, on listening to Da Lench Mob's "Fuck You and Your Heroes," that "That's a song for white folks. If you want to shock niggas, you gotta say, 'fuck Malcolm X, fuck Martin Luther King.'"

But so what? Rap's young white fans are hardly the first of their race to get off on black music. The problem with focusing on what percentage of rap's audience is white and whether the militancy of some of its performers panders to white sexual fantasies is that such questions leave black adults out of the equation. Reading any of those recent trendy books and magazine articles contrasting the tastes and values of Boomers with those of their offspring, you might think that generation gaps were an exclusively white phenomenon. Yet a visit to a record store in which you'll find one section for rap and another for soul should be proof enough that black America has its own generation gap, of which differing tastes in music are only the tip. As the essayist Gerald Early has pointed out,

> Each new generation [of African Americans] views its elders with suspicion, thinking them failures who compromised and accommodated themselves in order to survive among the whites. And each generation, in some way, wishes to free itself from the generation that produced it.

African Americans now in their late thirties or early forties, already resentful of their marginalization by mass media that tend to present black culture only in terms of new directions in jive, must sometimes feel as though everything they grew up believing in is under attack in some of the music their children are listening to. "When we first started, everything was black-this and black-that—the whole positive black thing," Easy E, the former drug dealer who was a founder of N.W.A., once explained to an interviewer. "We said fuck that—we wanted to come out in everybody's face. Something that would shock people."

Parents have always been mocked for being convinced that their children are emulating poor role models and headed straight for trouble. But given such grim statistics as the one showing that black teenage males have a greater chance of serving prison sentences than of attending college, today's black parents are justified in thinking that their children genuinely are at risk. And this particular generational clash is exacerbated by class friction of a sort seldom experienced by whites. In *Juice*, an otherwise forgettable 1992 action movie directed by Ernest Dickerson (Spike Lee's cinematographer), a young man named Quincy who is an aspiring hip-hop DJ from the projects introduces himself as "Q" (his street name) to the estranged husband of the older woman he's been sleeping with. "What, did names like Mustafah and Akbar become too hard to spell?" the husband sneers. His equal disdain for the African or Islamic names given to children by roots-conscious black parents in the 1970s and for the breezy street names many of those kids have since adopted is a tip off that this man in a suit is a member of the black bourgeoisie, or at least aspires to it. Both kinds of names reek of the ghetto to him, and this makes him an unsympathetic character in the movie's scheme of things. But what gives the scene its surprising complexity is the glimpse it provides of the alienation felt by many middle-class African Americans at a time when the ghetto street culture celebrated in rap is increasingly viewed as the only authentic black experience (apparently even by a black achiever like Dickerson).

MY OWN FEELINGS ABOUT RAP ARE SO CONFLICTED THAT I HARDLY KNEW how to answer when somebody asks (usually incredulously) if I'm a fan. I'm not, exactly. The first requisite for being a fan of anything is to think of it as somehow *yours,* and I no longer feel entitled to think of any pop music as "mine," rap least of all. Yet I listen to a fair amount of rap out of a combination of professional obligation and curiosity, and wind up enjoying much of what I hear—though even that often saddens or troubles me. The rapper most admired by my colleagues is Chuck D, of the group Public Enemy, who has, in effect, put a beat to the bluster of the Black Panthers and the Nation of Islam. Marshall Berman, a professor at the City University of New York and the author of *Everything That Is Solid Melts into Air,* an influential text on modernism, has likened Public Enemy's "breakthroughs" in rap to "Picasso's in painting, Eliot's and Pound's in poetry, Faulkner's and Joyce's in the novel,

Parker's in jazz." If you say so, professor. All I hear in Chuck D is a rapper whose delivery is too sententious to be convincing and whose worship by the pop intelligentsia is evidence of the extent to which black racism is now deemed a legitimate response to white oppression.

The rap performers I enjoy are those who emphasize production values, songcraft, and that quality of playfulness endemic to all good pop. These include P. M. Dawn, Neneh Cherry, De La Soul, and a new group from Los Angeles called The Pharcyde. Another new group, the Digable Planets, are nothing if not playful in attempting to fuse rap with elements of bebop, but what finally turns me off about them is their reduction of jazz to walking bass lines, finger-snaps, and bohemian vogueing.

These performers (I'll add Arrested Development, if only for their "Tennessee," an evocation of the agrarian South as a place filled with both harrowing and idyllic memories for black Americans) suggest the wide range of approaches possible in a genre as seemingly inflexible as rap. My very favorite among all recent pop albums is one generally spoken of as an example of alternative rap, though it might not be if the young performer responsible for it weren't black and didn't employ sampling and other hiphop studio conventions.

Michael Ivey is the leader of a group called Basehead, which—at least on its debut album, *Play with Toys*—turns out not to be a group at all but just Ivey on guitar and vocals, a drummer named Brian Hendrix, and a handful of other musicians drifting in and out of the studio. Ivey sings in a small voice as uvular as any we've heard since Donovan. When he isn't singing, he's speeding up and slowing down the tape to alter his speaking voice: what are presented as arguments between him and his friends are actually Ivey's stoned interior monologues. Although "basehead" is street slang for someone who freebases cocaine, the illegal substance of choice in Ivey's songs is marijuana, and even it takes second place to beer—Ivey or one of his imaginary buddies is always popping the top off a cold one.

Ivey is a musical as well as a verbal ironist who delights in subverting both rock and gangsta-rap conventions. His guitar riffs demonstrate pop's boomerang effect: played a little faster and with more thunder, they could be the riffs that Led Zeppelin and other British protometal bands appropriated from Delta bluesmen. The bass-heavy sound mix on *Play with Toys* is similar to those favored by the gangstas, but Ivey turns the tables on them by sampling N.W.A.'s "8 Ball" on a song called (what else?) "Ode to My Favorite Beer."

Ivey's melodies are slightly woozy and doggedly minimalistic: a key change is a big event. Not much happens in his lyrics, either, and that's probably what I like about them. "It's the existential hero—what I like to call 'a man and his room' stories," the film director Paul Schrader once said of his screenplays for *American Gigolo, Light Sleeper,* and Martin Scorsese's *Taxi Driver, Raging Bull,* and *The Last Temptation of Christ.* Schrader would love Ivey, who recently graduated from Howard University with a degree in film and who opens and closes *Play with Toys* leading an imaginary country band called Jethroe and the Gram Crackers in a redneck honky tonk, but otherwise never seems to leave his apartment (rendering moot the question of his street credibility, I guess). Ivey drinks beer, writes songs, broods over breaking up with his girlfriend, and frets over his own future and the fate of other young black men as he watches the evening news. Although compared by critics to the aimless postadolescents in Richard Linklater's movie *Slacker,* Ivey can no more be said to represent a type than his music can be reduced to sociology.

Basehead's new *Not in Kansas Anymore* is a disappointing follow-up on which Ivey—whose cult listenership is mostly white, to judge from the audience that turned out for a show he gave in Philadelphia last winter—makes what sounds like a deliberate attempt to blacken up, at least in terms of his lyrics. Leaving his apartment for a change, he's treated as a potential shoplifter in a clothing store and stopped and frisked by the police for no apparent reason other than that he's young and black, and therefore assumed to be armed and dangerous. Though I don't doubt for a minute that Ivey is writing from experience, his touch is almost too light to convey his indignation.

This turf belongs to the gangstas, whose ghetto narratives forcefully express the rage a middle-class monologist like Ivey can hardly bring himself to feel. What gives a song like Ice-T's "Cop Killer" or Paris's "Coffee, Doughnuts & Death" its troubling power is the performer's sense and ours that he isn't speaking just for himself. Such songs are the only ones on the radio now in which more seems at stake than a position on next week's charts. But the fact of their social significance doesn't allow us to overlook all that's reprehensible about them; issues are rarely that simple, and neither is pop.

I'm someone whose tolerance of—no, *enthusiasm* for—such violent films as Quentin Tarantino's *Reservoir Dogs,* Carl Franklin's *One False Move,* and Abel Ferrara's *Bad Lieutenant* renders him vulnerable to charges of practicing a racial double standard in feeling such dismay over rap's bloodlust. And I do admit that rap troubles me in a way that movies rarely do. But there are differences between movies and pop music, the most obvious of which is that movies, by their very nature, are capable of presenting multiple points of view. In *Reservoir Dogs,* for example, Tarantino stops just short of showing us a cop having his ear sliced off by a sadistic, razor-wielding hood played by Michael Madsen. This is a scene that sickens some moviegoers and sends others stumbling for the exits, either in fear of what they're about to see or in fear of their response to it. The camera follows Madsen throughout the scene, and it's difficult not to become caught up in his delirium as he turns up the volume on the radio, does a series of graceful little dance steps to Stealers Wheel's "Stuck in the Middle with You," and closes in on his defenseless, screaming captive. "Was that as good for you as it was for me?" Madsen asks the cop afterward. Then he douses him with gasoline and pulls out his lighter. Madsen might as well be asking those of us who sat through the scene without averting our eyes if it was good for us—the embarrassed answer would be yes. But along with Madsen's dance steps, what stays in the mind are the cop's screams and his dazed reaction to his mutilation and imminent death.

Pop songs are theoretically as capable as film of representing this kind of emotional and moral complexity. Randy Newman and Lou Reed are among the pop songwriters who have provided it, or at least come close. Rap is strictly first-person singular at this point. Its young performers have yet to develop the artistic (and moral) gift of empathy. Maybe when they grow up, if this isn't asking too much of pop.

(OCTOBER 1993)

MIXED MEDIA

At the Movies

Everycat

In jazz circles, the early word on *'Round Midnight,* the French director Bertrand Tavernier's nicotine-stained valentine to bebop in European exile in the late fifties, went roughly as follows: critics would loathe the movie for its trivialization of jazz history, but musicians—flattered to see one of their own on the big screen—would adore it for validating their existence (the "I'm in Technicolor, therefore I am" impulse that made longhairs embrace *Easy Rider* in the late sixties, and black urban audiences embrace *Shaft* and *Superfly* a few years later). Musicians for, critics against, is indeed the way the sides are lining up, now that *'Round Midnight* has opened. You can probably guess which side I'm on, but I'm not saying that musicians are wrong.

'Round Midnight—starring the tenor saxophonist Dexter Gordon as Dale Turner, a fictional composite of Lester Young and Bud Powell—is about jazz as a religious experience, with all the stigmata and stations of the cross presented in jumbled, vaguely sacrilegious fashion. Gordon's Dale Turner is a tortured black innovator who, like Young, memorizes the lyrics to songs before interpreting them instrumentally, addresses even male acquaintances as "Lady," and spent time in the stockade during World War II for carrying a photograph of his white wife. Like Bud Powell, Turner was once beaten repeatedly on the head with billy clubs, and like many musicians of Powell's generation, he is easy prey for obsequious drug pushers and sleazeball promoters (typified here by Martin Scorsese, in a distracting cameo). He has an old sidekick nicknamed Hersch (presumably Herschel Evans, Young's sparring partner in the Count Basie Orchestra), a daughter named Chan (after Chan Richardson, Charlie Parker's common-law wife), a lady friend called Buttercup (just like Powell's widow), and another who sings with a white gardenia pinned in her hair (just like you-know-who, though the buppie princess Lonette McKee is unlikely to remind you of Billie Holiday). When

the man standing next to Dale at the bar passes out, Dale says "I'll have what he's been drinking," just as legend has it Young once did. And like Young, he calls someone shorter than himself "half-a-motherfucker"; the only problem is that Lester was talking to Pee-wee Marquette, the midget master of ceremonies at Birdland, whereas Dale is addressing the normal-sized Bobby Hutcherson.

You get the point: Turner is Everycat, less a character than an accumulation of fact and lore. Despite this, 'Round Midnight, in its meandering middle stretches, is less a jazz film than another buddy-buddy flick, replete with unacknowledged homoerotic undertones (one scene in which Turner is writing music at the opposite end of the table from his French graphic-designer roommate and benefactor—played by François Cluzet and faithfully modeled on Powell's keeper, Francis Paudras—plays like an inadvertent parody of the successful two-career marriage). The only difference is that one of the buddies is a black, dypsomaniacal, six-foot-seven *down beat* Hall-of-Famer.

Even so, it's easy to understand why musicians are pleased with 'Round Midnight. Clichés and all, it s as sympathetic an account of the jazz life as has ever been presented in a feature film, erring on the side of compassion rather than exploitation, guilty of sentimentality but not sensationalism. The uncertainty of Gordon's line readings betrays that he's no actor and that he was given no real character to work with. But his presence and dignity—his paunch-first stagger, his big-man's daintiness, his rasped expletives, and his vanquished Clark Gable good looks—rescue the movie from banality. A former alcoholic, drug abuser, and longtime expatriate himself, he's obviously drawn from personal experience to give a performance that one suspects would have been beyond the ability of a more experienced actor. His peers will recognize themselves in him, and they can be proud of what they see.

Oddly, the drawback to casting Gordon in the lead role was musical. When he's in peak form, Gordon's tone is as bracing and aromatic as freshly perked coffee. But he was recovering from assorted illnesses and an extended period of inactivity during filming, and as a result, his solos have a spent, desultory air. In dramatic terms, this may be just as well, inasmuch as we are given to understand that Dale Turner is a man slowly snuffing himself out, capable of summoning up his former brilliance only in flashes, convinced that death is nature's way of telling him to take five. (You wonder what Francis is using for ears when he says that Turner is playing "like a god."[*]) But a

---

[*]You also wonder what Tavernier is using for ears, because, contrary to what our own ears tell us, Francis is supposed to be telling it like it is. It's worth passing along an astute comment that the pop critic Ken Tucker made about this sketchily drawn

sub-par Gordon makes the soundtrack album (Columbia SC-40464) pretty tough going. Gordon isn't the only culprit; the soundtrack's supporting cast is made up of musicians ten to twenty years his junior, for whom bebop is little more than a formal exercise, and Herbie Hancock's incidental music is flat and uninvolving when divorced from the film's imagery. Gordon deserves the plaudits he's winning as an actor, but it would be a pity if the lay audience now discovering him accepts the music from *'Round Midnight* as characteristic.

Although *'Round Midnight* is the only recent movie to star a jazz musician, it's not the only one with a jazz soundtrack. Spike Lee's sleeper hit *She's Gotta Have It* boasts a fine soundtrack by his father, the bassist Bill Lee, which has just been released on Island 7 90528-1. The elder Lee's modest, by turns moody and frolicsome small-band score goes awry only once, exactly where the black-and-white movie does: in the too-sweet Ronnie Dyson vocal accompanying an oversaturated Technicolor ballet. But in its mix of disciplined composition and footloose improvisation, Lee's music recalls earlier film scores by such jazz composers as Duke Ellington (*Anatomy of a Murder*), Miles Davis (*Frantic!*), Sonny Rollins (*Alfie*), John Lewis (*Odds Against Tomorrow*) and Cato Barbieri (*Last Tango in Paris*). It also brings to mind Henry Pleasants's conjecture that the collaborations between composers and film directors have the potential to become the modern equivalent of lyric theater. Writing before the corporate takeovers of both film and record companies, and before the success of *Easy Rider, The Graduate,* and *Saturday Night Fever* made soundtrack albums little more than K-Tel greatest-hits collections in disguise, Pleasants had no way of knowing that film composers would eventually rank lower than the music- acquisitions lawyers in the overall scheme of things. It's becoming more and more unusual to hear a score like Bill Lee's, brashly original and homogenetic to the film it serenades. If Dexter Gordon's haunting portrayal in *'Round Midnight* suggests that jazz musicians can be riveting onscreen subjects, Lee's score confirms that they also have plenty to offer behind the scenes. Here's hoping that more film producers take them up on the offer.

(NOVEMBER 1986)

---

character, after the screening we both saw. Francis is a commercial artist; we see one of his posters for an American film starring Jeff Chandler. Tucker pointed out that such a Frenchman would almost certainly be obsessed with American popular culture in general, not just jazz. But when Francis accompanies Dale to New York, he doesn't go looking for paperbacks by Erskine Caldwell or movies by Nicholas Ray. For that matter, he doesn't even hear any live jazz, except for Dale's.

Birdland, Mon Amor

Charlie Parker assured himself of immortality when he recorded "Ko Ko" for Savoy Records, on November 26, 1945. This wasn't the first time that bebop was performed in a recording studio, nor was "Ko Ko" the first jazz "original" extrapolated from the chord sequences of an existing tune—a practice that didn't begin with bop, contrary to popular belief. For that matter, Parker wasn't the first improviser to recognize that despite the nondescript melody of Ray Noble's "Cherokee," its fast-moving chords held the potential for tour de force; Charlie Barnet had beaten him to it by six years. Yet there was really only one historical precedent for "Ko Ko": Louis Armstrong's 1928 recording of "West End Blues." As Armstrong had done (and as John Coltrane would later, with "Chasin' the Trane"), Parker with one performance reshaped jazz into his own image by establishing an exacting new standard of virtuosity. Listeners encountering "Ko Ko" for the first time are likely to be astonished by Parker's faultless execution at a tempo that starts off reckless and seems to speed up as it goes along. But the most remarkable aspect of "Ko Ko" is Parker's reconciliation of spontaneity and form—the impression of economy despite the splatter of notes; the surprising continuity of suspenseful intro, staccato bursts, pulsating rests, and phrases so lengthy they double back on themselves at the bar lines. Parker's contemporaries faced the challenge not only of matching his technique, but also of emulating his harmonic and rhythmic sophistication, and his successors still face the same challenge.

Parker's innovations—and those of Dizzy Gillespie and Bud Powell—are today so ingrained in jazz that it's difficult to remember that bebop was initially considered so esoteric and forbidding that only its originators could play it. "Ko Ko" would seem to prove the point. Stimulated by Parker, Max Roach made a breakthrough of his own on "Ko Ko," with an unyielding polyrhythmic accompaniment that amounted to a second melodic line. But Gillespie, who had been forced into service as a pianist in relief of Sadik Hakim (listen to Hakim's disoriented intro on "Thrivin' on a Riff," recorded earlier at the session, and you'll know why), also had to spell Miles Davis on "Ko Ko." Davis, then still in his teens and making his recording debut, declined even to try to his luck on the piece.

Parker was twenty-five but already addicted to heroin; he would be dead in less than ten years. Two weeks after recording "Ko Ko," he traveled with Gillespie to Hollywood for a nightclub engagement that lasted almost two months, despite the generally hostile reaction of Southern California audiences to bebop (the new style had been nurtured in secret on the East Coast, its dissemination hindered by a musicians' union ban on new recordings and by wartime restrictions on materials needed to manufacture discs). Parker didn't return to New York with his bandmates; instead, he cashed in his airline ticket to buy drugs. He found himself stranded in Los Angeles during a time when police crackdowns on heroin sent street prices soaring and often made the drug unavailable at any price. In August, 1946, Parker was confined at Camarillo State Hospital after being arrested for setting fire to his hotel room in the aftermath of a disastrous recording session.

Parker spent six months at Camarillo, returning to New York in April of 1947. He then began a period in which he could do no wrong, at least in the recording studio, where he produced an unbroken succession of masterpieces for Dial and Savoy, including his most memorable ballad performance, a harmonic tangent on George Gershwin's "Embraceable You." Already married and divorced twice, he wooed two women almost simultaneously, marrying one in 1948 and setting up house with the other two years later, without bothering to divorce the first. In 1949, he scored a triumph at the International Jazz Festival in Paris, and a year later made the first of several records on which he was accompanied by woodwinds and strings, the format that brought him his greatest popular success.

But he never kicked his drug habit for good, and he drank to such excess that his weight ballooned to more than two hundred pounds. Despite his drawing power, nightclub owners became increasingly reluctant to book him, for fear that he'd show up in no shape to perform, or not show up at all. At one point, he was banned from Birdland, the Broadway nightclub named in his honor in 1950. Although he somehow eluded arrest for possession (there were rumors that he pointed detectives to other users in order to save his own skin), the cabaret card he needed in order to perform in New York City nightclubs was taken from him without due process, at the recommendation of the narcotics squad, in 1951. The incident that is said to have finally broken him was the death from pneumonia of his two-year-old daughter by his common-law wife, Chan Richardson, in March, 1954. Later that year, he swallowed iodine in an unsuccessful suicide attempt. He died of lobar pneumonia on March 12, 1955, while watching television in the New York apartment of the Baroness Panonica de Koenigswarter, a wealthy jazz patron. He was thirty-four, but physicians estimated his age at fifty to sixty.

Forest Whitaker plays Parker in *Bird*, a film produced and directed by Clint Eastwood and written by Joel Oliansky. Miming to Parker's actual solos, with his eyes wide open and his shoulders slightly hunched and flapping, Whitaker captures the look we recognize from Parker's photographs and the one surviving television kinescope of him (a 1952 appearance on Earl Wilson's *Stage Entrance*, which is featured in the excellent jazz documentaries *The Last of the Blue Devils* and *Celebrating Bird: The Triumph of Charlie Parker*). Unfortunately, even though he's been outfitted with a gold cap over one incisor to make his smile shine like Parker's, Whitaker is less convincing offstage, where most of *Bird* takes place. On the basis of his brief but effective turn as the young, possibly psychotic pool shark who spooks the master hustler played by Paul Newman in Martin Scorsese's *The Color of Money,* Whitaker was the right choice to play Parker—a master con, among other things. But Whitaker's performance is too tense and pent-up to bring Parker to life, and by the end of the movie, the actor seems as much the victim of heavy-handed writing and direction as the character does.

Why is it always raining in jazz films, and why are the vices that kill musicians always presented as side effects of a terminal case of the blues? It merely drizzled throughout *'Round Midnight,* and though the movie was false in other ways, the mist was in keeping with the slow-motion music performed by the ailing Dexter Gordon. The music in *Bird* is supposed to be defiant and ebullient, but the *mise en scène* is downbeat, with rain gushing against the windows of melodramatically underlit interiors. (You come out of the theater squinting, just like Eastwood.) Like Milton's Lucifer, whither this Bird flies is hell. He brings rain and darkness with him wherever he goes. His unconscious is haunted by symbols—or, to be more specific about it, by a literal cymbal that flies across the screen and lands with a resounding thud every time he drifts off or nods out. The vision is based on a (perhaps apocryphal) incident to which Eastwood and Oliansky have given too much interpretive spin. As an untutored seventeen-year-old in Kansas City, Parker is supposed to have forgotten the chord changes to "I Got Rhythm" while playing at a jam session with the drummer Jo Jones, who, legend has it, threw one of his cymbals to the floor as a way of gonging the teenager off the stage. Except for overwrought conjecture by Ross Russell in a purple passage toward the end of *Bird Lives!,* there is nothing in the voluminous literature about Parker to suggest that this public humiliation haunted him for the rest of his life. To the contrary, it's usually cited as the incident that strengthened his resolve to become a virtuoso. But in *Bird*'s retelling, the echo of that cymbal deprives Parker of all pleasure in his accomplishments. *Bird*'s Parker wants to rage but can only snivel, even when hurling his horn through a control-room window in abject frustration. You don't believe for a second that this frightened sparrow could have summoned up the self-confidence to make a name for himself in the competitive world of jazz in the 1940s, much less set that world on its ear with "Ko Ko." Parker was a compulsive, which is another way of saying that he was a junkie, but he was also obsessive, which is another way of saying that he was an artist.[*] Parker's torment is here, but not his hedonism or his genius or the hint of any connection between them.

---

[*]Charlie Parker to Paul Desmond (as quoted by Stanley Crouch, in *The New Republic,* February 27, 1989): "I put in quite a bit of study into the horn, it's true. In fact, the neighbors threatened to ask my mother to move once when I was living in the West. They said I was driving them crazy with the horn. I used to put in at least eleven to fifteen hours a day. I did that for over a period of three or four years."

MUCH OF WHAT *BIRD* TELLS US ABOUT PARKER IS HOOEY, AND AT LEAST
one of its inventions is an abomination—a character, a slightly older saxophonist who knew Parker as an upstart in Kansas City, who becomes jealous
when he finds out that Parker is the talk of New York. A final encounter with
this saxophonist seals Parker's doom. Parker stumbles down Fifty-second Street,
dazed to find that the jazz clubs that were the settings for his early triumphs
have given way to strip joints. (The excuse for his surprise is his having been
holed up in the country with Chan for a few months, but anyone who knows
anything about jazz during this period has to wonder if he's been on the moon—
articles in the national press were bemoaning the departure of jazz from "The
Street" as early as 1948, and this is supposed to be 1955.) Told by another
acquaintance that he hasn't seen anything yet, Parker wanders into a theater
where his old Kansas City rival is knocking 'em dead with a greasy rhythm 'n'
blues *à la* King Curtis. This triggers Parker's final breakdown. Even assuming
that it was necessary to invent a fictional nemesis for Parker, why name that
character "Buster," which the filmmakers should have known was the name of
one of Parker's real-life Kansas City mentors, the alto saxophonist Buster Smith?
And why pretend that Parker, who reportedly found good in all kinds of music,
would have been shocked into a fatal tailspin by the advent of rock 'n' roll?*

Jazz fans appalled by the fraudulent portrayal of Parker won't be the only
moviegoers displeased with *Bird*. It's a mess. Even at the epic length of two
hours and forty-five minutes, the narrative feels hurried and absentminded,
with more flashbacks within flashbacks than any movie since Jacques
Tourneur's 1947 *noir, Out of the Past.* You're never sure who's remembering
what, what year it is, how famous Parker has become, or how long he has to
live—Whitaker has the same puppy-dog look no matter how far gone he's supposed to be, so the only way of telling is by the hair style on Diane Venora,
the actress who plays Chan Richardson (she gives up her bohemian bangs and
braids after becoming a mother). In terms of explaining to an audience that
knows nothing about jazz (most moviegoers, in other words) what made
Parker's music so revolutionary, *Bird* is about as much help as *The Ten Com-
mandments* was in explaining the foundations of Judeo-Christian law—you
almost expect someone to point to Parker and proclaim, like Yul Brynner as
Pharaoh, "His jazz *is* jazz." The script primes us for ironic payoffs it never
delivers; as when, for example, Parker hears his blues "Parker's Mood" sung by
King Pleasure, whose lyrics envision six white horses carrying Parker to his

---

*"Gigi Gryce on Charlie Parker (as quoted by Orrin Keepnews in *The View from
Within,* Oxford University Press, 1988): "We might be walking along and pass some-
place with a really terrible rock and roll band, for instance, and he'd stop and say 'Listen to what that bass player's doing,' when I could hardly even hear the bass."

grave in Kansas City; he makes Chan promise not to let his body be shipped back to K.C. for burial. What we're not told is that, against Chan's wishes, that's exactly what happened—to tell us this would require acknowledging that Parker was separated from Chan at the time of his death, and still legally wed to Doris Snydor, who is conveniently never mentioned in *Bird*. This movie is probably going to be praised in some quarters for its "unsensational" depiction of an interracial relationship. But the relationship between Whitaker and Venora could stand some sensationalizing. The only sparks that fly between them are acrimonious; they bicker from the word go. Although the script makes Chan an awful scold, Diane Venora brings unexpected shadings to the role: you believe in her as a thrill-seeking hipster who's just as glad when motherhood forces her into a more conventional way of life. Venora's is the film's only convincing performance. Michael Zelnicker is affectless as Red Rodney, the white trumpeter who sang the blues in order to pass as a black albino while on tour with Parker in the segregated South in the late forties. Zelnicker wouldn't have had to worry about white sheriffs; black audiences of the period would have hooted this yuppie off the stage. (He and Parker play a Jewish wedding, and when the cute little rabbi says about Parker and the other sidemen, "These boys are not Jewish, but they are good musicians," you feel as though you've witnessed this scene in a hundred other movies. Eastwood and Oliansky are delivering a sermon on the need for unity among oppressed minorities, and what's unbearable about it is that they think they're being subtle.) As the young Dizzy Gillespie, Sam Wright is sanctimonious and old before his time, and (as the jazz critic Bob Blumenthal has pointed out) the audience that knows nothing about the real-life Dizzy is going to wonder how he ever got that nickname. The first time we see Diane Salinger as the Baroness Nica, she's wearing her beret at a tilt that casts half of her face in shadow, and she watches Parker with predatory eyes. She's a shady lady from Grand Guignol. Why this visual insinuation about a woman who made her apartment into a salon for black musicians with whom she maintained platonic relationships, and whose only possible "crime" was that of dilettantism? She had no responsibility—symbolic or otherwise—for Parker's death.

The music in *Bird* has a phoney ring to it, even though Parker's recordings were used for most of the soundtrack. There were fans who used to follow Parker around the country, sneaking cumbersome wire recorders into nightclubs to preserve his work and shutting them off when his sidemen improvised. Eastwood and music supervisor Lennie Niehaus go these ornithologists one better (or one worse) by filtering out Parker's sidemen altogether in favor of new instrumental backing. In addition to being unfair to Parker's sidemen, many of whom were indeed capable of keeping pace with him, this removes him from his creative context and gives no sense that bebop was a movement.

But Parker is out of context throughout *Bird*. The movie would have us believe that he had little curiosity about the world beyond jazz, which in turn showed only oppositional interest in him. In reality, the musicians who worshiped Parker remember him as well-read, with a consuming interest in twentieth-century classical composition. And black jazz musicians of Parker's era had a direct influence on those white artists from other disciplines—the nascent hipsters and beats who people such early fifties novels as Chandler Brossard's *Who Walk in Darkness* and John Clellon Holmes's *Go*. Parker was a source of fascination to these poets, novelists, and abstract impressionists who were beginning to define themselves as outlaws from middle-class convention. They recognized his artistic drive and suicidal self-indulgence as the yin and yang of a compulsive nature pushing against physical limitations and societal restraints. In *Bird*, few white characters, except those from the jazz underground, seem to know or care who Parker is, and he isn't sure himself.

The pity of all this is that Clint Eastwood is a jazz fan, and *Bird* is supposed to have been a labor of love. In 1982, Eastwood directed and starred in *Honky-tonk Man*, the gentle, admirably straightforward story of a Depression-era Okie troubadour called Red Sovine, who succumbs to tuberculosis before realizing his dream of performing at the Grand Ole Opry. Among its other virtues, that film managed to suggest the succor that music can give both performers and audiences. Perhaps believing that Parker was subjected to a harsher reality than the fictional Sovine by virtue of being black and a drug addict, Eastwood's tried to find a more insistent rhythm for *Bird*, but the one he's come up with feels choppy, disconnected, and pointlessly arty, with dated experiments in time and point of view forcing him against his best natural instincts as a storytelling director.

Charlie Parker first appeared on screen in the guise of Eagle, a heroin-addicted saxophonist played by Dick Gregory in the forgotten *Sweet Love Bitter* (1967), which was based on John A. Williams's novel *Night Song*. A lthough Gregory's performance was surprisingly effective, Eagle was a peripheral figure in a civil-rights-era melodrama about a white liberal college professor on the run from his conscience. In the late 1970s, Richard Pryor was supposed to star in a film about Parker that never got made—which is probably just as well, because Pryor brings so much of his own persona to the screen that Charlie Parker would have gotten lost. That leaves us with *Bird*, a jazz fan's movie in the worst possible sense—a movie with the blues, a *Birdland, Mon Amor* that wants to shout "*Bird lives!*" but winds up whispering "Jazz is dead." Bird communicates the melancholy that every jazz fan feels as a result of the music's banishment from mainstream culture. In projecting this melancholy on Charlie Parker—whose music still leaps out at you with its reckless abandon, and whose triumph should finally count for more than his tragedy—Eastwood has made another of those movies that make jazz fans despair that mainstream culture will ever do right by them or their musical heroes.

(NOVEMBER 1988)

Obsession

Bruce Weber's *Let's Get Lost* is an extraordinary two-hour, black-and-white film portrait of Chet Baker, the trumpeter who fell to his death from a third floor window of an Amsterdam hotel May 13, 1988, shortly after Weber finished shooting. Only the way that Baker died was surprising (the Dutch police ruled his death a suicide, but the U.S. Consulate declared it an accident, and Baker's intimates believe that he was murdered). Baker, who was fifty-eight, had been a drug addict for most of his adult life, and he looked like he was dying from a cumulative overdose the last time I saw him perform, at Fat Tuesday's in New York in 1986. He also looked like he didn't particularly give a shit. Once the most photogenic of jazz musicians, he still had his hair, and was still attractive in that lined and ravaged way that's frequently described as "rugged"—though not in his case. The lower half of his face was caving in (looking at him, I thought for a moment that he'd forgotten his dentures— he'd lost his teeth eighteen years earlier, in a drug-related mugging); all that was left of him were his wary, cooly appraising eyes. He spoke slowly and without inflection, as though in a permanent narcotic stupor, exactly the way he does in *Let's Get Lost.* "What's your favorite kind of high?" Weber asks him at one point. "The kind of high that scares other people to death," Baker answers without hesitation, his face a Nosferatu mask. "I guess they call it a speedball. It's a mixture of heroin and cocaine. . . ."

The obits explained Baker's less-than-brassy trumpet style in terms of a specific era and locale, crediting him with helping to spawn "cool" as a member of Gerry Mulligan's pianoless quartet in Los Angeles in 1952. But Baker's greatness was a matter of essence, not consequence: his ability to inhabit a melody was more important than his role in any movement or school. People will tell you that he played with *heart,* and as vague and romantic as the word sounds, it's the right word for what Baker projected: the white jazzman's equivalent of soul. His knowledge of chord changes was rudimentary, and his projection was weak. But with no flash to hide behind, he had to make every note count, and by the end of his life, his solos had become as deep and indelible as the lines of his face.

The current party line among jazz critics, in the wake of Albert Murray's influential *Stompin' the Blues,* is that jazz, like the blues that spawned it, is a celebration of shared cultural values between performers and audiences. Anyone who's heard Louis Armstrong or Charlie Parker knows that this is generally true. But anyone who's heard Bix Beiderbecke, Pee Wee Russell, Lester Young, or Paul Desmond knows that jazz can also be a vehicle for the expression of isolation and melancholy. It may be significant that all these soloists, with the exception of Young, were white men playing a black-identified music. Theirs was a song of isolation rather than community, and this is the lineage to which Baker belonged.

Music was only part of his appeal in the mid-fifties, when he was finishing ahead of Louis Armstrong, Miles Davis, and Dizzy Gillespie in the jazz magazine polls. He was often said to resemble Montgomery Clift, James Dean, or Marlon Brando; the Hollywood screenwriter Lawrence Trimble—the most articulate of the "witnesses" in *Let's Get Lost*—likens Baker to PFC Robert E. Lee Prewitt, the moody army bugler played by Clift in *From Here to Eternity*. Baker's resemblance to these actors (and, later, to Clint Eastwood) was more than a matter of laconic delivery and a good jaw line; like them, he was, in Trimble's apt words, "a slightly antisocial role model to look up to," in an era of college football heroes. What audiences responded to when listening to the young Baker or watching those actors, paradoxically, was the private nature of their blues.

Baker also sang, and, until nicotine dyed his timbre a manly brown, the adjective most frequently used to decry his crooning was "epicene." No one thought he was gay, but he sounded effeminate to some—an equally grave offense in the 1950s, a testosterone-counting decade in which the pianist Horace Silver's denigration of West Coast cool as "fag" jazz was widely and approvingly quoted, and in which two men meeting for the first time each felt obliged, as Norman Mailer once put it, to prove he was "less queer" than the other. But it was Baker who was in touch with the sexual tenor of the times: androgyny is now recognized as having been central to the appeal of Brando, Clift, and Dean, and most movie audiences probably recognized as much even then, if only subliminally.

If this talk of sexual ambiguity seems tangential to *Let's Get Lost*, consider that Weber, a commercial photographer known for the superrealist eroticism of his ads for Calvin Klein and Ralph Lauren, used Baker's early vocals as mood music for most of *Broken Noses* (1987), a wet dream of a documentary about a self-adoring Adonis of a prizefighter named Andy Minsker and the school-age Adonises-to-be he's grooming in the manly arts (but mostly just grooming, from what Weber shows us). In a written prologue to *Broken Noses*, Weber tells us that Minsker is a dead ringer for the young Chet Baker, to whom the film is dedicated. Though both of Weber's films are about unequivocally hetero men (and though his own sexual preference is, of course, none of our business), both films are homoerotically charged, and both demonstrate the extent to which the gay male sensibility that pervades the fashion professions (including commercial photography) has eroticized what even straight men see when they gaze at other men.

Weber tries your patience in *Let's Get Lost* (named after an escapist pop tune that Baker recorded in 1955, though the title also suggests perdition). Minsker, the punchy hunk from *Broken Noses,* is here for no apparent reason, cavorting on a Santa Monica beach with others from Weber's retinue, including a bonbon named Lisa Marie (described in the press kit as "a voluptuous young actress/model") and a jazzbo poseur called Flea ("member of the rock group The Red Hot Chili Peppers [and] a Chet Baker lookalike and fan"—and if you buy that, I got a vice-president for you who's the spittin' image of Robert Redford). Minsker and Flea, who condescend to Baker as an admirable old stud, are a reminder that we're on Weber's turf, not Baker's. So is the poster of Jean-Paul Belmondo in *Breathless* behind Baker during the interview sequences in Cannes, where Weber is presumably showing *Broken Noses.* There's a poignant moment at Cannes when Baker has to plead for silence from a crowd of second-string glitterati before singing and playing Elvis Costello's "Almost Blue." But instead of being moved, you're just angry: why did Weber drag Baker to Cannes in the first place? Shouldn't Weber be birddogging his subject, instead of the other way around? (If Weber remade *Nanook of the North,* Nanook would be wearing Calvins). Weber's self-reflexiveness almost spoils what should have been a powerful final scene in which Weber (off-camera) tells Baker how "painful it's been to see you like this" (strung out on heroin for five days, before methadone could be obtained for him). "Will you look back on this film in years to come and remember it as good times?" Weber asks Baker, who—understandably flattered by the attention he's been receiving as the subject of a million-dollar documentary, but otherwise opaque—asks how the hell else he could be expected to feel.

But even when you're staring as *Let's Get Lost* in disbelief, you can't take your eyes off it—a sympathetic reflex, in part, because you know that Weber can't take his eyes off his beautiful loser of a subject. It's an autobiographical film about somebody else (every journalist who's ever become hopelessly wrapped up in one of his subjects will know what I mean). "I remember, for the first time, [knowing] what photogenic meant, what star quality meant, or charisma," William Claxton, whose early album-jacket photos of Baker helped to make him a star, tells Weber—and you know that Weber experienced palpitations in first looking at those photos (like the narrator of Mishima's *Confessions of a Mask* looking at drawings of St. Sebastian). Jazz fans are going to complain that *Let's Get Lost* is more about Baker's mystique than his music, but the mystique was what drew Weber to the music, and the movie is finally as much about Weber's Chet Baker fixation as it is about Chet Baker—it's that fixation that gives this meditation on the nature of cool (replete with 1950s-style lower-case graphics) its sexual heat. Without the intensity of Weber's gaze, *Let's Get Lost* would be dull hagiography, like many of the documentaries shown at jazz film festivals and on PBS. When it's over, you know you've seen a movie. Trimble could be talking for Weber when he says, "Jazz musicians had names like Buck and Lockjaw and Peanuts and Dizzy, and he was just named Chet, which was sort of a soft sound. . . . The way he played, what he looked like, his name, everything—it all went together."

So could the trumpeter Jack Sheldon, who complains, good-naturedly, that "[Baker] didn't know what note he was hitting. He just pressed the valves down. It was *easy* for him. . . . I played the trumpet, too, and it was real *hard* for me." You get the feeling that Baker's unnegotiable independence is a large part of his attraction for Weber, who comes from a world in which making the right contacts and being seen in the right places is paramount. (And in contrast to Minsker and Flea, whom Weber no doubt spent hours dolling up to resemble Baker, the genuine article probably spent as little time worrying about how he looked as he did practicing.) When Weber badgers Baker's mother to admit that Baker disappointed her as a son (one of two instances when he ignores an interview subject's request to go off the record), the scene is moving because you know that Baker ultimately disappointed Weber, too: though he lived fast, he didn't die young and leave a good-looking corpse. The Chet Baker we see under the closing credits is the dreamboat from *Ulatori alla Sharrar,* a 1959 Italian quickie so obscure it's not listed in David Meeker's definitive *Jazz in the Movies.* (Nor is *Hell's Horizon,* another delightful curio Weber has dug up—a 1955 B-movie about the Korean War, with a surprisingly callow and athletic Baker as the kid in a battalion that also includes the Beaver's dad and Jerry the dentist from *The Dick Van Dyke Show.*)

Weber also interviews Baker's estranged third wife and her three grown children by him in Stillwater, Oklahoma, and two of his lovers: the singer Ruth Young, a tough cookie who disputes Baker's version of the beating that cost him his teeth, and characterizes his wives as "the crazy, the frigid, and the Virgin Mary" (she herself is "the bitch"); and Diane Vavra, a pathetic burn-out who tells how he beat her and once stood her up, and who flatters herself that he needed her to help him figure out how to phrase lyrics in the recording studio. This is riveting stuff, but *Let's Get Lost* is most seductive when no one on camera is speaking: when light and shadows and cigarette smoke are playing across Baker's aged face, or when, to the accompaniment of Baker's youthful singing, Weber and the cinematographer Jeff Preiss pan old album covers, publicity stills, and baby pictures. These deliriously shot sequences, which are tactile in their intimacy, flaunt something discreetly hinted at in

Francis's worship of Dale Turner to the exclusion of all other jazz musicians in *'Round Midnight:* fandom as another name for fetish.

CHET BAKER WALKS THROUGH *LET'S GET LOST* IN A DAZE, THOUGH HE seems to be enjoying the antics of Andy Minsker and Flea. The scenes in which Baker seems most alive are those in which he's shown recording the movie's soundtrack album—especially when he's whispering lyrics close to the mike, shaping the words with his mouth. Or at least, that's the way it looks in the movie. But the soundtrack (RCA Novus 3054-1-N) is the sort of album you're reluctant to listen to very closely—not because it doesn't reward undivided attention, but because you're afraid it'll get to you. It isn't just that the tempos are so funereal. Baker's trumpet tone is slack, his vocal phrasing is labored and gasping, and his sense of time is uncertain (though the pianist Frank Strazzeri gallantly tries to keep him in proximity to the beat, and just as gallantly covers up for him when he falters.) Wobbling between the diatonic, the pentatonic and the catatonic, Baker has never sounded worse—and no one has ever sung better. He was an intuitive musician, and these battered interpretations of "Every Time We Say Goodbye," "You're My Thrill," and "Imagination" show that intuition, unlike technique, is something that can't be lost. The album's final track is Baker's only recorded version of "Almost Blue," which Elvis Costello says he wrote while thinking about Baker. In the movie, Baker pleads with the revellers at Cannes for quiet, explaining that "It's one of those songs." It certainly is. It's so enveloping, in its almost inaudible way, that nothing could possibly follow it. You don't even feel like putting another record on.

(APRIL 1989)

Cause of Death: Jazz

In 1967, when he was still a groundbreaking comedian and not yet himself a joke, Dick Gregory made his film debut in Herbert Danska's *Sweet Love, Bitter,* giving a remarkable performance in the role of Richie Stokes, a.k.a. "Eagle," an alto saxophonist and junkie loosely based on Charlie Parker. Also starring Don Murray (Marilyn Monroe's romantic interest in *Bus Stop*), Robert Hooks (Clay in the original production of Amiri Baraka's *Dutchman* and a founder of the Negro Ensemble Company), and Diane Varsi ("the female James Dean," best remembered for her roles in *Peyton Place* and *Wild in the Streets*), *Sweet Love, Bitter* is superior in every way to *Bird,* Clint Eastwood's dark (or maybe just underlit) 1988 Parker biopic. It should have been mentioned in the reviews of *Bird,* but few film critics knew of it. In fact, until

Sweet Love, Bitter's resurrection at New York's Film Forum as part of last summer's JVC Jazz Festival, and its release on videocassette earlier this year (Rhapsody Films), only independent film buffs and those vigilant enough to have caught one of its infrequent showings on late-night TV had ever seen it.

Shot mostly in Philadelphia (despite an implied New York setting) on a shoestring budget of $260,000, this black-and-white film is so brutally honest in its depiction of the jazz demimonde of the 1960s that more than one viewing is required to realize that there's very little jazz in it, apart from Mal Waldron's moody small-band score. Only one scene takes place on a bandstand and it's a doozy, dramatically as well as musically. After borrowing a horn and sitting in with a band in a nightclub, Eagle rudely dismisses his fellow musicians' request for an encore: "You jive niggers must be crazy to think I'm gonna stand up here all night and blow a freebie." While this is going on, the pragmatic club owner, instead of being pleased to have a living legend playing for free, frets that the presence in his dive of a convicted drug user might cost him his cabaret license. On his way out, Eagle bums $15 from a young white woman trying to put the make on him. He promises to meet her at the club the next night, but warns her, "I have to tell you in front: it ain't gonna rub off, baby."

Gregory inhabits his character so forcefully it hardly matters that the screenplay by Danska and Lewis Jacobs (also the movie's producer) takes even greater liberties with Parker's life than did the script for *Bird.* Sauntering but rocking slightly on his heels as he enters or leaves a room, and isolating every syllable in his bitter pronouncements on jazz or race (as if he's trying to give the impression that he's stoned even when he's not), Gregory captures his real-life model's arrogance and intellect—his talent for putting people on. For a nonactor, Gregory makes surprisingly efficient use of props, tilting his beret just so and wearing his sunglasses in such a manner that he looks not just bloodshot but somehow diminished when he takes them off. And there's a reminder of what a gifted comic he once was, in a scene in which he riffs at length about an imaginary biblical epic starring "the late J.C. Himself." But even when delivering lines lifted verbatim from John A. Williams's *Night Song,* the 1961 novel on which *Sweet Love, Bitter* was based, Gregory succeeds in making it seem as if he's making everything up as he goes along.

Thanks to Gregory's wit (Woody King, Jr., a veteran actor featured in the nightclub scene, was his dialogue coach), we accept Eagle as a great improviser on faith, even before hearing him play his horn (Charles McPherson, the Parker-influenced alto saxophonist who ghosted for Gregory and taught him fingerings, would perform the same services for Forest Whitaker in *Bird* twenty-one years later). But *Sweet Love, Bitter* has more going for it than

Gregory's powerful performance as part of a fine ensemble cast. In telling the story of an on-the-skids white college professor (Murray) and his ambivalent relationships with Eagle, a black coffeehouse owner named Keel (Hooks), and Keel's white lover (Varsi), Danska demonstrated an unerring eye for the claustrophobic jazz milieu of the 1960s.

Ironically, this faithfulness to its world helps to explain how *Sweet Love, Bitter* stayed "lost" for almost twenty-five years. A movie steeped in jazz ambiance practically demanded a greater commitment to the music's nocturnal subculture than most moviegoers of the time were willing to make. Unless you count *Lady Sings the Blues* (1972), in which Diana Ross seemed to be playing Susan Hayward or Lana Turner instead of Billie Holiday, no jazz movie has generated much action at the box office. With their usual subtexts of drugs, black rage, and genius sociologically programmed to self-destruct, jazz movies tend to be downers. *Sweet Love, Bitter* was no exception. Finding Eagle dead of an overdose, Keel says, "Cause of death: resisting reality." (This isn't giving anything away, because Eagle's death occurs in a flash-forward precredit sequence, before we even know who he's supposed to be.) He might just as well have said, "Cause of death: jazz," an autopsy report that could have extended to the movie's commercial prospects.

In an era in which Sidney Poitier could create a fuss just by coming to dinner, and in which impotence was alluded to only in adaptations of Tennessee Williams, *Sweet Love, Bitter* further sealed its doom with scenes such as one of Varsi pleading with Hooks not to flee her bed after he's failed to become aroused. As in the novel on which it was based, the movie's climactic incident is one in which the professor betrays Eagle, after having earlier helped to save his life. Released at a time when black leaders were publicly questioning how far well-meaning whites were prepared to go in support of civil rights, Danska's movie delivered a message not even the liberal arthouse audiences of its day were ready for.

But *Sweet Love, Bitter* was probably doomed from the start, on account of its low budget, its uncelebrated source material (Williams later became much better known for *Click Song* and *The Man Who Cried I Am*), and an apparent lack of faith on the part of its executive producers. Although Danska's frequent use of hand-held camera and a mise-en-scène as murky as the dishwater in the sink of Keel's coffeehouse made a virtue out of penury, the point must have been lost on the movie's backers, who cut about twenty minutes' worth of subplots, secondary characters, and what Danska calls "layering" from his and Jacobs's "final" edit. Streamlined into a more conventional narrative than Danska had intended, *Sweet Love, Bitter* bypassed a proper theatrical release and went straight to drive-ins and grindhouses under the mildly salacious title *It Won't Rub Off, Baby.* Danska, who's based in New York and still active in television, says that no one knows what became of the discarded footage, which he'd like to find if only to rescue an outstanding performance by Carl Lee in a role based on Miles Davis ("Yards" in Williams's novel).

So in one sense, no one's ever seen *Sweet Love, Bitter*—at least not the version that Danska wanted seen. Even so, what's still there on the Rhapsody Films video shapes up as quite possibly the best feature-length film ever made about jazz.

(JUNE 1992)

Talking Kerouac

I read *On the Road* when I was sixteen, in 1963, probably imagining myself to be one of the "frenetic young men" in search of "Kicks and Truth" described on the back cover of the original Signet paperback edition. I say "probably" only because I like to think that my perception of Kerouac differed slightly from that of Signet's copywriters and my own teenage peers, as a result of having practically memorized another of his novels earlier that year.

Written in 1953 but not published until six years later, after *On the Road* had created a market for Kerouac's scraps, *Maggie Cassidy* tells a tale of "adult love torn in barely grown-up ribs" in prose as fuchsia all the way through. Set in Kerouac's hometown of Lowell, Massachusetts, during his senior year in high school, it's slight as can be. But growing up across the street from a gasworks and a lumber yard in a sooty West Philadelphia neighborhood that might as well have been a New England mill town, I found more of myself in *Maggie Cassidy* than in *The Catcher in the Rye*. I still do, though I now realize that I was confusing its idealized version of Kerouac's blue-collar, Catholic adolescence with my own.

Except for the fact that he's a varsity jock and French Canadian instead of Irish, Kerouac's Jack Duluoz could have been me. He runs track, mopes in front of the radio, plays hooky with buddies he's known since grade school, and necks with his high school sweetheart (the eponymous Maggie) without going all the way—blaming his virginity on excess chivalry, not on inexperience, just as I did:

> In there, by the hissing radiator, on the couch, we did practically everything there is to do but I never touched her in the prime focal points, precious trembling places, breasts, the moist star of her thighs . . .

Sigh. The prose stabs with its pubescent longing, but it's written from the vantage point of a disillusioned man who knows (as I do, paging through it twenty-seven years later, and as Kerouac himself put it in *Doctor Sax*, another of his Lowell novels) that "you'll never be as happy as you are right now in

your book-devouring boyhood." So no wonder I have a soft spot for Kerouac.
But who reads him today? That's the question prompted by the arrival of
Rhino's *The Jack Kerouac Collection,* a deluxe, three-CD boxed set reissue of
the long-out-of-print spoken arts LPs Kerouac cut in 1958 and '59, two for
Hanover (*Poetry for the Beat Generation,* with Steve Allen on piano; and *Blues
and Haikus,* with the tenor saxophonists Al Cohn and Zoot Sims) and one for
Verve (the unaccompanied *Readings by Jack Kerouac on the Beat Generation*).
My guess is not even sixteen-year-olds, though he remains one of the most
read about of American authors, thanks to the memoirs of Joyce Johnson and
Carolyn Cassady, the women he and Neal didn't take on the road.

Lacking his friend Allen Ginsberg's flair for self-promotion and wisdom that
the beat goes on, Kerouac was already out of favor by the time I left college in
1968, a year before his death. That fall, he appeared drunk, sweating, and
grossly overweight on *Firing Line*—the painful footage, with Kerouac playing
the stooge to the reptilian William F. Buckley and rebuking his hippie and
Vietnik progeny, is included in the documentary film *What Happened to Kerouac?* He appears fully reconciled to the lifelong Roman Catholic death wish
that he had earlier snookered himself into believing was Buddhist enlighten-
ment on the transient nature of human existence ("dead already and dead
again," as he put it in "Praised Be Man," a poem included on the Rhino box).

If there's one thing that growing up Celtic teaches you, it's that people who
drink themselves to death seldom need a reason. Still, in Kerouac's case, the
process was speeded along by the adoration of wanna-bes who thought of him
as Dean Moriarty to their Sal Paradise, not having read him closely enough to
realize that he still lived at home with Mamere and was comfortable only on
the periphery of the beat subculture he named. As John Clellon Holmes once
put it, Kerouac "was never famous, only notorious," and it must have broken
his heart that he was idolized for his exploits rather than for writing about them.

The Jack Kerouac Collection isn't likely to sway those who refuse to take Kerouac seriously as a writer. Bombed on Tokay and onomatopoeia, he romanticizes every bum and railroad break man as a Bodhisattva, while indulging in
far too much Slim Gaillard-level jive ("Dem eggs & dem dem / Dere bacons,
baby, . . . All that luney & fruney / Fracon, acons, & beggs . . .) and sub-
Joycean bullshit ("Whilst tee-kee-kee pearl the birdies and mummums murk
and ululate in this valley of peaceful firewood"). But, my god, you'd need an
ear as deaf to the tones of actual American speech as that of your average 1990s
tenured professor to resist something like this, from *Jack Kerouac on the Beat
Generation*'s "Lucien Midnight: The Sounds of the Universe in My Window":

> Friday afternoon in the universe and all the directions in and out you got
> your men, women, dogs, children, horses, ponies, tics, perks, pots, pans,

pools, pauls, pails, parturiences, and petty thieveries that turn into Heavenly Buddha. I know boy what's I talking about 'cause I made the world and when I made it . . . I had Lucien Midnight for my name and concocted up a world so nothing you had forever thereafter make believe it's real . . .

This is language chasing its own tail, but its dizziness is contagious, especially as read by its author, his voice occasionally imitating Neal Cassady's barroom cowboy drawl or Allen Ginsberg's crazed rabbinical rant, his gulps and pauses for breath making it easier for you by implying punctuation he didn't always remember to type. Kerouac's literary career was a sustained feat of anamnesis, and his triumph here—on the passage quoted above and numerous others—is in reexperiencing the rush of first putting these words down on paper years earlier. It's something like the rush you get reading him for the first time, and it's thrilling to hear him feeling it, too.

The booklet that comes with the *Collection* amounts to a thirty-two-page mash note, with avid (if generally unilluminating) words from everybody from Ginsberg and William Burroughs to a columnist from the *Lowell Sun* and Kerouac's novelist daughter, Jan. (It also includes rare photos from the private collections of Ginsberg and others. In one, Joyce Johnson, Kerouac's girlfriend in 1957, when *On the Road* was published, is misidentified as Edie Parker, Kerouac's second wife—an inexcusable gaffe, because it's the photo Johnson used on the cover of her memoir, *Minor Characters*). In 1990 no reissue is complete without previously unreleased material, and Rhino has unearthed some doozies, including outtakes and studio chatter from *Blues and Haikus,* Kerouac's tense readings from *Visions of Cody* and *On the Road* on *The Steve Allen Show,* and his drunken contribution to a 1957 Hunter College symposium on "Is There a Beat Generation?"

Even ignoring these extras, the *Collection* expands the Kerouac canon by including a number of items not readily available in print—most notably his thirty-odd, freestyle "American Haikus," with Cohn and Sims majestically filling the silences between each. These three-line poems present Kerouac at his best; atypically for him, they give the impression of having been worked over, compressed.

> *Well, here I am,*
> *2PM.*
> *What day is this?*

> *Blackbird!*
> *NO! BLUEBIRD!*
> *The branch still jumping.*

Unfortunately, the rest of *Blues and Haikus* (with Cohn frequently switching to piano) is an inebriated hoot that becomes downright embarrassing when Kerouac attempts to wail the blues (though he's no worse than Mark Murphy or Ben Sidrian, I suppose). But the session with Steve Allen is an unexpected success, even though Steverino doesn't curl a lick you haven't heard a hundred times before. His backing is giving and unobtrusive, and Kerouac reads his single most affecting poem (about his mother) and his single most apocalyptic one ("The Wheel of the Quivering Meat Conception"), both from the undervalued *Mexico City Blues*.

Still, I have to agree with Kerouac biographer Gerald Nicosia's liner note assertion that Kerouac's "spontaneous bop prosody" most approaches the actual rhythms of bebop when he reads unaccompanied, as on the excerpts from *The Subterraneans* and *Desolation Angels* on the Verve LP. In a way, Kerouac's unrequited love for jazz—his perception of which was clouded by his unconsciously racist view of black Americans as *On the Road*'s "happy, true-hearted, ecstatic" primitives—supplies a dramatic subtext for these recordings. The irony is that Amiri Baraka and countless other black poets in the contemporary oral tradition echo Kerouac's rhythms more than they do those of Charlie Parker or John Coltrane, the forebears they'd claim.

In light of this, one of the most startling cuts on the Rhino box is Kerouac's lengthy, unaccompanied reading of "Fantasy: The Early History of Bop." This 1959 magazine piece is riddled with factual errors (Kerouac has the vibraphonist Lionel Hampton "wailing his tenor saxophone," for example), but however dubious it is as history, it now amounts to prophecy:

> Bop is the language from America's inevitable Africa. . . . And you can't
> believe that bop is here to stay. Or modern music, call it what you will. . . .
> And figure it with histories and lost kings of immemorial tribes and jungle
> and *fellaheen* town . . .
>
> He is here at last. His music is here to stay. His history has washed over
> us. His imperialistic kingdoms are coming.

Jack Kerouac, folks—a white man with no fear of a black planet. Even if his readings fail to convince you that there was more to him than met the eye, this ought to.

(AUGUST 1990)

Standup Sitcom

Those of us who are inclined to feel guilty about watching too much television are sometimes startled to realize that we actually watch very little. We eat dinner and do the dishes, catch up on our reading, have friends over or chat with them on the telephone, and generally go about our lives with the TV on in the background. In its infancy television was advertised as radio with pictures, and the fact that many of us still tend to use it that way helps to explain the enduring popularity of news and talk shows, soap operas, sketch humor, and situation comedies—formats in which what we hear is at least as important as what we see.

What's wrong with television is demonstrated by examining what I've just named as its strengths: newspapers remain a more dependable source of information, soap operas are an inducement to sloth (the least scintillating of the Seven Deadly Sins), and anybody in his right mind would prefer the company of his own friends (or solitude) to that of the celebrities welcomed by Arsenio or Leno or of the abuse victims exhibited by Oprah, Phil, and Sally Jesse. Comedy, on the other hand, is something television now does better than any other medium, including the movies. Before arguing the contrary, recall the inspired sketches performed by such comics as Bill Murray, Eddie Murphy, Martin Short, Rick Moranis, and the late John Belushi as members of TV ensembles. Then take a look at their movies, which almost without exception have been imbecilic.

The failure of these transplants (and of Damon Wayans, who was nothing short of brilliant on TV's *In Living Color* but just annoying in last summer's *Mo' Money*) can be rationalized by observing that it's one thing to sustain a comic conceit for five minutes and quite another to try to sustain one for two hours. But that hardly explains the adolescent excess of most recent Hollywood comedies. What might is that only teenagers regularly attend the movies anymore—and only they spend much money at the candy counter, where theater operators make their profits. Television, although also guilty of aiming low, at least includes in its target audience adults forced by parenthood or heavy work loads into becoming stay-at-homes.

Like TV's sketch comedians, its sitcom auteurs have floundered in attempting to master longer narrative forms. I wasn't among the many moviegoers infatuated with James L. Brooks's *Broadcast News,* which struck me as a stretched-out and only slightly updated episode of *The Mary Tyler Moore Show,* one of the sitcoms for which Brooks was co-executive producer. Garry Marshall's *Pretty Woman* and *Frankie and Johnny* were more "adult" than his *Happy Days* and *Laverne and Shirley,* but not necessarily more profound or even funnier.

Dark humor never has been television's strong suit (don't tell me about *Twin Peaks*); the medium offers nothing to compare to Robert Altman's *The Player,* Jim Jarmusch's *Night on Earth,* or John Boskovich's *Without You I'm Nothing* (a vehicle for Sandra Bernhard, herself largely a creature of TV). But the best sitcoms now regularly provide the sort of literate, unequivocal humor for which we used to depend on the movies. Some of TV's sorriest hacks, taking consolation from the fact that Shakespeare wrote for the masses, argue that if he were alive today he, too, would be writing for TV. (Writing what? *Prospero's Island? Fresh Prince of Denmark? Polonius Knows Best?*) This is extremely doubtful. I do think, though, that S. J. Perelman, the screenwriter for many Marx Brothers movies, would today be writing sitcoms. So would Preston Sturges and the team of Billy Wilder and I.A.L. Diamond, if only because now the movies probably could not accommodate them. And possibly Ring Larder and Dorothy Parker would too.

TYPICALLY SET IN THE HOME OR THE WORKPLACE, THE HALF-HOUR sitcom has evolved into our comedy of manners, its prevalent theme being how the people closest to us can drive us crazy. Because those who work in TV (and those who write about it for daily newspapers) are painfully aware of occupying a low cultural rung, TV is a medium in which artistic aspiration often passes for artistic achievement, and in which self-congratulatory liberalism regularly passes for biting social satire. This explains why *All in the Family* and *M*A*S*H* were overpraised in the 1970s and why *Designing Women* and *Murphy Brown* are overpraised now. The best sitcoms seldom tackle big issues except as little disturbances. In the wittiest of the current crop—*Coach, Roseanne, Roc, The Simpsons,* and, on cable, *Dream On* and *The Larry Sanders Show*—the biggest laughs derive not from predictable zingers but from the characters' often nettled takes on one another and on the mundane stuff of life in general. In this regard the funniest and best-written of all current shows might be *Seinfeld,* an NBC sitcom now in its third season, starring Jerry Seinfeld as a standup comedian, also his identity in real life.

Although shot in Hollywood, *Seinfeld* is set mostly in the title character's apartment on New York's Upper West Side, with one or two scenes in each episode taking place in a nondescript coffeeshop similar to that on almost any

Manhattan street corner. The coffeeshop is the equivalent of the family dinner table in *Father Knows Best* or *Leave It to Beaver* for Seinfeld and his surrogate family of thirty-somethings, which consists of his ex-girlfriend, Elaine Benes (Julia Louis-Dreyfus), his best friend, George Costanza (Jason Alexander), and Jerry's across-the-hall neighbor, a hipster doofus known simply as Kramer (Michael Richards). *Seinfeld* is the only show for which I could imagine the novelist Nicholson Baker someday writing a script; a lunch hour highlighted by an escalator ride (the subject of Baker's *The Mezzanine*) wouldn't be a stretch for a series that has already devoted one entire half-hour episode to waiting for a table in a Chinese restaurant and another to an attempt, by Seinfeld and his companions, to remember on which level of a New Jersey shopping-mall parking lot they left their car.

So much in *Seinfeld* is new to TV, beginning with its acknowledgment of the absurdity in the ordinary, that you tend to forget that it's based on a premise as old as the medium. As originally conceived by Seinfeld and Larry David, the show's head writer and executive producer, himself a failed standup, *Seinfeld* was strictly a vehicle for its star, whose monologues were to be juxtaposed with the (fictional) daily comings and goings that supplied the material for them. Sort of like George Burns or Jack Benny or, more recently, Garry Shandling, but minus their winking self-reflexiveness by virtue of showing Seinfeld delivering his material to a nightclub audience instead of directly to us. The problems caused by Seinfeld's inexperience as an actor are minimized because he more or less plays himself.

Although this founding premise hasn't been completely abandoned, Seinfeld's monologues have become shorter and fewer in number as the series has evolved. This is just as well, given the generic ring of his material. His specialty used to be called "observational" humor but has been renamed "recognition" humor, and the difference is more than semantic. Instead of generalizing from his own experience, as Mort Sahl, George Carlin, and Richard Pryor do and Lenny Bruce used to, Seinfeld, like most of his standup contemporaries, internalizes everybody's experience. The result is peevish bits about airports and dating and the candy we ate as children, which—timing and other tricks of the trade aside—you feel as though you could have come up with yourself.

FORTUNATELY, SEINFELD'S MONOLOGUES ARE WOVEN INTO EPISODES vibrant with the sort of acute observation that his monologues fail to deliver. True, the show may have begun as an outgrowth of Seinfeld's routines, but with the collaboration of Larry David it has gone far beyond that. Half a dozen writers have contributed funny scripts. The most hilarious episodes tend to be those written by David, frequently in collaboration with Seinfeld. Despite his failure on the comedy circuit, David remains something of a legend to his peers, less, one gathers, for his stinging material than for his absolute lack of showmanship (he was likely to throw down the microphone and stalk offstage if an audience was inattentive or didn't laugh in the right places—something all standup comedians have probably wanted to do). David has made the show's unofficial motto "No hugging, no learning," which capsulizes the difference between *Seinfeld* and those sitcoms in which the characters "grow," as a result of marriage, parenthood, new careers, or some other dramatic midlife passage. David once told an interviewer, "A lot of people don't understand that *Seinfeld* is a dark show. If you examine the premises, terrible things happen to people. They lose jobs; somebody breaks up with a stroke victim; somebody's told they need a nose job. That's my sensibility."

It's also the sensibility that pervades the show—a synthesis of angst and shtick best realized in the character of George Costanza. At face value George—short, pudgy, bald, and implicitly Jewish, despite his Italian surname—lives up to *New York Newsday*'s description of him as "the most fully realized schlemiel in the history of television." Jason Alexander, a Tony Award winner for his role in *Jerome Robbins' Broadway* and a crackerjack actor, transcends this stereotype by zeroing in on George's deviousness, his raging libido, and his volatile combination of arrogance and low self-esteem. (Alexander admits that his interpretation of George is based in large part on Larry David.) In his own way George is as vain as he is needy. His first reaction on hearing that a bulimic woman with whom he has recently been intimate has missed her period, probably owing to a defective condom, is to shout, "I did it! My boys can swim!"

It tells you everything you need to know about George's underdeveloped inner life to learn that he has a favorite explorer (De Soto, if memory serves) and that his favorite author is the sports writer Mike Lupica. George is tight with a dollar, a trait understood to predate his having lost his job as a real-estate broker because he tried to poison his boss. (The character Elaine found him a job at the publishing company where she works as a manuscript reader, but he was fired for having desktop sex with a cleaning woman; the sight of her vacuuming turned him on—which, given that he says his mother reminds him of Hazel, the sitcom maid played by Shirley Booth, provides food for thought.) "It's like going to a prostitute," he tells Elaine, explaining why he drives around looking for a parking space instead of just pulling into a lot. "Why should I pay when, if I apply myself, maybe I can get it for free?" Every word out of George's mouth is raw material for Freudian analysis, but never more so than when he compares the "completely uninhibited" sex that Jerry is having with a new girlfriend to "going to the bathroom in front of lots of people and not caring." ("It's not like that at all," Seinfeld, a surprisingly effective straight man, exclaims after a stunned pause.)

Despite his image of himself as a lonely guy, George seems to have little difficulty in meeting women. His problem, for obvious reasons, is holding on to them. A single woman friend of mine recently told me that her new ambition in life is to not date George—the way she put it being an admission that she has already dated plenty of him and expects to date many more. After giving the matter some thought, she agreed that the self-satisfied character played by Seinfeld would be no bargain either.

Jerry's problem with women is that he's a perfectionist. The woman with whom he has been enjoying the completely uninhibited sex fails to measure up, because she's a bad actress who insists that he read lines with her between trips to the bedroom. Elaine is the only woman Jerry really seems to be comfortable around, but you can see why they were unsuccessful as a couple. A self-righteous nonsmoker unable to restrain herself whenever she spots a woman wearing animal fur, even if it's at a party, Elaine is as spoiled as Jerry. She's the one who breaks up with a stroke victim, a novelist thirty years her senior who suffers his stroke on the afternoon she was planning to tell him good-bye. Breaking up with him is one thing, but she talks to him as if he were an infant, just because he's temporarily paralyzed and unable to feed himself.

TELEVISION USED TO WORK LIKE THIS: DAD WATCHED COP SHOWS, MOM followed each new miniseries, and the entire family gathered around for sitcoms. This has changed, partly because American lifestyles have and partly because cable and multiple household TVs have expanded our viewing options. Although Seinfeld's ratings have been mediocre, its demographics have been spectacular. Despite ranking only thirty-eighth among last season's regularly scheduled primetime shows (and finishing second in its time slot so far this season to ABC's *Home Improvement*), it finished at number eleven for male viewers between the ages of eighteen and thirty-four—the audience most desired by advertisers. An NBC spokesperson I talked with called it "a network ad salesman's dream."

This success is somewhat surprising in light of *Seinfeld's* regional and ethnic specificity. What do viewers beyond New York's five boroughs make of references to Ray's Pizza and Moe Ginsberg's? A knowledge of Jewish senior-citizen condo culture and Long Island families whose every conversation sounds like an argument was necessary in order to savor all the details in last season's single funniest episode (written by Larry David), in which Jerry and Elaine visited his parents in their Florida retirement community.

Despite *Seinfeld's* New York ambience, there are constant reminders that the action is unfolding on television (which is to say, nowhere in particular), not on West Eighty-first Street. In what is in fact one of Manhattan's best-integrated neighborhoods, the show's regulars cross paths with few people of color not in menial service positions. The only homeless person they encounter is

George and Jerry's old high school gym teacher, now living on the steps of the Forty-second Street library. Of Jerry's friends, only Elaine has a visible means of income. Despite his unemployment, George doesn't seem to be hurting. Jerry, who seems to have as much free time on his hands as Ozzie Nelson used to, is never shown at his computer working on his gigs. Although he's a big name on the comedy circuit and has even been on the *Tonight* show, he doesn't pal around with anybody else in show business.

Where *Seinfeld* achieves the ring of authenticity is in its characters, the likes of whom have never before been seen on television. Insofar as there is such a thing as a typical *Seinfeld* plot, it involves a character who tries unsuccessfully to keep a secret or to avoid hurting somebody else's feelings by telling the truth. These are people who can't keep anything to themselves-the sort of people we all know, whose irreverence we might admire but who we sometimes wish would just grow up. Garry Marshall, presumably thinking of his own Fonzie, Mork and Mindy, and Laverne and Shirley, once said that the secret of a successful sitcom is creating characters whom viewers will be happy to welcome into their living rooms week after week. Not necessarily. *Seinfeld* is a sitcom (like *The Honeymooners,* come to think of it) that presents us with characters we might wish to keep our distance from in real life, but whose misadventures we delight in following from week to week on TV.

IS *SEINFELD* A PREVIEW OF SITCOMS TO COME OR AN EVOLUTIONARY DEAD end? Probably the latter, if only because this is a show whose formula even its creators would be hard pressed to reproduce. It's sitcom stripped to is essentials, with any and all situations tangential to character quirks—the ultimate source of comedy in most shows anyway. *All in the Family* spawned *The Jeffersons* (Archie Bunker upscale and black) and *Maude* (Archie female and liberal). *The Mary Tyler Moore Show* spawned *Rhoda* and *Phyllis* (also about single women making it on their own) and contributed to the gene pool for *WKRP in Cincinnati* (also about people in broadcasting, just like Mary and Ted and Lou). What would be the point of another sitcom about an unmarried standup and his friends, or of a spinoff for Kramer, George, or Elaine? The only one of this season's new sitcoms arguably influenced by *Seinfeld*'s deliberately prosaic style of humor is *Mad About You*, the show that now follows it Wednesday nights on NBC. *Mad About You* is similar to *Seinfeld* in that it, too, stars a standup comedian, in this case Paul Reiser. *Entertainment Weekly* described it as "Seinfeld gets married." But it's finally another of those shows about a mismatched couple, a formula long ago perfected by *Cheers* and also copied this season by *Hearts Afire* and *Love & War*.

Seinfeld, meanwhile, has been moving in unpromising directions, beginning with a two-part broadcast last summer in which George and Jerry find themselves in Hollywood trying to free Kramer, who has been apprehended under suspicion of being a serial killer. (These episodes were written by Larry Charles, the show's supervising producer and its most prolific scriptwriter, aside from David and Seinfeld.) Why was it necessary to transport the characters to the West Coast? Last season the writers would have built an entire episode around making it to the airport in time. There were distracting cameos by Fred Savage of *The Wonder Years,* George Wendt of *Cheers,* and Corbin Bernsen of *L.A. Law.* This season there have been continuing episodes, an odd twist for a show whose signatures have been its sense of day-to-dayness and recurring gags that sometimes move the plot along and sometimes don't. In one of last season's episodes Jerry and Elaine started sleeping together again. By the next episode they were back to being just friends, with no explanation of what had happened to change their minds in between. It didn't matter, because each episode was such a brilliant non sequitur. There has been too much of Kramer, a one-dimensional character whose problems with gravity used to provide just the right amount of physical humor to this intensely verbal show.

The Hollywood episodes and a running plot line in which Jerry and George negotiate with NBC for a show much like the one we're watching—about "nothing," as George describes it—might prove to be ominous in light of a remark that Seinfeld made to *TV Guide* earlier this year. He said that when he wearies of doing the show, he'll write a final episode in which "my character will get a TV show and have to move to Los Angeles." In other words, *Seinfeld* isn't about "nothing" anymore. It's increasingly about itself. This cute touch could mean that Seinfeld and the show's other writers, including David, are running out of ideas. We'll have to wait and see. In the meantime, barring an unlikely outbreak of hugging and learning, this remains one of the few shows worth making it a point not just to turn on but to stop everything to watch.

(DECEMBER 1992)

A few months after this was published, Seinfeld *became television's top-rated show—but also become a tedious self-parody, which it remained for the duration of its long network run.*

Onward

When [I] first opened at the hungry i in San Francisco [in 1953], I used to do about fifteen minutes. . . . Since then, a lot of people think I've lost my discipline, and they say . . . 'Why does it take you an hour to cover a subject?' Believe it or not, it's not me. It's that there wasn't that much wrong in the country then and you could cover it a lot quicker," Mort Sahl quipped in *Heartland,* his 1977 memoir.

Mort Sahl on Broadway! the political satirist's 1987 one-man show at New York's Neil Simon Theater, ran just under *two* hours. But don't jump to conclusions about Sahl's current opinion of the state of the union. Sahl doesn't play favorites. Reagan is "a nine-to-five president—make that nine-to-ten. . . . George Washington could not tell a lie, Richard Nixon could not tell the truth, Ronald Reagan cannot tell the difference." The surplus of Democratic presidential hopefuls "in the Kennedy mold" causes Sahl to wonder, "Is there anyone in the party who's not like Kennedy? Yes—Teddy Kennedy." He confides that he's not against funding the contras as long as it's for "humanitarian" purposes, "like a suite for Arturo Cruz at the Ambassador Hotel when he does *Nightline.*" Turning his attention to Hollywood, he tells how, with tears in his eyes, he threw away all the popcorn, salad dressing, and spaghetti sauce in his refrigerator after an ideological disagreement with Paul Newman. But it isn't only Hollywood's liberal cause celebs who amuse him: Charlton Heston is "a cerebral fascist," who thinks, "I, unfortunately, won't live to see it, but someday my grandchildren will live under a military dictatorship.'" If Heston were "more perceptive, he'd be happy now."

This is funny stuff, but, except for the rip at Heston, no more seditious than the gentle tweaking that Johnny Carson regularly gives the high and mighty. It's impossible to tell from these nonpartisan one-liners what Sahl's own politics are—which is all right for Carson and Bob Hope, who depend on writers and give you the feeling that comedy is a job, but not all right for Sahl, who's too egotistical to let anyone else write his material, and who used to entertain audiences with the news that the military and the CIA were running the country.

That was the message of *Heartland,* which was written during a period when few club owners or television producers would touch Sahl, for fear that he might read aloud from the Warren Report. This was the low point of Sahl's career, and what a drop it must have been for someone who had reached such pinnacles as co-hosting the 1960 Academy Awards (with Hope, Jerry Lewis, Laurence Olivier, and Tony Randall) and being profiled in *The New Yorker* and featured on the cover of *Time* that same year.

Did Sahl fall or was he pushed? In *Heartland,* he claimed he'd been black-listed as punishment for going to work for New Orleans D.A. Jim Garrison on the Kennedy assassination and daring to speculate about the CIA's involvement. Sahl may have been right, just as Garrison may have been. But those who shunned Sahl would probably argue that he had become a paranoid and crank; significantly, he did find work on two-way talk radio, where being a paranoid and crank is among the job qualifications.

My own guess is that Sahl's career would have gone into reverse even without Garrison. Sahl was the most innovative comedian to gain access to a mass audience in the comedy-happy fifties (you'll have to take my word for it, because the albums that would prove it are long out of print). Lenny Bruce was still doing *shtick* when Sahl began walking onstage with a newspaper, extemporaneously riffing on the headlines. A cool-jazz buff, Sahl derived from musicians not only his timing, but also their habit of traveling light—schnooky dialects and comic personas like the ones Bruce was still hiding behind would have been excess baggage for Sahl, who spoke to audiences in his natural voice, that of a pseudo-intellectual positive he was smarter than the assholes running things. In 1960, Richard Nixon, long one of Sahl's favorite targets, and never more eager to prove that he had a sense of humor than in an election year, told *Time* that Sahl was "the Will Rogers of our time." Sahl's comeback: "Rogers . . . impersonated a yokel who was critical of the federal government. . . . I impersonate an intellectual who is critical of the yokels who are running the federal government. Other than that, we're similar in every respect."

Nixon's quote is reprinted in the *Playbill* for *Mort Sahl on Broadway!*—but without Sahl's rejoinder. As Nixon's blessing might suggest, Sahl got away with as much as he did because the people he skewered assumed he was only kidding, and maybe they were right. He thought of himself as "the loyal opposition," critical of whoever was in power, liberal or conservative. The bigwigs saw him as a court jester, and they dropped him when his humor turned sour (it was one thing to rib JFK about his father's wealth, another to make wholesale accusations about his murder). At the same time, Sahl's show-biz veneer and in-ness with Hugh Heffner and various New Frontiersmen made him an unlikely candidate to be speaking truth to power, in the eyes of the audience that was coming to prize irreverent humor most—disaffected, vaguely leftist youth. The biggest barrier for this audience was Sahl's misogyny, which was always there, but which became more virulent in response to feminism. Here was a man who, as late as 1977, was capable of writing: "When I went to New York in the '50s, you had to be Jewish to get a girl. In the '60s you had to be black to get a girl, and now you have to be a girl to get a girl." That's at least funny—the sort of joke feminists are likelier to laugh at than "sensitive men, if only because no man has ever experimented with homosexuality for ideological reasons. But what about this: "A writer and I were talking about a picture called *How to Make Love in Three Languages*. We idealized the last scene, in which a girl who insists on being an actress falls in love with an analyst. She tears up her Social Security card, throws it in the Trevi Fountain, and decides to be a woman, which is the only decision for a woman to make." In the seventies, politics gradually became as much a question of values as issues, and Sahl stubbornly refused to make the transition. He was soon left with no audience at all.

Now Sahl is back and Broadway's got him, which is, respectively, the good news and the bad. The audience for the matinee performance I attended was considerably smaller but otherwise not much different than the middle-aged-to-elderly and moneyed-looking crowd lined up around the corner for *Cats*. A typical Broadway crowd, in other words, which Sahl seemed to interpret to mean a mostly Jewish crowd. Although Sahl is both Jewish and a comedian, he's never come on like a *tummler*, so it was shocking to watch him courting favor with easy put-downs of Vanessa Redgrave and inanities about second-generation Jews who don't speak Yiddish. Sahl's only previous show on Broadway was the 1958 revue *The Next President*, the title of which, although it referred specifically to who would be Eisenhower's successor in Washington, was a dead giveaway that Sahl was (as fellow egoist Norman Mailer once said about himself) running for president in the privacy of his mind. Now that Sahl is back on the campaign trail, as it were, Jackie Mason's successful comeback has persuaded him of the wisdom of going after the Jewish vote.

Without the cocksure ebullience he possessed in the fifties or the bilious anger that ate away at him later, Sahl is in danger of becoming Mark Russell with sharper incisors and a hipper delivery. But after the dues he's paid, who has the heart to accuse him of selling out? Besides, he can be outrageously funny, especially when he isn't joking—when he addresses sexual politics and betrays his rancor at the way cultural values have shifted against him. You know you shouldn't be laughing, but you can't help yourself, and part of it is the ironic realization that it took a self-described "puritan" who wouldn't dream of using profanity on stage to identify our new taboos. "The new woman doesn't want to get married," he says, and adds that that's fine with him, because "men have never wanted to get married. So we now live in a country with two-hundred-and-forty-million people and nobody wants to get married and have children—except for the occasional Catholic priest." Watching his wife dance with George Bush at the White House, Sahl is troubled: "and not only because it was the first time I saw her smiling since she met me," but also because he suspects that he has more in common with Bush than he would with a liberal Democrat vice-president "who would probably be saying to her, 'Why don't you leave that crumb? After all, *you're* a person, too. Go back to college and study the social sciences. You can help lesbians to adopt children!'"

Sahl's wife—China Lee, a 1964 *Playboy* centerfold—gets her turn around the floor with Bush during a discursive but brilliantly sustained narrative that reveals Sahl to be a monologist as well as a comic—sort of an outer-directed Spalding Grey. Sahl is in his office at the Warner Brothers lot, where he makes a living writing screenplays that get optioned but never filmed (and where, to stay in good graces, he must "maintain the illusion of still being a liberal"). He's going through his mail, and there at the bottom of the pile is an invitation to a state dinner in honor of Israeli Prime Minister Yitzhak Shamir. Paul Newman, Warren Beatty, Dustin Hoffman, and other liberal friends urge him not to accept, but his wife thinks he should. Mort is undecided. "'You don't know how to be happy . . .'" China nags him: "You're not happy when they accept you, you're not happy when they don't accept you. You're not happy when you're inside, you're not happy when you're outside. . . ."

Sahl finally decides to go: "It's only a dinner." In the reception line, he's impressed that the president has a different joke for each couple. After exchanging pleasantries with Ron and Nancy, Mort meets Shamir, who, upon learning that Sahl is an entertainer, instructs him to beseech his audiences to urge their government not to sell arms to the Saudis ("Israelis are lots of fun at parties"). Later, he overhears an argument between Shamir and Caspar Weinberger over whether the U.S. is indeed already instructing the Saudis in the use of U.S.-supplied weaponry. He informs Reagan, who dissolves the tension with an anti-Arab joke. As the President and First Lady stand waiting with Mort and China for their limo, Ron tells Mort how much he's looking forward to his retirement, and charms him with an apocryphal story about Jimmy Carter and Menachem Begin meeting at the Wailing Wall on the anniversary of the Camp David accords.

This is Sahl's *Swimming to Washington.* From the retelling, it might seem as though he's fallen in love with Reagan for the reason he once fell head over heels for JFK—he's a sucker for a leader with a sense of humor. But the story isn't really about Reagan. It's about Sahl's ambivalent relationship to power. He knows that, as a political satirist, it's his calling to reveal that the emperor has no clothes. But when actually in the emperor's presence, he's like a painter who becomes infatuated with his nude model. Not having an audience must have been an ordeal for Sahl—he gives the impression of being the talkative sort who, if all else failed, would consider becoming an alcoholic just for the pleasure of sounding off to strangers in bars. But the worst part of being considered washed up must have been that it cut him off from his best source of material: the behind-the-scenes machinations of the Hollywood and Washington power elites. His inclusion of China Lee's harangue seems intended to show that, given seventeen years of marriage, even an Asian-American Playmate can become a yenta. But it also shows that Lee has her husband's number. Presidents—can't live with 'em, can't live without 'em. He's not happy when they accept him, but he's not happy when they don't accept him, either, because he's learned that he needs them more than they need him.

Like most one-man shows, *Mort Sahl on Broadway!* is negligible as theater. But Sahl himself is the stuff of drama. Despite raves in the *Times* and *The New Yorker,* the show closed on November 1, exactly as first announced: it wasn't held over, as Sahl confidently told the *Times* it would be. But it wasn't a flop, either, and the middling result hardly seems fair—someone with Sahl's sense of self-importance deserves either complete redemption or crushing failure. I don't know where he goes from here, but I'm hoping it's back up.

(NOVEMBER 1987)

Bob Hope, Prisoner of War

═══

War correspondents frequently suffer from what might be diagnosed as Ernie Pyle syndrome. At least one colleague of the late Michael Kelly, the *Washington Post* columnist and former editor of *The Atlantic Monthly,* who was killed while traveling with the Third Infantry Division in Iraq, confessed to being angry with Kelly on hearing of his death. The colleague had argued that having written brilliantly about the first Gulf War entitled Kelly to sit this one out, especially since he was now the father of two young children. Bob Hope was a showman, not a reporter, but until old age stopped him, he obeyed the same itch.

Not bending the truth by much in *Don't Shoot, It's Only Me*—one of his many memoirs, published in 1990—Hope quipped that the closest the United States came to formally declaring war on North Vietnam was in 1963, when he was invited over to perform for our military, as he had during World War II and the Korean War. Probably the only U.S. civilian ever targeted for assassination by the Vietcong, Hope donned camouflage and entertained U.S. troops on foreign soil as recently as Desert Storm. But to our men and women in Bosnia in 1996, he merely sent a video and his prayers. Iraq was out of the question for Hope, who celebrated his hundredth birthday on May 29; the old casting-couch general no longer has the strength to appear on his own television specials, much less escort a harem of beauty queens and Sinatra discards into war zones. So on April 20, with the fighting in Iraq more or less over, though not the homefront flagwaving (nor the Pentagon and the newsmedia's exploitation of our rescued POWs-an invasion of their privacy unanticipated by the Geneva Convention), NBC presented a two-hour retrospective called *100 Years of Hope and Humor,* thirty minutes of which consisted of clips from Hope's 1940s USO tours and his 1960s Vietnam Christmas specials.

The special was watched by 12.6 million people—nothing compared to the numbers that Hope racked up in the age before cable, but enough now to dominate its timeslot and finish in Nielsen's Top 20 for the week. I have a hunch that these ratings surprised NBC, given that (along with patriotic fever) the logic in jumping the gun on Hope's centenary by several weeks seemed to be to avoid showing chicken skin and black-and-white archival footage during a sweeps month, when advertising rates are set and the only viewers who count are loutish young men between the ages of eighteen and thirty-five.

The ratings surprised me, even though I wouldn't have dreamed of missing the show. I have a soft spot for Bob Hope dating back to my childhood in the 1950s, when I saw him in *That Certain Feeling, Beau James,* and *The Seven Little Foys*—movies in which he was so funny and appealing it hardly mattered that he epitomized an era of popular culture being pushed aside by mine. But I don't think I know anybody else who watched, which tells you something about the company I keep. I know plenty of people who loathe Hope, on general principle, as a hideous relic of a time when young actresses were referred to as "sex kittens" and war was embraced as a masculine rite of passage, a team sport with fatalities.

These people tend to be my age and older; no one under forty seems to think much about Hope one way or the other, which might be the greater insult. "To most of my friends, Bob Hope is the guy in the blazer who's doing a monologue off cue cards or who's dressed up like a Cabbage Patch doll and doing a sketch with Brooke Shields," Conan O'Brien, the host of NBC's *Late Night* and a former writer for *The Simpsons* and *Saturday Night Live,* told *The New York Times* in 1998, describing the decrepit Hope his generation grew up with in the 1970s. "If you were a comedy fan, you knew that he was one of the faces on Mount Rushmore, but you thought it was based on that. It wasn't."

O'Brien recommended taking a look at Hope's movies of the 1940s and early 1950s—good advice, because there was a difference between this Hope and the later one from television. In his prime, the smug TV stand-up had no equal at working an audience or milking a laugh; he was the CEO of comedy, with his own celebrity golf classic included among the perks. The character that Hope played to perfection in movie after movie was something else—the weasel who got by on his wits, but just barely. He was a boastful coward who was the only one ever fooled by his bravado, a loser who could be manipulated by anybody clever enough to pretend he wasn't, a wolf who came on to every pretty girl he met and kept coming on after being rebuffed, as if seduction were a war of attrition.

Of course, W. C. Fields was all of these things a good decade earlier than Hope. But Hope added something new, something that I think that James Agee unwittingly put his finger on when he complained (in a 1949 piece he wrote for *Life* in praise of the great silent-movie comedians) that most of the humor in Hope's movies was verbal. This wasn't completely true; part of what made Hope a terrific comic actor, as opposed to a radio gagman hauled in front of a camera, was his face—I mean his double-takes, of course, which were almost a match for Jack Benny's, but also the inspired way he put his very *features* to work for him. His chin stuck out so far, for example, that he might as well have been leading with it, just begging for a punch even as he backpeddled away from an assailant just itching to land one (he'd been a prize-fighter as a young man, and he still had the moves).

But Agee had a point. Hope never stopped talking, even when running from a punch or holding a lover in his arms, and if frequently nobody on screen seemed to being paying attention to anything he said, that was all right because his funniest remarks were aimed straight at the balcony anyway (many of his best vehicles, including *The Paleface, My Favorite Brunette,* and his borderline-surreal "road" pictures with Bing Crosby, were genre parodies that depended on the supporting cast playing it straight). Modeling his delivery on Walter Winchell's hard-boiled rat-tat-rat (itself a modification of Hemingway's tough guy), Hope was perhaps the first star of vaudeville and Broadway to compre-hend the different requirements of radio and what many people still referred to as "talking pictures" when he made his screen debut in *The Big Broadcast* of 1938, stealing the show right out from under Fields's bulbous nose.

The Big Broadcast, one of seventeen films included in *The Bob Hope DVD Tribute Collection,* a series of DVDs released by Universal to coincide with Hope's landmark birthday, was also the movie in which Hope and Shirley Ross, playing a wised-up divorced couple who are still half in love with each other, sang "Thanks for the Memory." As much as anything else, it was Hope's singing in this scene that made him a star, yet anyone seeing the movie for the first time is likely to be surprised by what a wonderful singer Hope was. Before going to Hollywood, Hope introduced a number of immortal songs on Broadway, beginning with Vernon Duke and Ira Gershwin's "I Can't Get Started." What virtually ended his singing career was being cast opposite Crosby, who was the most popular recording artist of the first half of the twen-tieth century. Although Hope did occasionally join Crosby for a comic duet, the formula called for Crosby to do the romantic ballads it took to woo Dorothy Lamour. Crosby more or less invented a sensational style of pop singing in the 1920s, but by the time he teamed up with Hope, he'd become a crooning self-caricature. Unlike Lamour, I happen to prefer Hope's looser, more conversational phrasing; and before calling me crazy, you ought to hear his four duets with Ross on *Thanks for the Memories,* a new compilation on MCA that should force you to think twice.

HOPE'S INFLUENCE HAS BEEN UBIQUITOUS, BOTH AS A STAND-UP comedian and as a comic actor. Without him as the prototype, there would be no Johnny Carson, Steve Martin, or Bill Murray—to say nothing of Austin Powers, George Costanza, Deputy Sheriff Barney Fife, and even *M*A*S*H**'s

Captain Franklin "Hawkeye" Pierce, an idealist-become-cynic whose nonstop wisecracking outweighed the fact that he was Hope's political antithesis (many of his quips were the work of Larry Gelbart, the creator of the series, who did his own tour of duty in Korea as Hope's head writer). Conan O'Brien, when announcing that his guests that night include a supermodel or leggy movie star, might lick his index fingers and use them to smooth his eyebrows, like Hope primping for what he's only been led to believe will be a rendezvous (it's usually some sort of scheme, with him as the sucker). The host of *Late Night* also occasionally growls when an attractive female guest says something provocative, a variation on Hope's ejaculatory *woof!* And the premise of many of O'Brien's best sketches is either that he's sexually inadequate or that nobody thinks he's funny—two more pages straight out of Hope's book, as O'Brien would be the first to admit.

Hope's other most adoring fan among fellow professionals might be Woody Allen, who once admitted that "it's all I can do at times not to imitate him," and who has himself often been accused of being overly verbal in his approach to comedy. "It's hard to tell when I do," Allen said in 1973, while filming *Sleeper*, "because I'm so unlike him physically and in tone of voice, but once you know I do it, it's absolutely unmistakable." (Forget that Hope was funny-haha, and Allen more often funny-weird. The real difference between them is that Allen, in his movies, is usually desperate for our approval, whereas Hope dared us to dislike him, confident that he was irresistible.) Allen more or less credited Hope with inventing the one-liner, which I think is going a little too far. What Hope does seem to have originated, for better or worse, is the celebrity in-joke—a type of humor that assumes the audience is familiar with the foibles of the stars. (It resembles ethnic humor in presupposing such knowledge, but hasn't celebrity become a type of ethnicity? Many older people in show business adored Ronald Reagan when he was president not because they agreed with his policies, but because he was one of theirs. Their feelings for him were similar to those of my Irish-American grandmother for JFK.) Jokes about the famous flatter the rest of us, in making us feel like part of the clan. But no other brand of humor has a shorter shelf-life.

A telling moment on the NBC special came during a clip from an unspecified military base in Southeast Asia, circa 1965. It's Christmas, and Hope badgers a soldier into singing "Silent Night" with Les Brown's orchestra. The soldier sings surprisingly well; he has good pitch and a pleasing baritone, and despite the stiffness in his body, he doesn't rush the beat. Giving in to the moment, he lifts the microphone off its stand and brings it close to his mouth, like a pop crooner. "I tell ya, that Bing has children everywhere," Hope wisecracks. Cut to the soldier, now a lot older, who tells us that everybody laughed at that, including him. If so, weren't they just going along with the implied script? We now know that our soldiers were as radicalized by the 1960s as the college protestors. By the end of the war, they were booing Hope. What possible sense did they make of a Hollywood Canteen-era joke about—what exactly? Crosby's Roman Catholic disdain for birth control?

What other comics have always admired about Hope isn't necessarily his material, but his mechanics—the smoothness of his setups and payoffs. My favorite joke of his, in a way, is the one he opened with after being announced as the winner of a Jean Hersholt award during an Oscar broadcast: "I don't know what to say," he admitted, seemingly humbled, then waited a beat. "I don't have writers for this kind of work." "Bob Hope is supposed to employ so many gag-men they are organizing a union," the film critic Otis Ferguson once remarked, making a joke that only sounded like one written for Hope. The new *Bob Hope: My Life in Jokes,* assembled by his daughter Linda, proves that Hope's humor doesn't really translate to the page. His gift, hardly a small one, was delivering scripted material as if he were ad-libbing.

IN THE 1960S, HOPE FOUND HIMSELF ON THE WRONG SIDE OF BOTH A WAR and a generation gap. How did someone with such unerring timing so misjudge the cultural moment? In *Don't Shoot, It's Only Me,* he sought to give the impression that he went to Vietnam only to show his concern for our troops, not necessarily to endorse our foreign policy—a distinction that no one would argue with today (indeed, that such a distinction needs to be made was among the most painful lessons of Vietnam). But by 1990, even Robert McNamara was claiming to have been a closet peacenik. In the 1960s, when Hope wasn't onstage making sour fun of hippies and draft-card burners, he was giving interviews in which he mouthed the domino principle: "If the Commies ever thought we weren't going to protect the Vietnamese, there would be Vietnams everywhere," he said in 1965. He has more in common with Jane Fonda than either might realize—they both were casualties of Vietnam. She's always going to be "Hanoi Jane" to right-wing talk-show hosts, and the left is never going to forgive him for mistaking Vietnam for Iwo Jima. I say it's time we granted Hope amnesty, not because we owe it to him but because we owe it to ourselves. Maybe he never made a movie as good as *Klute* or *They Shoot Horses, Don't They?* but at least he never made one as sappy as *On Golden Pond* or as heavy-handed as *Coming Home.*

(JUNE 2003)

America Surrenders

ast year, beginning in early September, the Film Forum, a theater on Houston Street in lower Manhattan, presented a four-week retrospective of films directed by William Wyler, in honor of his birthday centennial. Whether by coincidence or design, just days after the one-year anniversary of the attack on the Twin Towers, the theater—three stops from Ground Zero on the Number 1 subway line—screened *The Best Years of Our Lives,* Wyler's 1946 melodrama about a trio of World War II veterans and their difficulties in readjusting to civilian life (including the rituals of courtship and marriage).

Although it might be dimly remembered today only for the novelty of featuring a real-life amputee (and nonprofessional actor) in the role of a sailor outfitted with hooks after losing both of his hands when his ship was sunk by a torpedo, *The Best Years of Our Lives* was once revered. Its first engagement was at a theater in Times Square, a week before Thanksgiving in a year when many families were still mourning their loses as they sat down to count their blessings. Bosley Crowther, who was the most influential film critic of the day, by virtue of publishing in *The New York Times,* immediately recognized the stuff of greatness in it, as did James Agee, of *The Nation* and *Time,* the critic with the most literary cache. *The Best Years of Our Lives* won seven Academy Awards, including the one for best picture from among a field of nominees that also included *It's a Wonderful Life* and Laurence Olivier's *Henry V.* (Wyler won for best director, and Fredric March was chosen best actor for his performance as a disillusioned bank officer and former infantry sergeant. Harold Russell, the amputee, won for best supporting actor and was also awarded a special Oscar "for giving hope and encouragement to his fellow veterans." The other winners were Robert E. Sherwood, for his screenplay, Daniel Mandel, for his editing, and Hugo Friedhofer, for his lovely, Aaron Copland-like score.) Released nationwide in 1947, soon after the Oscar ceremony, *The Best Years of Our Lives* grossed more in its first run than any movie since *Gone with the Wind,* seven years earlier.

This seems to me proof that *The Best Years of Our Lives* captured the ambivalence of Americans who, though rejoicing in victory and looking forward to sharing in the postwar prosperity, secretly doubted that peace would be long-lasting or that their lives would ever return to normal. On the other hand, it's possible that the movie's box office was a triumph of marketing—that millions of moviegoers were duped by all those Oscars and a coming attraction (now a DVD bonus feature) that promised not just "the love story of today that will live with you for all your tomorrows," but "the greatest thing that ever happened!" (*The Best Years of Our Lives* or the return of our troops from overseas? The coming attraction treated these as one and the same.) The inevitable backlash wasn't long in coming. Writing in *The Partisan Review* while the movie was still being shown in neighborhood theaters, Robert Warshow denounced it for its "denial of the reality of politics," by which he meant its reduction of widespread postwar problems into matters of individual psychology that could be solved by the application of good, old-fashioned American virtues (hard work, patience, cheerfulness, and the like). Though Warshow was practically the only naysayer, his point of view gradually came to prevail in intellectual circles—so that in 1957, when Manny Farber, writing in *Commentary*, dismissed *The Best Years of Our Lives* as "a horse-drawn truckload of liberal schmaltz," he was telling his readers something they felt they already knew (then as now, the only ones more disdainful of liberal ideals than conservatives were those on the extreme left).

Skepticism is the critic's stock in trade, but I think Farber and Warshow let theirs run away with them—as have we. We're so used to being manipulated by movies that we instinctively distrust one that stirs something real in us. Seeing *The Best Years of Our Lives* again last year, in the aftermath of the media blitz that surrounded the September 11 observances (and amid vague new terrorism alerts and the virtual certainty of a war with Iraq), filled me with regret that today's popular culture has responded to our current national predicament only in ways that seem crass—witness the many commemorative books for which 9/11 represented both a marketing opportunity and a sell-by date—or, worse, ineffectual. Pop music was the first responder, and the most anticipated and publicized album was Bruce Springsteen's *The Rising*, whose individual songs strained so hard to represent the perspective of so many different people—rescue workers, victims' relatives, even the hijackers—that Springsteen seemed without a point of view of his own. (Talk about a truckload of liberal schmaltz: he was so vague that he could have been running for president, not just taking his band on tour. At least with the maudlin "Where Were You When the World Stopped Turning?" the country singer Alan Jackson came right out with what was on his mind, even if it wasn't very much.)

There have been plenty of new war movies in the last eighteen months, but *Black Hawk Down, We Were Soldiers*, and the rest were in production long before September 11, inspired by *Saving Private Ryan* and the anticipated success of *Pearl Harbor*—an epic that took in hundreds of millions of dollars at the box office without causing much of a stir culturally. *Pearl Harbor* was like a 1940s double feature: it combined action and dewy romance in a transparent attempt to please younger moviegoers of both sexes and become a favorite "date" movie—*World War 90210.* It may also have been the first blockbuster ever to incorporate its own sequel, ending not with the bombing of Pearl Harbor, which would have been too sobering, but with Doolittle's raid on Japan the following year, which demonstrated American pluck and represented a great psychological victory. War movies since *Saving Private Ryan* have emulated it in mixing period sentimentality with the graphic bloodletting characteristic of today's action movies. *Pearl Harbor,* dreadful as it was, also felt like a prototype. Audiences want happy endings, and this probably means that we won't be seeing any movies about 9/11 any time soon. As I watched the September 11 observances on television and heard repeated mention of that day's "heroes," it took me a few minutes to realize that the word was also meant to refer to the thousands of innocent people who died in the Twin Towers. There was a reluctance to call them "victims," even though that's what they were. I think that Hollywood has a similar reluctance, given that the directors now likely to be called to make war specialize in crowd control. They lack the talent to portray the emotional toll that war exacts even on the victors—the subject of *The Best Years of Our Lives.*

I WAS BORN THE YEAR *THE BEST YEARS OF OUR LIVES* CAME OUT, A DEAD soldier's nephew and namesake, and circumstantially as much a war baby as a Boomer. My generation was the first to grow up with television, but thanks to the endless after-school hours that local channels once filled with diversions originally shown at kiddie matinees during the Depression (Popeye, Our Gang, the Three Stooges, Hopalong Cassidy, and Johnny Mack Brown), we were also the first generation weaned on our parents' popular culture as well as our own. Even *Superman, The Lone Ranger,* and *Gunsmoke* were radio hand-me-downs. Vietnam is said to have been the first television war, because it was the first in which nightly newscasts delivered fresh kill to our dinner tables. But World War II was refought endlessly on *The Early Show* all through my childhood, in movies such as *Bataan, Thirty Seconds Over Tokyo,* and my personal favorite, William Wellman's *The Story of G.I. Joe* (the one with Burgess Meredith as Ernie Pyle, the wizened, chain-smoking war correspondent who did for U.S. foot soldiers on their advance through Nazi-occupied Italy what Albert Camus did for Sisyphus). When my friends and I weren't playing Cowboys and Indians, we played "war," throwing clumps of dirt from a forgotten neighborhood victory garden at one another and calling them grenades.

Rock 'n' roll—our music—was rarely permitted on television before Elvis Presley and *American Bandstand.* Along with numbers from the latest Broadway smashes, the songs we heard performed on the big nighttime variety shows were likely to be ones that our mothers and fathers had courted to during the war. To us, these songs sounded hopelessly mushy, or just plain silly. Our parents weren't about to tell us that "Don't sit under the apple tree with anyone else but me" once meant "Promise me that you'll be faithful while I'm away," much less that "So love me tonight, tomorrow was meant for some, tomorrow may never come, for all we know," was an elegant way of saying "Fuck me now, for Christ sake, because I might be sent home in a box." The nuns who taught me catechism used to say that God showed mercy toward the men like my uncle who died on the battlefield, without benefit of extreme unction. It went without saying that the first commandment was waived for men putting their own lives at risk in defense of their country. As I grew older, I wondered if other bans had been lifted during the war. Those songs should have given me the answer. They were the first manifestos in a sexual revolution whose beginnings are usually traced back only to *Playboy* and the Pill in the late 1950s.

For me, seeing *The Best Years of Our Lives* for the first time on television several years ago was like having a recovered memory. Part of what I was responding to was Gregg Toland's lifelike cinematography and a kind of bourgeois neo-realism. Much of the shooting was done on location in Cincinnati, rather than on a studio back lot, and the barrooms and high rises and row houses in which much of the action takes place looked much like those in the eastern city where I grew up. There are no stylized close-ups in the movie, and even the women are wearing outfits bought off-the-rack, which they were asked to break in for a few weeks before shooting started. But *The Best Years of Our Lives* also felt like my notion of 1946.

THOUGH ITS CREDITS SAY THAT *THE BEST YEARS OF OUR LIVES* WAS adapted from MacKinlay Kantor's novel *Glory for Me,* its actual genesis was in a news story that the producer Samuel Goldwyn read in *Time* magazine in 1944, set aboard "The Home Again Special"—a cross-country train taking members of the First Marine Division to their hometowns to start a thirty-day furlough after more than two years in battle. The unsigned piece often reads surprisingly like many we read during Vietnam:

> In another war there might have been brass bands at every stop. But in this pagentry-less, slogan-less war, the train just rumbled on toward New York, through the big towns and the whistle-stops.

"I'm a little worried about how I'll look to them, about how much I've changed," one man says as the train nears his hometown. Another confides, "I haven't shaken so much since the night we went around Cape Hatteras, leaving the States."

Knowing a good idea when somebody else had it, Goldwyn commissioned a treatment by Kantor, hardly expecting the 400-plus-page manuscript written in blank verse that Kantor published as *Glory for Me* after Goldwyn, understandably, passed on it. The project might have ended there if not for Wyler's desire to make a movie about returning veterans, rather than the star-spangled biography of General Dwight D. Eisenhower that Goldwyn had him penciled in for.

Wyler, who died in 1981, eleven years after the release of his final movie (*The Liberation of L.B. Jones,* a lurid, near-blaxploitation southern potboiler), began his career in the silent era, directing western two-reelers. He directed plenty of hypermasculine fare: World War II combat documentaries, Humphery Bogart and the Bowery Boys in the muckraking *Dead End,* and Charlton Heston riding a chariot in *Ben-Hur.* Yet he's remembered today mostly for his work with actresses—Bette Davis in *Jezebel, The Little Foxes,* and *The Letter;* Greer Garson in *Mrs. Miniver;* Olivia de Havilland in *The Heiress;* Audrey Hepburn in *Roman Holiday* and *The Children's Hour*; and Barbra Streisand in *Funny Girl.* Inasmuch as its drama comes from the working out of personal relationships, *The Best Years of Our Lives* could almost be one of Wyler's "women's" pictures. The difference is that the characters who are in danger of being immolated by their emotions are disaffected fighting men whose reunion with their wives and sweethearts does not go smoothly.

WORLD WAR II PROVIDED A BACKDROP FOR ROMANCE IN *CASABLANCA*; IN *The Best Years of Our Lives,* it's the backstory. "Remember what it felt like when you went overseas?" Dana Andrews, the movie's third veteran, asks March, echoing a line from that story in *Time,* as their transport plane makes its way to Boone City, the movie's fictional Midwestern setting. "I feel the same way now, only more so." Andrews and the others have been men without women. War has changed them, and the women have gained a measure of independence in their absence. The liquor cabinet is nearly empty when March arrives home, and there's only enough bacon in the refrigerator for his wife (Myrna Loy) and their two children. At one point, March offers her a cigarette, forgetting she doesn't smoke. *Since You Went Away,* a bona fide women's picture made during the war—a morale booster for homemakers counting their rationing coupons and praying for the safe return of their husbands—began with the caption "This is the story of the Unconquerable Fortress: the American Home . . . 1943." It was still unconquerable three years later, only by then the troops storming the home front were ours.

What makes March's situation especially poignant is that this is no nagging housewife he's alienated from: to that day's audiences, Loy was Nora Charles, from *The Thin Man*—not just a spouse but an ideal partner in every way. Loy and March obviously adore each other, but after having lived apart for so long, they're at a point in the marriage where they need to start courting again, and neither of them has the energy.

Russell's problem is more acute: he worries that Cathy O'Donnell, his sweetheart since adolescence, feels only pity for him now. A scene in which she undresses him and puts him to bed after convincing him that she still loves him is just about perfect, and it isn't until afterward that you realize that Wyler was quietly shattering a long-standing taboo by allowing an unmarried couple such intimacy in a bedroom. Part of what makes the scene so moving is that you don't feel you're being unduly manipulated. The scene is expository, not exploitative: we've watched Russell impressing people by showing them how nimble he's become with his hooks, and now we're being shown how helpless he is once he removes them for the night—"as dependent as a baby who doesn't know how to get anything except to cry for it." O'Donnell helps him remove his arm harnesses, and we, too, get our first look at his bandaged stumps. "I'm lucky to have my elbows," he says. "Some of the boys don't." He wiggles into his pajama top, and she buttons it for him, tucks him in, and kisses him goodnight. On her way out, she closes the door behind her and then, as if remembering that he might need the bathroom in the middle of the night, reopens it and leaves it ajar. We see him crying in the shaft of light, with no hand to wipe away his tears.

Robert Warshow observed that not just Russell but each of the other main male characters has "a scene in which the woman he loves undresses him . . . and puts him to bed." Warshow saw in this "an unusually clear projection of the familiar Hollywood [and American] dream of male passivity."

> And when it is the sailor who is put to bed, the dream becomes almost explicit. He is the man (the real man) who has lost his hands—and with them the power to be sexually aggressive . . . Every night, his wife will have to put him to bed, and then it will be her hands that must be used in making love.

He might have added that when Teresa Wright undresses Andrews soon after meeting him, he's dead drunk and the bed she puts him in to sleep it off is hers—an ultra-feminine one, with a lace canopy and a billowy comforter. He begins talking in his sleep as she prepares to leave; she knows, from having volunteered at a veterans' hospital, that he's having a battle nightmare. She sits at his bedside, attracted to him because of his vulnerability. (Their first kiss comes much later, after she finds him working behind a drugstore perfume counter.)

Despite his harsh judgment of *The Best Years of Our Lives,* Warshow was the only contemporary critic to detect its undercurrents of male surrender, emotional and sexual, Warshow, who died of a heart attack in 1955 at the age of thirty-seven, once wrote, "A man watches a movie, and the critic must acknowledge that he is that man"—a defense of subjectivity as an analytical tool that has become a rallying cry for many of today's critics, including me. (In his own case, though, the man watching the movie was sitting awfully close to Dr. Freud.) Among other things, Warshow called the male characters "inarticulate," which at first seems an odd word for so talkative a movie. But these men *are* inarticulate in a way: they've witnessed things and done things they feel unable to discuss in mixed company, and words are unnecessary when they're alone with one other. They're hurting and their women sense this, but back then nobody spoke today's language of recovery.

The women's pictures of the 1940s that *The Best Years of Our Lives* resembles were altogether different from today's "chick flicks," like *My Big Fat Greek Wedding* and *Real Women Have Curves,* with their flattering messages of self-empowerment. Old-fashioned women's pictures wallowed in suffering and sacrifice, but the best of them—Wyler's with Bette Davis, for example—were among the few movies of their era to tackle the issue of class without mounting a proletariat soapbox. *The Best Years of Our Lives* qualifies as something of a woman's picture in this regard as well, even though much of its dialogue verges on hard-boiled—especially as delivered by Andrews, who frequently still seems to be playing the homicide detective he'd starred as in *Laura* two years earlier (his former Air Force captain and bombardier is the kind of guy who describes his citations for bravery as "just a lot of words that don't mean anything").

Boone City, like the real-life towns that Wyler and Sherwood based it on, is changing, its self-sufficiency undermined by postwar expansion. The drugstore where Andrews goes back to work as a soda jerk has been taken over by a chain, and the local savings and loan where March returns to a desk job has become a branch of a Midwestern trust. But it's still the sort of place where a family's social standing remains the same for decades, and personal growth is interpreted as a threat to the status quo. (Boone City's nearest equivalent in literature would be Updike's Brewster.) Fired from the drugstore for slugging an obnoxious customer, Andrews arrives home after looking for work one day to find his flashy blonde wife (Virginia Mayo) openly entertaining another man. In a departure from the conventions of 1940s melodrama—one of many in the screenplay by Sherwood, a former speechwriter for Franklin D. Roosevelt and the winner of three Pulitzer Prizes for drama—being cuckolded bothers Andrews only in principle, and the news that his wife wants to call it quits is a relief. Like many wartime couples, they were married on impulse soon after meeting, when he was in basic training and awaiting assignment overseas. He married a pin-up, and she married a uniform. They start living together for the first time, and despite their obvious incompatibility (money is a constant argument, and she scolds him for crying out in his sleep while having vivid war nightmares), he stays with her, because a stand-up guy doesn't walk out on his wife. But he's fallen in love with March's daughter, played by Teresa Wright. (The friendship between the two men hits a bump when Wright—the aggressor in the relationship—informs her parents that she intends to do whatever it takes to rescue Andrews from his unhappy marriage.) What prevents Andrews from following his heart and running straight to Wright after his final confrontation with Mayo is his lack of prospects—the worry that he isn't good enough for a banker's daughter.

Andrews heads for the airport and buys a ticket on the first plane out. The destination doesn't matter, because anywhere else has to be better than Boone City. With time to kill before catching his flight, he wanders into a nearby scrap yard filled with engines and propellers disassembled from aircraft like the ones he flew. The planes are being junked, their parts to be reused in building houses. Passing a row of planes that are still more or less intact, he hoists himself into a B-17, brushes away a few cobwebs, and climbs into the bombardier's post up front. As the music on the soundtrack grows dissonant and militaristic, with the roar of engines beneath it, the camera pans the row of propellerless jets as if each were taking off in succession. We see Andrews through the Plexiglas nosecone of his plane; then we see him from behind, moving his hands as if releasing a bomb; and then in tight close-up—he's sweating and staring straight ahead with a look of determination that could be a disguise for shock. We've heard Andrews dismiss his citations, but we also know from hearing his father read one of them aloud that Andrews was awarded the Distinguished Flying Cross for carrying out a mission despite being wounded and losing a massive amount of blood. He's having a flashback, but we don't see whatever it is that he's seeing. There are no combat scenes in *The Best Years of Our Lives,* unless you count the battle of the sexes.

THE BEST YEARS OF OUR LIVES EPITOMIZES A LARGE-SCALE APPROACH TO storytelling no longer favored by our culture, although the success of *The Sopranos* and Jonathan Franzen's *The Corrections* suggests that it might be staging a comeback. What else keeps people away from the movie, I think, is the belief (first voiced by Warshow) that it presented an officially sanctioned, overly optimistic view of postwar American life.* *The Best Years of Our Lives* is

---

*There are people who reject Robert Frost as overly optimistic, too, not realizing that those famous lines about having "promises to keep" and "miles to go before I sleep," from "Stopping by the Woods on a Snowy Evening," refer to unhappy obligations and the inevitability of death, which at least puts an end to them. (It doesn't help that there are rah-rah types who insist on reading Frost as though he were a coach giving a fourth-quarter pep talk. Years ago, I worked in a campus bookstore whose manager quoted those lines from "Stopping by the Woods" on business cards he had printed to announce that we'd be staying open late during fall registration.)

actually a femme fatale, a double cross, and a few menacing shadows shy of being a film noir. The amputee gets the girl at the end, but what else does he get? In Edward Dmytryk's *Till the End of Time*—another movie about maladjusted veterans that beat Wyler's film to theaters by a few months—a prizefighter who has lost both legs in the war stops sulking when it dawns on him that he can make himself useful to society by training younger, able-bodied pugs. Russell has nothing but the love of a kind woman to fill his days; he's content to live off his monthly disability checks and amuse his friends by using his hooks to uncap beer bottles and play "Chopsticks" with his Uncle Butch (Hoagy Carmichael, looking as always like a corn-belt Samuel Beckett). And as Warshow suggested, the question of whether he and his new bride will prove to be sexually compatible is left hanging—possibly in their minds as well as in ours. (This isn't *Coming Home*, where Jane Fonda straddled Jon Voight, who was supposed to be paralyzed below the waist from wounds suffered in Vietnam, and humped herself to a noisy climax in his wheelchair, answering whatever prurient questions anyone may have had.) Andrews and Wright wind up together, true, but the only work he can find—and keep—is as a beginner in the scrap yard where he had his flashback. A more optimistic scenario would have ended with him taking out a loan on the G.I. Bill and opening his own flight school (he could go on wearing that bomber jacket in which he cuts such a handsome figure). March stays on at his bank, even though he knows he's in for a fight every time he approves a loan for a veteran with no collateral. Along with a social conscience, he's also developed a drinking habit, and this is still an issue in his marriage at the end. It's also worth noting that the sort of thing that Manny Farber mocked as liberal schmaltz from the safe distance of the late 1950s—a Carmichael wisecrack about a nuclear doomsday, Andrews's one-punch knockout of a loudmouth who thinks we should have fought "the Limeys and the Reds" instead of the Nazis, a speech March gives at a banquet in his honor that could be interpreted as antibusiness—was subversive enough in 1947 to land *The Best Years of Our Lives* on a congressional list of movies that supposedly contained "anti-American content." The mighty Samuel Goldwyn was subpoenaed to testify before HUAC as a direct result of his involvement in the film, before the committee was forced to settle for smaller Hollywood fish.

The Best Years of Our Lives was Wyler's masterpiece, but its reputation has depreciated along with his. Though Wyler still has his devotees (apparently including the programmers for the Film Forum), he wasn't on the short list of directors hailed as auteurists by François Truffaut, Eric Rohmer, Claude Chabrol, Jean-Luc Godard, and the other argumentative young Frenchmen who reviewed the latest American movies for *Cahiers du Cinèma* in the late 1950s, before going on to make their own. Along with his versatility, his reputation as a director of ingenues and grand dames earned Wyler the animosity of the French auteurists and their followers in the United States and England (they much preferred John Ford and Howard Hawks, who took turns making the same John Wayne movie well into old age). Though hardly anyone today subscribes to the theories put forth by the auteurists, their rankings of directors are still the ones trusted by most film critics and historians.

During the years when Wyler was venerated within the film industry, his champion among intellectuals was André Bazin, a founding editor of *Cahiers du Cinèma* who had been a Socrates to Truffaut and the others. Along with Siegfried Kracauer and Sergei Eisenstein, Bazin was one of the first to write about movies not just as dramatic narratives, but as examples of a visual art similar to photography, with the advantage of motion and sound. Both an empiricist and something of a religious mystic—a dual temperament that put him in an ideal position to theorize about a medium that was at once a technological breakthrough and a vehicle for artistic expression—Bazin believed that because motion pictures were capable of capturing a semblance of reality, they had what was practically a moral obligation to do so. Distrustful of montage and other forms of editing on account of their potential for falsehood (a potential fully realized by Eisenstein in his films about the Bolshevik Revolution, and by Leni Riefenstahl in *Triumph of the Will*), Bazin admired Wyler for relying instead on mise-en-scène—a term borrowed from theater, where it refers to the placement onstage of actors, props, and scenery, though in Wyler's case, it meant long, uninterrupted takes in which the actors moved freely while the camera remained more or less stationary.

This was the issue on which his disciples parted ways with Bazin. To them, Wyler's mise-en-scène just looked stagy (and, in fact, many of his films were adapted from plays). But what made Wyler's approach fully cinematic—and what thrilled Bazin—was his use of a technique called "deep focus": a way of shooting a scene so that everyone and everything in it, whether in the foreground or the background, in the center of the frame or toward the margins, was photographed with equal clarity, eliminating the need for frequent cuts or shifts of focus to redirect the audience's point of view. A trademark of Gregg Toland, the cinematographer for *Citizen Kane* and *The Grapes of Wrath*, as well as this and other Wyler films, deep focus credits audiences with having enough intelligence to follow more than one action at a time. It involves a viewer more directly in a scene by inviting him "to do his own cutting," as Wyler once put it. Cinema's fourth wall is the camera, and there are moments in *The Best Years of Our Lives* when you almost forget it's there. The movie concludes with Russell and O'Donnell's wedding, a scene that reconciles several divergent plot lines by bringing together all six of the principal characters amid a much larger gathering. Andrews is the best man, and when he turns his head from the ceremony to stare at Wright, who's all the way in back, it's as if he's showing *us* where to look. As the other guests rush to congratulate the bride and groom, Andrews and Wright keep looking at each other for a long moment, with the left side of the screen all to themselves.

BUT IT ISN'T ONLY ANDREWS WHOSE EYES OURS FOLLOW DURING THE wedding. Standing before the minister, O'Donnell clasps Russell's right hook and gazes at him with a look of courage and swooning devotion that she has in all of their scenes together. (O'Donnell, who was making her screen debut and whose only other movie roles of any consequence were in Wyler's *Detective Story* and opposite Farley Granger in both Nicholas Ray's *They Live by Night* and Anthony Mann's *Side Street,* is being called on here to portray not just innocence but something like absolute goodness, and that you find yourself willing to believe in such a thing is as much a tribute to her acting as it is to the way she's lit, which makes it seem as though the light is emanating from her.) As Russell slips the ring on her finger, using his pincers, there is a look of apprehension in the eyes of the wedding guests—that is to say, in the eyes of the actors, who were painfully aware (as we are, by that point) that Russell's hooks weren't just props. The rest of the cast looks embarrassed to be caught staring at him—as we are—even though the joyous occasion calls for it.

RUSSELL, WHO WAS A MEAT CUTTER BEFORE JOINING THE ARMY AND whom Wyler cast after seeing him in a documentary about disabled veterans, comes across in that numbed way that nonactors often do in front of a camera—his face is slack, and he doesn't know what to do with his body. Wyler vetoed acting lessons for him, which was a wise decision. This is a character who has every right to feel numb and to be physically unsure; professional coaching might have resulted in his overacting in a role that needed to be underplayed to avoid excess pathos. Even Russell's Boston accent gives him away as an amateur, because we're not used to hearing regional accents—authentic ones, anyway—in 1940s movies, except as comic relief. (Andrews and O'Donnell were from Mississippi and Alabama, respectively, but you'd never guess it to listen to them.)

Russell's casting was in keeping with a Hollywood trend toward greater realism in response to World War II. Wyler and the other established Hollywood directors who had served in the military were put to work making combat documentaries that required them not only to forego elaborate technical resources but also to place themselves and their crews at risk from enemy fire. "[Wyler] came back, I think, with a better perspective on what was and wasn't important," Gregg Toland once told an interviewer, referring to Wyler's work on *The Memphis Belle,* which was shot aboard a B-17 during a bombing raid of Germany, and *Thunderbolt,* for which cameras were rigged to the wings, tails, and cockpits of a fleet of fighter jets. Even many wartime features qualified as semi-documentaries: *The Story of G.I. Joe,* for example, includes combat footage from John Huston's documentary *The Battle of San Pietro,* and the extras were identified in the opening credits as "combat veterans of the campaigns in Africa, Sicily, and Italy." Many of them were dead by the time the movie was released in 1945. (So was Ernie Pyle, who survived the liberation of Italy only to be killed on an island near Japan.)

In much the same way that auto manufacturers diverted their assembly lines into the production of tanks and submarines during the war, Hollywood rolled out movie after movie that substituted Nazis for mobsters. War lent moral urgency to even the most conventional sort of romantic melodrama: a kiss was no longer just a kiss, no matter what the song said. Today's movies are produced for the global market, which we tend to think is a fairly recent development. But according to figures provided by Clayton R. Koppes and Gregory D. Black in their informative 1987 book *Hollywood Goes to War,* American movies already occupied 80 percent of the world's screens by 1939, and the studios earned 40 percent of their profits overseas. Along with pressure from congressional isolationists, who threatened legislation that would have forced the major studios to relinquish their monopolistic control of theatrical distribution and exhibition, and interference from the Hays Office, the motion-picture policing agency, which frowned on political themes almost as much as it did on suggestions of sexuality, this dependence on foreign receipts initially kept Hollywood from taking sides when war broke out in Europe. The turning point wasn't Pearl Harbor; it was with Hitler's ban on American films in Germany and Italy in August 1940 that Hollywood screenwriters won an editorial freedom long enjoyed by novelists and playwrights. During the war, producers were required to submit their scripts not only to the Hays Office but also to the Bureau of Motion Pictures, a branch of the Roosevelt administration's Office of War Information staffed with ardent New Dealers who urged studios to emphasize the important roles being played by women as factory workers and temporary single parents, and to make it clear that our fight was against fascist forces in Europe and Asia, not the entire populations of enemy countries—and certainly not Americans with roots in those countries.[*]

---

[*]In general, the bureau was more successful in convincing screenwriters to create sympathetic German characters than it was in persuading them to extend the same consideration to the Japanese. But at least our movie military was more fully integrated than our real one. The BMP's chief script reviewer was Dorothy B. Jones, who later wrote an article defending the Hollywood Ten, and the head of the OWI's overseas division, which approved movies for distribution to our allies, was the very Robert E. Sherwood who wrote *The Best Years of Our Lives.*

In return for putting up with all of this, directors and screenwriters routinely got away with things they couldn't possibly have gotten away with before the war. Although homosexuality was permissible only if the character showing unmistakable signs of it wore a Nazi officer's uniform, the circumstances under which something first appears on screen eventually cease to matter. Once it's there, it's there for good—hopefully to be treated with more dignity as the years pass. Many wartime movies were lurid and sensationalistic, including (I confess) two of my personal favorites, both directed by Edward Dmytryk, the Quentin Tarantino of his day: *Hitler's Children,* in which a young American woman played by Bonita Granville is tied to a post and whipped on her bare back in sight of the swastika, and *Behind the Rising Sun,* in which a Chinese baby is tossed in the air and speared on a Japanese bayonette (the camera pulls away not an instant too soon).

But there also were scenes of surprising intimacy, not necessarily sexual in implication. Death pervades *The Story of G.I. Joe,* as it does many of the Hollywood movies made during the final stages of World War II, when certain victory eliminated the need for home front morale boosters and audiences were finally given permission to weep. Toward the end, a weary soldier touches his mud-splattered hand to his dead lieutenant's cheek before hobbling to catch up to his platoon. Had one man ever touched another so tenderly in an earlier movie? All of these breakthroughs in movies during World War II culminated in *The Best Years of Our Lives* just after, but it took victory to allow such an unguarded expression of male surrender.

(MARCH 2003)

Only in the Movies

=====

ilm Culture was the name of an arcane critical journal, but those two words always make me think of the goo from candy and spilled soda that accumulates on the floors of movie theaters, and then of the habits of those of us who spend so much of our lives in theaters that others must think us indigenous to them—candidates for ethnological study. One of our most cherished customs is seeing movies in the early afternoon or very late at night, when the rest of the world is working or getting ready for bed. The first time I saw Quentin Tarantino's *Reservoir Dogs* (1992), on a weekday afternoon soon after it opened, about a third of the audience seemed to be black teenagers—an unfamiliar presence in arthouses like the one closest to me in Philadelphia. If these kids had been lured by the promise of reckless bloodshed, they weren't disappointed. "*Damn,*" one of them cried out in seeming approval on several occasions when a round of bullets hit a human target. (Sometimes it was a drawn-out "*Dey—em*"; other times, a quick *"Dang!"*) Although I was used to this sort of thing, from having seen so many action movies with integrated audiences in multiplexes, where expressions of astonishment by teenagers are pretty routine (and often prompted by lavish on-screen displays of money, drugs, or stolen goods, rather than by carnage), others in the audience apparently were not. Several people turned to see where the noise was coming from—at first alarmed, then amused, and finally just annoyed. The only ones who paid no mind were the young men who made up about another third of the audience, whose intense concentration suggested they might be film students weighing the logic of Tarantino's edits or keeping a running count of his allusions to Hong Kong action movies. They looked as if nothing short of gunplay in the aisles would break their trance.

I remember wondering if these two groups of young men were seeing two different movies—and which of those movies I was seeing. Possibly a third. A scene from *Reservoir Dogs* that many people recall with a shudder (actually, a scene they only *think* they remember, because the camera moves away a horrible second after the squeamish in the audience have closed their eyes) is one in which a hoodlum slices a cop's ear off with a razor and then douses him with gasoline. The dialogue from the movie that people tend to remember involves the crayon aliases—"Mr. Brown," "Mr. Orange," and so on—that the leader of a gang of criminals assigns to the total strangers he's brought together for a heist. These aliases are a way of keeping anybody from ratting on anybody else. The wonderful Steve Buscemi—a bug-eyed, motor-mouthed actor who slightly resembles Don Knotts and plays many of his parts like Deputy Sheriff Barney Fife with a coke habit and a rap sheet—objects to being called "Mr. Pink," because he thinks it makes him sound gay.

The bit of dialogue from *Reservoir Dogs* that made a lasting impression on me is from a scene that finds Harvey Keitel dragging Tim Roth, who's noisily bleeding to death after being shot, into the gang's warehouse hideout. "Come on," Keitel says. "*Who's* a tough guy?" Unaware that Roth is an undercover cop, Keitel is making one last attempt to bond with him, man to man. But his tone is that of a father giving a pep talk to a little boy who's fallen off a bike and skinned his knee. It's as if what he most wants is to get Roth to stop his caterwauling. Roth gives the right answer. "*I'm* a tough guy," he yowls through his pain, and there you have it—the real subject matter of *Reservoir Dogs* and practically every movie ever made about lowlife bruisers. They're okay with breaking any law except for the unwritten one about keeping your mouth shut, which includes not letting on when you've been hurt.

SELF-CONSCIOUSNESS OF THIS KIND CAN BE DETRIMENTAL TO A MOVIE. Yet Roman Polanski's *Chinatown* (1975) was a masterpiece largely because of its self-consciousness. It was the definitive 1940s film noir, even though it was made three decades later and depended on a final twist that would have been taboo in the days of Sam Spade and Philip Marlowe. And sometimes, as with Tarantino's articulation of the most basic and knuckleheaded of male codes, a line or two of movie dialogue will be so knowing and full of sass—so clearly meant as a comment on the movie and others in the genre—that I find myself glancing around the theater to see if anybody else caught it.

We expect witty flourishes from Tarantino, who is extremely literary, even if his idea of literature is some people's idea of trash, and whose characters talk and talk and talk—whether it's John Travolta, in *Pulp Fiction,* going on about what the French call a Quarter Pounder with cheese, or Samuel L. Jackson, in *Jackie Brown,* delivering an impromptu lecture on the relative merits of various automatic weapons. What's surprising is to find ourselves laughing along with the script in an action blockbuster of the kind made for an international market, where the assumption is that any dialogue not essential to the plot will be lost in translation—and is probably over the head of most domestic audiences. The veteran action director James Cameron, despite the step up in class that *Titanic* (1997) was supposed to represent for him, might be the last man in Hollywood from whom one would expect much in the way of word-play.* But there's plenty of it in Cameron's *True Lies* (1994), with Arnold Schwarzenegger and Jamie Lee Curtis, which is as enjoyable for its banter as for its special effects.

True Lies, for which Cameron also wrote the story (based on the screenplay of an obscure French movie called *La Totale*), stars Schwarzenegger as a har-ried secret agent simultaneously trying to spice up his marriage and crush the Crimson Jihad, a foreign terrorist group in possession of weapons of mass destruction. What struck some people as shameful about the movie seven years ago, and might seem especially irresponsible now, if it weren't so cheeky, is that the threat of a nuclear holocaust is a McGuffin—a device to keep the charac-ters running from place to place in what's really a bedroom farce. Toward the end, as Schwarzenegger kisses Curtis and slips her wedding ring back on, as if to renew their vows, the sky lights up with a nuclear explosion over the Florida Keys, in a wicked parody of those Freudian fireworks displays that used to stand in for sex in the movies.

True Lies is like *American Beauty* played for broader laughs and interrupted every so often by a shootout or a helicopter chase. The underlying comic premise is that the brute strength and animal cunning that we've seen Schwarzenegger rely on to thwart evildoers in movie after movie are of no prac-tical value to his character in everyday life.** His wife and teenage daughter, who believe he's a computer sales rep, think of him as an awful drudge, a buff Willie Loman. "Whenever I can't sleep, I just ask him to tell me about his day," the wife complains to a friend. (Ironically, she's drifting into an affair with a sleezy used-car salesman who's only *pretending* to be a secret agent, which he's found it to be a surefire come-on with bored married women.) When the terrorists kidnap Schwarzenegger, they also bag Curtis. The terrorists inject Schwarzeneg-ger with a truth serum, and taking advantage of the situation despite her fear, Curtis asks him a few questions of her own. After establishing that he's a spy, she asks if he's ever killed anyone. "Yah," he says, "but they were all bad."

SCHWARZENEGGER SAYS THIS TO CURTIS STRICTLY ENTRE NOUS, BUT HE'S not telling her anything we don't already know from having watched him mow

---

*Cameron is essentially a toymaker, like Spielberg before he started taking himself too seriously. The difference is that Cameron's toys aren't intended to reawaken child-hood wonder; he's usually blown them to smithereens by the closing credits. *Titanic* showed that Cameron knew how to manufacture toys for girls, too—the Leonardo DiCaprio doll. On TV's *Dark Angel,* which Cameron produces, the toy *is* a girl.

**And do not qualify him to be governor of California, it has become necessary to point out.

down terrorists for close to two hours without hitting a single innocent bystander. Not until later does it sink in that this wry rationale for his blood-letting, and for the bloodletting in action movies in general, has been used throughout history to justify capital punishment, vigilantism, and even geno-cide. And it brings a shudder to realize that the terrorists who carried out the attacks on the Pentagon and the World Trade Center probably felt justified in doing so because they believed their victims to be infidels.

Even before September 11, those of us who enjoy action and subgenre movies that are done with some flair were sometimes hard put to defend them. Many people find such movies objectionable not because they portray vio-lence but because they glorify it, cheapening regard for human life—particu-larly among adolescents, who may not be sophisticated enough to recognize that some forms of behavior are acceptable only in the movies. (Although I categorically dismiss this argument when it's made by the sort of politician who accepts contributions from the NRA—if you're going to insist that guns don't kill people, how can you say movies do?—I admit it's a legitimate con-cern. Two years ago I went to see Denzel Washington in *The Hurricane* at a theater where there had recently been gang violence; it was Martin Luther King's birthday, a school holiday, and everyone in line was frisked for weapons and made to pass through a metal detector.) My feelings about even the best of these movies—another exceptional one is John Woo's *Face/Off* (1997)—tend to be so conflicted that I'm usually forced to begin my defense of them by conceding that I have what I suppose is a gift for intellectualizing movie violence along with the fine points of a director's mise-en-scène. Now I would argue that our response as a nation to the events of September 11—typified for me by a photograph in *Time* of a group of stricken Iowa high school stu-dents watching the horror unfold on a television in their classroom—suggests that even the youngest and most impressionable of moviegoers can tell the dif-ference between depictions of slaughter and the real thing.

The accusation that movies like *True Lies* stereotype Arabs as bloodthirsty religious fanatics is more difficult to answer, and the fact that the hijackers actu-ally fit the stereotype hardly makes the job easier. In the weeks following the attacks and preceding the first air strikes on Afghanistan, the Hollywood stu-dios treated action films as something shameful and best kept out of sight. The opening dates of several fall movies were pushed back, some for a few weeks and others indefinitely—decisions I suspect were motivated by fear that these movies would do poorly at the box office, rather than by genuine sensitivity to what audiences might be feeling. The producers of *Collateral Damage,* starring Schwarzenegger as a firefighter whose wife and child are murdered by Colom-bian terrorists, closed down their Web site and ordered the return of the posters for the movie, which had been on display in theater lobbies all summer.

Topical humor was also put on hold, while Letterman and Leno posed as journalists. Yet people hungry for political humor continued to log onto *The Onion,* and video-store chains reported no decrease in sales and rentals of movies like *Armageddon* and *Independence Day.* One Blockbuster manager told the *Los Angeles Times* that last September people wanted "anything where terrorists got the stuffing kicked out of them." Our popular culture is our collective dream life, and it has never been easy to predict what directions it might take, especially in times of national crisis. Along with escapist comedies and patriotic battlefront epics vetted by the Office of War Information, the movies made during World War II also included those in which Humphrey Bogart and John Garfield gained stardom as existential antiheroes—wisecracking loners not about to sit still for sanctimonious speeches or to put their shoulders to the wheel without asking questions first. It's possible that bitter memories of the attacks and the anxiety that followed will cause audiences to avoid the likes of Schwarzenegger and Sylvester Stallone. But it's just as possible that audiences will be ready for action—that in the face of uncertainty, they'll flock to movies that offer them the illusion of control.

Last year, I saw John Singleton's remake of *Shaft* with a mostly middle-aged, working-class black audience that seemed to love the idea that the hero was willing to turn in his badge and play dirty if that was what he had to do to remove a vicious drug dealer and murderer from the streets. Despite their cheers when Shaft finally took out his nemesis, these people didn't strike me as likely to resort to similar measures to make their own neighborhoods safe. The movie was their way of letting off steam—escapist fantasy ennobled by an element of social consciousness. Action movies might fill a similar need.

WHAT'S MISSING FROM EVEN THE BEST ACTION MOVIES BECOMES obvious when they are compared with an Alfred Hitchcock masterpiece that I and many others consider to be the greatest of American movies: *Vertigo* (1958), a story of unconsummated love that ends with one lover dead and the other broken, in which Hitchcock gave suspense a moral dimension. More forcefully than in his earlier and much lighter *Rear Window* (1954), in *Vertigo* we encounter the themes of helplessness, guilt, obsession, and absence that have dominated so many of the finest movies of the last ten or fifteen years, such as Brian De Palma's *Casualties of War* (1989), Michael Tolkin's *The Rapture* (1991), Neil Jordan's *The Crying Game* (1992), Atom Egoyen's *Erotica* (1995), Paul Thomas Anderson's *Boogie Nights* (1997), Billy Bob Thornton's *All the Pretty Horses* (2002), and Christopher Nolan's *Memento* (2001). As different as they are from one another, these movies have in common a character who is either powerless to stop tragedy from befalling another person or to halt his own slide. The murder of someone innocent—the young Vietnamese woman raped by American soldiers in *Casualties of War,* for example, or the kidnapped British soldier played by Forest Whitaker in *The Crying Game*—can be disturbing evidence of a movie's integrity. The problem with most action movies is that nobody worth caring about is ever truly put at risk in them; when the villains kidnap the hero's wife or child or partner, we know he'll come storming to the rescue. And even if he doesn't (as in *Face/Off,* which begins with John Travolta's young son taking a bullet meant for him), his manly tears and the revenge he vows give us an even greater stake in rooting for him.

Everything in hit action movies is exaggerated, beginning with their heroes' overdeveloped torsos, and everything about them is cynical (*Charlie's Angels* introduced a surefire new commercial formula—jiggle for him, allusions to female self-empowerment for her). Still, I enjoy many of these movies—for the acting as for anything else. Schwarzenegger, for example, has a fine comic touch, especially now that he has as many crow's feet as muscles and doesn't try to make a secret of it. (Though his conventional comedies have been dreadful, he's never funnier than when he's flexing his muscles, firing a round of bullets, and daring us to keep a straight face.) Yet the people who are most appreciative of good acting—the people who read reviews and pride themselves on confining their movie-going to the arthouse—tend to shun figures like Schwarzenegger. He doesn't need these people, but the directors of daring little independent films do, and the violence in their films, or something else that might be troubling or unsavory about the characters, frequently keeps the arthouse audience away. More than an understandable aversion to violence seems to be involved—namely, snobbery. Even though cineplexes keep getting bigger and bigger, their screening rooms keep getting smaller and smaller, reflecting not just profit motives but a growing distrust between different types of moviegoers that has as much to do with race and class and age as with taste.

Ten years ago, *Reservoir Dogs* became a surprise hit by appealing simultaneously to two very different cults: budding cinéastes and sensation-hungry kids. Last year, the reviews for Mike Hodges's *Croupier* were so consistently favorable that people who claim to be forever on the lookout for good movies could hardly ignore it. This year *Memento* attracted a large number of young people, even though (to judge from the audience I saw it with, and from what I heard being said about it for months afterward) they seemed more impressed by the protagonist's tattoos and the movie's gimmick of a narrative in reverse than by the mood of sorrow and the drumming panic that I thought were the best things about it. It almost seems like a miracle these days when a good little movie finds the large audience it deserves, because so many of these movies feature shady or unpleasant characters, and so many of those who might enjoy them are reluctant to see a movie about people they wouldn't vote into their co-ops.

Though one rarely hears "*Damn*" shouted in pleasure in arthouses, the audiences in them have their own method of acting out. At a comedy there are always a few who clap their hands loudly several times as they laugh and then sigh, letting the rest of the audience know that not only did they get the joke but they also recognize the Importance of Laughter. When this audience does embrace a crime movie, it's usually the wrong one—Jonathan Glazer's *Sexy Beast,* for example, with a cardboard performance by Ben Kingsley as a thug feared by other thugs, rather than Andrew Dominick's horrifyingly funny *Chopper,* with a lively and complex performance by Eric Bana as Mark "Chopper" Read, Australia's most famous career criminal and one of its best-selling authors, a good-natured jailbird whose violent eruptions frequently surprise even him.

IF NOT VALUES, MAYBE WHAT WE GET FROM MOVIES IS SOMETHING equally essential to determining who we are, though more ambiguous and harder to pin down—something often referred to as sensibility. As a child, I went to the movies so regularly that my bewildered mother would say that I'd do so even if she were dying. She didn't know how prophetic she was. Despite the stroke she had suffered three months earlier, my mother's death felt terrifyingly sudden. I saw *15 Minutes,* a dreadful movie starring Robert De Niro (who these days seems to make no other kind), after visiting my mother in the hospital one night last spring and trusting that she was in no immediate danger. Approximately forty-eight hours later she underwent emergency brain surgery as the result of a fall she had taken before she went into the hospital. She never regained consciousness.

A hospital nurse had told me that it was standard practice in neurosurgical intensive-care units to leave the television turned on in an unconscious patient's room, preferably to a channel on which the patient might recognize some of the voices. I suggested American Movie Classics for my mother, hoping that the voices of actors familiar from her youth would be reassuring to her. She lay there unconscious with the television on for three days, her head bandaged and her face gruesomely bruised from the fall and the blood thinner she'd been taking, her neck and shoulders tensed like those of someone stunned by a blow to the head and instinctively braced for another. She looked like the victim of an unspeakable act of violence—but who was there to blame? My mother's hands were like ice, but for two days I had been able to warm them by squeezing them in mine. On the last morning my hands were as cold as hers, when I reluctantly unclasped them.

Though raised Catholic, I have never been religious. I often joke that as a child I preferred the movies to church, because the movies were air-conditioned and started in the afternoon. But I knew that my mother would have wanted a Catholic funeral. After the priest read the verses from John in which Jesus raises Lazarus, I delivered the eulogy. Trying to reconcile my mother's beliefs with my own, I spoke of memory as a form of afterlife. I also talked about how she and I often watched old movies on television together when I was a kid. Her favorites were Bette Davis and Joan Crawford; I was drawn to Bogart and Garfield, in their roles as tough guys with big hearts who were so used to keeping their lips sealed that their way of saying goodbye, perhaps forever, to someone they loved might be just to say, "I'll be thinking of you." At one point there was a collective sob from the other mourners, perhaps as much in grief for me as for my mother. My wife, who had lost her mother just six weeks earlier, was still weeping when it was time for us to follow the casket up the aisle. "Come on," I whispered, holding her tight, though maybe I was the one more in need of hearing it. "Who's a tough guy?"

(JANUARY 2002)

Index